Bioinformatics Tools and Big Data Analytics for Patient Care

Nowadays, raw biological data can be easily stored as databases in computers but extracting the required information is the real challenge for researchers. For this reason, bioinformatics tools perform a vital role in extracting and analyzing information from databases. **Bioinformatics Tools and Big Data Analytics for Patient Care** describes the applications of bioinformatics, data management, and computational techniques in clinical studies and drug discovery for patient care. The book gives details about the recent developments in the fields of artificial intelligence, cloud computing, and data analytics. It highlights the advances in computational techniques used to perform intelligent medical tasks.

Features:
- Presents recent developments in the fields of artificial intelligence, cloud computing, and data analytics for improved patient care.
- Describes the applications of bioinformatics, data management, and computational techniques in clinical studies and drug discovery.
- Summarizes several strategies, analyses, and optimization methods for patient healthcare.
- Focuses on drug discovery and development by cloud computing and data-driven research.

The targeted audience comprises academics, research scholars, healthcare professionals, hospital managers, pharmaceutical chemists, the biomedical industry, software engineers, and IT professionals.

Bioinformatics Tools and Big Data Analytics for Patient Care

Edited by
Rishabha Malviya
Pramod Kumar Sharma
Sonali Sundram
Rajesh Kumar Dhanaraj
Balamurugan Balusamy

CRC Press
Taylor & Francis Group
Boca Raton London New York

CRC Press is an imprint of the
Taylor & Francis Group, an **informa** business

A CHAPMAN & HALL BOOK

Cover image: LeoWolfert/Shutterstock

First edition published 2023
by CRC Press
6000 Broken Sound Parkway NW, Suite 300, Boca Raton, FL 33487-2742

and by CRC Press
4 Park Square, Milton Park, Abingdon, Oxon, OX14 4RN

CRC Press is an imprint of Taylor & Francis Group, LLC

Library of Congress Cataloging-in-Publication Data
Names: Malviya, Rishabha, editor. | Sharma, Pramod Kumar, Dr., editor. |
Sundram, Sonali, editor. | Dhanaraj, Rajesh Kumar, editor. | Balusamy,
Balamurugan, editor.
Title: Bioinformatics tools and big data analytics for patient care /
edited by Rishabha Malviya, Pramod Kumar Sharma, Sonali Sundram, Rajesh
Kumar Dhanaraj, Balamurugan Balusamy.
Description: First edition. | Boca Raton : Chapman & Hall/CRC Press, 2023.
| Includes bibliographical references and index. | Summary: "Nowadays,
Raw biological data can be easily stored as databases in the computers
but extracting the required information from the quantum of data is the
actual challenge for researchers. For this reason, bioinformatics tools
perform a vital role in extracting and analyzing information from the
databases. Bioinformatic Tools and Big Data Analytics for Patient Care:
Future of Healthcare describe the applications of bioinformatics, data
management and computational techniques in clinical studies and drug
discovery for patient care. This book gives details about the recent
developments in the fields of artificial intelligence, cloud computing
and data analytics for improved patient care. This book highlights the
advancement in computational techniques which are used to perform
intelligent medical tasks"-- Provided by publisher.
Identifiers: LCCN 2022009889 (print) | LCCN 2022009890 (ebook) | ISBN
9781032129310 (hardback) | ISBN 9781032129372 (paperback) | ISBN
9781003226949 (ebook)
Subjects: MESH: Patient Care | Computational Biology--methods | Big Data |
Medical Informatics--methods | Artificial Intelligence
Classification: LCC R119.95 (print) | LCC R119.95 (ebook) | NLM W 26.5 |
DDC 610.285--dc23/eng/20220625
LC record available at https://lccn.loc.gov/2022009889
LC ebook record available at https://lccn.loc.gov/2022009890

ISBN: 978-1-032-12931-0 (hbk)
ISBN: 978-1-032-12937-2 (pbk)
ISBN: 978-1-003-22694-9 (ebk)

DOI: 10.1201/9781003226949

Typeset in Times
by SPi Technologies India Pvt Ltd (Straive)

Contents

List of Figures

List of Tables

Preface

Healthcare is an important sector of any economy. For a society to realize its dream and vision of sustainable growth, it is important that the physical and mental health of its individuals be ensured. The development of a nation is dependent on the state of the health of its citizens, hence the popular saying "health is wealth." Therefore, any technology or system that is tailored towards improving the healthcare system is most likely to enjoy favorable public perception. This book includes various data from bioinformatics and healthcare informatics domains coupled with analytics that are estimated to deliver in the near future preventive, predictive, and personalized healthcare aids. This is expected to contribute to national growth and development. This book describes the applications of bioinformatics, data management, and computational techniques in clinical studies and drug discovery. This information has been compiled from recent developments in the fields of artificial intelligence, cloud computing, and data analytics for improved patient care.

The book discusses recent developments in machine learning techniques and includes an overview of intelligent tutoring systems as well as describing new learning concepts for researchers. It contains 11 chapters written by important researchers from around the world and is well referenced and copiously illustrated.

This book should be of immense interest and usefulness to researchers and industrialists working in clinical research and disease management, pharmacists, formulation scientists working in R&D and remote healthcare management, health analysts, and researchers in the pharmaceutical industry.

Finally comes the best part to thank you everyone who helped to make this book possible. First and foremost, we express our heartfelt gratitude to the authors for their contribution, dedication, participation, and willingness to share their significant research experience in the form of written testimonials, which would not have been possible without them. lastly, we are feeling fortunate to express our gratitude to CRC, Taylor & Francis Group (publisher) for his unwavering support.

Acknowledgments

Having an idea and turning it into a book is as hard as it sounds. The experience is both internally challenging and rewarding. We fail to find adequate words, with only a limited vocabulary to our command, to express our gratitude to the Almighty, whose eternal blessing, divine presence, and masterly guidance helped us to fulfill all our goals.

We especially want to thank Mr Dhruv Galgotia, CEO, Galgotias University without his encouragement this book would not exist. We express our heartfelt gratitude to the authors for their contribution, dedication, participation, and willingness to share their significant research experience in the form of written testimonials, which would not have been possible without them.

No words can describe the immense contribution of our parents and friends.

Last but not least, we would like to thank our publisher CRC, Taylor & Francis Group for his unwavering support., innovative suggestions, and guidance in bringing out this volume.

Editors' Biographies

Rishabha Malviya completed his B. Pharmacy from Uttar Pradesh Technical University and his M. Pharmacy (Pharmaceutics) from Gautam Buddha Technical University, Lucknow Uttar Pradesh. His Ph.D. (Pharmacy) work was in the area of novel formulation development techniques. He has 11 years of research experience and has worked as Associate Professor in the Department of Pharmacy, School of Medical and Allied Sciences, Galgotias University for the past eight years. His areas of interest include formulation optimization, nanoformulation, targeted drug delivery, localized drug delivery, and characterization of natural polymers as pharmaceutical excipients. He has authored more than 150 research/review papers for reputable national and international journals. He is an editorial board member/reviewer of more than 40 journals. More than ten patent grants from different countries are to his credit while 40 patents are published/under evaluation.

Pramod Kumar Sharma completed his M. Pharm and Ph.D. at Jadavpur University, Kolkata, India. He has around 27 years of teaching, research, and administrative experience. He has supervised more than 50 M. Pharm and ten Ph.D. students. Currently he is working as Dean of the School of Medical and Allied Sciences, Galgotias University, Greater Noida, India. He has published more than 150 articles in prestigious journals. He has eight patents to his credit. He is the author of eight books and six book chapters.

Sonali Sundram completed her B. Pharm and M. Pharm (Pharmacology) at AKTU, Lucknow. She has worked as a research scientist in a project of Indian Council of Medical Research (ICMR) at King George's Medical University, Lucknow after which she joined Babu Banarasi Das Northern India Institte of Technology (BBDNIIT); she is currently working at Galgotias University, Greater Noida. Her Ph.D. (Pharmacy) work was in the area of neurodegeneration and nanoformulation. Her area of interest is neurodegeneration, clinical research, and artificial intelligence. She has attended more than 15 national and international seminars/conferences/workshops. She has more than eight patents to her credit.

Rajesh Kumar Dhanaraj is Associate Professor in the School of Computing Science and Engineering at Galgotias University, Greater Noida, India. He holds a Ph.D. degree in Information and Communication Engineering from the Anna University, Chennai, India. He has contributed more than 20 books on various technologies and more than 35 articles and papers in various refereed journals and international conferences, and contributed chapters to books. His research interests include machine learning, cyber-physical systems, and wireless sensor networks. He is Expert Advisory Panel Member of Texas Instruments Inc., USA.

Balamurugan Balusamy is Associate Professor at VIT University, Vellore, where he has taught and researched over the past 14 years. He completed his Bachelors from Bharatidasan University, Tiruchirappalli and masters from Anna University, Chennai, PhD from VIT University, Vellore. His passion is teaching and he adapts different design thinking principles while delivering his lectures. He has published over 30 books on various technologies and visited more than 15 countries for his technical course. He has several top-notch conferences on his résumé and has published over 150 quality journal articles, conference papers, and book chapters combined. He serves on the advisory committee for several start-ups and forums and does consultancy work for industry on the industrial IOT. He has given over 175 talks at various events and symposia. He is currently working as a professor at Galgotias University and teaches and conducts research on blockchains and the IOT.

List of Contributors

Md. Aftab Alam
School of Medical and Allied Science
Galgotias University
Greater Noida, India

Deepika Bairagee
Oriental College of Pharmacy and Research
Oriental University
Jakhiya, India

Manisha Bharti
Department of Pharmacy
School of Medical and Allied Science
Galgotias University
Greater Noida, India

Akash Chauhan
School of Medical and Allied Sciences
Galgotias University
Greater Noida, India

Tatheer Fatima
Mahatma Gandhi Institute of Pharmacy
Dr. A. P. J. Abdul Kalam Technical University
Lucknow, India

Neeraj Kumar Fuloria
Faculty of Pharmacy
AIMST University
Bedong, Malaysia

Shivkanya Fuloria
Faculty of Pharmacy
AIMST University
Bedong, Malaysia

Deepti Jain
Rajiv Gandhi Proudyogiki Vishwavidyalaya
Bhopal, India

Neelam Jain
Oriental College of Pharmacy and Research
Oriental University
Jakhiya, India

Anushka Joshi
School of Pharmaceutical Science
Rajiv Gandhi Proudyogiki Vishwavidyalaya
Bhopal, India

Gaurav Kumar
School of Basic and Applied Sciences
Galgotias University
Greater Noida, India

Simran Ludhiani
Shri Govindram Seksaria Institute of Technology
and Science
Indore, India

Rupa Mazumder
Noida Institute of Engineering and Technology
(Pharmacy Institute)
Greater Noida, India

Prem Shankar Mishra
School of Medical and Allied Science
Galgotias University
Greater Noida, India

Rakhi Mishra
Noida Institute of Engineering and Technology
(Pharmacy Institute)
Greater Noida, India

Sudhanshu Mishra
Madan Mohan Malaviya University of
Technology
Gorakhpur, India

Aishwarya Rajput
School of Pharmaceutical Science
Rajiv Gandhi Proudyogiki Vishwavidyalaya
Bhopal, India

Shilpa Rawat
School of Medical and Allied Sciences
Galgotias University
Greater Noida, India

Mahendran Sekar
Faculty of Pharmacy and Health Sciences
Royal College of Medicine Perak
University Kuala Lumpur
Ipoh, Malaysia

Urvashi Sharma
Oriental College of Pharmacy and Research
Oriental University
Jakhiya, India

Nitu Singh
Oriental College of Pharmacy and Research
Oriental University
Jakhiya, India

Shilpa Singh
School of Medical and Allied Sciences
Galgotias University
Greater Noida, India

Ambarish Kumar Sinha
School of Basic and Applied Sciences
Galgotias University
Greater Noida, India

Shashimala Tiwari
India Health Action Trust
Uttar Pradesh Technical Support Unit
Lucknow, India

Sandesh Varshney
School of Medical and Allied Science
Galgotias University
Greater Noida, India

Swati Verma
School of Medical and Allied Science
Galgotias University
Greater Noida, India

1 The Role of Bioinformatics Tools and Technologies in Clinical Trials

Sandesh Varshney, Manisha Bharti, Sonali Sundram, and Rishabha Malviya
Galgotias University, Greater Noida, India

Neeraj Kumar Fuloria
AIMST University, Bedong, Malaysia

CONTENTS

DOI: 10.1201/9781003226949-1

1.1   INTRODUCTION

Bioinformatics may be a new interdisciplinary field of study that combines clinical informatics, bio-informatics, medical informatics, information technology, mathematics, and proteomics research. This chapter will examine Watson and Crick's 1953 revelation that they had found the blueprint for DNA, the growth of organic chemistry, and the understanding of polypeptide structure in the 1960s. Pauling, Coren, and Ramachandran classified the information of the polypeptide stereoscopic framework, which Margaret O. Dayhoff considered to be the heart of BI [1]. Clinical BI can be defined as a new emerging science which combines the effort of clinical informatics and omics science with mathematics and information technology [2]. BI plays a very important role in biological research including niches like microarray technology, proteomics, pharmacogenomics, cancer studies, and systems biology [3]. This field is related to biological molecules which require expertise in fields like biochemistry, molecular biology, molecular evolution, and biophysics. It also requires the use of computer science, mathematics, and statistical approaches [4]. In the beginning, it was used to provide biomedical and medical data for personalized healthcare. The use of an internet-based biomedical database for study and medical practice makes the process easier. It aids in the selection of suitable software for the analysis of microarray data for medical purposes. It may even improve tasks including disease-specific biomarker generation, therapeutic target selection, and clinical validation [5]. Clinical research is an area of science concerned with ensuring the therapeutic efficacy and safety of medication, equipment, diagnostic products, and treatment regimens intended for human use. Many pharmaceutical firms still adopt a conservative approach to drug development, with the goal of finding a novel therapeutic target and a unique molecule that modifies the function of that goal. As a result, an efficient and novel way to speeding up the drug development process is critical [6]. BI tools and technology apply an excellent statistical algorithm, directional approaches for the identification of the target, validation, and optimization. They help in developing databases, identifying the functions of proteins, structure modeling, or determine the sequence of nucleic acid and so on. They reduce the burden by allowing AI to locate a suitable molecule based on the provided parameters from a wide group of candidates; they also conduct information extraction, analysis, and interpretation at a much quicker pace, resulting in time savings and increased accuracy, as well as cost savings. The correlation is shown in Figure 1.1 [7]. Jonathan Pevsner typified the space of BI and genomics from three points of view: (1) the cell and the central dogma of molecular biology; (2) the organic entity and reflex alteration among various phases in advancement and also in locales within organs; (3) the tree of life, where a huge number of species are gathered into three transformative branches. These points re stated to be an organization of the information in compiled form, which makes it easily available to specialists to develop apparatus and assets that assist in handling information and investigation and the utilization of devices to explore the data and decipher them all together [1].

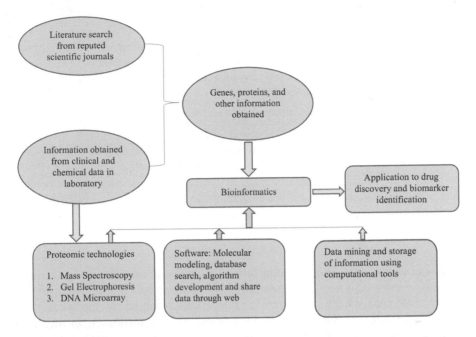

FIGURE 1.1   Relationship between BI, biological sciences, proteomics, and information technology.

1.2   CLINICAL RESEARCH

Clinical studies are a discipline of medicine that includes biological investigations that are systematic, observational, and experimental. Its primary purpose is to improve people's quality of life. Observational and experimental research are the two broad areas of clinical research. The selection criteria are simple: the researcher/investigator may choose whether they are allocated to exposures, such as treatments, or if they are seen in medical care. For investigational research, it is necessary to determine if the exposure allocated is genuinely randomized or incorporates some kind of allocation method, such as alternate assignment [8]. There are several forms of medical investigation, depending on the investigators and the type of answer they seek. They include the following. Healthcare investigation includes the development or improvement of any pharmaceutical, psychoanalytic, new equipment, or novel surgical or radioactive treatment approaches. Preventive investigation involves the avoidance of illnesses from occurring or resurfacing and may include the investigation of medication, supplements, or lifestyle changes. Diagnostics investigation is the process of discovering a more accurate approach to diagnosing a certain ailment or situation. Screening research is focused on finding problems which exist in health domains. Genetic studies involve the prediction of disorders by looking at how genes and disorders are related and how to combat them. Epidemiological studies involve the identification of patterns, on the basis of the physiological division [9].

One of the most important areas of clinical research is clinical trials. A medical study is a scientific effort that tests whether a new healthcare therapy or a new way of employing an existing medication is better in terms of preventing, diagnosing, or treating a disease. Pre-clinical tests must be passed before a novel medicine may join a clinical trial. *In vitro* experiments and preliminary meta-analyses are examples of biomedical models. To obtain primer viability, toxicity, and pharmacokinetic data, a wide range of measures of the examined medication needs to be supplied to animal participants or *invitro* substrates [10]. Before the initiation of the clinical trial, it must pass the approval stage of the FDA, which involves a preclinical investigation. There are five phases in the clinical trials: Stage 0, Stage I, Stage II, Stage III, and Stage IV. They are elaborated below.

1.2.1 PRE-CLINICAL INVESTIGATIONS

Pre-clinical investigations include *in vitro* studies and other preliminaries on animal populations. Wide-angle measurements of the test chemical are given to animal material or *in vitro* substrates in an attempt to provide initial viability, toxicity, and pharmacokinetic data and to aid drug corporations in determining if more testing is required [11].

1.2.2 STAGE 0

Stage 0 might also be a new option for the preliminary, first-barbaric preliminaries, according to the FDA (US-FDA) 2006 guidelines. Exploratory Investigational New Medication (IND) Studies Directions Stage 0 preliminary studies are designed to speed up the development of potential drugs or imaging experts by determining early on whether the medication or specialist work with the biological participants is as predicted from pre-clinical studies [12].

1.2.3 STAGE I

The first phase of testing is the Stage I preliminaries. Ordinarily, a small (20–80) gathering of sound volunteers is assembled who may be chosen. This stage incorporates preliminaries used to survey the wellbeing, tolerance, pharmacokinetics, and pharmacodynamics of the medication. These preliminary examinations are typically cleared out of any medical institution, in which the person is seen by entire professionals. The issue of who gets this medicine is usually not addressed until a few half-lives have elapsed. This stage of clinical trial frequently incorporates fraction moving, also known as fraction boosting, which focuses on finding a suitable piece for remedial usage. Stage I regularly incorporates solid volunteers. However, there are very limited circumstances in which real people are used, such as individuals who are nearing the end of their illness and want alternative treatment options. Volunteers are compensated for their time spent within the voluntary community by way of a burden fee. The payment varies from a little financial value for a brief time at home to a significantly bigger sum of up to £4000 depending on the length of collaboration [13].

1.2.4 STAGE II

When the primary safety of the investigated drug has been established in Stage I, Stage II clinical preliminaries are conducted on larger cohorts (20–300) and are to illustrate how well the medication functions; likewise on the continuation of clinical test Stage I clinical preliminary wellbeing measures used on a greater gathering of volunteers and patients. The point when the occasion cycle for a substitution drug fall flat normally happens during Stage II when the medication is found to not fill in as arranged or to have poisonous impacts. Stage II clinical preliminary examinations are partitioned into two sub-stages: Stage IIA and Stage IIB. Stage IIA is intended to independently check dosing prerequisites, while Stage IIB is exclusively intended to survey intensity. A few preliminaries bridge the gap between Stage I and Stage II clinical preliminaries, evaluating either viability or toxicity [14].

1.2.5 STAGE III

In this stage studies are controlled trial multicenter preliminary studies on large treatment populations (300–3000 or more, depending on the illness/ailment under consideration) and are intended to be the authoritative assessment of the medication's viability in comparison to this "best quality level" medication. Because of their size and near-indefinite duration, Stage III medical studies are more costly, time-consuming, and complex to plan and perform, particularly in the treatment of severe disorders. It is a common procedure to decide that the Stage III clinical preliminary will go forward while chief approval is being awaited from the suitable administrative organization. While not needed for all cases, it is ordinarily expected that there will be at least two effective Stage III clinical preliminaries, showing a medication's security and viability, so as to obtain endorsement from the requisite administrative organizations. When a medication has demonstrated its suitability after Stage III, the preliminary outcomes are normally consolidated into an outsized record containing a complete depiction of the techniques and results of human and animal investigations, delivery methods, planned subtleties, and periods. This gathering of information makes up the "administrative accommodation" that provides a survey to the regulatory administrative experts in a few nations. Most medications going through Stage III are frequently advertised under FDA standards with appropriate suggestions and rules, yet if there should be an occurrence of any untoward impacts, the medications should be removed promptly from the market. While most drug organizations retain from this training, it isn't uncommon to get numerous medications going through Stage III while on the market [15].

1.2.6 STAGE IV

Stage IV is also referred to as Post Showcasing Reconnaissance Preliminary. After a medicine has the authority to be marketed, Stage IV requires security observation and in-measure specialist assistance. Administrative experts may require Stage IV tests, and the supporting organization may accept them for significant or various reasons. The security review is completed so as to recognize any uncommon or long-haul antagonistic impacts among larger patient populations and an all-inclusive time of your time, and it had been conceivable during the Stage I–III clinical preliminaries. Harmful impacts found in Stage IV may end in a medication being not sold or limited to a specific employment [16].

1.3 THE ROLE OF (BI) TOOLS AND TECHNOLOGIES IN CLINICAL RESEARCH

BI utilizes natural data and numerical, measurable, and processing strategies to explore living things [17,18]. BI to a great extent affects logical examination in microarray innovation, proteomics, pharmacogenomics, oncology, and frameworks science [19]. Researchers may now analyze the trillion bytes of data collected in the Human Genome Project (HGP) because of BI's easy access to the data. Together, gene sequence databases, gene expression databases, and protein sequence databases assist to identify the pattern of a specific molecule's involvement in disease processes, and it aids in the discovery of novel and improved medication targets [4]. A drug design method, such as the one presented in Figure 1.2, may greatly reduce the time and expense of generating a

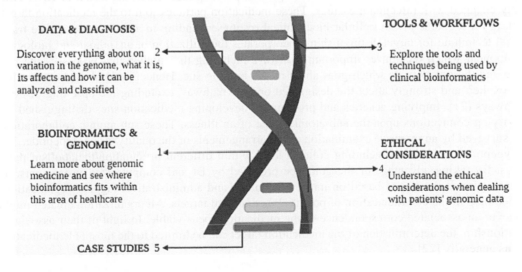

FIGURE 1.2   Clinical BI.

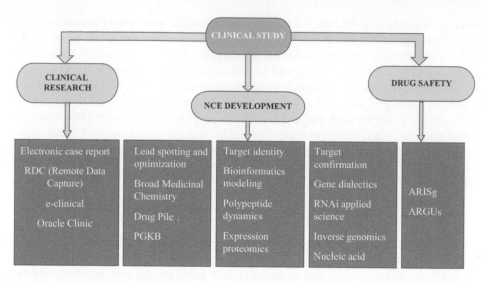

FIGURE 1.3 Representing the role of BI and programming instruments in clinical examination.

pharmacologic agent. Drug similarity may be predicted using computational techniques, which can be calculated using genomic algorithms and neuronal network methodologies [20]. As illustrated in Figure 1.3, the traditional method of drug development typically comprises four steps: target identity verification, lead discovery, lead optimization, and pre-clinical formation before moving on to clinical trials [5].

1.3.1 IDENTIFICATION OF TARGET

Formerly some advanced remedials have been found, the sickness viable should be perceived, to unravel the causative hidden condition. The infection instrument characterizes the conceivable reason or reasons for a specific issue, just as the way or aggregate of a sickness. The recognizable proof of new and clinically applicable sub-atomic focuses for drug medication is of remarkable significance. Medication sites can be binding sites, polypeptides, catalysts, DNA, or RNA critically engaged with infection measures. These medication particles join to the medication target, setting off a course of intracellular biochemical responses, ending in a cell response. The traditional technique for target distinguishing incorporates the utilization of an animal and biological component which recognizes important pathways including the catalyst that processes the particle and the polypeptide which goes about as the binding site. Hence, optimal medication sites are explicit and strongly affect the designated organic pathway, excluding the upsetting of other pathways [21]. Implying genetics and proteomics, developing medication sites distinguished via clarifying connections upon the sub-atomic stage of an illness. These sub-atomic collaborations are surveyed by an intensive examination of the arrangements of the quality else polypeptide, 3-D polypeptide construction including collaboration within different articulation/metabolism pathways. By taking advantage of the guidance provided by BI and computerized instruments, an organization is developed based on inner metabolism and administrative flagging organizations which help in the communication of potential mediational targets. An organization created might uncover an associated correspondence of the medication focus viable. In light of their associated relationship, the determination of the medication target can be limited to the most able medication focus generally [22].

1.3.1.1 Computerized Technique for Site Determination

1.3.1.1.1 Bioinformatic Modeling

Bioinformatic modeling is the strategy that determines the design of inter-molecular compounds originated in between two particles for tracking down the most appropriate direction of substrates that frame a composite compound by generally exercising the least power. The three-dimensional position of the attached substrate could utilize diverse imagining apparatuses. This provides outcomes like grades dependent on the modeling calculations created because of the differently conceivable primary compositions [23]. Through the activity indicated, different polypeptides assume a basic role. A modeling strategy can anticipate its partiality in the middle of these polypeptides and potent medication applicants. The first prerequisite of atomic modeling is the development of proteins. Construction is controlled by electromagnetic crystallography or atomic attractive spectrographic reverberation. Achievement capacity produces outcomes dependent upon compound up-and-comer most suitable to the objective be distinguished.

1.3.1.1.2 Polypeptide Dynamics

The polypeptide dynamic PC reproduction technique ascertains the time-subordinate conduct of a sub-atomic framework and provides the data encircling construction and tiny communication among particles. This is regularly utilized for the assurance of molecular modeling, the design of phospholipid double-layering, and the prediction of protein structure from protein chains by information created due to electromagnetic crystallography and nuclear magnetic resonance spectrograph [24].

1.3.1.1.3 Expression Proteomics

Expression proteomics concentrates upon the construction and the capacity of polypeptides. A complete examination of huge scope is performed on the change/variety of a polypeptide bounty, its particular collaborating accomplices, and organizations with the means to explain cell measurements. Utilizing BI instruments for proteomics, an enormous amount of information can be stored and investigation performed quickly. BI instruments and expression-proteomic data are likewise accessible so as to reveal biomolecules, incorporating biological fluids and cell data. This latest methodology exploits practical collaboration in the middle of precise biological fluids along with cells ripe for clinical critical discoveries [25].

1.3.1.1.4 Target Confirmation

By innovative progression in compound disclosure, the accessibility of possible objectives isn't amount restricting other than the issue of the decision of better serious medication site. This forces a test for the scientist to foster instruments which can choose a minimum quality other than medication targets to undergo the most grounded relationship to the most solid link to the sickness from a large amount of data. In any case, roughly 324 medication goals have been distinguished as clinically significant [26]. This shows how momentum drug innovative work is reliant and depends on a little pool of medication focuses, notwithstanding the accessibility of various genome information on a human just as the pathogen [27]. Countless medications come up short at the early pre-clinical stages because of some unacceptable objective ID. As of late, a medication target expectation technique, that is, a finite state machine, was developed [28]. This is determined by the physiological and chemical characteristics of polypeptide successions as opposed to homology explanation and polypeptide 3D construction. This strategy can recognize realized medication focuses from possible nondrug focuses by a precision of 84 percent.

1.3.2 Datasets and Computational Devices Utilized for Target Approval

1.3.2.1 Gene logic

Quality rationale has become a major incorporated genomics organization providing exhaustive genetic datasets and biomedical research center data to executive arrangements. It utilizes its enormous information base of the tumor and typical quality articulation to create a short rundown of focuses that are specially communicated in circumstances of disease. The objectives in this rundown would then be able to be evaluated for utilitarian objective approval. The utilization of the dataset gives the agent a differential articulation example of the objective as well as demeanor amounts in distinct organs and kinds of disease. This database also enables analysts to examine the degree of articulation of different proteins implicated in certain networks [29].

1.3.2.2 Ribonucleic Interference Technology

Intradigm's RNA interference (RNAi) technology may be utilized to effectively and specifically delete homologous mRNA (Rockville, MD, USA). Intradigm research focuses on cancer, inflammation, and autoimmune disease-related angiogenesis pathways. Target validation *in vivo* through clinically viable siRNA injection may be beneficial for determining the role of specific genes or proteins in the illness pathway, as well as the involvement of several genes in a single pathway and their impact on sickness. This information may be utilized to create more effective medicines. This understanding is critical for the future development of therapeutic siRNAs, in addition to medication discovery [6].

1.3.2.3 Immusol

Immusol (San Diego) has created an effective and safe *in vivo* target validation approach using siRNA vectors in numerous disease models as a consequence of this innovative methodology. Immusol provides inducible RNAi vectors for target validation, which may be injected into tumor cells in culture or cell lines to trigger RNAi expression. A xenograft mouse tumor model might be used to investigate the inducible vector [30].

1.3.2.4 Aptamers

Nascacell employs aptamers to verify and test targets since they are synthesized nucleic acids. Antibodies may be deactivated by binding to the active site of an antidote and binding to its active binding site. Aptamers are then used to imitate the effects of a tiny pharmacological agent. By inactivating the stable protein at a regular turnover rate, aptamers may be able to distinguish between distinct post-translational modifications [31].

1.3.3 Lead Identification/Optimization

The screening of compound libraries is the first step in the lead identification procedure. Compounds that interact with and influence the activity of a target protein have been found. Pre-clinical drug candidates are developed by a process known as lead optimization, in which the chemical structure of a verified hit is thoroughly improved [32]. The main and secondary structures of the chemical are modified to optimize the potential lead contender. As a result of recent advances in computing and invention, a lead candidate may be identified in this complicated process. Toxicology prediction is also a serious challenge.

- A broad understanding of the pharmaceutical chemistry: These databases offer information on physiochemical features such as drug class, pKa, and Log P data for about 840 active therapeutic compounds.

- Drug bank: This database links compounds and their pharmacological qualities to a variety of therapeutic targets, as well as providing detailed sequencing, structural, and route data. It combines physical, chemical, and therapeutic information and the appropriate therapeutic targets, which are sequencing, structural, and route [33].

1.4 MANAGEMENT OF CLINICAL DATA (CDM)

This is crucial to medical trials because it assures the validity, quality, and integrity of data obtained from trial participants at the investigator site. As a result, this database provides trustworthy, high-quality data that is statistically valid. Clinical trials are much more cost-effective and time-efficient using CDM, enabling medications to be created more swiftly and at a lesser cost. Throughout the trials, the quality of a variety of activities is checked regularly, including database structure, database input, information verification, and various critical operations including CRF design and data freezing. CDMS is presently in great demand for clinical trials to make them more efficient, to meet regulatory standards, and to lead the pharmaceutical sector in terms of innovation [34].

Some of the clinical data software are as follows.

1.4.1 E-CLINICAL SOLUTIONS

Cutting-edge e-clinical technologies are becoming increasingly dependent on clinical data collecting, compilation, evaluation, and judgment, allowing for a novel product. The major clinical solution suppliers are e-clinical Solutions and works. There is no better alternative for organizing clinical trials and facilitating electronic data exchange (EDI) than an e-clinical application. Using e-clinical procedures, each trial stage may be effectively organized.

1.4.2 ORACLE CLINICAL DATA COLLECTION, AS WELL AS ORACLE REMOTE DATA CAPTURE

Oracle Clinical and distant data collection RDBMS (relational database management system) is software that handles the design and data collection for clinical investigations. Allowing items to be reused across experiments results in uniformity and consistency in data collection and reporting. In Oracle Clinical, data may be seen in a number of ways that can be customized. Data validation is embedded into the system's error messages. Throughout the production, modification, maintenance, and transfer of electronic data, the Oracle Clinical application ensures its validity, integrity, and security [35].

1.4.3 ELECTRONIC CASE REPORT FORM

The Electronic Case Report Form (eCRF) is a digital device that captures clinical trial participant data in an electronic format, similar to the paper CRF. All clinical and non-clinical data from the patient, including medical treatments, are captured via a single clinical database interface and sent directly to the advertiser. In a multicenter experiment, the usefulness of eCRF is increased since data administrators have access to all of the data at the same time. Data collection is therefore made more efficient, which has a significant influence on the overall efficacy of the clinical study [36].

1.5 UTILIZATION OF BI

BI is a multidisciplinary approach that interconnects the various fields and leads to a precise approach for pinpointing unidentified problems and solutions. Some of the common processes which utilize BI are phylogenetics, omics studies, homology modeling, sequence alignment, protein structure prediction, functional annotation, and systems biology [37]. As previously mentioned, BI serves a crucial part in the drug development and clinical trial processes. It is also a significant feature that makes research and development simpler and more convenient. Rapid advances in technologies like gene projects and BI along with their merging with industry and academics leads to the true potential for the HGP for utilization in healthcare services. It makes finding many things easier and more precise, such as identification of the gene, SNP detection, genotype, and genetic analysis [38]. Due to this, a large quantity of data is generated, so its organization and storage are the most important things, which brings us to the point of creating databases [39]. There are two kinds of databases: primary and secondary. Primary databases contain the results of experimental data which are not very refined; examples are NCBI, DDBJ, and EMBL, whereas secondary databases include the information which passed through the curation process; examples are PIR, PDB, and SCOP. They also help with pharmacogenetics, which involves the fact that combining the data with the right phenotype can help to determine SNPs or halotypes which are related to disease susceptibility or drug response [40]. This involves the function-like analysis of biological sequences, which means the comparison of two or more nucleotide substances, that is, DNA or RNA. It helps to establish an evolutionary relationship, individual genes, and the functions related to it [1]. Proteomics is related to proteins and includes the structure and amino acid sequence. For the majority of proteins whose designs are still up, computational construction forecast techniques can provide significant data. These can be designed by considering different factors, for example CMGC is a typical methodology which is used to isolate proteins and help in the investigation of proteins via ionization mass spectrometry [41]. There is numerous software tools available to make the processing of the data easier.

1.6 BI TOOLS AND DATABASES

Since the 1960s, biomedical researchers have used computerized databases (Neufeld and Cornog, 1999). When BI was first introduced in the mid-1980s, it was a game-changer. The National Centre for Biological Diversity has been established by the US government. In 1988, a law was passed requiring the disclosure of biotechnology information. A section of the National Library of Medicines is devoted to this. The government's official information and support agency is the National Centre for Biotechnology Information (NCBI). A huge amount of open-access websites, datasets, applications, and programs have been made accessible on the internet as a consequence of the growing use of digital technology in biomedical sciences. In addition, there is a vast quantity of material accessible for easy reference. The internet has changed the method by which data are saved in a central database. The Data Warehouse [38] is open to researchers from all across the globe. Some of the databases are described further below, as well as in Table 1.1.

1.6.1 Online Mendelian Inheritance in Man (OMIM)

This is an exhaustive, definitive, and ideal information space of human qualities and hereditary issues. It accumulates data to help in the exploration of human hereditary qualities. It was started by Dr. Victor A. McKusick on the basis that Mendelian Inheritance in Man was the irrefutable reference. The National Center for Biotechnology Information [42] is now disseminating it online.

1.6.2 3D Tooth Atlas

This alludes to the gross life structures and intelligent 3D tooth chartbook. This is user friendly in which clients can check in with a particular user name and password and can select "3D Tooth Atlas 7-Dental Edition."

TABLE 1.1

List of Software in BI and Their Functions [27,36,48–51]

Field Used in	Name of Software	Description
Microarray data	Cluster	SOM, for clustering
	Tree view	Provide graphical browser analysis of clustering result
	Scan Alyze	Process fluorescent image in microarray
	Array Miner	Set of analysis tools
Next generation sequencing	Phylogenetic p-values (PhyloP)	Compare various effects like positive and negative on the basis of clinical evolution
	Combined Annotation Dependent Depletion (CADD)	For detecting disease-causing variants
	Sorting Intolerant from Tolerant (SIFT)	Detect protein mutation on the basis of homologous sequence
Protein analysis	Psort II	Predict amino acid code
	WOLF Psort	Calculator for peptide protein

1.6.3 CARDIO SOURCE PLUS

This is a scholarly asset from the American College of Cardiology, which covers heart data and subsequently the clinical preliminaries database [43].

1.6.4 RD-CONNECT

This is an incorporated stage associated with datasets, vaults, biobanks, and clinical BI on uncommon infections research. It is funded via the European Union's Seventh Framework Program via the International Rare Diseases Research Consortium (IRDiRC) [44].

1.6.5 EVIMalaR

This is a dataset which has been in operation for a very long time jointly with the FP7 Network of Excellence. It is backed by the European Commission, and it now has 42 partners representing 34 organizations throughout India, Africa, Australia, and Europe. It works on jungle fever research that is coordinated toward an improved understanding of the basic facts of the pathogen, its vector, and the science of parasite–host interactions [45].

1.6.6 FLORINASH

This is a five-year European Commission-funded FP7 research looking at the function of intestinal microbiota in non-alcoholic fatty liver disease (NAFLD). Patient metadata and transcriptomic and proteomic profiles allow clinical research to be conducted.

1.6.7 CHERNOBYL TISSUE BANK (CTB)

The CTB is a multinational partnership to gather, store, and disseminate biological specimens comprising tumor cells and healthy tissues of individuals whose illness etiology is unclear or known—childhood radioiodine exposure as a consequence of the Chernobyl nuclear power plant catastrophe [46,47] (Table 1.2).

TABLE 1.2
List of Various Tools and Their Uses [52,53]

Name of Tool	Use
geWorkbench	Hierarchical clustering
BioPerl	Computational and molecular biology
Biopython Test Genomic Software	Sequence analysis in BI
InterMine	Integration of biological data source
GROMACS	Parameter files and topology

1.7 DATA MANAGEMENT IN BI

The unavoidable reality is that the high rate of increase and diverse nature of biological data makes them far more difficult to handle than traditional data analysis approaches [54]. As a consequence, more advanced theoretical methodologies and techniques for analyzing and extracting relevant data from the complicated bio-data described above are needed. Categorization, prediction, grouping, outlier identification, sequence processing, and so on are some of the essential ideas underpinning the various efficient and scalable methodologies and tools. To extract useable information from the original raw data, item querying regularly, deep network architecture development, analysis and presentation of spatial/temporal data transferring, and information extraction strategies using a fundamental technique dubbed computer intelligence are utilized. This is demonstrated to be a viable method that has been frequently used through developing replicas, creating estimates, and performing organizations and clump, followed by the discovery of related rules, and lastly locating desired patterns. The most crucial thing is to combine modern information analytic techniques with BI to appropriately integrate the two domains. This involves various processes, which are discussed briefly.

- Data pre-processing is the method for the rectification of primarily acquired data. It is an important step and can be said to be a preselection. The data obtained practically might be raw, incomplete, or inconsistent, which cannot be subjected to data mining directly. Cleaning of data, integration, transformation, and reduction are some of the sub-stages. It significantly increases data efficiency and cuts down on processing time during the real extraction operation [55].
- Data cleaning is a routine in which data is revised for any missing values, for smoothing of noise, formatting any outliers, and resolving inconsistencies. Software like MIAME is the perfect example [56].
- Data integration is the process in which data is combined with multiple sources as such flat files, databases, data cubes, or data warehouses. It gives a user-friendly interface and a unified outlook of data. Five types of data incorporation combine information into useful formats: consolidation, which is the collection of data in storage; propagation, which is the copying of data between source and destination; virtualization, which provides a unified view from a real-time interaction from various information designs; federation, which is the creation of a simulated database on heterogeneous data sources; and storeroom, which is the collection of data in a warehouse [57].
- Data transformation is the process of transforming data into a certain format that can be mined, which is accomplished by smoothing aggregation, information generalization, and standardization. Jiawei et al. suggested a seven-step methodology that includes a variety of computer training algorithms for data cleansing [58].
- Data reduction is the process that is used to acquire a reduced representation of the dataset. Its effective range is well-known to lower a dataset's storage capacity. This is accomplished by removing any inaccurate entries from an archive and aggregating the data attributes into the data columns. Some of the strategies used to cope with data reduction challenges include compression, deduplication, thin provisioning, and efficient snapshots. Andrews and Patterson proposed combining SVD with clustering [59].

Following pre-processing, categorization is the most critical stage in identifying the relationships between different situations and the characteristics of distinct entities. Some examples are KNN, NB, and DT. Clustering is the method that divides the wanted sample data into different groups/clusters, which is based on the similarities of characteristics. Examples are HC, PRC, and GBC [54].

1.7.1 Data Mining

All these steps are necessary before proceeding to data mining. From a technical aspect, a data mining or machine learning approach is equally important. Information extraction can accomplish its stated aim of accurate and consistent performance thanks to abstraction information representation. Because of the enormous complexity of the data and the massive number of instances, it is impossible to analyze and abstract huge volumes of data using human abilities. It is also much faster than traditional manual data analysis methods. We also lose our purpose for being if we can't provide individuals with original information by translating it into a more understandable form. That is why we need an automated method for analyzing high-level data that may aid in clinical diagnostics and help to analyze the clinical effects of drugs on experimental data as shown in Figure 1.4. As a consequence of years of study and development, machine learning approaches are increasingly being used in BI.

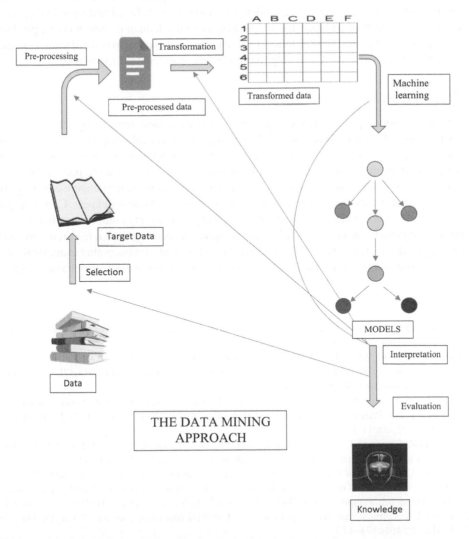

FIGURE 1.4   The general chain of work of a common data mining task [61].

BI and machine learning biology, bioimaging, picture computation and visualization, gene engineering, medical cell biology, nano-biological analysis, nuclear magnetic resonance/CT/ECG, physiological signal processing, and other biomedical research areas all use data mining techniques [60].

1.8 CHALLENGES AND OPPORTUNITIES

The huge challenge in the field of BI is the compilation of clinical and biomedical data obtained from extensive research. Clinical BI has fallen short in showing the precise relationship between clinical observation, molecular mechanisms, and digital informatics [62]. It also involves the cooperation of different fields and diverse groups of experts associated with it, such as research sponsors, clinical investigators, patients, physicians, and regulators of clinical trials [63]. Technical issues like data integration and modeling involve relations between scaling and coupling, coding, and so on. Mathematical issues relate to a mismatch between theory and practice and geometrical complexity. The management of data may face problems like algorithm managements and data servers.

The modernization of clinical research opens up a lot of possibilities for improving the drug development process. As a result of these tests, the pharmaceutical companies benefit greatly not only in terms of profits but also in terms of public perception, and not only in countries like North America and Western Europe, but also in a variety of other places such as Asia, South America, and Eastern Europe. As a result, the overall development cost is reduced and significantly increases the reach to large groups of patients. It may even result in the launch of new medical products in a variety of regions around the globe. Clinical trials can be viewed as a two-edged sword. Studies that are well-designed and carried out can help to improve the efficiency of medicines [64].

1.9 CONCLUSION

BI was being developed prior to DNA sequencing. This was made feasible by the collaboration of genomics research, clinical informatics, and IT. Many pharmaceutical companies continue to be cautious when it comes to medication development. We urgently want an innovative and efficient way to accelerate pharmaceutical development. Clinical trials are closely related to innovation in medical research technologies that lead to developments in healthcare. It is an important element of medical health research since it tries to discover the causes and remedies of human sickness. Conducting a clinical investigation for a novel medicine candidate is growing increasingly complicated, time-consuming, and expensive. When electronic clinical trials and computer-aided drug design research were launched, they caused a paradigm change in drug discovery and development. It is becoming increasingly usual for academics and regulators to utilize BI in novel and complicated ways to evaluate potential new products.

REFERENCES

1. Diniz WJ, Canduri F. Bioinformatics: An overview and its applications. *Genetics and Molecular Research* 2017 Mar 16;16(1):10–4238.
2. Kugler KG, Hackl WO, Mueller LA, Fiegl H, Graber A, Pfeiffer RM. The impact of sample storage time on estimates of association in biomarker discovery studies. *Journal of Clinical Bioinformatics* 2011 Dec;1(1):1–8. doi:10.1186/2043-9113-1-1.
3. Yao T. Bioinformatics for the genomic sciences and towards systems biology: Japanese activities in the post-genome era. *Progress in Biophysics and Molecular Biology* 2002 Jul 1;80(1–2):23–42. doi:10.1016/s0079-6107(02)00011-1.
4. Ou M, Ma R, Cheung J, Lo K, Yee P, Luo T, Chan TL, Au CH, Kwong A, Luo R, Lam TW. Database. bio: A web application for interpreting human variations. *Bioinformatics* 2015 Dec 15;31(24):4035–4037.
5. Chang PL. Clinical bioinformatics. *Chang Gung Medical Journal* 2005 Apr 1;28(4):201–211.
6. Gill SK, Christopher AF, Gupta V, Bansal P. Emerging role of bioinformatics tools and software in evolution of clinical research. *Perspectives in Clinical Research* 2016 Jul;7(3):115 doi: 10.4103/2229-3485.184782.
7. Zerhouni EA. Clinical research at a crossroads: The NIH roadmap. *Journal of Investigative Medicine* 2006 May 1;54(4):171–173.

8. Grimes DA, Schulz KF. An overview of clinical research: The lay of the land. *The Lancet* 2002 Jan 5;359(9300):57–61. doi:10.1016/s0140-6736(02)07283-5.

9. https://www.fda.gov/patients/clinical-trials-what-patients-need-know/what-are-different-types-clinical-research

10. Piantadosi S. *Clinical Trials: A Methodologic Perspective*. John Wiley & Sons; 2017 Aug 28.

11. Thorat SB, Banarjee SK, Gaikwad DD, Jadhav SL, Thorat RM. Clinical trial: A review. *International Journal of Pharmaceutical Sciences Review and Research* 2010, 1;101–106.

12. Hatfield I, Allison A, Flight L, Julious SA, Dimairo M. Adaptive designs undertaken in clinical research: A review of registered clinical trials. *Trials* 2016 Dec;17(1):1–3. doi:10.1186/s13063-016-1273-9.

13. Kulkarni SK. *Hand Book of Experimental Pharmacology*. Vallabh Prakashan; 1987.

14. Clinical trial wikipedia, the free encyclopedia. Jan 28 2008. Available from: http://en.wikipedia.org/wiki/clinical_trial. 28 Jan 2008

15. Mahan VL. Clinical trial phases. *International Journal of Clinical Medicine* 2014 Dec 4;5(21):1374.

16. Gawai AA, Shaikh F, Gadekar M, Deokar N, Kolhe S, Biyani KR. A review on: Phase '0'clinical trials or exploratory investigational new drug. *Turkish Journal of Pharmaceutical Sciences* 2017 Apr;14(1):84.

17. Gibas C, Jambeck P, Fenton JM. *Developing Bioinformatics Computer Skills*. "O'Reilly Media, Inc"; 2001.

18. Lesk AM, Chothia C. How different amino acid sequences determine similar protein structures: The structure and evolutionary dynamics of the globins. *Journal of Molecular Biology* 1980 Jan 25;136(3):225–270.

19. Oliver GR, Hart SN, Klee EW. Bioinformatics for clinical next generation sequencing. *Clinical Chemistry* 2015 Jan 1;61(1):124–135.

20. Skounakis E, Farmaki C, Sakkalis V, Roniotis A, Banitsas K, Graf N, Marias K. DoctorEye: A clinically driven multifunctional platform, for accurate processing of tumors in medical images. *The Open Medical Informatics Journal* 2010;4:105; Geller G, Holtzman NA. Implications of the human genome initiative for the primary care physician. *Bioethics* 1991 Oct 1;5(4):318–325.

21. Wang X, Liotta L. Clinical bioinformatics: A new emerging science. *Journal of Clinical Bioinformatics* 2011 Dec;1(1):1–3.

22. Schwarz E, Leweke FM, Bahn S, Liò P. Clinical bioinformatics for complex disorders: A schizophrenia case study. *BMC Bioinformatics* 2009 Oct 1;10(S12):S6.

23. Zhou XJ, Gibson G. Cross-species comparison of genome-wide expression patterns. *Genome Biology* 2004 Jun;5(7):1–5.

24. International Society of Translational Medicine (ISTM) n.d.. http://www.stmed.org

25. Lin JD. Levels of the first-phase insulin secretion deficiency as a predictor for type 2 diabetes onset by using clinical-metabolic models. *Annals of Saudi Medicine* 2015 Mar;35(2):138–145.

26. Li Q, Lai L. Prediction of potential drug targets based on simple sequence properties. *BMC Bioinformatics* 2007 Dec;8(1):1–1.

27. Wang JT, Liu W, Tang H, Xie H. Screening drug target proteins based on sequence information. *Journal of Biomedical Informatics* 2014 Jun 1; 49:269–274.

28. Su Y, Wang S, Li E, Song T, Yu H, Meng D. Analysis of gene logic networks for arabidopsis. *Current Bioinformatics* 2013 Apr 1;8(2):244–252.

29. Kour A and Gupta N. "RNA inference: A new technology for genetic improvement of major fruit species." *International Journal of Current Microbiology and Applied Sciences* 2019;8(3): 1209–1218.

30. Lee JF, Hesselberth JR, Meyers LA, Ellington AD. Aptamer database. *Nucleic Acids Research* 2004 Jan 1;32(suppl_1):D95–D100. doi:10.1093/nar/gkh094.

31. Phoebe Chen YP, Chen F. Identifying targets for drug discovery using bioinformatics. *Expert Opinion on Therapeutic Targets* 2008 Apr 1;12(4):383–389.

32. Shaikh SA, Jain T, Sandhu G, Latha N, Jayaram B. From drug target to leads-sketching a physico-chemical pathway for lead molecule design in silico. *Current Pharmaceutical Design* 2007 Dec 1;13(34):3454–3470.

33. Rondel RK, Varley SA, Webb CF, editors. *Clinical Data Management*. Wiley; 2000 Jan.

34. Krishnankutty B, Bellary S, Kumar NB, Moodahadu LS. Data management in clinical research: An overview. *Indian Journal of Pharmacology* 2012 Mar;44(2):168. doi:10.4103/0253-7613.93842.

35. Chang J, Zhu X. Bioinformatics databases: Intellectual property protection strategy. *Journal of Intellectual Property Rights* 2010 Nov 1;15(6):447–454.

36. Clark DE, Pickett SD. Computational methods for the prediction of 'drug-likenesses. *Drug Discovery Today* 2000 Feb 1;5(2):49–58.

37. Neufeld ML, Cornog M. Database history: From dinosaurs to compact discs. *Journal of the American Society for Information Science* 1986 Jul;37(4):183–190.

38. DiMasi JA, Hansen RW, Grabowski HG. The price of innovation: New estimates of drug development costs. *Journal of Health Economics* 2003 Mar 1;22(2):151–185.

39. Prosdocimi F (2010). Introdução à bioinformática. *Curso Online*. Available at [http://www2.bioqmed.ufrj.br/prosdocimi/FProsdocimi07_CursoBioinfo.pdf]

40. Rao VS, Das SK, Rao VJ, Srinubabu G. Recent developments in life sciences research: Role of bioinformatics. *African Journal of Biotechnology* 2008;7(5).

41. Hamosh A, Scott AF, Amberger J, Valle D, McKusick VA. Online Mendelian inheritance in man (OMIM). *Human Mutation* 2000 Jan;15(1):57–61.

42. http://libdatabase.uchc.edu/databases/databases.asp

43. Thompson R, Johnston L, Taruscio D, Monaco L, Béroud C, Gut IG, Hansson MG, Peter-Bram A, Patrinos GP, Dawkins H, Ensini M. RD-Connect: An integrated platform connecting databases, registries, biobanks and clinical bioinformatics for rare disease research. *Journal of General Internal Medicine* 2014 Aug;29(3):780–787.

44. Waters AP. EVIMalaR: A model for international cooperation in scientific research. *Nature Reviews. Microbiology* 2013 Aug;11(8):505–506.

45. http://www.florinash.org/hypotheses

46. http://www.chernobyltissuebank.com/

47. Martin-Sanchez F, Iakovidis I, Nørager S, Maojo V, de Groen P, Van der Lei J, Jones T, Abraham-Fuchs K, Apweiler R, Babic A, Baud R. Synergy between medical informatics and bioinformatics: Facilitating genomic medicine for future health care. *Journal of Biomedical Informatics* 2004 Feb 1;37(1):30–42.

48. Lynn DJ, Lloyd AT, O Farrelly C. Bioinformatics: Implications for medical research and clinical practice. *Clinical and Investigative Medicine* 2003 Apr 1;26(2):70–74.

49. https://www.techjockey.com/blog/

50. Majhi V, Paul S, Rachna J. Bioinformatics for healthcare applications. *Amity International Conference on Artificial intelligence*, 204–207, 2019.

51. Overington JP, Al-Lazikani B, Hopkins AL. How many drug targets are there? *Nature Reviews Drug Discovery* 2006 Dec;5(12):993–996.

52. Kellis M, Wold B, Snyder MP, Bernstein BE, Kundaje A, Marinov GK, Ward LD, Birney E, Crawford GE, Dekker J, Dunham I. Defining functional DNA elements in the human genome. *Proceedings of the National Academy of Sciences* 2014 Apr 29;111(17):6131–6138.

53. Alanazi HO, Abdullah AH, Qureshi KN. A critical review for developing accurate and dynamic predictive models using machine learning methods in medicine and health care. *Journal of Medical Systems* 2017 Apr 1;41(4):69.

54. Han J. How can data mining help bio-data analysis? In *Proceedings of the 2nd International Conference on Data Mining in Bioinformatics* 2002 Jul 23 (pp. 1–2).

55. Antonie ML, Zaiane OR, Coman A. Application of data mining techniques for medical image classification. In *Proceedings of the Second International Conference on Multimedia Data Mining* 2001 Aug 26 (pp. 94–101).

56. Dasu T, Johnson T, Muthukrishnan S, Shkapenyuk V. Mining database structure; or, how to build a data quality browser. In *Proceedings of the 2002 ACM SIGMOD international conference on Management of data* 2002 Jun 3 (pp. 240–251).

57. Han J, Pei J, Kamber M. *Data Mining: Concepts and Techniques*. Elsevier; 2011 Jun 9.

58. Andrews H, Patterson CL. Singular value decomposition (SVD) image coding. *IEEE Transactions on Communications* 1976 Apr;24(4):425–432.

59. Lan K, Wang DT, Fong S, Liu LS, Wong KK, Dey N. A survey of data mining and deep learning in bioinformatics. *Journal of Medical Systems* 2018 Aug;42(8): 1–20. doi:10.1007/s10916-018-1003-9.

60. Matthiesen R, Amorim A. Proteomics facing the combinatorial problem. In *Bioinformatics Methods in Clinical Research* 2010 (pp. 175–186). Humana Press. doi:10.1007/978-1-60327-194-3.

61. Serra A, Galdi P, Tagliaferri R. Machine learning for bioinformatics and neuroimaging. *Wiley Interdisciplinary Reviews: Data Mining and Knowledge Discovery* 2018 Sep;8(5): e1248.

62. Ohno-Machado L, editor. Data science and informatics: when it comes to biomedical data, is there a real distinction? *Journal of the American Medical Informatics Association*. 2013 Nov 1;20(6):1009.

63. https://www.ncbi.nlm.nih.gov/book/NBK25461/

64. https://www.policymed.com/2010/05/the-importance-of-clinical-trials.html

2 Bioinformatics Tools and Software in Clinical Research

Deepika Bairagee, Nitu Singh, and Neelam Jain
Oriental University, Indore, India

Urvashi Sharma
Medi-caps University, Indore, India

CONTENTS

2.1 BIOINFORMATICS

In the early 1970s, Ben Hesper and Paulien Hogeweg coined the term "bioinformatics" and described the extensive research they intended to do as the "study of informatics processes in biological systems." *In situ* hybridization was used by Marvin Carruthers and Leroy Hood in 1981 to find 579 real human genes and build a programmable DNA sequencing system. The Human Genome Project began in 1988. Huaung et al. used these ideas to conduct a year-long experiment in molecular biology in the year 2000. Based on temporal gene expression data, these ideas improved their ability to reveal distinct paths of neutrophil growth.

Bioinformatics (BI) is a branch of computer science that deals with the evaluation, explanation, and management of biological indicators. The researchers founded the European Molecular Biology Laboratory (EMBL) and GenBank to be able to produce a large database of biological sequences and structures. The various DNA sequences can be supplemented by the DNA data available from massive information basics. When it comes to BI, the current focus is on functional details of proteins/genes, structural protein evaluation, and metabolic route comparison for different species through pre-clinical/clinical studies [1].

Clinical research assures that personal-use medications, products, diagnostics, and treatment regimens are safe and effective. Many different software programs are capable of predicting communications like potential toxicities and indications, correctly identifying the accomplishment of a unique chemical, or even readjusting for novel applications. Clinical investigation is distinct from medical practice in that it looks into both existing and novel treatments [2].

2.2 BI APPLICATIONS

BI's goal is to make vast amounts of data created by molecular biology technology accessible. A large-scale DNA range, as well as resources for the production of protein-coding regions, will be produced.

The DNA processor chip, which is made up of thousands of nucleotide fragments, is found using the concept of multiple gene phrase dimensions. It is the only method for identifying gene coding DNA in a sample and locating genetic subgroups. Data mining technologies are strangely more useful in genomics and proteomics accomplishments. The rate of success in recognizing genetics-related diseases is measured in terms of the creation of new drugs and their efficacy. Several international, national, autonomous, and charitable organizations are collaborating to preserve data that is genetically related to a digital health record. The computation and interpretation problems associated with the molecular level can be solved by using mathematics and statistics. The Process Computational (PC) research and development can be leveraged to create appropriate computational tools [3,4]. Figure 2.1 depicts the many BI applications, which are described in the following.

2.2.1 SEQUENCE ANALYSIS

The cornerstone of this is unquestionably generic and is reliant on the entire genome's genetics. Sequence analysis is a method for determining the structure, function, and presentation of a sequence. There are various sophisticated tools available in computer research, each with its own set of pros and cons. These resources have been adapted to detect sequences linked to an organism's DNA mutations. The shotgun sequence approach can be used to quickly evaluate the sequences of several pieces.

2.2.2 PROTEIN FRAMEWORK PREDICTION

It is possible to anticipate the three-dimensional structures of amino acids. Finding secondary, quaternary, or tertiary structures of proteins is problematic. This function should be performed using either crystallographic or BI resources [5].

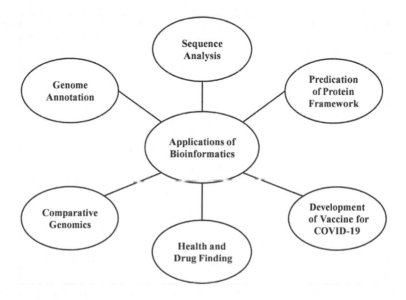

FIGURE 2.1 Applications of BI.

2.2.3 ANNOTATION OF THE GENOME

The regulatory sequence and required protein-coding are used in this genome annotation. This is how all genes, coding sections, and the genome's structure are found.

2.2.4 COMPARATIVE GENOMICS

Proportional genomics is the study of genetics through comparison. The genomic roles of genes, CDs, mRNA, tRNA, and rRNA will be explored to find the genomic structure and functional relationship among biological species. Researchers utilize inter-genomic maps to follow the whole chain of events that take place in the genomes of various animals. These maps can reveal a lot about the chromosomal organization and point mutations.

2.2.5 DRUG DISCOVERY AND HEALTH

Drug discovery based on molecular infection is carried out using BI resources. Scientists develop medicines that can suit significantly more than 500 genotypes based on disease and diagnosis. The distribution of specific medications is based on the cells into which they are targeted, as well as other computing resources [4,5].

2.2.6 DEVELOPMENT OF COVID-19 VACCINE

BI pipeline programs are crucial for predicting possible biomolecules that can help with infectious disease detection, prophylaxis, and treatment. BI tools and methodologies for analyzing biological data provided by genomes, transcriptomics, proteomics, and structural omics are gaining traction and providing immediate biological solutions [2]. BI has evolved into a system that analyzes reliable data gathered from epidemiological investigations, thanks to the growing number of databases and other curated web archives. As a result, pathogen identification, molecular pathogenesis, and the development of a good diagnostic tool are all highly likely. BI has recently been coupled with next-generation sequencing techniques to investigate infectious microbial and viral illnesses [6].

The methodologies for medication and vaccine repurposing have been revolutionized by these omics tools. Proteomics and transcriptomics can be employed in conjunction with genomes to detect proteins, for example, in surface host–pathogen communication [7]. Traditional lead screening in vaccine and pharmaceutical manufacturing took years to complete in the past. Before additional validation for clinical trials, a few computer algorithms were used to predict vaccine candidates. New ways were devised to shorten the length and expense of medication production, particularly with the use of a complex computer pipeline. These computational systems could be utilized to predict antigenic peptides and identify immunogenic companies in array responses for vaccines [8].

In December 2019, Wuhan, China, reported an unusual pneumonia outbreak. The epidemic quickly spread from the epicenter to other nations throughout the world, affecting tens of thousands of people and killing a large number of individuals, raising the disease to pandemic status. The WHO had connected the disease outbreak to a specific coronavirus strain known as SARS-CoV-2 (severe acute respiratory syndrome coronavirus 2), as well as the infection COVID-19, by December 31, 2019 [9].

During the 2003 epidemic, SARS-CoV-2 was a novel group 2B coronovirus strain with roughly 70 percent genetic affinity to SARS-CoV. The virus is thought to have been transmitted by bats because it shows a 96 percent resemblance to a bat coronavirus. The epidemic caused unprecedented statewide and worldwide travel restrictions, as well as serious financial difficulties, in many countries [10].

St the beginning of the COVID-19 pandemic, researchers were focusing their efforts on developing a viable vaccine candidate for the virus. This has led to unparalleled levels of collaboration between the federal government, academic institutions, and commercial enterprises in the development of vaccines and antibody counter-measures based on the structural and non-structural proteins of the viral genome [11]. Such collaboration has an impact on current technology, notably BI, to accelerate the response to an illness that is unquestionably spreading. This has resulted in the most well-known vaccine research endeavor in history, with a few teams developing vaccine candidates and completing medical trials in as little as a month or two. BI techniques such as reverse vaccinology (RV), immune-informatics, and structural vaccinology are only a few of the BI techniques available today for designing and developing safe, consistent, and effective vaccinations [11,12].

RV is a vaccine development method that involves identifying novel antigens by analyzing data that is nearly certainly genetic. Based on the pathogen's genetic makeup products, a method uses BI resources to discover target allergen information. RV can identify genes that code for proteins that may lead to favorable epitopes. This leverages appropriate programming tools to detect the open reading frames (ORFs) of the organism's genome and determine various antigenic and physicochemical parameters linked with antigenic epitopes using resources like the VaxiJen host [13].

RV is profitable and saves time as compared to standard pharmaceutical development methods. It enables the recognition of antigens that are present in lower quantities or are only expressed at certain points of the organism's life cycle, reducing the number of proteins studied. It enables more efficient allergen screening and scientific research into diseases that cannot be grown *in vitro* [14].

RV's viability is contingent on pathogen genetic data being available. It should potentially be possible to recognize both standard antigens and novel antigens that work on a completely different notion when novel antigens that work on a completely different concept become widely available. Few scientists employed RV in the development of the COVID-19 vaccine, and instead relied on data from the SARS-CoV-2 genome. SARS-CoV-2 chimeric multi-epitope vaccines have also been developed using it [8,14].

Immuno-informatics, or the BI approach to immunology, necessitates a thorough examination of an organism's immunomics and the use of the resulting data to aid in the prediction of immune reactions to specific particles. In the loyalty for humoral and mobile cells, which can be immune websites or the COVID-19 virus, immuno-informatics methods were utilized [9]. Several such methods have also been employed to see if a section of the genome linked to SARS-CoV-2, which is generally a necessary protein, can trigger a protective response. This is referred to as antigenicity, and it should be included. Some of the tools available are TEpredict, CTLPred, NetMHC, and Epitopemap. Deep machine learning approaches were used in a study [8,15,16] to forecast likely immunogenic components from viral genome arrangements.

These methods support researchers in better understanding genetic polymorphisms in Major Histocompatibililty Complex (MHC)classes I and II in target human populations, as well as in anticipating cytotoxic and helper T cell epitopes. Furthermore, in terms of existing vaccination for COVID-19 [8], these technologies shorten the time required to discover immunogenic sites and raise the possibility of a safe vaccine.

Several studies have gone even further, combining SARS-CoV-2 protein epitopes and immunogenic domain names to create truly unique vaccines, such as multi-epitope vaccines or chimeric vaccine construction, with or without predicted adjuvants to recover the immunogenicity of their potential products. Architectural vaccinology, on the other hand, addresses the viral epitope's conformational popular characteristics, resulting in good candidate antigens [9]. This necessitates a thorough examination of the vaccine candidate to see if it contains any conformational features or a home that could trigger a well-organized response. This is most likely immunological monoclonal antibodies, based on van Regenmortel's observations that monoclonal antibodies recognize conformational rather than linear epitopes [8,17].

To map antigenic epitopes and find conformational properties that may affect immunogenicity, architectural metrics such as peptide architectural stability, solvent visibility, hydrophobicity, and codon optimization are often utilized. To determine antigens and create antibodies, molecular docking, characterization simulations, and homology modeling are used. Structural vaccinology techniques were utilized to anticipate vaccine possibilities in the case of SARS-CoV-2, resulting in the identification of structurally stable, safe, and efficacious vaccine candidates [18].

2.3 TOOLS OF BI

Computational techniques are used to create data and knowledge about character depiction, phylogeny studies, and the determination of additional and physiochemical properties of proteins. These data are useful for determining how biomolecules behave within a living cell. The BI that can be employed for different projects is as follows [19].

2.3.1 SEQUENCE ANALYSIS AND GENE IDENTIFICATION

Through grouping examinations, it becomes possible to comprehend and distinguish several manifestations of a biomolecule, such as a nucleic protein or an acid. This method is thought to have started with the retrieval of sequences of related molecules from public databases. In terms of the need for distinct resources to enable its functions, nucleic acid and protein emphasize the importance of selecting capacity, frameworks, and homologues with extraordinary accuracy [20].

2.3.1.1 Basic Local Alignment Search Tool (BLAST)

BLAST is a program that searches for areas of local similarity between two sequences. The program calculates a statistical value by comparing nucleotide or protein sequences to databases of sequences. BLAST can assist in inferring practical and evolutionary sequence links as well as identifying homologous protein sequences from individuals. BLAST can be used for a variety of purposes. A handful of them is discussed as follows [21].

- Looking at species. If you are sequencing DNA from unidentified types, BLAST may help recognize the correct species which are homologous.
- Hunting for domains. For a necessary protein series (or perhaps a translated nucleotide series) To understand necessary protein series (or a translated nucleotide series BLAST domains can be used.
- Evaluating phylogeny. You can make use of the BLAST website to build a tree this is definitely phylogenetic of BLAST results.
- Mapping DNA to a chromosome that is definitely understood. If you're sequencing a gene coming from a recognized species but don't have any elementary concept of the chromosome site, BLAST will allow you to do this. BLAST explains to you the position regarding the unidentified sequence within the target. Note: BLAST can also be used to map annotations from one system to another or look for common genetics in two types that can be related.
- Searching for homology [22].

Many research projects involving sequencing of either DNA or necessary proteins require obtaining biological information associated with a newly sequenced series that is possibly unknown. If the scientists do not have information that can frequently be obtained, BLAST is utilized. The BLAST algorithm investigates for homologous series in predefined and annotated databases connected with the user's choice. The specialist can gain an understanding of a gene or necessary protein's purpose and its last evolutionary relations amongst the recently sequenced DNA and more developed information in an easy and quick method [20]. The user will receive a written report specifying found homologous sequences and their regional alignments to your question series following the BLAST search.

BLAST identifies homologous sequences employing a technique that is heuristic initially and finds quick matches between two sequences; therefore, the strategy will not use the entire series for the analysis. After the preliminary match, BLAST tries to start neighborhood alignments from the initial matches. This also means that BLAST doesn't guarantee the alignment, and so the use of the Smith-Waterman algorithm should be used for optimal results [23].

The type of query sequence (DNA or protein) and the database utilized distinguish five different BLAST programs:

BLASTP matches an amino acid arrangement to the database of protein sequences that are required.

BLASTN compares a series of nucleotide queries to a database of nucleotide sequences.

BLASTX compares the six-frame translation of a nucleotide query series to a protein series database; this is conceptual.

TBLASTN matches a necessary protein query arrangement to a series that has been nucleotide-dynamically changed in at least six reading frames.

TBLASTX compares the six-frame translations of a nucleotide query series against the six-frame translations of a sequence database to guarantee the query series is a nucleotide one.

2.3.1.2 FASTA

FASTA (pronounced FAST-AYE) is a heuristic for finding significant suits from a question string q and a database sequence d. FASTA's basic method is to find the most important diagonals when you look at the dot-plot or powerful programming matrix. The overall performance of a word size affects the algorithm parameter k, frequently 6 for DNA and 2 for amino acids [24–26].

2.3.1.3 HMMER

Sean Eddy created HMMER, a free and widely used software suite for sequence analysis. Its primary use is to find the required proteins with homologous nucleotide sequences and to perform series alignments. It discovers homology by comparing a profile-HMM with either a single sequence or a sequence database. Sequences that score significantly higher on the profile-HMM than a null design are considered homologous to the sequences utilized to create the profile-HMM [27]. The program build is used to create profile-HMMs from a multiple sequence alignment within the HMMER bundle. The HMMER program's profile-HMM execution is based on Krogh and colleagues' work. HMMER is a system tool that has been ported to Linux, Windows, and the macOS. Pfam and InterPro are two well-known protein databases that rely heavily on HMMER. Several additional BI tools, including UGENE [27,28], utilize HMMER.

2.3.1.4 European Molecular Biology Open Suite Software (EMBOSS)

EMBOSS is a large reported package of open resource software for molecular biology. It includes over 200 applications for molecular series analysis as well as other tasks which can typically be BI. It combines a core command-line user interface that is effective [29]. The software contains a number of characteristics that can be useful, such as the ability to deal with data in a variety of forms and the ability to retrieve series information from the internet in a transparent manner.

EMBOSS includes C that has been considerably developed by having a clean and consistent Active Pharmaceutical Ingredient (API). There is much inbuilt that is of good use, for example, the control regarding the command line and common file formats, which makes it a strong and convenient system to build up and launch BI programs. True to the character of open source, EMBOSS is free to any or all in addition to being certified to be used by everyone else under the General Public Licenses (GPL) and the Lesser General Public License (LGPL). No institute or individual owns the code, nor previously has. Underneath the terms of the permits, it can be installed via the internet, copied, customized, and passed on, as long as the same freedoms are maintained for other people [30].

EMBOSS is established. It has been used in demanding manufacturing environments, reflecting the readiness of this code base. A significant brand new version is gradually released each year. If you require the latest code, the present resource rule tree can be downloaded via Consumer Value Stores (CVS). There are thousands of packages on sites all over the world. Many interfaces with EMBOSS can be obtained, including simple to use internet interfaces and workflows that are powerful, enabling programs to become combined into analysis pipelines [29–31].

2.3.1.5 THREADER

THREADER is another program. The purpose of this software is to "thread" a sequence of amino acid side chains onto a backbone structure (a fold) and analyze this proposed three-dimensional structure using a set of potentials and a separate salvation potential. Cluster [32] presented many computational BI practices.

2.3.1.6 Clustral Omega

The most recent Multiple Sequence Alignment (MSA) algorithm from the Clustral family is Clustral Omega. Only aligned proteins are suitable for this approach. When working with big series sets, Clustral Omega beats other MSA algorithms in terms of completion time and overall placement quality. Clustral Omega can align 190,000 sequences for a processor that has been alone for several hours. The Clustral Omega algorithm creates multiple series positioning by first using the k-tuple approach to perform a pairwise alignment. Following that, using the mBed approach, the sequences are grouped. Following that, the k-means approach is used to cluster the data. The Unweighted Pair Group Method with Arithmetic meaning (UPGMA) algorithm is then used to build the guide tree. Finally, the HHalign bundle, which aligns two profile hidden Marko designs (HMM) [33], creates an unquestionably numerous sequence.

2.3.1.7 SEQUEROME

Using a tool named "Sequerome," the Bioinformatics and Computational Biosciences Unit (BCBU) produced an outline layout. Sequerome is a web-based series that combines the outcomes of a unique sequence-alignment report with outward research tools and hosts that perform advanced level series modifications and allow users to record the assessment's steps. Sequerome is nucleic web-based Java software that functions as a front-end to BLAST queries and enables easy access to web-distributed resources for protein and acid research [34].

The device has been featured in *Science* since its inception in 2005, and it is formally linked to BI, which is used by many people all over the world. The characteristics of a sequencerome are: profiling BLAST sequence positioning reports by linking the results page to a panel of alternative party services; tabbed browsing allowing the user to go back to earlier operations; seeing the third party perform personalized sequence manipulations; allowing one-box any-format sequences input; and alternative options for sequence feedback, such as seeing third party websites, cached storage and retrieval of input sequences, and a three-pane browsing environment. There is direct access to the software application. There are three panels on the website: the Query pane, the Results pane, and the Search History pane. Any of these windows can be resized to perform activities that are parallel to each other. Running concurrent BLAST lookups on numerous sequences, analyzing them all, or seeing the constraint digests for each document may all be done within a browser.

2.3.1.8 ProtParam

"ProtParam" is a computational device that calculates a variety of physiochemical parameters found inside a required protein. The gene models are identified using series positioning utilizing Gene Manufacturing Using Multiple Sources of Evidence (JIGSAW). In comparison to existing identification algorithms like Ensembl and UCSC's well-known Gene track, it is expected to generate significantly higher accuracy. Single nucleotide polymorphisms (SNPs) will be utilized to identify the genetic disorders that are being studied. ORF stands for open-frame reading which is used for a variety of BI analysis, graphical viewing, and data management. The prokaryotic cost promoter (PPPT) is used to upstream the conventional promoter sequence. Virtual Footprint is a tool for studying the bacterial zone [35].

2.3.1.9 WebGeSTer DB

In the "WebGeSTer DB" information base, a transcription that is intrinsically detected in microbial genome sequences and plasmids is stored. It is a collection of the intrinsic terminators of transcription and is unquestionably the best. It contains over 2,200,000 bacterial terminators from all 2036 chromosomes and 1508 plasmids. The database is the repository for the WebGeSTer program, which can search for and determine intrinsic terminators in virtually any fully sequenced genome, including microbial genomes [36]. When searching the database, users will find data on the structural parameters of individual terminators such as the sequence, stem and cycle period, mismatches and spaces, the U-trail, genomic locations, gene name, and accession quantity in both tabular and composite form. In addition, summary statistics for terminator pages of the entire genome are obtained. For step-by-step research, raw documents for individual genomes (.zip files) are obtained.

Users can fine tune their search by inputting a name linked with the species, a taxon ID, or a number that is specific to their genomes.

To depict the event for the terminators, an interactive map is generated using the quality of a single gene level [36,37].

2.3.1.10 GENSCAN

GENSCAN is BI software. Its main function is to acquire a DNA series and locate a reading this is definitely open (a series of DNA that may encode a necessary protein) that accords with the genetics. GENSCAN was created by Professor Chris Burg who is currently working on his thesis. The "GENSCAN" method is used to identify the total number of genes in genomic DNA. "Soft berry" technologies are primarily used to research genome alignment, contrast, and control in genomic plants, including pets [37]. In point of fact, there are primarily four profiles in a parameter file and each profile is equivalent to C+G%.

Primarily two types of structure predictions are found: proteins and genes. For knowledge of the gene forecast and analysis terms, one should know for sure what genes there tend to be. Genes are the biological device of heredity; they are situated at a distinct place (locus) for a chromosome and is specific. Essentially genes are of two sorts.

Coding genes or exons are a sequence of DNA that carries instructions to convert amino acids into protein. For instance, there are globin genes that give directions for the production of the hemoglobin protein. An individual contains 50,000 various genes that work collectively in intricate combinations to perform functions that are different.

The total structure prediction of genes simply by using computational advances is done by looking for the location and function of a gene. The situation mainly requires splitting up and establishing the exon–intron boundaries of a gene [38].

Two techniques are followed by gene forecast:

- Statistical habits identification: This approach of gene prediction utilizes all-purpose information about the gene framework, for example, statistics and guidelines. Knowledge of gene structure as discussed earlier includes the promoter region and the start and end sequences of exon and intron.
- Sequence similarity comparison: As similarity is founded on evolution, either our sequence is homologous or not. This approach is dependent on similarity which takes benefit of the fact that if the series is similar it will have a function that is the same. Nevertheless, the construction of genes cannot accurately be predicted based on sequence information alone [38,39].

2.3.2 Phylogenetic Investigations

The hereditary relationship between a group of identical chemicals, organisms, or life kinds is in terms of transformative commitment. To predict the peak of a chemical with unknown capabilities and a poor stream track, phylogenetic studies are used. Molecular Evolutionary Genetics Evaluation (MEGA) is a powerful and user-friendly program for analyzing protein arrangement information from courses and populations [39]. It is built with phylogenetic trees in mind to obtain transformative results from proximity. "MOLPHY" is a software application that uses the likelihood approach to analyze sub-atomic phylogenetic trees. The possibility approach to phylogenetic evaluation is used by both phylogenetic analysis by maximum likelihood (PAML) and by a phylogeny inference package (PHYLIP), and each bundle contains a few computational resources. Improvements to phylogenetic trees can be found in open-source libraries such as Bio, Js tree, and Treeview. "Jail view" is well-known software used for editing and analyzing a large number of [5] series.

2.3.3 Protein Structure and Function Predication

The essential protein particles in the preliminary phase are usually unstructured amino acid sequences. During the last step, a three-dimensional (3D) construction of organic traits is developed. The collapse of proteins into a pre-imperative structure is required for the performance of biological activities. This leads to the conclusion that 3D dwelling is required for feature extraction and that this type of framework can be investigated using X-ray crystallography or Nuclear Magnetic Resonance (NMR). The thermodynamic balancing physio-chemical criteria, with a global minimum free energy of protein surface and minimum free energy, determine the contrast of estimating structures and the quality of the imitation technique. Table 2.1 lists the many methods for determining the requisite protein structure and function [40,41].

2.3.4 Drug Discovery

The drug discovery process entails the identification and validation of a disease target, as well as the synthesis and growth of a chemically transmitted molecule that interacts with that target. The pharmaceutical business requires High Throughput Screening (HTS) data, computational chemistry, combinatorial chemistry, Absorption, Distribution, Metabolism and Excretion (ADME) informatics, cheminformatics, toxicology, metabolic modeling, BI in health materials, drug discovery and metabolism, and other multidisciplinary informatics. Within and across divisions, there is advancement and development of information methods [42].

TABLE 2.1

The Numerous Tools Used to Determine the Structure and Purpose of Proteins

Name of the Tool	Applications
CATH	A self-loading tool for arranging protein associations.
RAPTORX	Predicts protein structure based on multi-layout threading or solitary threading.
APSSP2 and JPRED	Protein auxiliary structure is predicted using this method.
PHD	Forecasts the structure of a neural network.
HMMSTR	Predicts the organization's structural correlations in proteins.
MODELLER	Based on comparative modeling, forecasts the 3D structure of a protein.
PHYRE and PHYRE2	These web-based systems are used to forecast protein structure C.

1. *Identification of the drug targets.* The current strategy is to identify the physiologically active applicant. Medicines are typically only generated when the specific medication for those drug activities required has been identified and investigated. The number of possible medical innovation targets is continually increasing. The use of BI to mine and store the human genome has aided in defining and classifying the nucleotide configurations of those genetics accountable for target protein-coding, as well as identifying new targets that may lead to new treatments. It is a location where people's genes are supposed to unwind and take center stage. Pharmaceutical breakthrough time is becoming more data-intensive as a result of the unnaturally good quality of genes discovered by drug developers [41]. BI is employed to decide on and analyze more biological drugs in the pipelines of pharmaceutical companies. This is expected to increase the number of drugs available considerably.

2. *Validation of medicine targets.* BI also provides methods and algorithms for predicting novel medicine objectives as well as storing and managing drug target information. Following the development of "possible" pharmacological goals, there is a clear need to initiate a robust organization based on a putative target and a disease of high interest. When it comes to medicine enhancement, this method is known as target validation, and the organization of these organizations is a crucial rationale. It is a region where BI is almost always involved and crucial. Drug target validation can help to reduce the risk of failure at the medical approval stage of the examination.

3. *From target discovery to preclinical development.* From target selection to preclinical development, there are various stages to drug breakthroughs. A breakthrough in today's medicine demands the transformation of small protein particles into massive volumes of data. High throughput screening (HTS) is used to find the bulk of hit compounds [5]. HTS is a high-tech drug discovery approach that is gaining popularity among professional researchers for proving how precise compounds are for a given target. This system can monitor 10,100 chemicals per day, whereas ultra high throughput screening (UHTS) can provide results for up to 100,000 tests per day.

   Procedures such as particle count measurement for variable test concentrations, 2D fluorescence power circulation analysis for florescence interference, and color quenching adjustments in scintillation proximity assays (SPAs) have recently been developed to reduce some aberrations [22].

4. *Lead optimization.* This is a procedure that comes after the lead finding procedure. The lead's purpose is to make lead compounds, which are new analogies with more strength. It reduces the number of target tasks and optimizes leads, as well as other characteristics like selectivity and metabolic stability. If architectural information about the target can be gathered, this optimization can be achieved through chemical customization of the hit structure, with structure-activity evaluation (SAR) and framework-based design being preferred. This molecule has a high drug similarity and will never interact with the P-glycoprotein or any of the cytochrome P450 enzymes [40].

2.4 DRUG DEVELOPMENT

The growth method is afflicted by material that has a new identity and has just been discovered. When looking at the R&D divisions of pharma businesses, chemical ability is mostly demonstrated. SARs (dwelling task relationships) are usually established. Preclinical animal scientific investigations and clinical pharmacology are the two types of pharmacology used for substances (individual studies).

2.4.1 PRECLINICAL RESEARCH

A putative medicine is put through rigorous pharmacological and *in vivo* testing on animal models (mice, rats, pigs, dogs). The most important research areas are persistent toxicity that might be acute, subacute, or chronic (toxicity profile). The evolution of therapeutic safety and efficacy concerns the ratio of the median efficient dosage to the median effective dose, called (ED50). Absorption, Distribution, Metabolism and Excretion (ADME) investigates the processes of consumption, circulation, elimination, and metabolism (pharmacokinetics) [41].

2.4.2 CLINICAL STUDIES

Clinical trials are used to assess a medicine's metabolic and pharmacologic action in people, as well as the risks associated with raising the dose, to conduct early efficacy research. Approximately 90 percent of medical students who enrolled in medical school were unsuccessful in the clinical trials of medication. In 1991, the primary cause of clinical studies on drug failure was Pharmacokinetics (PK)/bioavailability issues (40 percent), followed by insufficient effectiveness (30 percent), and toxicity (10 - 12percent)). In the year 2000, inefficiency was the leading reason for failure (27 percent), followed by profitability and market concerns (20 percent). There are four stages of clinical testing:

Phase 1:Clinical pharmacology advancement;
Phase 2:Managed clinical development;
Phase 3:Extended clinical advancement;
Phase 4:Surveillance during post-marketing general clinical use.

2.5 NEW APPROACHES

One of the most used BI-based drug development strategies is computer-aided drug design (CADD). This term refers to a technique of modeling drug-receptor interactions. CADD techniques are influenced by BI tools, software, and databases. In BI CADD, many crucial aspects need to be investigated. BI approaches are used in two phases of medication development to abstract data that is exciting for revealing significant genes and proteins, speeding up the process of medicine creation, and lowering the cost. Gene identification is an essential step in the process for all of them [42].

2.6 DEVELOPMENT OF A DRUG DATABASE

BI innovation has prevented the above-mentioned therapy and encouraged disclosure and preparation in the field of medicine. Before inventing the BI tools, the researchers belonged to various fields, including pharmacology, clinical sciences and chemistry, and they worked together to introduce the new compound to the world. When opposed to traditional practice processes, computer software allows you to quickly break down the molecules. CADD was discovered as a method of generating efficient medicines as a result of developments in computer software design and information technology. The following are examples of common medications offered by various companies to assist researchers and scientists who are interested in designing this new medication:

- Potential Drug Target Database (PDTD);
- Therapeutic Target Database (TTD);
- Target Database (TDR);
- Manually Annotated Targets and Drugs Online Resource (MATADOR);
- Drug Bank;
- Tropical Disease Research;
- Tuberculosis (TB) Drug Target Database.

Ion transportation, conformational alteration of important protein-nucleic acids, and structures that occur in biological systems are studied using strong molecular resources like Abalone, Ascalaph, Discovery studio, Amber, and FoldX.

2.7 BI AND HEALTHCARE INFORMATICS

Preclinical, clinical, post-clinical, and healthcare management data and information are collected in health informatics. When it comes to information technology, researchers and professionals now have no-cost tools at their disposal for improving public health, the healthcare system, and industry [5]. This is unmistakably a biological situation. The major goal of healthcare informatics is to give healthcare providers comprehensive data on their patients' health. This knowledge tends to make their job easier in terms of making the best treatment decision at the appropriate moment. Furthermore, by utilizing healthcare informatics, in-patients in outlying locations can obtain advice from the best healthcare professionals on the list of options available.

BI and analytics are concerned with the analysis, interpretation, storage, development, and optimization of large amounts of biomedical data. The shift in capabilities, as well as the notion of electronic health records (EHRs), which allows for the establishment of a vast data warehouse, is certainly computational. It can be used to figure out how phenotypes and genotypes are linked. Many computational methods are utilized to examine and analyze massive biological databases to better understand the illness, and these forecasts are useful for connecting to healthcare data quickly. Researchers in this field are currently working on developing new approaches and algorithms for analyzing genomic and proteomic data available in a range of industries, including drug discovery, medication, and location-related data [43].

Artificial intelligence (AI) is a higher-level technology targeted at restoring partial/complete human intelligence. The field of molecular BI has seen a surge in interest in computational biology research. When compared to other computational techniques, AI formulae provide better performance and accuracy for DNA sequencing. To classify microarray disease data, Shi et al. highlighted the requirement for AI in gene selection resources [44]. In the field of BI, Serra et al. examined the application of device finding methods for dimensionality reduction in difficult data and feature selection for biomarker assignment in natural data. Single nucleotide polymorphism analysis and category device learning are used to accomplish this. Drug repositioning and patient categorization based on neuroimaging data are examples of BI applications [45].

2.8 SOFTWARE FOR CLINICAL TRIALS

Medical research studies are an endeavor to test novel medical treatments or simply a new way of using an existing treatment to see if it could be an easier way to prevent, monitor, diagnose, or treat an ailment. Any drug that is being tested in a clinical trial for the first time must pass pre-clinical tests. *In vitro* scientific investigations and trials on animal populations are included in pre-clinical studies [46]. To obtain initial effectiveness, toxicity, and pharmacokinetic information, a wide variety of dosages for the study medicine are focused on animal subjects or even an *in vitro* substrate. The information presented in the medical trial is obtained and reviewed by various software, the majority of which are listed below [46,47].

2.8.1 ELECTRONIC DATA CAPTURE (EDC)

In clinical trials, the EDC information system, also known as the electronic case report form (eCRF), is a crucial program. Clinical trials rely on accurate data, and EDC solutions are used to gather, clean, and analyze clinical research data. To improve data collection and minimize the time it takes to advertise medical treatments and products, EDC substitutes the old paper-based data collection process [47]. EDC solutions are popular among pharmaceutical corporations and contract research firms (CROs).

EDC has the potential to increase data accuracy while also shortening the time it takes to collect data for medication and other health-related investigations. Many drug developers have to make a trade-off when employing an EDC system to drive their drug development: there is a lengthy setup process followed by significant gains in terms of trial time. If an EDC is affordable in general, the savings during the trial's lifetime should exceed the setup costs [48].

In 2013, the US Food and Drug Administration (FDA) announced eSource assistance, which involves gathering medical test data electronically from the start and moving it to the cloud, as opposed to EDC's more typical manner of collecting data on paper and transcribing it into the EDC system [49]. Because eSource adoption was slow at first, the FDA prepared a webinar in 2015 to help promote the July recommendation. According to the TransCelerate eSource Initiative (founded in 2016) this was to: "enable the understanding of the eSource ecosystem as well as the best use of electronic data sources on the market to boost worldwide research that is clinical international medical trial execution for stakeholders." "The majority of firms" expected to deploy eSource in the following three years, according to research done by the Tufts Center for the Study of Drug Development in 2017. With 87 percent of analytical websites indicating that combining eSource with today's EDC will be "useful" or "very beneficial" [48,49], a move away from EDC is possible.

2.8.2 REMOTE DATA CAPTURE (RDC)

This is the method for automatically counting scientific data. It is commonly utilized in medical investigations, where it is referred to as electronic data capture. In actual sciences, mobile automated observation equipment is linked to a laboratory observer by a cellphone or any other communication website link, such as in hydrology. The EDC system was influenced by RDC procedures [50,51].

2.8.3 ORACLE CLINICAL

Oracle Clinical is a medical data management system that includes subsystems for research design, randomization, data input, batch data loading, laboratory ranges, custom validation and derivation treatments, discrepancy management, and data extraction. Oracle Clinical is compatible with the Thesaurus Management System (TMS), the Life Sciences Data Hub (LSH), and queries.

Oracle Clinical Remote Data Capture (RDC) is an EDC solution that works with studies created by Oracle Clinical. RDC can be used to collect, analyze, and report clinical data acquired during the subject check-out phase of a clinical trial [52].

2.8.4 ECRF

This is software used to collect data for a medical investigation. eCRFs are often web-based programs that incorporate a variety of data types and industries and are used to collect data in medical testing or observational research. eCRFs are critical components of medical research since they are the tool that research coordinators and detectives use to enter data from source documents, which is then exported and sanitized before being entered into a database for statistical analysis [49].

This has increasingly revolutionized paper-based CRFs, resulting in various benefits for sponsors, such as faster data collecting, better data cleansing, and, overall, a reduction in the efforts and costs associated with the information administration process. Simplicity (simple design, ease of use), security (access control, information encryption), dependability (information backups, seamless solution), and compliance are only a few of the important aspects that eCRFs should have (positioning with 21CFR Part 11 requirements).

2.9 DRUG RESEARCH AND DEVELOPMENT

A significant number of pharmaceutical companies have built enormous throughput testing facilities and are increasingly dedicating automation to screen a large number of chemicals. BI advancements have made it possible to evaluate a wide range of analysis domains across the genome. The trillions

FIGURE 2.2   Steps of drug development.

of bytes of data generated by the Human Genome Project can be analyzed using BI technologies. Gene sequence databases, gene expression databases, protein arrangement databases, and related assessment tools all help to control whether and how a particular molecule is linked to a disease procedure, enabling the development of new and improved therapy targets [50]. An approach that is both effective and medically sound could cut the time and cost of developing effective pharmaceuticals in half. Computational approaches are used to forecast drug-likeness, which involves lowering and identifying potential compounds that are unlikely to survive later stages of discovery and development. Hereditary algorithms and network-based neural techniques could be used to predict drug similarity. The traditional pharmaceutical discovery process begins with the drug target and progresses through the lead element to the medicine.

The first and most crucial element in this technique is the ability to set different treatment goals for future scientific studies. According to statistics, the majority of pharmaceuticals now on the market are based on 483 pharmacological targets (45 percent receptors, 28 percent enzymes, 5 percent ion stations, and 2 percent atomic receptors) [51]. The steps of drug development are depicted in Figure 2.2.

2.9.1   TARGET IDENTIFICATION

Before any potential novel therapy is identified, the mental state must be grasped in order to identify the underlying causal problem. The conditioned apparatus specifies an explanation for a condition's possible causes, as well as the condition's route or phenotype. The need of recognizing the most recent and clinically relevant molecular medicine input is enormous. Receptors, proteins, enzymes, deoxyribonucleic acid (DNA), and ribonucleic acid (RNA) are all closely linked to disease processes and could be used as medication targets. These medication molecules connect to the medication target, triggering a series of intracellular metabolic activities and, ultimately, a cellular reaction [51]. The application of metabolicand cellular that identifies important avenues involved in the traditional technique of target recognition comprised enzymes that metabolized the chemical (drug) and proteins that function as receptors. As a result, ideal therapeutic targets are narrow in scope and have a favorable influence on the biological route of interest while avoiding interference with other pathways.

By revealing how molecules interact with one another at the molecular level of an illness, genomics and proteomics are routinely used to develop viable therapeutic goals. These molecular connections are studied by looking at the sequence of the gene or protein, the 3D protein framework, and their interconnections in the various expression/metabolic, regulatory, and signaling networks with which the drug interacts. The drug target's interaction relationships with one another can be inferred from the community that forms [52]. The medication target may be limited to the most skilled drug target to an extent that is unquestionably great depending on their devotion to the conversation. The identification of targets is done using computational techniques.

2.9.1.1   Molecular Docking

This system can anticipate the location of an intermolecular complex formed between two molecules, as well as the ligand orientation that will result in the least energy complex. Various visualization tools, like pymol and rasmol, can be used to examine a ligand's 3D posture, which can aid in determining the best appropriate ligand match. This calculates the score using docking algorithms created by a huge number of architecturally conceivable combinations [53]. Signal transduction involves a variety of biomolecules, including nucleic acids, proteins, and lipids. It is very promising to employ a docking technique to estimate the affinity among these biomolecules or receptors (medicine targets) and drug candidates. The most important docking requirement may be the structure of the protein or receptor of interest. The residence is determined via X-ray crystallography or magnetic nuclear resonance (NMR) spectroscopy. The rating is dependent on how well a medication candidate fits within the target, which is determined by the scoring purpose.

2.9.1.2 Proteomics

Proteomics is a branch of biology that studies protein function and structure. It is a large-scale study that looks at how important protein abundance changes over time, as well as their interaction partners and communities, to understand cellular processes. Massive volumes of data can be stored and analyses may be conducted quickly when employing BI tools for proteomics [54]. Biomarker discovery, biofluid integration, and muscle data are all covered by today's proteome BI resources and information. This technology is of brand-new benefit to practical cooperation among certain bio-fluids and cells, with the potential to produce therapeutically substantial effects.

2.9.2 TARGET VALIDATION

The choice of the most powerful pharmaceutical target, rather than the availability of prospective targets, is a rate-limiting issue when using technical breakthroughs in drug development. This provides a challenge to bioinformaticians in terms of building tools that can select from a large data collection a small quantity of genes or possibly a pharmacological target with an organization that is most efficient in fighting infection.

Despite this, 324 therapeutic targets with clinical significance have been discovered. This means that, despite the abundance of genetic data on both humans and pathogens, current pharmaceutical development research is focused on and dependent on a small number of therapeutic targets. Because of incorrect target identification, a huge number of medications fail in the early stages of pre-clinical research. A support vector device based on the physiochemical features of critical protein configurations, rather than a homology protein and annotation 3D framework, has recently been built as a pharmaceutical target prediction approach [55].

For target validation, the following databases and tools are used.

2.9.2.1 Gene Logic

Gene logic is a well-known integrated genomics firm that delivers a wide range of information. This is a data management solution for genomics and life science labs. It will produce a short list of aims that can be expressed more frequently in sick conditions using its huge library of cyst and normal genes. This set of goals can be used to verify functional targets. The investigator can use this database to find a distinct phrase for the target as well as its level of presence in a variety of muscle and disease types. Researchers can also use the database to look into the levels of expression of other proteins connected with various pathways.

2.9.2.2 Ribonucleic Interference Technology

Intradigm (Rockville, MD, USA) employs RNA interference (RNAi) technology, which employs short interfering RNA (siRNA) oligos to selectively and effectively eliminate homologous mRNA. Intradigm is a medication that inhibits angiogenesis, which has been linked to cancer, inflammation, autoimmune disease, and other diseases [55]. The capacity to perform effectively *in vivo* target validation with medically viable siRNA is particularly useful in evaluating the importance of a single gene or protein in the infection process, as well as numerous genetics of the same path and the role of this pathway in infection. These findings are critical not just for medication research, but also for the creation of siRNA, which is a very useful tool.

2.9.2.3 Immusol

Immusol (San Diego) has developed a patented method for *in vivo* target validation for utility and protection in a variety of disease models using siRNA vectors. Immusol possesses inducible RNAi vectors that can be securely implanted into developed tumefaction cells or cell lines to produce RNAi, which will be utilized to validate targets. The inducible vector will be tested using a mouse xenograft tumor model.

2.9.2.4 Aptamers

To validate and evaluate targets, Nascacell works with aptamers, a nucleic acid-based artificial acid. Aptamers bind to the small-molecule drug's active binding site and inactivate the helpful epitope on protein without affecting the other components. Aptamers duplicate the effect of a very small pharmaceutical molecule as a consequence. Furthermore, an aptamer can distinguish between distinct post-translational modifications by inactivating a protein at a steady physiological turnover rate [54].

2.9.3 LEAD IDENTIFICATION/OPTIMIZATION

The testing of element libraries is the first step in the lead recognition process. Substances that interact with a specific essential protein and affect its function are increasingly being discovered. Lead optimization is a complicated medicine discovery technique in which the substance framework of a confirmed hit is significantly refined to provide a pre-clinical medication candidate. The optimization associated with the potential lead is carried out due to the element's main and secondary structure being modified. This stage, which is unquestionably complex, will be increased thanks to innovation and improvements in computation, which analyze important ingredients to produce a lead prospect. The alternative chief issue is the precise prediction of drug toxicity. To identify and optimize leads, the following software is used.

2.9.3.1 Comprehensive Chemistry that Is Health

This database contains vital information on biochemical features such as medication course, pKa, and Log P data for over 8390 pharmaceutical particles.

2.9.3.2 The Drug Bank

This is a database that connects a substance's pharmacological data to a variety of therapeutic goals while also providing detailed sequence, construction, and pathway information. It combines detailed medication information with broad medical target information. The drug bank's medicine is undeniably vast, and target data has allowed the creation of many present drugs to treat a wide range of unusual and newly discovered ailments.

2.9.3.3 PharmaGKB

This is a computer program that predicts how medicine will react based on individual genetic characteristics. The PharmGKB is a pharmacogenomics knowledge base that includes medical dosing guidelines and pharmaceutical labels, as well as gene–drug correlations and genotype–phenotype interactions that may be clinically useful. PharmGKB is a database that collects, curates, and disseminates information about how genetic variants affect pharmacological responses [2].

2.9.4 Pre-clinical Development

Pre-clinical research includes drug testing of potential therapeutic interventions in cells and animals. After that, clinical trial candidates could be chosen based on their efficacy and safety in illness models. Before clinical trials can begin, all drugs must have data from several toxicological pre-clinical tests to support their likely safety in people. Pharmacogenomics is a novel area based on molecular pharmacology and functional genomics that arose in the late 1990s. Genome analysis can be used to investigate the related genes that cause differences in drug metabolism in the body and diverse genotype reactions to drugs. As a result, drug effects and safety evaluations are completed more quickly. This is an important tool for studying rational drug usage and personalized treatment [56].

2.9.5 Clinical Trials

Clinical trials are used to evaluate pharmaceutical safety and efficacy, whereas clinical research is used to find and develop new treatments. Target discovery, validation, and lead optimization are all steps in the drug development process. Pre-clinical investigations, rigorous clinical trials, and post-marketing vigilance for medication safety are the next steps. Not just in drug discovery, but also in drug development, software and BI technologies are crucial. The use of informatics in the discovery of new health and illness data, data management during clinical trials, and the secondary use of clinical data are all discussed.

Computerized data capture and remote data collection are used in clinical trials. The information is collected and stored using an eCRF. Clinical software such as eClinical and Oracle Clinical are two examples [2].

2.10 PHARMACOVIGILANCE

Pharmacovigilance is a pharmacological method for detecting, assessing, analyzing, and preventing drug side effects, particularly long and short-term unfavorable effects. Typically, pharmacovigilance refers to the technology of collecting, recording, researching, assessing, and evaluating data from doctors and patients on the adverse effects of drugs, biologics, herbal medicine, and traditional remedies with the purpose of:

- Identifying new drug hazards;
- Protecting patients from injury.

Pre-marketing (medical phase) and post-marketing pharmacovigilance are the most prevalent types of pharmacovigilance, which begin in the clinical phase and continue throughout the product life cycle for the medicine. The process of collecting a huge number of such details regarding a pharmaceutical begins in Phase I of this medical trial and continues even after approval; a few post-market safety scientific investigations are typically undertaken, with several deemed mandatory by drug regulating corporations around the world [53].

Adverse drug reactions (ADRs) are defined by pharmacovigilance as "an unpleasant and unexpected reaction to a drug that occurs at doses commonly used for the prevention, diagnosis, or treatment of disease, or the adjustment of physiological purpose."

As the frequency of media reports about pharmaceutical recalls has increased, pharmacovigilance has become more essential among doctors and scientists. ADRs are typically neglected since clinical trials only involve a few thousand people at most, and research groups are small. Post-marketing surveillance uses data mining of natural reporting systems and patient registries, as well as case report studies, to establish the link between medications and ADRs [53–55].

2.11   SOFTWARE FOUND IN PHARMACOVIGILANCE

We will now discuss some software used in pharmacovigilance.

2.11.1   ORACLE ARGUS SAFETY

Starting with medical development and continuing through post-marketing surveillance, companies are gradually turning their focus to a more holistic approach to safety. Oracle Argus Safety is a comprehensive solution created primarily for the pharmacovigilance requirements of the life sciences industry. Argus Safety's comprehensive database maintains global regulatory compliance, enables intelligent security decisions, and streamlines security and risk management chores [15]. Oracle Argus Safety can help companies:

- Ensure global regulatory compliance and make faster, science-based protection decisions;
- Integrate risk and safety management;
- Reduce pharmacovigilance costs.

2.11.1.1   Ensures Global Regulatory Compliance

Global standards and directives, such as those issued by the European Medicines Agency (EMEA), FDA, International Council for Harmonisation of Technical Requirements for Pharmaceuticals for Humas Use (ICH), and other national agencies, should be followed by life science companies. Significant license partnerships, as well as the outsourcing of numerous services, further complicate the situation, and the industry's global reporting needs are becoming increasingly complex to manage. Businesses rely on Argus Safety to help them stay on top of their regulatory compliance obligations in a timely and proactive manner.

Managers and executives can gain visibility into reporting metrics and compliance by utilizing Argus Safety's extensive reportability functions, which include complete dashboards and data [20]. The flexible structure of Argus Safety enables the creation of virtually any business procedure, as well as crisis management and compliance reporting both within and across license partner systems.

Argus Safety encourages compliance by offering a robust reporting engine that allows customers to tailor particular rules to satisfy regulatory standards. It assures 100 percent conformance and lowers the cost of regulatory reporting when paired with additional automated options like "Auto/Force distributes" and "Auto-Submit."

2.11.1.2   Offers Better Data Insights and Faster Decision-making

With the help of scientists, scientific institutions, and industry thought leaders, Argus Safety was developed, resulting in an efficient and successful administration.

For swiftly entering safety information, the device is appropriate. Advanced capabilities like sophisticated workflows, wordlist management, company-defined reporting needs, and considerable automation are available to achieve optimum case effectiveness.

End users can query the device without knowing SQL or having to rely on IT. As a result, security data is readily available for reporting and analysis. Other segments can be fully connected with Argus Safety, allowing you to easily reconcile Serious Adverse Events (SAEs) from tests or handle routine reports [41].

Argus Safety's focus on business procedure efficiency allows pharmacovigilance teams to focus on drug clinical efficacy at a lower cost. It provides executives with the knowledge they need to make timely, science-based decisions regarding their products and portfolios, such as a drug's overall safety profile.

2.11.1.3   Integrates Risk and Safety Management

Pharmacovigilance divisions are dealing with an increase in the number of instances, a variety of data resources, and an unquestionably complex business environment, all of which provide a challenge to their ability to assess and understand security data. While dealing with real-time item risk profiles, the company is attempting to keep procedure efficiency.

Argus Safety is a complete solution that solves the safety and threat management needs of the business from beginning to end. It offers a full reporting system that includes the ability to reconcile clinical trial SAEs and manage partner adverse events [49].

Risk profiles, including reporting automation using higher-level problems, document storage space, and quantity of data points for advanced level visualization and tracking pregnancy registries, are all included in Argus Safety to fulfill regulatory criteria and manage a product's advantages. To provide proactive security, it can also be seamlessly connected with signal detection and administration systems. From medical research to marketing and advertising, companies may utilize the Argus Safety package to ensure that security is managed in a proactive manner.

2.11.1.4   Proven and Accepted in the Business

Argus Safety has worked for over a decade at some of the industry's most prestigious firms, including global pharmaceutical, biotech, Contract Research Organization (CRO), and medical device firms. Thanks to a well-thought-out product plan, it's always growing better.

The most important features and benefits of Oracle Argus Safety are:

- Ability of several affiliates to view and work out regional labeling from the same locked instance;
- Support for e-signatures;
- Duplicate search capabilities;
- A central staging location for analyzing submitted affiliate marketing cases;
- Electronic submission capabilities;
- Querying, asserting, and submitting cases;
- Audit trails.

The following are some of the advantages of adopting Oracle Argus Safety:

- Improve data security with a single situation administration database;
- Get an immediate return on investment by streamlining and integrating affiliate operations;
- By dethatching redundant data, you can boost worker productivity. Allowing safety reduces risk. This is vital in deciding whether or not to accept or reject a case.

2.11.2   ARISg

ARISg is the most commonly utilized pharmacovigilance computer program by pharmaceutical companies. It is used by over 300 companies around the world to keep their important medication safe. As required by numerous regulatory bodies throughout the world, ARISg provides all of the capabilities required to handle an occurrence that has an unfavorable and unpleasant effect. From case input to automatic generation of delivering prepared adverse event (AE) statements, it covers all pharmacovigilance processes, including CIOMS 1, MedWatch 3500A, and many more.

ARISg is a key component of a pharmacovigilance-integrated threat management system, helping companies to keep track of their goods and spot any safety issues ahead of time. With its adjustable workflow and advanced level automation functions, ARISg aids in the management of ADRs. By automating the routing of events as indicated in their workflow rules, people can create something that better meets their company process and standard operating procedure (SOP) expectations. Both on-premise and on-demand versions of ARISg are available.

2.11.3 ORACLE AERS

Biopharmaceuticals, vaccines, healthcare companies, and CROs all have to satisfy stringent regulatory deadlines while operating with limited resources. They must determine and oversee safety operations, as well as ensure strict adherence to evolving regulations before they become issues. This is certainly important for business management; and they may demand clear visibility in their data.

To solve the issues of processing global safety data, Oracle AERS provides a single international solution with effective automation and productivity features. Oracle AERS aids in the capture, management, reporting, and evaluation of significant events involving poor item compliance for all medical items, such as medications, medical products, vaccines, biologics, and gene treatments derived from both medical and natural sources [57].

Oracle AERS was developed by specialists in the field and is simple to use. The sensitive interface provides excellent functioning at the touch of a button. Each subsystem includes a navigator panel that serves as a broad foundation. The AERS graphical user interface dynamically displays critical case information, allowing users to visualize case elements and comprehend the overall case picture. Validated screens and an easy-to-use end-user interface are used for configuration and management.

2.11.4 PvNET

PvNET is a comprehensive pharmacovigilance system that is integrated into the industry's leading software for adverse event reporting, ADR information management, and individual case protection report (ICSR) reporting. By including safety information from the beginning of development to the completion of marketing and promotion, PvNET assists users in making vital decisions. PvNET's drug safety is rigorously audited across the board for Good Manufacturing Practice (GMP) compliance, 21CFR compliance, and ICH E2B compliance.

Some of PvNET's most popular features are:

- Workflow, which allows you to separate data entry, quality control (analysis), and scientific analysis;
- Significant data validation and cross-field situation data validation for E2B compliance;
- Dictionary assistance and management on a global scale;
- Audit records for tasks involving security information management;
- Management dashboard provides a dashboard with the ability to focus on the right domain personnel who are supplying the data to alert them to anomalies and outliers so they may act quickly;
- Crafting a narrative about a traumatic occurrence and providing multilingual text support;
- Checking for duplicate cases;
- Centralized triage before comprehensive case processing.

2.11.5 REPCLINICAL

repClinical is a safe, web-based solution that helps you manage critical pharmacovigilance responsibilities in a timely and cost-effective manner. repClinical can be used to record negative events, generate regulatory reports, and trade Integrated Care Records Service (ICRs) with a variety of regulatory systems and business partners. All of this is accomplished in a simple and effective manner. To assist in the generation of exact E2B reports, repClinical provides clutter-free displays with easy-to-use capabilities.

The information in the individual case safety report is closely designed by data in repClinical (ICRs). In all circumstances, information is tracked and stored. Safety reports can save and track administrative and identifying information from this comprehensive scenario report. Messages will eventually be able to track and save message data.

repClinical allows you to create, amend, and track cases. Other users are allocated to situations for examination or update. As detailed in the digital Transmission of Individual Case Study Reports Message Specification, case data matches information found in area B of the ICSR.

You obtain access to the information in repClinical with only a single click. This allows you faster access to information without having to navigate through the menu. repClinical also performs a minimal data check for scenarios arising during the earliest stages of data entering [57,58].

2.12 CONCLUSION

Clinical trials are an important link between advancements in health study technologies and improved medical care. Marketing is an important branch of health science that studies human disease, prevention, treatment, and well-being. Clinical trials for new drug candidates are becoming more complex, time-consuming, and costly procedures. The pharmaceutical industry is fiercely competitive, and there is a lot of pressure to have a novel medication licensed as soon as possible. As a result, pharmaceutical companies are under tremendous pressure to improve their performance and efficacy to achieve medication breakthroughs and development. The technology endeavor is widely seen as the only means of achieving that goal.

The introduction of electronic medical testing and computer-assisted drug analysis has revolutionized drug discovery and development. Genomic analysis, sequence analysis, hereditary formulas, phylogenetic inference, genome database business and mining, optical computation and holographic memory, structure identification, and image analysis are among the resources developed by application firms. As a result of their incorporation, several stages of medical trials, including target identification, validation, randomization, data collecting, data integration, and trial pharmacovigilance and management, have become more structured, efficient, and controllable. Pharmaceutical businesses and regulators have adopted technology to improve not only efficiency but also clinical data evaluation (i.e., the transformation of trial information into functional knowledge) and data safety, all while lowering the overall cost of testing. Establishing and using large data strategies for clinical studies, leveraging new ways to offer patient-centric tests, bringing development in existing procedures and methods with new practices, providing assistance in sample research from existing information resources for progressive tests, easier data sharing, and combating information confidentiality issues are all speculated BI features in medical research (Figure 2.3). As a result of the necessity to innovate, researchers and regulators have been experimenting with new and more challenging approaches to studying interesting services using BI and software tools, resulting in a design that is quicker, more flexible, and more complicated. We can only hope that, in the long term, faster technological advancements will lead to new levels of discovery that could never have been obtained with traditional natural data processing. Clinical trials use clinical research to examine the safety and efficacy of medications, treatment regimens, diagnostic products, and technologies. Drug discovery and development benefit greatly from BI software applications. BI tools are classified into standard and customized items to meet needs. BI is used daily to analyze sequences and predict structure using tools such as BLAST, EMBOSS, and THREADER. Software such as electronic data capture, remote data capture, and electronic case report form is especially beneficial for storing data in clinical trials. After a drug is approved for sale, software like Oracle Argus or ARISg is used to track its safety. Various software is being used for drug design, drug development, clinical trials, and pharmacovigilance. In this chapter, we have learned about the many modern software and BI tools utilized in clinical research.

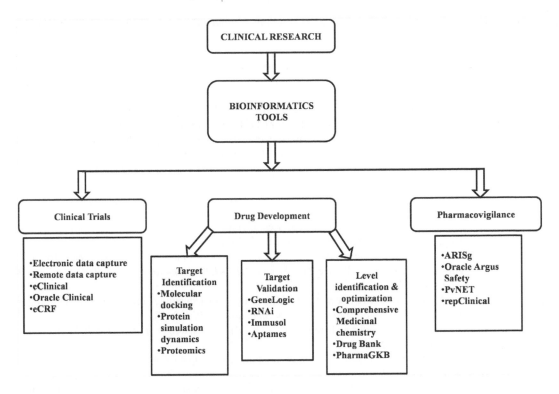

FIGURE 2.3 The role of BI and software tools in clinical research.

ACKNOWLEDGMENT

The authors are grateful to the administration of Oriental University, Indore, for their assistance.

REFERENCES

[1] Majhi, V., Paul, V. S., Jain, R., Bioinformatics for healthcare applications. *Amity International Conference on Artificial Intelligence (AICAI)*, 204–207, 2019.

[2] Gill, S. K., Christopher, A. F., Gupta, V., Bansal, P., Emerging role of bioinformatics tools and software in evolution of clinical research. *Perspectives in Clinical Research*, 7, 115, 2016.

[3] Oyelade, J., Soyemi, J., Isewon, I., Obembe, O., Bioinformatics, healthcare informatics and analytics: an imperative for improved healthcare system. *International Journal of Applied Information System*, *13*, 1–6, 2015.

[4] Qadrie, Z. L., Wani, S. U. D., Gautam, S. P., Contribution of pharmacist for transforming global health care system: roles and opportunities. *International Journal of Current Pharmaceutical Research*, *11–12*, 2020.

[5] Jain, S., Sood, M., and Paul, S. (Eds.), *Advances in computational intelligence techniques*. Springer Nature, 2020.

[6] Lefterova, M. I., Suarez, C. J., Banaei, N., and Pinsky, B. A., Next-generation sequencing for infectious disease diagnosis and management: a report of the Association for Molecular Pathology. *The Journal of Molecular Diagnostics*, *17*, 623–634, 2015.

[7] Weinstock, G. M., Genomic approaches to studying the human microbiota. *Nature*, *489*, 250–256, 2012.

[8] Chukwudozie, O. S., Duru, V. C., Ndiribe, C. C., Aborode, A. T., Oyebanji, V. O., Emikpe, B. O., The relevance of bioinformatics applications in the discovery of vaccine candidates and potential drugs for COVID-19 treatment. *Bioinformatics and Biology Insights*, *15*, 11779322211002168, 2021.

[9] Zhu, H., Wei, L., Niu, P., The novel coronavirus outbreak in Wuhan, China. *Global Health and Research Policy*, 5, 1–3, 2020.

[10] Zhou, P., Yang, X. L., Wang, X. G., Hu, B., Zhang, L., Zhang, W., ... Shi, Z. L. A pneumonia outbreak associated with a new coronavirus of probable bat origin. *Nature*, 579, 270–273, 2020.

[11] Burwell, S. M., *Improving pandemic preparedness: lessons from covid-19*. Council on Foreign Relations, 2020.

[12] Sempowski, G. D., Saunders, K. O., Acharya, P., Wiehe, K. J., Haynes, B. F., Pandemic preparedness: developing vaccines and therapeutic antibodies for COVID-19. *Cell*, 181, 1458–1463, 2020.

[13] Ullah, M. A., Sarkar, B., Islam, S. S., Exploiting the reverse vaccinology approach to design novel subunit vaccines against Ebola virus. *Immunobiology*, 225, 151949, 2020.

[14] Rappuoli, R., Reverse vaccinology. *Current Opinion in Microbiology*, 3, 445–450, 2020.

[15] Chukwudozie, O. S., Gray, C. M., Fagbayi, T. A., Chukwuanukwu, R. C., Oyebanji, V. O., Bankole, T. T., ... Daniel, E. M., Immuno-informatics design of a multimeric epitope peptide based vaccine targeting SARS-CoV-2 spike glycoprotein. *PLoS One*, 16, e0248061, 2021.

[16] Yang, Z., Bogdan, P., Nazarian, S., An in silico deep learning approach to multi-epitope vaccine design: a SARS-CoV-2 case study. *Scientific Reports*, 11, 1–21, 2021.

[17] Van Regenmortel, M. H., Requirements for empirical immunogenicity trials, rather than structure-based design, for developing an effective HIV vaccine. *HIV/AIDS: Immunochemistry, Reductionism and Vaccine Design*, 163–188, 2019.

[18] Salmaso, V., Moro, S., Bridging molecular docking to molecular dynamics in exploring ligand-protein recognition process: an overview. *Frontiers in Pharmacology*, 9, 923, 2018.

[19] Thapar, P., Bioinformatics-tools and applications. In *The proceedings of the 12th INDIACom Int. Conference*, 5044–5047, 2018.

[20] Koonin, E., Galperin, M. Y., Sequence—evolution—function: computational approaches in comparative genomics, 2002.

[21] Pertsemlidis, A., Fondon, J. W., Having a BLAST with bioinformatics (and avoiding BLASTphemy). *Genome Biology*, 2, 1–10, 2001.

[22] McGinnis, S., Madden, T. L., BLAST: at the core of a powerful and diverse set of sequence analysis tools. *Nucleic Acids Research*, 32, W20–W25, 2004.

[23] Wheeler, D., Bhagwat, M., BLAST quickstart. In *Comparative genomics*, pp. 149–175, Humana Press, 2007.

[24] Gertz, E. M., Yu, Y. K., Agarwala, R., Schäffer, A. A., Altschul, S. F., Composition-based statistics and translated nucleotide searches: improving the TBLASTN module of BLAST. *BMC Biology*, 4, 1–14, 2006.

[25] Pirooznia, M., Perkins, E. J., Deng, Y., Batch blast extractor: an automated blastx parser application. *BMC Genomics*, 9, 1–5, 2008.

[26] Using Sequence Databases and Search Tools, http://csmbio.csm.jmu.edu/biology/courses/bio480_580/mblab/database.html 2008

[27] Finn, R. D., Clements, J., Arndt, W., Miller, B. L., Wheeler, T. J., Schreiber, F., ... Eddy, S. R., HMMER web server: 2015 update. *Nucleic Acids Research*, 43, W30–W38, 2015.

[28] Information Resources Management Association, ed. *Bioinformatics: Concepts, Methodologies, Tools, and Applications*, IGI Global, 2013.

[29] Introduction to EMBOSS, http://emboss.open-bio.org/html/use/pr02s01.html

[30] Rice, P., Longden, I., Bleasby, A., EMBOSS: the European molecular biology open software suite. *Trends in Genetics*, 16, 276–277, 2000.

[31] Martin, D., Norway, E., Rice, P., The EMBOSS Administrator's Guide, 2000.

[32] Peng, J., Xu, J., Low-homology protein threading. *Bioinformatics*, 26, i294–i300, 2010.

[33] Daugelaite, J., O'Driscoll, A., & Sleator, R. D., An overview of multiple sequence alignments and cloud computing in bioinformatics. *International Scholarly Research Notices*, 2013.

[34] A Bigger BLAST, NetWatch. *Sciences*, 309, 1971, 2005.

[35] Gasteiger, E., Hoogland, C., Gattiker, A., Wilkins, M. R., Appel, R. D., Bairoch, A., Protein identification and analysis tools on the ExPASy server. In *The proteomics protocols handbook*, 571–607, 2005.

[36] Brooks, L., Kaze, M., Sistrom, M., A curated, comprehensive database of plasmid sequences. *Microbiology Resource Announcements*, 8, e01325–e01418, 2019.

[37] Mitra, A., Kesarwani, A. K., Pal, D., Nagaraja, V., WebGeSTer DB—a transcription terminator database. *Nucleic Acids Research*, *39*, D129–D135, 2011.

[38] Korf, I., Flicek, P., Duan, D., Brent, M. R., Integrating genomic homology into gene structure prediction. *Bioinformatics*, *17*, S140–S148, 2001.

[39] Flicek, P., Gene prediction: compare and contrast. *Genome Biology*, *8*, 1–3, 2007.

[40] Majhi, V., Paul, S., Jain, R., Bioinformatics for healthcare applications. In *2019 Amity Int. Conf. Artif. Intell. (AICAI)*, 204–207, IEEE, 2019.

[41] http://chromatic.tellmag.ro/cast-of-ybuuw/role-of-bioinformatics-in-pharmacy-and-healthcare-6f1d65

[42] Siddharthan, N., Prabu, M. R., Sivasankari, B., Bioinformatics in drug discovery a review. *International Journal of Research in Arts and Science*, *2*, 11–13, 2016.

[43] Samuel, P., Bioinformatics on health system. *European Journal of Biomedical Informatics*, 2021.

[44] W Shi, T., S Kah, W., S Mohamad, M., Moorthy, K., Deris, S., F Sjaugi, M., … Kasim, S., A review of gene selection tools in classifying cancer microarray data. *Current Bioinformatics*, *12*, 202–212, 2017.

[45] Thorat, S. B., Banarjee, S. K., Gaikwad, D. D., Jadhav, S. L., Tharat, R. M., Clinical trial: a review. *International Journal of Pharmaceutical Sciences Review and Research [Internet]*, *1*, 101–106, 2010.

[46] Rao, V. S., Srinivas, K., Modern drug discovery process: An in silico approach. *Journal of bioinformatics and sequence analysis*, *3*, 89–94, 2011.

[47] Amrutkar, S. P., Patil, P. A., Patel, R. S., Review on modern drug discovery process. *Research Journal of Pharmacology and Pharmacodynamics*, *12*, 137–141, 2020.

[48] Urquhart, C., Hamad, F., Tbaishat, D., Yeoman, A., Chapter 13: health information systems: clinical data capture and document architecture. *Information Systems: Process and Practice*, 233–253, 2017.

[49] Neuer, A., At the source, *International Clinical Trials*, *40–44*, 2015, Retrieved 24 May 2018.

[50] Kellar, E., Bornstein, S. M., Caban, A., Célingant, C., Crouthamel, M., Johnson, C., … Wilson, B., Optimizing the use of electronic data sources in clinical trials: the landscape, part 1. *Therapeutic Innovation & Regulatory Science*, *50*, 682–696, 2016.

[51] Aitkenhead, M. J., Cooper, R. J., Neural network time series prediction of environmental variables in a small upland headwater in NE Scotland. *Hydrological Processes: An International Journal*, *22*, 3091–3101, 2008.

[52] Chow, S. C., *Encyclopedia of biopharmaceutical statistics*. CRC Press, 2010.

[53] Shuka, S. S., Gidwani, B., Pandey, R., Rao, S. P., Singh, V., Vyas, A., Importance of pharmacovigilance in Indian pharmaceutical industry. *Asian Journal of Research in Pharmaceutical Sciences*, *2*, 4–8, 2012.

[54] Suke, S. G., Kosta, P., Negi, H., Role of pharmacovigilance in India: An overview. *Online Journal of Public Health Informatics*, *7*, 2015.

[55] Jahan, N., Hossain, M. A., Hossain, M. A., Amran, M. S., Review on pharmacovigilance practice for safety of medication system in Bangladesh. *Bangladesh Pharmaceutical Journal*, *20*, 105–114, 2017.

[56] Kaye, J. B., Schultz, L. E., Steiner, H. E., Kittles, R. A., Cavallari, L. H., Karnes, J. H., Warfarin pharmacogenomics in diverse populations. *Pharmacotherapy: The Journal of Human Pharmacology and Drug Therapy*, *37*, 1150–1163, 2017.

[57] Types of Pharmacovigilance Software's, https://sollers.edu/types-of-pharmacovigilance-softwares/ 2020

[58] Software used in Pharmacovigilance, https://www.clinskill.com/software-used-in-pharmacovigilance/ 2019

3 Computational Biology for Clinical Research

Rakhi Mishra

Noida Institute of Engineering and Technology (Pharmacy Institute),
Greater Noida, India

Rupa Mazumder

Noida Institute of Engineering and Technology (Pharmacy Institute),
Greater Noida, India

Prem Shankar Mishra

Galgotias University, Greater Noida, India

CONTENTS

3.1 INTRODUCTION

In recent years the combination of biological science and computer science (CS) have emerged as essential aids for investigating complex natural systems [1]. Computational biology is a biological study done to collect and analyze data related to the biological, medical, and health status of a single or group of patients [2]. Computational biology uses the science of computers, statistics, mathematics, and biological science to compute different databases in a brief period [3].

This is an emerging discipline, and computational biology is gaining momentum in the medical and tech worlds as an excellent means of quantifying vast datasets. Computational biology is an area in which there is a great deal of overlap with bioinformatics (BI) [4,5]. The two fields have developed in tandem with one another and often find use in systems where biological data and data models are

DOI: 10.1201/9781003226949-3

necessary. Information from different databases can be collected from various BI sources, which may be a specimen of patient tissue or genetic molecular research studies which have already been conducted [6–8]. This science has been directly used for the modeling of complex biological systems [9].

Nowadays, there is an extensive role of computational biological science for clinical research in which different diseases and their effect on one's health can be interpreted [10,11]. It also aids in finding new and better ways for the detection, diagnosis, treatment, and prevention of any particular disease [12]. New outcomes in detection, diagnosis, and treatment are only possible when a particular disease effect on different patients can be studied and correlated. The technique of computational biology makes this task easy by analyzing the patient database quickly and steadily in a short period [7,13].

Medical research has become increasingly dependent on sophisticated modeling, analysis, and computational techniques [7]. Clinical research makes use of new clinical trials as well as history studies to understand how a specific disease develops and also how it progresses over time [14,15]. Computational biology imparts support to clinical research study to generate data-driven hypotheses or even answer other research questions. The interaction between clinical research and computational techniques has been fruitful and synergistic [16,17].

Perhaps this has extensive applications in biomedical research. Despite using trial and error methods, doctors are prescribing medicine based on patient genetic and physiological conditions [18,19]. The biomedical approach is helping in the advancement of disease prevention as it aids the understanding of the genetic mechanism of disease, which makes it possible to take preventive measures before the onset of that particular disease [20]. The phase of drug development also helps to identify, validate, and develop new targets by correlating the study done through genes and gene therapy [21,22].

Thus, both disciplines, that is, bioinformatics and computational biology, are considered to be interdependent and essential studies in data science and biotechnology advancement and growth [23]. Computational biology, in contrast, helps the more complex issues, problems, and hurdles that arise during the same BI studies. It is also helpful to identify and examine the report of in silico results defining protein folding, motion, and interaction [24,25]. It also helps in the mapping of genomes and aids in modeling biological systems [26].

This chapter focus on the same new approach of computational biology, which can contribute to a new revolution in the field of BI and also in the health-care sector. We hope that the content and meritorious applications discussed in this chapter will benefit all readers [27,28] (Figure 3.1).

3.2 SOFTWARE USED IN COMPUTATIONAL BIOLOGICAL STUDIES

With the help and use of innumerable computer resources and tools, one can perform the processing and analysis of data at the molecular and cellular levels [29]. Sometimes different computational software is also available for a wide range of clinical research at the tissue, organ, or whole-body system level [30].

The following software is used in the field of computational biology for undertaking clinical, cellular, and molecular work [1,13,31]:

- PLOS Computational Biology Software;
- Nature Computational Biology Tools;
- Institute for Systems Biology List of Open-Source Computational Biology Software.

This software helps to give information on the progression of a disease; a clinician can also link specific patient characteristic patterns to the biology of a target through this software [3]. For the development of personalized medicines, linking patient body physiology with distinct phenotypes is an essential task for providing specific treatment [32]. The software used for computational biology successfully performs two functions [33]. Firstly, to identify and analyze measurable biochemical data of the patient related to the patient's prevention, diagnosis, and treatment—known as "GOLD STANDARD PARAMETERS" [4,23].

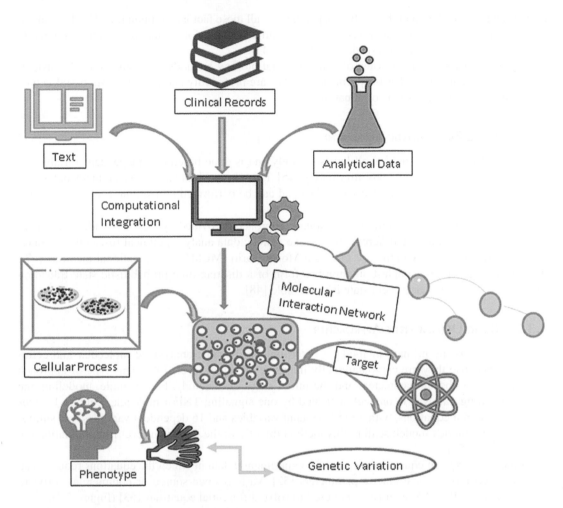

FIGURE 3.1 Computational biology and clinical research.

Secondly, to develop protocols and parameters based on the above reported biochemical parameters, which clinicians can use for following efforts of disease treatment [34].

Thus, very broadly, one can see that one uses a computational biology method and related software for (i) the discovery of a biochemical pattern for the reported and diagnosed disease and (ii) for the generation of patient data-driven reports for assessing and directing patient care [35,36].

3.3   COMPUTATIONAL BIOLOGY METHODS

The biological process involved in any illness or disease is different and involves a profound change of many physical processes involved in the entire human-natural system [37]. Various conditions also apply different extracellular and intracellular signaling mechanisms, which will produce other disease symptoms, responses, and so on [38,39].

Thus, in the treatment of a particular disease and for the development of personalized medicine, different factors are involved:

- The cellular, molecular, and genetic level(s) under study;
- Already reported and diagnosed literature reports of the disease [40,41];
- The system level(s) under study, from molecules to organisms;
- The available data;
- What biological processes are under study, within what context, and for what goals.

Fundamental is the "goal of the study." Depending on all these factors, computational biology methods are selected as different methods can produce different types of results; thus, before moving to the study, the study's goal must be decided first [42,43].

Discussed below is an overview of computational biology methods and some general considerations of different approaches [44]. The approaches are probability and deterministic-based, which can be used individually or in combination.

3.3.1 Basic Probabilistic Approaches

This type of approach is used at all levels of study and is done based on independent variables; it does not incorporate any previous information [45]. It can be used for static measurement and analysis of any injury response with sufficient data and can be performed in a simple test like Student's t-test [46].

In recent studies the "conditional probability approach" provided by Bayes is widely and more commonly used to analyze different studies like genetic data analysis, clinical research, and diagnostic medicine types, with the use of Chain Monte Carlo (MCMC) computational methods [47]. A Markov chain is the simplest autonomous form of a discrete-time probabilistic state-transition Markov model where the system state is observable [48].

3.3.2 Basic Deterministic Approaches

This approach is the primary method for deterministic dynamic analysis at molecular and cellular levels because they are computationally intensive at higher levels [49]. This type of approach depends on the chosen parameters and the initial stage of the study. For example, modeling one NFκB signaling pathway in one cell activated by one signaling TNF-α molecule requires 18 nonlinear differential equations, with 33 independent variables and 16 dependent variables in a simplified reaction kinetics model; scaling this method directly to the organism level is computationally intractable [50,51].

Sometimes explicit equations are used for experimental data in which the equations require data for estimated biochemical kinetic parameters [52]. Various open-source or commercial software such as MATLAB and Mathematica are used to solve differential equations [53] (Figure 3.2).

3.3.3 Graphical Approaches

The study of computational biology can be used to interpret cascades of molecular interactions, which are obtained as graphs to explore pathways within the chart [54]. For higher analytical studies, the graphical approach can be used. Graph theory is observed by a series of studies of computer science. Biological pathways can be abstracted as network graphs with nodes for molecules and edges for molecular interactions [55,56].

Computational methods are usually analysis-specific. They can measure the structural properties of the chart in many ways, such as counting the number of nodes and edges, the number of edges per node or nodes per edge, or identifying primary hubs and sub-network motifs [57]. For example, the web-based Hub Objects Analyzer identifies important hubs in a protein interaction network by using a combination of software including databases, graph generators, and topology calculators [58].

3.3.4 Symbolic Approaches

A symbolic approach is a formal qualitative modeling approach that can answer questions at various levels of data information extrusion [59]. Different computational methods for symbolic biology have been developed based on specific intracellular functions such as signaling. Extended models can be analyzed or run as simulations; models can be checked and verified formally [60].

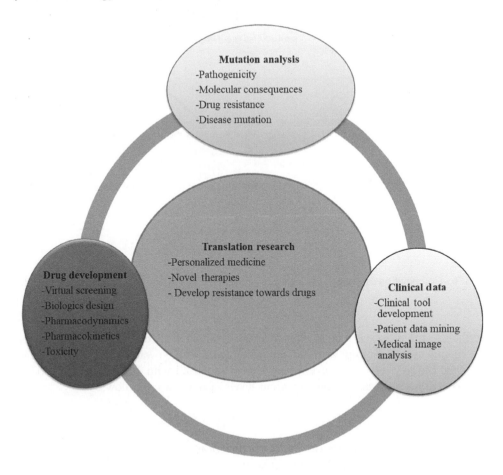

FIGURE 3.2 Computational biology and clinical informatics laboratory.

3.3.5 MECHANISTIC APPROACHES

Artificial neural networks and agent-based models are two mechanistic approaches that can be run and implemented through special computationally intensive software with the help of multiprocessor hardware [8].

In computational biology studies, the artificial neural network can mechanistically learn nonlinear patterns from a set of observations [61].

3.4 APPLICATIONS OF COMPUTATIONAL BIOLOGY IN CLINICAL RESEARCH

Computational biology methods extract biological science information from complex data, which have sufficient detail to reproduce the results. The integration of many interdisciplinary sciences such as biology, computer science, engineering, and mathematics initializes, evaluates, and develops the study [62,63] (Figure 3.3).

Biological systems differ regarding two variables, that is time and space, and thus their interactions in each patient are often nonlinear. Computational biology methods are therefore used to quantify each study parameter with all the physical and chemicalconstraints [64].These methods are significant for the development of new theories by leveraging omics data [65].

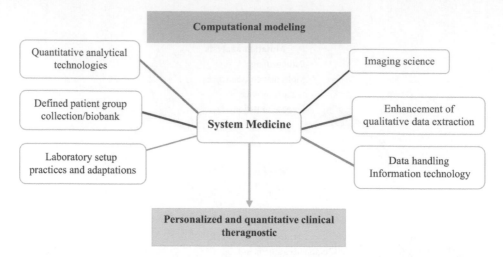

FIGURE 3.3 Computational biology approaches for modern medical research and drug development.

Nevertheless, life science is a big challenge involving all medical, environmental, and bioprocess fields for linking system biology with different parameters [66]. Nowadays the wide application of computational biology serves to solve the problems associated with clinical research [67]. Other applications of computational biology in various levels of study are as follows.

3.4.1 COMPUTATIONAL ANALYSIS OF DIFFERENT BIOLOGICAL LEVELS (MOLECULAR, CELLULAR, TISSUE/CONSORTIA LEVEL)

The biology of the human system is an inherently dynamic process. Computational biology can perform an analysis of active processes at the molecular, cellular, and tissue levels. Such a study makes use of molecular-level processes; gene studies are used for the optimization of different parameters [68].

In recent years the frontiers of biological and medical research have become increasingly dependent on sophisticated modeling, analysis, and computational techniques. Computational biology has emerged as a vital tool for investigating complex biological systems [69]. In turn, biomedical research has spawned new mathematical developments in computational biology.

With the aid of the computational analysis of cardiac arrhythmias, the associated calcium channel gateway of cardiac cells have been studied by application of the bifurcation theory and its methods, numerical bifurcation analysis, and geometric singular perturbation theory to study nonlinear multi-time scale systems [70,71].

Scientists and clinicians have also reported on the study and result of interactions between mammalian cells and bioreactor environments for optimizing different mammalian bioprocesses [72]. The dietary requirements for a healthy individual have also been studied by looking for the exchange of intra- and extracellular processes associated with lipoprotein and cholesterol metabolism. These studies also give an idea on the influence of statins and diet on the metabolism of ordinary individuals [73,74].

The study of different microbial infections and of the interactions of microbial metabolites with their host can also be studied to quantify the growth rate of microbes in the host [75]. With the help of this technology cellular and tissues are also studied for interpreting the interactions between the tumor and host immune cells [76].

3.4.2 Analysis of the Interface of Biotic and Abiotic Processes

Human life depends on two variables that are dependent on each other. Of the two, one comprises different biological processes according to the form of life present. The other variable consists of numerous physical variables such as chemical transport to and from the cell [77]. The biological process involves the metabolic system of humans also. Scientists in their research have shown that other micro-organisms create a balance between their cells' natural reaction rates and abiotic diffusion rates by pointing to the spatial distributions of cell types and often enhanced system robustness [78,79].

Computational biology studies discuss this type of interface of mammalian cells and convective transport processes, which ultimately influence the local chemical, thermal, and mechanical environments [80].

3.4.3 Processing of Large Data Sets for Enhanced Analysis

Recently clinical studies have become a reservoir of large sets of data from which the extraction of information is a tedious and complex process. Computational biology can very efficiently extract and represent the output from these databases [81]. For rapid and simplified data formatting a software is also there that enables the visualization of metabolic flux data with the use of a graphical user interfaceing [82].

Other scientists have used this computational biology tool for extracting additional information from microRNA removed from breast cancer cells by measuring 50,000 recurrent editing sites. The data identify additional levels of complexity in microRNAs, which influence how the molecules interact with target mRNA [48,83].

3.4.4 Selection of Parameters and Their Optimization

For a specific biological study, selecting an appropriate parameter and its optimization study is a challenging task and represents the hallmark of many studies. For optimization of the parameter selected, a biphasic system must be created that involves all contributions like generalized mass action networks relevant to gene signaling and metabolite networks, calcium-induced oscillation, and so on [84].

Computational biology and various associated software help in the identification of suitable parameters, and also for finding the required conditions for their optimization for related study which can be done and focused for producing very different results based on the interaction of electron balances and metabolism [85,86].

3.4.5 For Systems Analysis and Systems Biology Study

Systems biology is defined as a subcategory of computational biology and is given by the National Library of Medicine (NLM) as the "comprehensive, methodical analysis of complex biological systems by monitoring responses to perturbations of biological processes and using the large scale, computerized collection, and analysis of the data to develop and test models of biological systems," while systems analysis focuses on the identification of the fundamental units of a specific biological system, and also a description of the interaction between a large number of processes or components of a system in a generalized way [87,88].

Research can be performed either qualitatively or quantitatively. Both these studies, that is, systems analysis and systems biology, can be done with the help of computational biology as both involve an interaction with a complex biological system. Research can be done by taking into account different and specific assumptions and constraints [89]. Physical system analysis can be static or dynamic, stochastic or deterministic, or combinations of these. The fundamental units (components or processes) of natural systems and their involvement may be nested within a hierarchy, overlapping with computational biological studies [90].

3.4.6 FOR SYSTEMS APPROACH IN TRAUMA

Trauma is a severe bodily injury of sufficient intensity and magnitude that it leads to different systemic inflammatory responses [91]. It can also lead to slight organ injuries as it is accompanied by severe effects in normal human physiology and other protective biological mechanisms [92]. In trauma-associated critically ill patients, the different and affected pathophysiology is incompletely associated, which leads to a high fatality rate of a disease [93].

The complex and often rapid progressions of trauma and critical illness provide a vast quantity of patient data that can be collected and evaluated through real-time monitoring in an intensive care unit (ICU) continuously, hourly, or on a daily basis. Thus, today's challenge is to understand the meaning of all data in the context of the progression of the disease, which further can provide a data-driven protocol for implementing any newly available technology. Computational biology serves this intermediary response by providing a complete study of data based on pathophysiology and disease progression [94,95].

Other applications of computational biology in the modern-day world are as follows [96,97]:

- Molecular medicine;
- Microbial genome application;
- Comparative studies;
- Analysis and interpretation of various kinds of data;
- Development of new algorithms and statistics;
- Gene therapy;
- Drug development;
- Preventive medicine;
- Climate change studies;
- Analysis of gene expression;
- Computational evolutionary biology;
- Data-driven biology;
- Pharmacogenomics;
- Toxic genomics;
- Waste cleanup;
- Microbial genome application;
- Antibiotic resistance;
- Sequence analysis;
- Forensic analysis.

3.5 CONCLUSION

A level of understanding of the components and the organizational structure of the system is necessary to formulate initial hypotheses about how the system operates. Computational biology consists of a series of theories and applications used to translate biology into mechanisms for advancement in the discovery of medicines. This helps in the understanding of biological testing more practically and rigorously and aids in forming a bridge to hold different insights on a single platform. While technical developments provide opportunities, conceptual advances are the proper drivers of progress. This chapter has reviewed the principles of systems biology, which further can be applied to translational research. The molecular and cellular level of data studies can be performed with the use of different computer tools, among which is one of the latest and most advanced resources for research. The ultimate object of computational biology is to develop predictive computational models of a disease, which will provoke a revolution in the diagnosis process and provide the mechanistic understanding necessary for personalized therapeutic approaches. To obtain the factor of causes and their effect on the severity of the disease, it is necessary to understand and analyze the patient and the disease data which can be done by the computational approach. Additionally, biologically meaningful information can be derived from diagnostic tests if interpreted in functional relationships rather than as independent measurements. Such systems-biology-based diagnostics will transform disease taxonomies from the phenotypical to the molecular and allow physicians to select optimal therapeutic regimens for individual patients. Combining computational methods and computational modeling with systems thinking can lead to the development of a "virtual sandbox" in which researchers can utilize their creativity and intuition to try out and explore multiple different hypotheses and lines of investigation.

ACKNOWLEDGMENT

The authors are very grateful to the Management of the Noida Institute of Engineering and Technology (Pharmacy Institute) Greater Noida for providing all necessary support for completion of this work.

REFERENCES

1. Markowetz F. All biology is computational biology. *PLoS Biol* 2017;15:e2002050.
2. Nathan DG. The several Cs of translational clinical research. *J Clin Invest* 2005 Apr;115(4):795–797.
3. Butte AJ. Translational bioinformatics: coming of age. *J Am Med Inform Assoc* 2008 Nov-Dec; 15(6):709–714.
4. An GC. Translational systems biology using an agent-based approach for dynamic knowledge representation: An evolutionary paradigm for biomedical research. *Wound Repair Regen* 2010 Jan-Feb;18(1):8–12.
5. Kirkwood TB. Systems biology of ageing and longevity. *Philos Trans R Soc Lond Ser B Biol Sci* 2011 366:64–7010.
6. Ideker T, Galitski T, Hood L. A new approach to decoding life: systems biology. *Annu Rev Genomics Hum Genet* 2001;2:343–372. doi: 10.1146/annurev.genom.2.1.343.
7. Kohl P, Crampin EJ, Quinn TA, Noble D. Systems biology: an approach. *Clin Pharmacol Ther* 2010;88:25–33. doi:10.1038/clpt.2010.92.
8. Yildirim MA, et al. Drug-target network. *Nat Biotechnol* 2007; 25:1119–1126.
9. Khoury MJ, Gwinn M, Dotson WD, Schully SD. Knowledge integration at the center of genomic medicine. *Genet Med* 2012; 14:643–647.
10. Dammann O, Follett P. Toward multi-scale computational modeling in developmental disability research. *Neuropediatrics* 2011; 42:90–96.
11. Tegnér JN, Compte A, Auffray C, et al. Computational disease modeling - fact or fiction? *BMC Syst Biol* 2009;3:56.
12. del Sol A, Balling R, Hood L, Galas D. Diseases as network perturbations. *Curr Opin Biotechnol* 2010;21:566–571.
13. Vodovotz Y, Csete M, Bartels J, Chang S, An G. Translational systems biology of inflammation. *PLoS Comput Biol* 2008;4:e1000014. doi:10.1371/journal.pcbi.1000014.
14. Stephens SM, Rung J. Advances in systems biology: measurement, modeling and representation. *Curr Opin Drug Discov Devel* 2006;9:240–250.
15. Martin-Sanchez F, Iakovidis I, Norager S, Maojo V, Groen Pd, Van der Lei J, Jones T, Abraham-Fuchs K, Apweiler R, Babic A. et al. Synergy between medical informatics and bioinformatics: facilitating genomic medicine for future health care. *J Biomed Inform* 2004;37(1):30–42.
16. Butcher EC, Berg EL, Kunkel EJ. Systems biology in drug discovery. *Nat Biotechnol* 2004; 22(10):1253–1259.
17. Service RF. Biology's dry future. *Science* 2013;342(6155):186–189. doi: 10.1126/science.342.6155.186.
18. Ding F, Dokholyan NV, Buldyrev SV, et al. Molecular dynamics simulation of the SH3 domain aggregation suggests a generic amyloidogenesis mechanism. *J Mol Biol* 2002;324:851–857.

19. van Wieringen WN, Kun D, Hampel R and Boulesteix A-L. Survival prediction using gene expression data: A review and comparison. *Comput Stat Data Analy* 2009;53:1590–1603.

20. Kumar S, Jayaraman K, Panchanathan S, Gurunathan R, Marti-Subirana A, and Newfeld SJ. BEST: a novel computational approach for comparing gene expression patterns from early stages of Drosophila melanogaster development. *Genetics* 2002;162:2037–2047.

21. Boissel JP, Auffray C, Noble D, Hood L, Boissel FH. Bridging systems medicine and patient needs. *Pharma Syst Pharmacol* 2015;4:135–145.

22. Saqi M, Pellet J, Roznovat I, Mazein A, Ballereau S, De Meulder B, Auffray C. Systems medicine: the future of medical genomics, healthcare, and wellness. In: Schmitz U, Wolkenhauer O, editors. *Systems Medicine. Methods in Molecular Biology* vol. 1386. New York: Springer; 2016. p. 43–60.

23. Clermont G, Auffray C, Moreau Y, Rocke DM, Dalevi D, Dubhashi D, Marshall DR, Raasch P, Dehne F, Provero P, Tegner J, Aronow BJ, Langston MA, Benson M. Bridging the gap between systems biology and medicine. *Genome Med* 2009;1:88.

24. McGartland Rubio D, Schoenbaum EE, Lee LS, Schteingart DE, Marantz PR, Anderson KE, Platt LD, Baez A, Esposito K. Defining translational research: implications for training. *Acad Med* 2010; 85:470–475.

25. International Society for Computational Biology. Mission, Vision & Values. 2003.

26. Stacey Finley, Department of Biomedical Engineering, Quantitative and Computational Biology, and Chemical Engineering & Materials Science, University of Southern California, USA.

27. Ayoob, JC, and Kangas, JD. 10 simple rules for teaching wet-lab experimentation to computational biology students, I.e., Turning computer mice into lab rats. *PLoS Comput Biol* 2020;16 (6):e1007911.

28. Eddy, SR. 'Antedisciplinary' Science. *PLoS Comput Biol* 2005;1 (1): e6.

29. Levet, F, Carpenter AE, Eliceiri KW, Kreshuk A, Bankhead P, and Haase R. Developing open-source software for bioimage analysis: opportunities and challenges. *F1000Research* 2021;10 (April):302.

30. Loman, N, and Watson, M. So you want to be a computational biologist? *Nat Biotechnol* 2013; 31 (11):996–998.

31. Karvunidis T, Mares J, Thongboonkerd V, Matejovic M. Recent progress of proteomics in critical illness. *Shock* 2009 Jun;31(6):545–552.

32. NIH. [Accessed Aug 28, 2009];*NIH Roadmap for Medical Research.*

33. Clermont G, Auffray C, Moreau Y, et al. Translating systems biology into medical applications: report of the 3rd bertinoro systems biology workshop. *BioMed Central* 2009.

34. Buchman TG. The digital patient: predicting physiologic dynamics with mathematical models. *Crit Care Med* 2009 Mar;37(3):1167–1168.

35. An G. Agent-based computer simulation and sirs: building a bridge between basic science and clinical trials. *Shock* 2001 Oct;16(4):266–273.

36. Yamamura S, Kawada K, Takehira R, et al. Artificial neural network modeling to predict the plasma concentration of aminoglycosides in burn patients. *Biomed Pharmacother* 2004 May; 58(4):239–244.

37. Lin CY, Chin CH, Wu HH, Chen SH, Ho CW, Ko MT. Hubba: hub objects analyzer--a framework of interactome hubs identification for network biology. *Nucleic Acids Res* 2008 Jul 1;36(Web Server issue):W438–W443.

38. Wixon J. Pathway databases. *Comp Funct Genom* 2001;2(6):391–397.

39. Caspi R, Altman T, Dale JM, et al. The MetaCyc database of metabolic pathways and enzymes and the BioCyc collection of pathway/genome databases. *Nucleic Acids Res* 2010 Jan;38(DataEbase issue):D473–D479.

40. Altman RB Introduction to translational bioinformatics collection. *PLoS Comput Biol* 2012; 8(12):e1002796.

41. Ouzounis CA. Rise and demise of bioinformatics? Promise and progress. *PLoS Comput Biol* (2012);8 (4):1–5. Bibcode:2012PLSCB...8E2487O.

42. Shah, NH, Jonquet, C, Lussier, YA, Tarzy-Hornoch, P, Ohno-Machado, L. Ontology-driven indexing of public datasets for translational bioinformatics. *BMC Bioinform* 2009;10 (2):S1.

43. Lesko, LJ. Drug research and translational bioinformatics. *Clinic Pharmacol Therap* 2012;91 (6):960–962.

44. Sarkar, IN, Butte, AJ, Lussier, YA, Tarczy-Hornoch, P, Ohno-Machado, L. Translational bioinformatics: Linking knowledge across biological and clinical realms. *J Am Med Inform Assoc* 2011;18 (4):345–357.

45. Altman, RB. "Translational bioinformatics: The year in review". Retrieved November 16, 2012.

46. Butte, AJ. Translational bioinformatics applications in genome medicine. *Genome Med* 2009;1 (6):64.

47. Azuaje, FJ, Heymann, M, Ternes, A, Wienecke-Baldacchino, A, Struck, D, Moes, D, Schneider, R. Bioinformatics as a driver, not a passenger, of translational biomedical research: Perspectives from the 6th Benelux bioinformatics conference (PDF). *J Clin Bioinform*, 2012;2(7):1–3.

48. Massard C., Michiels S., Ferté C, et al. High-throughput genomics and clinical outcome in hard-to-treat advanced cancers: results of the MOSCATO 01 trial. *Cancer Discov* 2017;7(6):586–595.

49. Meric-Bernstam F, and Mills GB, Overcoming implementation challenges of personalized cancer therapy. *Nat Rev Clin Oncol* 2012;9(9):542–548.

50. Lander ES Initial impact of the sequencing of the human genome. *Nature*;2011 470(7333):187–197.

51. Visvanathan M, Breit M, Pfeifer B, Baumgartner C, Modre-Osprian R, Tilg B. DMSP--database for modeling signaling pathways. Combining biological and mathematical modeling knowledge for pathways. *Methods Inf Med* 2008;47(2):140–148.

52. MathWorks. [Accessed Aug 9, 2010];*MATLAB*.

53. Schilling CH, Palsson BO. The underlying pathway structure of biochemical reaction networks. *Proc Natl Acad Sci U S A* 1998 Apr 14;95(8):4193–4198.

54. Kowarsch A, Blochl F, Bohl S, et al. Knowledge-based matrix factorization temporally resolves the cellular responses to IL-6 stimulation. *BMC Bioinform* 2010;11:585.

55. Ma'ayan A. Network integration and graph analysis in mammalian molecular systems biology. *IET Syst Biol* 2008 Sep;2(5):206–221.

56. Russell S, and Norvig P. *Artificial Intelligence: A Modern Approach*. 3. Prentice Hall; 2009.

57. Sachs K, Itani S, Fitzgerald J, et al. Learning cyclic signaling pathway structures while minimizing data requirements. *Pac Symp Biocomput* 2009;63–74.

58. Heiner M, Donaldson R, Gilbert D. Petri nets for systems biology. In: Iyengar MS, editor. *Symbolic Systems Biology: Theory and Methods*. Sudbury: Jones & Bartlett Publishers; 2010. pp. 61–97.

59. Iyengar MS. *Symbolic Systems Biology: Theory and Methods*. Sudbury: Jones & Bartlett; 2010. pp. 101–107.

60. Knapp M, Briesemeister L, Eker S, et al. Pathway logic helping biologists understand and organize pathway information. Paper presented at: Computational Systems *Bioinformatics Conference*; 2005; IEEE; 2005. Workshops and Poster Abstracts.

61. Zhao S, Iyengar R. Systems pharmacology: network analysis to identify multiscale mechanisms of drug action. *Annu Rev Pharmacol Toxicol* 2012;52:505–521.

62. Besnard J, Ruda GF, Setola V, Abecassis K, Rodriguiz RM, Huang XP, Norval S, Sassano MF, Shin AI, Webster LA, et al. Automated design of ligands to poly pharmacological profiles. *Nature* 2012;492(7428):215–220.

63. Stuart JM, Segal E, Koller D, Kim SK. A gene-coexpression network for global discovery of conserved genetic modules. *Science* 2003;302(5643):249–255.

64. Goh KI, Cusick ME, Valle D, Childs B, Vidal M, Barabasi AL. The human disease networks. *Proc Natl Acad Sci USA* 2007;104(21):8685–8690.

65. Hidalgo CA, Blumm N, Barabasi AL, Christakis NA. A dynamic network approach for the study of human phenotypes. *PLoS Comput Biol* 2009;5(4): e1000353.

66. Cho DY, Kim YA, Przytycka TM. Network biology approach to complex diseases. *PLoS Comput Biol* 2012;8(12): e1002820.

67. Furlong LI. Human diseases through the lens of network biology. *Trends Genet* 2013;29(3):150–159.

68. Marcotte E, Boone C, Babu MM, Gavin A-C. Network biology editorial 2013. *Mol BioSyst* 2013;9(7):1557–1558.

69. Barabasi AL, Albert R. Emergence of scaling in random networks. *Science* 1999;286(5439):509–512.

70. Strogatz SH. Exploring complex networks. *Nature* 2001;410(6825):268–276.

71. Wagner A, Fell DA. The small world inside large metabolic networks. *Proc Biol Sci* 2001; 268(1478):1803–1810.

72. Alon U. Network motifs: theory and experimental approaches. *Nat Rev Genet* 2007;8(6):450–461.

73. Milo R, Shen-Orr S, Itzkovitz S, Kashtan N, Chklovskii D, Alon U. Network motifs: simple building blocks of complex networks. *Science* 2002;298(5594):824–827.

74. Babu MM, Luscombe NM, Aravind L, Gerstein M, Teichmann SA. Structure and evolution of transcriptional regulatory networks. *Curr Opin Struct Biol* 2004;14(3):283–291.

75. Schneider G. Virtual screening: an endless staircase? *Nat Rev Drug Discov* 2010;9(4):273–276.

76. Taylor IW, Linding R, Warde-Farley D, Liu Y, Pesquita C, Faria D, Bull S, Pawson T, Morris Q, Wrana JL. Dynamic modularity in protein interaction networks predicts breast cancer outcome. *Nat Biotechnol* 2009;27(2):199–204.

77. Abraham E, Marincola FM, Chen Z, and Wang X. Clinical and translational medicine: integrative and practical science. *Clin Transl Med* 2012 1, article 1.

78. Hörig H, Marincola E, and Marincola FM. Obstacles and opportunities in translational research. *Nat Med* 11(7):705–708, 2005.

79. Greenwood JC. Biotechnology: delivering on the promise. *Sci Transl Med* 2010;2(13):13cm1

80. Hay M, Thomas DW, Craighead JL, Economides C, and Rosenthal J. Clinical development success rates for investigational drugs. *Nat Biotechnol* 2014;32:40–51.

81. Rubio, DM, Schoenbaum, EE, Lee LS, et al. Defining translational research: implications for training. *Acad Med* 2010;85(3):470–475.

82. Portilla LM and Alving B. Reaping the benefits of biomedical research: partnerships required. *Sci Transl Med* 2010;2(35):35cm17.

83. Bernstein HA, Gough J, Cooper DN, et al. "Predicting the functional, molecular, and phenotypic consequences of amino acid substitutions using hidden Markov models," *Hum Mutat* 2013;34(1):57–65.

84. Sutskever I, Vinyals O, and Le QV, *Advances in Neural Information Processing Systems*, MIT Press, Cambridge, MA, USA, 2014.

85. Torracinta R and Campagne F. Training genotype callers with neural networks 2016, *bioRxiv*, 097469.

86. Poplin R, Newburger D, Dijamco J, et al. Creating a universal SNP and small indel variant caller with deep neural networks. 2018, bioRxiv.

87. Ballester PJ and Mitchell JBO. A machine learning approach to predicting protein-ligand binding affinity with applications to molecular docking. *Bioinformatics* 2010;26(9):1169–1175.

88. Gordon D, Abajian C, Green P. Consed: a graphical tool for sequence finishing. *Genome Res* 1998;8(3):195–202.

89. Choi K, Ma Y, Choi JH, Kim S. PLATCOM: a platform for computational comparative genomics. *Bioinformatics* 2005;21(10):2514–2516.

90. Li H, Leung KS, Wong MH, and Ballester PJ. Improving AutoDock vina using random forest: the growing accuracy of binding affinity prediction by the effective exploitation of larger data sets. *Mol Inform* 2015;34(2-3):115–126.

91. Meslamani J, Bhajun R, Martz F, and Rognan D. Computational profiling of bioactive compounds using a target-dependent composite workflow. *J Chem Inf Model* 2013;53(9):2322–2333

92. Behler J. Constructing high-dimensional neural network potentials: a tutorial review. *Int J Quantum Chem* 2015;115(16):1032–1050.

93. Gómez-Bombarelli R, Aguilera-Iparraguirre J, Hirzel TD et al. Design of efficient molecular organic light-emitting diodes by a high-throughput virtual screening and experimental approach. *Nat Mater* 2016;15(10):1120–1127.

94. Bryksin AV, Brown AC, Baksh MM, Finn MG, and Barker TH. Learning from nature-novel synthetic biology approaches for biomaterial design. *Acta Biomater*, 2014;10(4):1761–1769.

95. Rekhi R, and Qutub AA. Systems approaches for synthetic biology: a pathway toward mammalian design. *Front Physiol*, 2013;4:article 285.

96. Arpino JAJ, Hancock EJ, Anderson J et al. Tuning the dials of synthetic biology. *Microbiology* 2013;159(7):1236–1253.

97. Fox S, Filichkin S, and Mockler TC. Applications of ultra-high-throughput sequencing. *Methods Mol Biol* 2009;553:79–108.

4 Issues and Challenges Related to Clinical Bioinformatics Tools for Clinical Research

Tatheer Fatima

Dr. A. P. J. Abdul Kalam Technical University, Lucknow, India

CONTENTS

4.1 INTRODUCTION

A bioinformatics device can be specified as one using bioinformatic-associated innovations and sciences to evaluate and examine molecular systems and prospective treatments for human illness. Laying unique stress on utility in the medical field, clinical bioinformatics tools(CBTs)are charged with integrating molecular and medical information for fast understanding and exploration of therapies that work and are customized. CBTs utilize the techniques and objectives of translational bioinformatics (TBI), such as storage space advancement, evaluation, and analysis to enhance the transformation of biomedical information—genomic information particularly—into positive, anticipating, precautionary, and participatory health and wellness administration [1]. CBTs and TBI are roughly comparable terms, associated with the same establishment of technological information. CBT

DOI: 10.1201/9781003226949-4

objectives are to offer techniques and devices to assist in decision-making. This helps experts in handling medical genomics (the origin of a biomarker), medication in genomics (genotype recognition/phenotype correlations), pharmacogenomics, and hereditary epidemiology, and to assist scientists in the multiple use of medical information for a research study [2]. Due to this element, together with problems related to the administration, evaluation, and combination of "-omics" information, CBTs likewise have to handle the different problems and difficulties that go along with them. CBTs can be called a mixture of self-control, and ought to offer an extensive structure for the administration of all types of biomedical information, facilitating their change into information and understanding. The objective of a CBT might appear to be ambitious; however, there are lots of elements that motivate research study in this area. The starting element is that new genome sequencing and various other high-throughput speculative methods have created large quantities of molecular information, which have to be analyzed together with medical information for significant biomedical discoveries and their appropriate exploitation by scientists [2]. New analysis and prognostic examinations are being offered to clinicians which are based upon molecular biomarkers; therefore, the ability to deconstruct an illness is enhanced and, likewise, the chosen area is enlarged because of the enhanced evaluation of danger. The ever-increasing online ease of access to the "bibliomic,"that is, the biomedical text corpus, made with launched manuscripts, abstracts, textual comments, and documents, along with Direct-to-Web publications, develops new solutions concerning significance essential information obtained from these messages and provides it in computable designs [1]. These algorithms have been shown to have the capability to integrate the information offered in the text;keeping it in organised repositories has shown efficiency to be evaluated for hypothesis generation or corroboration of medical research. The ever-enhanced openly offered information and understanding resources and their inexpensive accessibility and high-throughput molecular innovation imply that computational innovation and bioinformatics are essential for medical research. Extra research and advancement are required in the development of information warehouses and Information and Communication Technology (ICT)centers for data sharing, implying a demand for sharing phenotypic information and the advancement of devices to execute effective computer services (Figure 4.1).

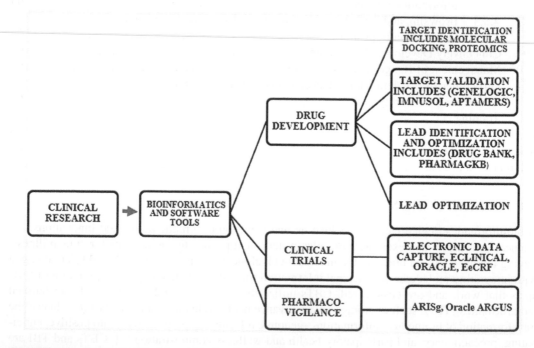

FIGURE 4.1   Scope of clinical research and bioinformatics.

4.2 ICT FACILITIES FOR SUSTAINING MEDICAL BIOINFORMATICS

Animportant function in the development of informatics for incorporating biology and biomedical computers is an incorporated structure for utilizing medical information for a research study. One section of the system includes a modular software application, which is charged with a storage space of information and ease of access. The access of various other sections is through an interface that helps scientists in browsing and evaluating the hidden information. The treatment prescribed is maintained in the software application and is accessed by individuals if needed and can be utilized at several websites around the world. It uses various techniques from cohort recognition and hypothesis generation to retrospective information evaluation [3]. Many functions consist of assistance in obtaining fast approval by the medical research community. They are maintained as open source to ensure that they are free to access and that there exists a neighborhood of collaborators—various other individuals—who are participating in assisting with inquiries and motivating development. The open source, self-service nature of the system allows researchers and individuals to obtain concepts easily with no monetary concern. The online and neighborhood documents are routinely upgraded and offer excellent individual assistance. Both these functions of modular development and open source guarantee compatibility with continuous research study, which is included in the system and does not become outdated. However, possibly one of the most essential particulars for the energy of the system is the simpleness in developing its data source. A research study information storage facility includes information from several resources, such as digital health and wellness documents, management systems, hereditary and research study information, and laboratory outcomes [4]. This information has to be aggregated and enhanced for fast cross-patient browsing. The data source ought to permit this to be done in a manner that's clear to the individual. The particular development of information design ought to be versatile so that it sustains the enhancement of new research study information for the data source; at the same time it ought to permit individuals to make complicated inquiries into the several resource systems. Its development ought to show the method by which individuals consider and utilize information, to ensure that they have accessibility to the information to develop inquiries. This should allow the advancement of real information without hindering effectiveness. Among one of the most important components of the information resource is the establishment of metadata, which is the vocabulary, all the medical terms that embrace real things in the information resource [4]. Metadata assists people in interacting with the information resource. A typical clinical information storage space center consists of 100,000 to 500,000 concepts, including CPT, NDC, ICD-9, CPT, HCPCS, and SNOMED-CT codes, as well as local codes from interior systems [4]. It needs to be user-friendly in the framework, so helps the individuals can comprehend and utilize the codes. The upkeep and upgrading of the metadata are essential and poses a challenge. Clinical codes are produced quickly, and old ones are disposed of or altered. The framework of metadata ought to be such that it can perfectly take in new codes while maintaining suitable old coding plans. The objective of the system is to help with a combination of information from various resources of modern health care organizations so it provides an extensive pool for the medical research study.

The business worth of information has never been higher than it is today. The loss of intellectual Property (IP) can affect future development and success

4.3 SPECIFY DATA INFORMATION MANAGEMENT

It is crucial to specify the range of information administration needed and establish steps to guarantee administration. An extensive information tracking method can be utilized to accomplish this in jobs including high-throughput advancement and information generation [5]. Generally, a core center ought to have an essential running treatment for information administration that covers information dealing with throughput to stimulate evaluation by enduring storage space and back-up. Since administration center generally handles information had by another center, a core's obligation might just encompass protected storage space of information and outcomes for the customer (for a brief orlengthyterm), whereas last information sharing is the information owner's obligation [6]. Nevertheless, data-generating researchers might telecall bioinformaticians to help with the advancement of a DMT for a research study to examine and analyze a project. Bioinformaticians in core centers are required to interact with extensive number of DMTs and information proprietors. Likewise, bioinformaticians ought to understand and interact with the degree of their coreDMTs [7,8]. Demands to establish a great DMT have been formerly talked about. Elements to think about when establishing a DMT are: identifying the lawful, ethical, and funder's requirements when having contact with the data; determining the kind of information to be collected; determining the needs and ontologies that will be employed; and identifying whetherthe information will be orderly, regulated to high quality, preserved, and distributed [9,10]. Additionally, core centers ought to think about specifying appropriate information dealing with techniques and preparing information administration budget strategy techniques. The objectives of extensive DMTs are: to deal with the ethical, administration, and source requirements obtained when in contact with the data; to advertise findable, providable, interoperable, and recyclable (FAIR) research; and to think about connected information safety. [11]. Eventually, the DMT offers a guarantee for the enduring conservation and ease of access to the produced information. Like the speculative styles, DMTs can be collaboratively designed or chosen by data-generating scientists and bioinformaticians [6]. Nevertheless, bioinformatics core centers might likewise decide to establish an essential DMT that can be changed as needed for individual jobs.

4.4   ADMINISTRATION OF INFORMATION TRACEABILITY

Information traceability of all instances in a research study is an important aspect of effective bioinformatics support. Traceability should be comprehensive and consist of instances to buy and fine-tune, along with information generation, assessment, storage space area, and protection. The best-case situation is an information source administration system that is safeguarded by and provided to both the data-generating researchers and bioinformaticians. In an exercise, this type of system is called a lab information administration system (LIMS) and might be carried out to enhance the traceability of circumstances and information;and for that reason decreases human mistakes and the manufacturing of erroneous information [8]. If a LIMS is not possible, a common cloud-based source might offer the same accurate work. These systems ought to allow the manufacturing of dependable outcomes at a quicker rate but set you back compared to hands-on systems and allow information monitoring from sequencing runs in time and through experiments in purchasing to enhance effectiveness and map down prospective mistakes. Additionally, these systems also promote quality control by highlighting quit functioning instances and identifying accountable events. Allowing example and information traceability is eventually among one of the most effective methods to determine resources and avoid the manufacturing of erroneous information. Significantly, bioinformaticians might not constantly belong to a sequencing core and are for that reason based on information proprietors offering precise information [5]. Extensive DMPs might have to represent the precise configuration appropriate to private customers.

4.5   DECISIONS OF METADATA

For bioinformaticians to perform suitable downstream information evaluation of an experiment, the connected metadata should be offered. Metadata ought to be as general as possible and to consist of the speculative variables of the cost of interest, all elements of circumstances dealing with, comprehended, or concept resources of developing variables, and lab errors such as circumstance mislabels and swaps [9]. Previously discussed aspects to consider include an efficient system to guarantee extensive metadata security. Preferably, data-generating centers ought to approve a system to allow the monitoring of important information connected with experiments and pass this information to the bioinformatics core. Since a good deal of research study analyzes teams that might not have the costs of a LIMS, the data-generating scientists and bioinformaticians ought to suggest or establish basic worksheets or web-based entryway kinds for metadata security, which assign the needed and optional places [8]. In the case of a lack of a fundamental method, metadata security might be offered in different ways (e.g., spreadsheets, remembered by the participants, etc);. Preferably, it may deserve preparation from the beginning where information will be openly offered. Oftentimes, the information will be transferred to a current public repository; because of that, comprehending the structure and deepness of the metadata collection required for the data source is important. For smaller-scale research study, metadata develop styles provided by the data source which can be used to file instances to guarantee that whatever is presently obtained is prepared for the last entrance. In the process of producing interoperable research study, metadata protection should comply with experiment-specific protection requirements, such as Very little Information Concerning a Microarray Experiment (MIAME), Very little Information required for a DMET Experiment (MIDE), and Very little Information Concerning a Proteomics Experiment (MIAPE) [10]. These can be accessed with FAIR sharing (a standard resource), BioSchemas. Also, metadata ontologies can be found in online repositories such as Bioportal and Ontology Lookup Service [12]. Selecting and using appropriate protection demands should be safeguarded in the DMP and may be required by journals or funders. Protection demands assurance that researchers comply with worldwide develop demands throughout their speculative therapies. Furthermore, utilizing information coverage requirements assists in advertisement recycling and contrastswithresearchformerly carried out. Eventually, this guarantees that both scientists and their neighborhoods enjoy the best advantage of their gathered and produced information.

4.6   SYNCHRONIZATION OF INFORMATION AND INTERNET SAFETY

Offering guarantees that information is both protected and steady is an essential element of offering efficient bioinformatics assistance. Although these elements are generally dealt with by an info-tech (IT) division or system manager, it is essential to interact with the demands of the accountable person(s) and might be an essential factor to consider in resource or capacity-limited centers. Information safety describes the avoidance of hazardous cyber-attacks and unoptimized web safety and safety problems, in addition to the establishing of information accessibility and movement restrictions. Typically, the people with accessibility to research study information ought to be restricted to share with appropriate obligation and responsibility. Situations relating to individual information, especially client information, might need bookkeeping of information accessibility also. The elements that have to be thought about when protecting information to preserve a high quality consist of: (1) privacy (preserving accessibility and transfer); (2) stability (guaranteeing the information is precise, legitimate, and reliable); (3) accessibility (sources and assistance are available); (4) responsibility (activities can be credited to appropriate parties); and (5) provenance (beginning and background of information are understood and well-specified)[13–15].

Internet security explains the use and safety of the internet, which is used to deal with and assess informationobtained by high-throughput experiments. To handle the computational problems (e.g., primary fine-tuning systems (CPUs), memory, storage space area) of high-throughput information assessment, a dark computer system has ended up being the popular solution. In these situations, the significance of guaranteeing information and web safety is additionally highlighted. Consequently, shadow individuals need to depend greatly on the provider for information on personal privacy and safety protection; because of that, information back-ups and recovery techniques should be protected and maintained track of; so GA4GH has introduced an information security and security toolkit for genomics and health-related information sharing [16]. This toolkit consists of recommendations for individual personal privacy and security safeguards and protect the suitable ease of access and stability of information. Useful recommendations to support this maintenance include: (1) developing the ease of handling data (that are assessed and updated periodically);

(2) performing information verification and protection processes; (3) performing risk management strategies; (4) establishing strong performance links with local IT support; (5) performing regular maintenance and upgrade processes; and (6) performing real-time internet web server monitoring systems and protecting security and security accreditations obtained via protected sites and software applications [17].

4.7 INFORMATION SAFETY

Information safety concerns safeguarding electronic information from unapproved accessibility, corruption, or burglary throughout its whole lifecycle. It is an idea that encompasses every element of information safety, from the physical safety of equipment and storage space gadgets to management and accessibility, in addition to the rational safety of software applications [18]. It likewise consists of business plans and treatments.

When correctly executed, durable information safety techniques will safeguard an organization's information possessions against cybercriminal tasks; however, they likewise protect against expert risks and human mistakes, which remain among the popular factors for information infractions today. Information security consists of launching gadgets and developments that enhance the organization's direct exposure to where its essential information is located and how it is used. Preferably, these devices ought to have the ability to use securities like file security, information concealing, and redaction of delicate data, and ought to automate coverage to improve audits and stick to regulative demands.

The large quantity of information that the system produces, controls, and keeps will expand and demand a higher requirement for information administration. Additionally, computer systems are more complicated compared to what they once were, regularly covering the information center, and various side gadgets varying from Web of Points (IoT) sensing units to robotics and remote web servers [19]. This intricacy produces a broadened assault surface area that is more testing to check and protect.

At the same time, understanding the significance of personal privacy is increasing. Sustained by enhancing the public need for information security efforts, several new personal privacy policies have lately been passed.

4.7.1 CONFIDENTIALITY

Confidentialityin healthcare describes the responsibility of experts that have access to client documents. Privacy is acknowledged by legislation as a fortunate interaction in between two centres in an expert connection, such as a client and a doctor, a registered nurse, or various other medical experts. The client expects private interaction in these connections. Efficient interaction relies on an environment of self-confidence and depends on the client being ready to make an honest and total disclosure.

When thinking about delicate health and wellness information needing unique layers of privacy, such as psychological health and wellness therapy, the system ought to offer assistance for health and wellness information administration experts [20].

4.7.2 PERSONAL PRIVACY

Personal privacy specifies and restricts the situations where an individual's safeguarded health and wellness information might be utilized or revealed. It strikes an equilibrium that licenses essential uses of information while safeguarding the personal privacy of individuals who require treatment and recovery. People are offered some aspects of management, such as appropriate accessibility of their own health and wellness information, in many cases, and the ability to demand a change of inaccurate health and wellness information [20]. This has enhanced the understanding of the subject of health and wellness information privacy, of problems bordering security, and of the patient's information at the same time. There is no doubt that such information administrators have been affected by their obligations to conform in personal privacy. these factors required that doctors record on an electronic data source information on the prescription of specific kinds of medications most likely to be misused. A specific doctor might feel this violates the physician–patient connection. The individual's strength of feeling over personal privacy security is kept in mind as a difficulty to be countered.

Disclosures of personal clinical information to physicians, to medical facility workers, to the insurance provider, and public health and wellness companies are frequently an important part of contemporary clinical exercise without individuals' having a say in it. This might result in expanding issues with the collection of personal information in digital format and the function of regulative standards.

4.7.3 SECURITY

Security refers straight to privacy, and particularly to the implies utilized to safeguard the personal privacy of health and wellness information and assist experts in holding that information in self-confidence.

As the use of the digital health and wellness document systems expands, and transmission of health and wellness information ends up being the standard, the requirement for regulative standards particular to digital health and wellness information ends up being more obvious. Dealing with technological and management safeguards, the objective is to safeguard separately identifiable information in digital form—a subset of information protected by the personal privacy rule—while enabling doctors suitable accessibility to information and versatility in the fostering of innovation, required accessibility by doctor and the security of individuals' health and wellness information [21].

The success of CBT in the area of health care research study depends greatly on the understanding of the patient's complete clinical background (e.g., various other illnesses, medicines, allergic reactions, and hereditary mutations) and its efficient use. This information is heterogeneous in its initial style [1,2]. Previously it could be put on the client's clinical documents if available in standard form. Currently, both information and understanding are produced by several resources, each having exclusive styles and idiosyncratic semiotics, frequently not understood clearly (e.g., if contextual information is disorganized it is challenging to deal with by choice assistance applications). The first activity in the evaluation of clinical information typically is handling the metadata, for example, the predefined schemas of clinical information systems [6]. Nonetheless, these schemas (typically relational) are unable to shape the intricacy of contextual information representation. For that reason, it winds up being obligatory to have a language adequate to allow the particular representation of the patient-specific context of each unique information item and of exposing its link to different various other information items. It should also relate to how it fits within the entire health and wellness history of a person. Medical files of a customer are often inconsistent and incoherent. A patient-centric, longitudinal, electronic health and wellness and health file according to around the world demands is needed to provide a coherent and particular representation of the data's semiotics [21]. New evidence is created by clinical research studies and is validated in clinical examinations. Its representation in accordance with clinical info representations is achieved by info mining. Raw information is provided today in research studies and clinical environments, for example, DNA sequences and expression information, along with uncommon variants are constantly improving [2,3]. Its depiction has to adhere, as long as feasible, to typical and agreed-upon recommendation designs that offer combined representations of the typical constructs required for health and wellness. Any type of monitoring can be used in regards to its associates, such as ID, timing, code, worth, technique, and condition. Utilizing the same recommendation designs will assist in the basic depiction of medical declarations (e.g., "tracking of gall bladder serious swelling recommended having a therapy of cholecystectomy," or "EGFR variations set off resistance to Gefitinib"), and for that reason can be fine-tuned by option support applications. The above-mentioned suggestion styles can be the basis of the logical styles of health and wellness information warehousing. Such warehousing will have the capability to protect the big semantic representation of information and comprehension. It will support this information to be interoperable with different other information systems. Various tasks, such as summarizing customer information or evaluating cohort information in research studies, require improved representations of the information. Information marts are improved representations, and each storage space center can provide many of these. The main design used to interact with customer information should strike a balance between physicians' accounts and orderly information. This would certainly assist in a progressive shift from disorganized medical mental notes to standard and organized information. The same change ought to likewise occur in understanding representations, from clinical documents in natural language to organized understanding, for instance. The initiatives to use All-natural Language Refining (NLP) to health and wellness information might be linked to health care information innovations [22]. The NLP basics can be decreased to the medical declaration components and therefore be a great "catcher" of the outcomes of NLP operating over disorganized health and wellness information.

4.8   SHARING DATA INFORMATION

Sharing information starts with constructing willful and devoted areas that consent to a common future over a worldwide range. On the one hand, public emergencies, such as upsurges and pandemics triggered by contagious illnesses, frequently require information sharing to help expedite the translation of huge amounts of information into understanding and treatments to enhance human health and wellness. On the other hand, we are currently being, and progressively so, equipped and empowered by lots of data-generating engines and devices, consisting of high-throughput sequencing innovations and high-performance computer systems, in addition to their collective products—large-scale genomic information that is produced at significantly expanding rates, the majority of the information being constantly created [3]. Information sharing ends up being critical for lots of factors for considering and preparing for activity in public emergencies, since the results from data-sharing are of significance in generating a total picture of the circumstances, speeding up clinical research study and understanding explorations, and making known practical and expeditious decision-making.

However, current methods bordering on information sharing are not efficient in accomplishing the optimal rate of progress from our financial investments. Information sharing is hindered or decreased by an absence of recognition of sustaining aspects for its application. What makes up "the aspects of information sharing" is, nevertheless, mostly undefined. For that reason, clarifying and specifying aspects of data-sharing is of essential importance, particularly when the world deals with unmatched worldwide risks and experiences a public emergency [23]. We, as a community of a common future, have to define important aspects of information sharing and develop fast, open, and efficient information launch standards.

4.8.1   Data Information Sharing Needs an Information Environment

Production information for the general public includes a collection of tasks that cover the whole life process of an information stream which symbolizes all appropriate centres in regards to plans for information sharing and launching (especially for information from public-funded research), requirements for information summaries and trade, in addition to data sources for information administration and accessibility [24]. All these appropriate entities and procedures develop a data-sharing community, where information sharing is started by information service companies and executed in data sources that play essential functions in information administration and offer information accessibility for the general public. For that reason, aspects of information sharing ought to cover two significant camps, one for information service companies (consisting of not just raw information generators, but also data sources that offer information annotations and connections) and the other for information supervisors.

4.8.2 PROMPTNESS, VISIBILITY, AND EFFECTIVENESS ARE OF SIGNIFICANCE FOR INFORMATION CARRIERS

As discussed above, difficulties constantly come in advance of information sharing. For example, variety in an information refining and sharing society in a broadlydefined area, such as biomedicine, say genomics-meets-pandemics, frequently creates challenges. Preferably, financing companies, journals, governmental companies, in addition to hands-on scientists should work collaboratively and develop common-practice procedures for data-sharing tasks. Their objectives are to develop a genomic epidemiological data source for worldwide recognition of micro-organisms to spot outbreaks and arising pathogens. Continuous initiatives for the present outbreak triggered by SARS-CoV-2 mainly consist of GISAID, GenBank in NCBI, and the 2019 unique Coronavirus Source in CNCB/NGDC[25]. Amongst them, 2019nCoVR functions in extensive combination with negative rtpcr assay generating large-quantity genome sequences with top quality annotations and offering a collection of solutions for viral genome information deposition, mining, and translation in actual time. Nevertheless, the requirements for information trade and synchronization between various data sources, connecting genomic information with essential metadata, and information standardization throughout nations and labs, end up being immediate and crucial. To handle worldwide outbreaks such as the COVID-19 pandemic, big and efficient collaborations with various data sources (e.g., 2019nCoVR, GISAID, and GenBank), self-controls, and nation information sharing are an immediate requirement [25] (Figure 4.2).

4.8.3 BROWSING AND REMOVAL OF APPROPRIATE INFORMATION FROM HUGE INFORMATION REPOSITORIES

The constantly increasing quantity of available information presents considerable technical and computational difficulties, both to their administration (collection, storage space, combination, conservation) and efficient utilization (accessibility, sharing, browsing, removal, evaluation). This difficulty in many areas has been dealt with using various methods, in accordance with each particular area's peculiarities. The internet is a paradigmatic area for this. A quickly expanding mass of information is swamping the internet. Yet, by leveraging the connected nature of internet

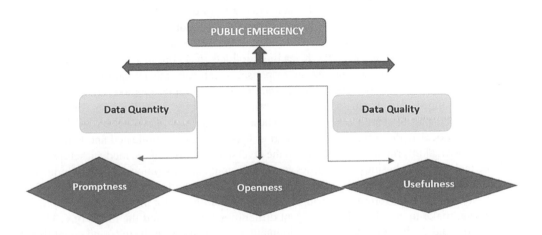

FIGURE 4.2 Data properties and emergency.

information, technical and computational developments avoid drowning [26]. Automated robotics have been used to search the internet sources, gather their big essential information, and keep them in effective data source administration systems.

Efficient indexing and positioning methods, such as the Google PageRank, have been used to effectively browse and search internet sources in accordance with their essential information and most likely significance. This allows internet online search engines to flag up products which frequently consist of their leading 10 or 20 products, the one(s) that can fairly respond to various, yet easy, individual browser's concerns. Such a capability, which is significantly increasing the internet as a remarkable user-friendly resource of information, is based upon the presumption that individual searches are primarily targeted at discovering "a minimum of one"or "one of the most apparent" products that can respond to his or her concern. The present internet browser innovations are insufficient when browsing concerns either ended up being more complicated, and at the same time include various subjects, or need the retrieval of the majority of the offered products responding to the concern, potentially purchased in accordance with various user-defined functions [10]. Additionally, an approximated and restricted section of information available on the internet can be discovered by contemporary search engines: the large "deep internet," consisting of vibrant web pages returned in response to an inquiry, sources safeguarded by a password, websites restricting accessibility by utilizing different safety innovations (e.g., CAPTCHAs), and those web pages which come with a link that produce manuscripts but are not revealed [8]. Especially in this field, the amount of collected information is continuously and rapidly improving, especially with the present collection of omics information. Also, compared to the web, today's ability to attract suitable biomedical information and react to common issues is much less, due to many factors. At first, biomedical-molecular information—which is of various kinds—is maintained in a variety of different designs within systems that are distributed, heterogeneous, and often not interoperable.

Additionally, a great deal of essential information is subjectively explained in free messages, within principal grievances, discharge letters, medical records, or recommendations, which are fundamentally disorganized. The fostering of digital clinical or health and wellness documents can considerably improve the accessibility and sharing of medical information, which is still just theoretically on many healthcare websites. Yet, the digitalization of health and wellness information alone is far from sufficient; having actual medical records and recommendations in PDF style is insufficient to remedy information removal and concerns responding to problems. Basic information depiction in accordance with a common recommendation design needs to be embraced, along with regulated terms and ontologies to objectively explain clinical and biomolecular searching. Furthermore, using progressed All-natural Language Refining methods fit for the medical domain name to safeguard info from previous clinical textual summaries can likewise significantly assist [22]. Second, typical biomedical-molecular concerns are more complicated compared to internet browser concerns. They frequently include more kinds of information, in addition to subjects with typically many associates. Oftentimes, retrieving just a few of the products relates to a biomedical-molecular browser concern, and even the K leading products in accordance with some user-defined position, might not suffice for an appropriate response, which can rather require the expedition of all offered products and their associates. Progressed browser computer methods are being designed to respond to complicated, multi-topic internet browser concerns including the combination of potentially placed partial search result pages. These methods can likewise be used in the CBT domain name to deal with such problems, in part at least. Yet, the complicated and heterogeneous nature of biomedical information, in addition to the diverse framework of the medical setups, present formidable technical and business difficulties for the efficient administration and use of biomedical-molecular information [2]. In particular, the incorporated browse and retrieval of bio-data, and their extensive evaluation for the removal of inappropriate information and for the inference of biomedical understanding, make up a few of the significant difficulties for today and the future of CBTs, with the prospective and desired effect on the development of medical research study and client therapy.

Medical bioinformatics is interested in the evaluation and visualization of complicated clinical datasets. As opposed to the classic "main stream" bioinformatics area which concentrates on the evaluation of organic information as an introduction to medical bioinformatics, is to correlate heterogeneous information collections from disparate resources (e.g., client medical documents, proteomics, and transcriptomics) and establish unique formulas for the evaluation of such heterogeneous information collections. Therefore, the essential objective is the simultaneous assessment of medical and fundamental research study information to enhance healthcare and treatment arrangement. For complicated illnesses such as psychological conditions, a rich base of information regarding clients is typically offered. This consists of medical information, basic lab evaluations, hereditary information, mind imaging information, and information acquired from molecular profiling experiments. The current advancement in technical developments enables the carrying out of high throughput experiments leading to a large enhancement in the quantity of biomedical information produced. Yet, the various resources of information are typically maintained differently which implies that important information is shed or overlooked. Because of this absence of an incorporated evaluation, the significance and connections between medical monitoring and the hidden molecular systems are not considered. In medical bioinformatics, a significant objective is to integrate these various resources of information and determine the problems arising out of the illness under examination. These functions might expose connections to various other pathologies and discover networks of connections between various illnesses.

Unique medical bioinformatics methods might therefore offer a much better comprehending and meaning of complicated illness leading to more precise, enhanced medical diagnosis and far better treatments [26]. Over the years a requirement for customized medication was progressively valued as it was obvious that basic therapy methods were seldom effective throughout the whole individual population.

4.9   COLLECTIVELY DEVELOP AN EXPERIMENT

Efficient bioinformatics analyses are based upon appropriate speculative development. Good speculative development begins with a well-defined hypothesis and covers circumstance techniques (e.g., number as well as frequency), relevant information, and information security. The speculation established should aim to minimize the variety and sources of variability, enhance the generalizability of the experiment, and make it replicable and recyclable. Because of that, conversation between data-generating scientists and bioinformaticians is much better and ought to happen as early as feasible throughout the job advancement and speculative development. However, bioinformaticians might not always be in a position to offer input on speculative development. In such situations, it might be advantageous to search for such development and emphasize issues that might be of importance throughout data analysis.

Throughout development conversations, a variety of problems ought to be dealt with, consisting of setbacks, confounding set impacts, impact dimension, technological and organic replicates, examples of stability and pureness, and management. Scientists might be lured into performing lots of contrasts within the structure of one experiment, including with large example dimensions (generally by compromising organic replicates). For that reason, it is essential to review the crucial function of suitable example dimensions and replicates (organic and technical), acquire a comprehension of the variables being examined, and review the significance of preventing confounding set impacts [27]. If several examples or problems are present in a job, batches ought to be built in a way that uniformly or arbitrarily distribute speculative problems throughout all the batches and procedures throughout each speculative phase. Likewise, the anticipated impact dimension of the examination problems ought to be thoroughly considered, as scientists might make unspoken presumptions regarding design system modifications while not preparing for sufficient replication to determine small impacts.

4.10   MANAGEMENT OF RANGES AND ASSUMPTIONS

Effectively performed experiments are connected with attentive speculative development and remove interaction. Interactions concerning the prospective restrictions and mistakes of a job (consisting of innovation, sources, and evaluation) ought to happen before carrying out the experiments. These interactions ought to aim to remove nonessential technological information without oversimplifying the subject (offering suitable recommendation products where needed). Subjects that ought to be protected consist of the utilized damp and completely dry lab process (openness ought to be offered from both sides) and, to prevent discontent from the anticipated and reasonable turn-around times. In these preliminary interactions, it is essential to state the techniques and accountable individuals for future interactions. To guarantee that interactions are efficient, a composed logical examine strategy (ASP) outlining the previously mentioned subjects ought to be ready and decided upon by all included centres[28]. The utilized process ought to be recorded and be made properly common to allow bidirectional understanding for future recommendation. The ASP ought to be extensive and describe speculative development. It ought to likewise consist of the decided upon timelines, the precise deliverables, and an options strategy, in a situation where the initial information evaluation strategy is considered inadequate.

To offer efficient assistance and provide the clinical vision of a job, range administration is crucial. The main range administration patterns to check are "range grope," where a job takes an undefined course without any view of a conclusion, leading to squandered sources without impact; "range swell," where the job broadens quickly without thoughtful allotment of sources and time, leading to tension on the core and impacting the variety of other jobs which can be supported; and "range sneak," where a job broadens gradually, however significantly, leading to postponed job ship-ment, loss of effect, and over usage of prepared sources. To flexibly handle the range of a job and the anticipated result, global fostering of the job administration approaches (consisting of arranging sources, establishing essential turning points, and interacting to-go/not-to-go strategies) is essential and among the main objectives of the designed ASPs. Eventually, all included celebrations ought to know the suggested research study vision and connected approaches. The ASP offers to advertise simple sharing and keeping of the examined information and speculative development and simple monitoring of the job from damp to completely dry lab. Removing interaction is therefore essential to offering efficient assistance since it allows shared understanding and comprehension.

4.11   DIFFICULTIES IN EFFICIENT CBT ADVANCEMENT AND CIRCULATION IN THE ACADEMIC COMMUNITY

Effectively executing and dispersing devices for clinical evaluation includes various distinct difficulties. In particular, essential distinctions between software application advancement processes in the academic community and market difficulties with the installability and archival security of unique devices designed by academics. These distinctions can be reducedto threebroad classifications:

- Software application created by scientists tends to be composed with the concept that individuals will be well-informed regarding the code and suitable system. This in some cases leads to devices that are challenging to set up, with directions and command-line choices that are uncertain and complicated yet crucial for the tool's working.
- Scholastic journals are the main resource for the information and paperwork of non-commer-cial clinical software applications, although the fixed nature of magazines implies this impor-tant information rapidly drops from the day of its incorporation [2–4].
- Rewards in the academic community greatly favor magazinesfor new software applications, not the upkeep of current devices.

Initially, software application designers in commercial setups get significantly more resources for developing easy-to-use devices compared to their equivalents in academic setups. The industrial software application is designed by big groups of designers that have specific individual experience (UX) designers [29]. In academic setups, software application is designed by smaller sized teams of scientists that might lack education in design, especially UX and cross-platform development. Lots of computational devices lack an easy-to-use interface to help with the setup or implementation procedure. Establishing a user-friendly interface is additionally made complex when the software application depends on third-party devices that have to be set up ahead of time, called "reliances." Setting up a reliance is a particularly complex procedure for scientists with restricted computational understanding. Well-defined UX requirements for software application advancement might assist designers in CBT to advertise extensive applications and usage of their recently designed computational devices [2].

Second, business effectively disperses industry-produced software applications utilizing devoted business systems or contractors—services that college and clinical financing companies don't generally offer academically-developed applications. The CBT neighborhood has embraced by default a practical, temporary structure for disseminating software application advancement, which typically includes publishing a paper explaining the application device in a peer-reviewed journal. The anticipated technique documents are devoted to discussing the rationale behind the unique computational device and showing its effectiveness with example datasets. Additional products such as outlined directions, tutorials, reliances, and resource codes are offered on the web and in the released paper as consistent source locators (URLs);. The high quality style and long-lasting accessibility of additional products differ amongst CBT designers and goes through much less examination in the peer-review procedure compared to the released paper itself. This method limits the installation ability of software application devices for utilization in research study and impedes the community's capability to assess the devices themselves [30].

Third, the academic frameworks of financing, employing, and promotion provide some benefit for constant, long-lasting advancement and the upkeep of devices and data sources; software application designers can also shed financing for the most commonly utilized devices. Loss of outside financing can result insluggish or even cease CBT advancement, possibly affecting the efficiency of research that depends upon these devices. Interrupted advancement likewise impedes the capability to innovate using released research that utilize technology of ceased devices [31,32]. Generally, an industry-developed software application is sustained by groups of software application designers devoted to establishing and executing updates for as long as the application is thought to be important. Lots of software application designers in the academic community don't have access to systems that might guarantee a comparable degree of upkeep and security.

4.12 TRAINING

For the facilitation of efficient bioinformatics devices, the advancement of a crucial mass of experienced bioinformatics professionals is important. Experienced bioinformaticians might exist at a few of the locations where bioinformatics advancement has been learnt; however, the bulk donot have bioinformatics proficiency. To conquer this lack of ability in the preliminary stage, in-person training sessions have to be designed. These sessions ought to be run at different nodes within the network. Preliminary training ought to be offered by expert instructors. They need to be resourced where required. The objective of these instructors ought to be to create regional trainingproficiency in particular information evaluation subjects. At specific locations and circumstances, previoustraining sessions can be encompassed to develop the Postgraduate Initial Bioinformatics workshop. This ought to cover various components to educate bioinformaticiansand should arrange for Train-the-Trainer occasions to concentrate on establishing local educating capability. Subsequently week-long workshops should be held which concentrate on specific bioinformatics evaluation subjects such as metagenomics, microbiomes, genome-wide organization studies (GWAS), information analytics, future generation sequencing (NGS), and advancement of bioinformatics capability [32]. Nevertheless, there are difficulties in accomplishing this. A lot are basic and not confined to a particular area; however, some might be restricted to one of the various other low-to-middle earning nations (LMICs) [12]. One such difficulty is the accessibility of the web. Good web connections might be considered a given in designer nations; however, the truth in the majority of under-developed nations is that they have restricted and sluggish web accessibility. Some colleges might have access to good regional web facilities [32]. These deals provide data transfer and download and install rate limitations. Moreover, these problems are intensified by unforeseen power outages and restricted backup resources [30]. Another difficulty is unsteady electrical power provision. Because of the much reduced power production compared to usage, unplanned rolling blackouts are an everyday occurrence in many nations. There are likewise problems of visa administration, endemic illness outbreaks, and so on. The provision of removing individuals from their parent institutes for prolonged periods likewise plays an essential function in the interest of the person in the setting of education. There may be individuals who do not have actual access to regional facilities to deal with after going back to their parent organization.

4.13 CONCLUSIONS

CBT has enthusiastic objectives, and there are different elements, like the accessibility of innovation and devices, the recognition of genomes and proteomes, and big enhancements in information storage space and computational power, which are offered by many current ICT systems and favor research in this field. Information warehousing is essential since CBT has to deal with a fantastic quantity of medical and biomedical information that is produced within the health andwellness company. CBT depends on information obtained from people, typically clients, and thus it can't solely depend upon data sources that are offered online from primary information service companies since itexists for the basic populace. On the other hand, essential information exists in an individual's medical and molecular information. These basic sources might only be utilized as a basic recommendation. Essential functions of an information storage facility for CBT have come to light after the evaluation of the user experience. Among the essential elements is the simpleness of the data source. This assists in the production of a modular and versatile system. This quality sustains constant advancement and enhancement of the system. It likewise helps with the optimization of inquiries and makes searches feasible. Modularity is an essential function that is important as it helps with the addition of different and heterogeneous information and resources in the information storage facility. It leads to multiple objectives and uses of domain names for the system. It is essential to have an opensource method. This assists the complete exploitation of partnerships amongst individuals both for software application advancement and for new function development. Collective advancement ends up being essential since it helps with the upkeep and upgrade of common metadata, which is utilized by individuals as it implies communicating with the data source. Its efficiency in establishing this communication identifies the actual effectiveness and success. People are in a state of continuous change, and lots of health and wellness companies and information systems are building constantly. The essential point at this moment is that these companies and systems have to interoperate, which results in a build-up of all feasible information on each client quickly and can be offered when it is required. This forms the basis for clinicians for an appropriate, molecular-enabled, medical diagnosis, prognosis, and enhanced therapy choice. Big populations under evaluation will help with availability of large information of global level. Ease of access to a sufficient amount of information is essential for clinical-related treatments as biomarker and acknowledgment of phenotype/genotype correlations. To accomplish this interoperation of information systems is extremely important. Interoperation ought to assist both combinations of information on solitary people and from lots of clients. For that reason the accomplishment of the objectives of CBT will deal with the provision of interoperability, and as mentioned regarding a few of the most current requirements for information modeling and information interchange. This makes it feasible to utilize CBT to conquer heterogeneity of initial information and understanding, which otherwise will position major difficulties. In the very early stage, current worldwide requirements need to be embraced, and there ought to be an arrangement which enables the appropriate addition of new proofs occurring as a consequence of genomic medication initiatives. The opportunity to apply a common recommendation design resulting in a basic, semiotics abundant, processable depiction of medical declarations has been highlighted. CBT ought to not be restricted to the evaluation of information by healthcare workers who can afford to purchase it to offer him/her better support. As currently discussed, it ought to likewise help with the recycling of medical information for research study functions and assist the scientists associated with this endeavor. Lots of scientists and designers are establishing new applications in the area, which mostly profit by accessing and browsing information sources with internet solutions. Such an open door to information might result in the development and recognition of new organizations, potentially resulting in ideas for the development of new biomarker recognition along with its evaluation. The primary problems in production accessibility and browsing of CBT-associated information resources have been explained. First of all, the concept that the fostering of typical information designs is the very best starting factor regarding executing a collection of information, enhance representations of information stored in repositories to carry out particular research study. CBT inquiries are complicated, include lots of information resources at the same time and, frequently, demand from each source more outcomes compared to the initiatives that are typically returned. Present methods and innovations offered for browsing information on the internet don't appear to be sufficient for CBT requirements. Accessibility to a great deal of information that is subjectively explained, in free messages, and is fundamentally disorganized is a required provision. The removal of information from clinical textual summaries can be helped by using regulated terms and ontologies, whenever feasible, along with the fostering of NLP devices fit for medical and organic domain names. The provision of browsing and drawing out of information in huge quantities is likewise essential. Because of feasible correlations amongst information in the outcomes may be absent, that might also not be sensible and significance to the general inquiry, CBT inquiries frequently need retrieving outcome collections larger compared to typical searches and queries. Of all these progressed browser computer methods, the essential one is targeted at incorporating search results arise from several resources. Among the greatest difficulties for the future is the incorporated browse and retrieval of CBT information from several resources and its extensive evaluation.

ACKNOWLEDGMENT

The author is very grateful to Galgotias University, Greater Noida for providing all necessary support for completion of the work.

REFERENCES

1. Sung, NS, Crowley, WF, Genel, M, Salber, P, Sandy, L, Sherwood, LM, Johnson, SB, Catanese, V, Tilson, H, Getz, K, Larson, EL, Scheinberg, D, Reece, EA, Slavkin, H, Dobs, A, Grebb, J, Martinez, RA, Korn, A, & Rimoin, D (2003). Central challenges facing the national clinical research enterprise. *Journal of the American Medical Association*, *289*(10), 1278–1287. https://doi.org/10.1001/jama.289.10.1278.
2. Payne PR, Johnson SB, Starren JB, Tilson HH, Dowdy D (2006). Breaking the translational barriers: The value of integrating biomedical informatics and translational research. *J Investig Med*;53(4):192–200.
3. American Medical Informatics Association (2007). AMIA Strategic Plan. Available at: http://www.amia.org/inside/stratplan/
4. Schena M, Shalon D, Davis RW, Brown PO (1995). Quantitative monitoring of gene expression patterns with a complementary DNA microarray. *Science*;270(5235):467–470. doi:10.1126/science.270.5235.467.
5. Lipshutz RJ, Morris D, Chee M, et al. (1995). Using oligonucleotide probe arrays to access genetic diversity. *Biotechniques*;19(3):442–447.

6. Golub TR, Slonim DK, Tamayo P, et al. (1999). Molecular classification of cancer: class discovery and class prediction by gene expression monitoring. *Science*;286(5439):531–537. doi: 10.1126/science. 286.5439.531.

7. Alizadeh AA, Eisen MB, Davis RE, et al (2000). Distinct types of diffuse large B-cell lymphoma identified by gene expression profiling. *Nature*;403(6769):503–11.

8. Clark TA, Schweitzer AC, Chen TX, et al (2007). Discovery of tissue specific exons using comprehensive human exon microarrays. *Genome Biol*;8(4):R64.

9. Kruglya KL, Nickerson DA (2001). Variation is the spice of life. *Nat Genet*;27(3):234–236.

10. Benson DA, Karsch-Mizrachi I, Lipman DJ, Ostell J, Wheeler DL. GenBank (2007). *Nucleic Acids Res Dec* 11.

11. Anonymous. Genetic Sequence Data Bank NCBI (2007)-GenBank Flat File Release 162.0 Distribution Release Notes; 162.0.

12. Barrett T, Troup DB, Wilhite SE, et al (2007). NCBI GEO: mining tens of millions of expression profiles—database and tools update. *Nucleic Acids Res*;35(Database issue):D760–D765.

13. Parkinson H, Sarkans U, Shojatalab M, et al. (2005). ArrayExpress—a public repository for microarray gene expression data at the EBI. *Nucleic Acids Res*;33(Databaseissue):D553–D555.

14. Dudley J, Butte AJ (2008). Enabling integrative genomic analysis of high-impact human diseases through text mining. *Pac SympBiocomput*; 580–591.

15. Martens L, Hermjakob H, Jones P et al (2005). PRIDE: the proteomics identifications database. *Proteomics*;5(13):3537–3545.

16. Anonymous. Taxonomy Nodes (all dates). (2007). Available at: http://www.ncbi.nlm.nih.gov/Taxonomy/ txstat.cgi

17. Mailman MD, Feolo M, Jin Y, et al. (2007). The NCBI dbGaP database of genotypes and phenotypes. *Nat Genet*;39(10): 1181–1186.

18. The Wellcome Trust (2003). *Sharing data from large-scale biological research projects: a system of tripartite responsibility. Fort Lauderdale: Wellcome Trust*; 14–15, 2003.

19. NIH Data Sharing Policy and Implementation Guidance. March 5, 2003. Available at: http://grants.nih. gov/grants/policy/data_sharing/data_sharing_guidance.htm

20. NIH, DOE Guidelines Encourage Sharing of Data, Resources (1993). *Hum Genome News*;4(5).

21. Saeed AI, Bhagabati NK, Braisted JC et al (2006). TM4 microarray software suite. *Methods Enzymol*;411:134–193.

22. Reich M, Liefeld T, Gould J, Lerner J, Tamayo P, Mesirov JP (2006). GenePattern 2.0. *Nat Genet*; 38(5):500–501.

23. Dahlquist KD, Salomonis N, Vranizan K, Lawlor SC, Conklin BR (2002). GenMAPP, a new tool for viewing and analyzing microarray data on biological pathways. *Nat Genet*;31(1): 19–20.

24. Gentleman R (2005). *Bioinformatics and Computational Biology Solutions Using R and Bioconductor.* New York: Springer Science Business Media.

25. Gentleman RC, Carey VJ, Bates DM et al. (2004). Bioconductor: open software development for computational biology and bioinformatics. *Genome Biol* 2004;5(10):R80.

26. HUGO—a UN for the human genome. *Nat Genet* 2003 Jun; 34(2):115–116.

27. Brazma A, Hingamp P, Quackenbush J, et al. (2001). Minimum information about a microarray experiment (MIAME)-toward standards for microarray data;29(4):365–371.

28. Rubin DL, Lewis SE, Mungall CJ et al (2006). National center for biomedical ontology: Advancing biomedicine through structured organization of scientific knowledge. *OMICS*;10(2):185–198.

29. Butte AJ. Medicine (2008). The ultimate model organism. *Science*;320(5874):325–327.

30. Guttmacher AE, Collins FS (2002). Genomic medicine—a primer. *N Engl J Med*;347(19):1512–1520.

31. Mootha VK, Lepage P, Miller K et al (2002). Identification of a gene causing human cytochrome c oxidase deficiency by integrative genomics. *Proc Natl Acad Sci U S A*;100(2):605–610.

32. English SB, Butte AJ (2007). Evaluation and Integration of 49 Genomewide Experiments and the Prediction of Previously Unknown Obesity-related Genes. *Bioinformatics*;23(21):2910–2917.

5 Artificial Intelligence
An Emerging Technique in Pharmaceutical and Healthcare Systems

Anushka Joshi
Rajiv Gandhi Proudyogiki Vishwavidyalaya, Bhopal, India

Sudhanshu Mishra
Madan Mohan Malaviya University of Technology, Gorakhpur, India

Deepti Jain
Rajiv Gandhi Proudyogiki Vishwavidyalaya, Bhopal, India

Simran Ludhiani
Shri Govindram Seksaria Institute of Technology and Science, Indore, India

Aishwarya Rajput
Rajiv Gandhi Proudyogiki Vishwavidyalaya, Bhopal, India

CONTENTS

DOI: 10.1201/9781003226949-5

5.1 INTRODUCTION

Artificial intelligence (AI) is the leading advancement in technology driven fields, and as stated in much research will be a fundamental benefit to the fourth industrial and technological revolution. AI as of now has been implemented in various domains. The concept of AI is aged yet venerable; nevertheless it has only been explored extensively since the 1950s. Due to the complexities involved in the development of AI, it was often misunderstood or poorly understood initially. As defined by one of its originators, John McCarthy, it is "the science and engineering of making intelligent machines." A simplified form of the same definition is: a machine resembling a human mind or its extended capabilities which is built up using computational advancements [1]. Several questions have arisen interrogating the practical implementation of AI, such as: Does a machine actually work like a human? Or can a machine be as intelligent as the human brain? The answer can be provided using Turing's test: to be considered intelligent, a machine must exhibit behavior that is indistinguishable from that of a human. It is well understood by this statement that this can be achieved once scientists and researchers reach the artificial general intelligence (AGI) level which is analogous to humans. Well, looking at the ongoing advancements of AI and its exponentially increased usage, it can be assumed that AI is passing the Turing test [2].

The concept of "intelligent agent" is used to understand AI theory; it integrates the abilities needed to pass the Turing test. This concept assumes that the agent is as skilled as humans, with logical and active senses, and utilizes its native environment to understand and act. An intelligent agent has the ability to bring about physical actions using sensors (Figure 5.1). The agent can bring out certain fundamental inputs that are originally fed into its system, such as the old or current nature of the working environment, observations of the environment, and past working experiences that the agent can use to learn and achieve objectives [3].

AI will be a progressive and optimistic impact on the coming future. Many nations are now seen to be readily investing in it; and it is set to transform medical conditions globally. It is extensively being used in healthcare and patient monitoring due to its ability of computer-based decision making [4]. There have been several advancements in healthcare using AI, some of them are already established and some are underway. The coming age of telemedicine and healthcare apps providing remote benefits to patients and users is a testament to the above statements. There are many studies highlighting the potential that AI driven healthcare applications have, and how well they are accelerating the whole healthcare system. Medical practitioners too can be seen to benefit, with a reduced

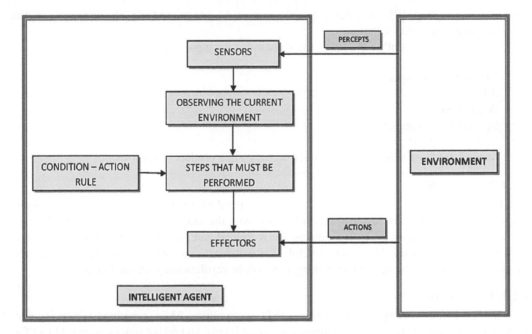

FIGURE 5.1 Theory of an intelligent agent.

administration workload, reduced burnout, and having more time for direct patient care. AI has the capacity to direct resources to the areas where they can make the most difference [5].

The EIT Health and McKinsey & Company report 2020 claims that the areas where AI- enabled healthcare delivery is most likely to make an impact are:

- Chronic care management
- Diagnostics;
- Self-care/wellness;
- Clinical decision support;
- Care delivery;
- Triage and diagnosis.

5.2 TYPES OF AI

AI can be simply put as intelligence which is incorporated into machines to perform functions, as humans do, or to make things easy for us, or we can say that AI machines are built up to resemble human intelligence. AI can go beyond human intelligence with its capabilities and functions [6]. In general the concept of AI can be understood by classifying it on two bases: the first on how capable the AI is, and the other on what function the AI will perform. The former has three subdivisions and the later has four, all which are described here.

5.2.1 ARTIFICIAL INTELLIGENCE: TYPE 1

5.2.1.1 Narrow AI (Weak AI)

Also known as artificial narrow intelligence (ANI), this is functional AI and is the most common type currently known to the world. Narrow AI as the name suggests has certain limitations and cannot perform tasks beyond its functional field; it turns out to be a failure if allowed to perform tasks beyond its capabilities [7]. To be more specific, narrow AI is restricted to performing only one task at a time, as it is trained for that only.

As narrow AI is currently functional, there are many examples that can be seen at present:

- IBM's Watson supercomputer;
- AI chess;
- Apple's Siri;
- Speech and image recognition;
- Self-running cars;
- Various functionalities on e-commerce websites like product suggestions.

5.2.1.2   General AI

Also known as artificial general intelligence (AGI), general AI is a next level AI in terms of capabilities, as it can be seen to be a substitute for humans with the same efficiency of work performance. The idea behind this concept is to eliminate the workload and give the same output as the human brain to make things easy. As of now, general AI is non-functional and still evolving, as researchers are still working to come up with something that will be revolutionary for the human race [8].

5.2.1.3   Super AI

Also known as artificial super intelligence (ASI), super/strong AI is something which is beyond human intelligence. It surpasses the human with more logical and active senses. Super AI can function to perform tasks better than humans and is one step ahead of general AI. Super AI is at the highest level of capabilities and can perform functions like making judgments, solving problems, reasoning things, questioning things, and planning, learning, and communicating all by itself. As it may seem, super AI is a hypothetical system which may lead to a changed era [9].

5.2.2   Artificial Intelligence: Type 2

5.2.2.1   Reactive Machines

This is the most basic type of AI in terms of function, and thus marks the beginning of AI's revolutionary era. As these machines are the oldest, they come with certain limits. This type of machine functions to perform tasks as per the current scenario only and react with suitable and best actions to complete the task [10]. They do not have stored memories of the functions performed in the past, nor can they utilize their performed work experience for future actions.

Examples of reactive machines are:

- IBM's Deep Blue;
- Google's AlphaGo.

5.2.2.2   Limited Memory

Limited memory AI has an updated function where machines can "learn" from their past working experiences. Along with the function to react they are trained to learn and thus take improved and intelligent decisions. As they are trained to learn, they have a lot of training databases fed into the AI system. But as the name suggests these systems can store the data of their past experience for a limited period of time only. As of now most machines utilize this system only [11].

There are basically three machine learning models that function at this level of AI:

1. Reinforcement learning. Through many cycles of experimentation, these designs figure out how to make accurate decisions.
2. Long short term memory (LSTM). Researchers hypothesized that using previous information to predict the next item in a series, notably in language, would indeed be beneficial, therefore

they devised a model based on LTSM. LSTM labels more recent data as more significant and those from the past as less essential when anticipating the following parts in a series [12].

3. Evolutionary generative adversarial networks (E-GAN). This concept stores memory in the form that it forge ahead with each advancement. This concept stores memory in a form that can be easily move. The model generates a developing entity, which does not always pursue the same route. The model may identify a better path each time, a path of least resistance, as a result of the changes [13]. We can say that E-GAN simulates human evolution, each succeeding generation comes with better advancements as compared to its parent generation.

Relevant examples of this system are:

- Fingerprint scanning;
- Self-driving cars (can memorize the recent speed and distance of nearby cars).

5.2.2.3 Theory of Mind

This is the non-active system of AI, and is still under development. The theory of mind system can be utilized to understand and depict human emotions, beliefs, and thought processes. They are also made to become involved socially and interact with people around them.

5.2.2.4 Self-awareness

This system too is a hypothetical one and can be seen as the future of AI or the ultimate goal of the AI system. This system will work ahead of human subconsciousness. These machines will be self-aware, self-resilient, and will use their own consciousness to act and react.

At present we have successfully surpassed the first system which is the reactive machine and improved the second system which is limited memory. Not much information is available about the latter two types of AI, as they are under development or beyond the scope of currently defined AI. It may take years before they are activated [14].

5.3 AI TIMELINE IN HEALTHCARE

The history of AI goes back to the 1950s when Alan Turing explained that machines and computers can mimic human cognitive abilities and critical thinking. He demonstrated an imitation game in his publication "Computing Machinery and Intelligence" which is most commonly known as the Turing test to analyze whether computers have acquired these abilities; it is still used as a reference test. John McCarthy, a mathematician and computer scientists from the United States, in 1956 introduced the world to the term "artificial intelligence" along with his colleagues Marvin Minskly (at MIT), Claude Shannon, and Nathaniel Rochester, who later devised organized research into unleashing the further potential of AI [15]. In 1961, Unimate, the first ever industrial robot, came into existence and which was developed by George Devol. Later on the development of "shakey—the first electronic person" in 1966 by the AI center at the Stanford Research Institute (SRI) and ELIZA, a computer program used as a natural language processing tool, created by Joseph Weizenbaun in 1964–1966 were huge milestones in the world of AI. After this revolutionary achievement, the road ahead for further development was blocked; the period from the late 1960s until 1997 has no mentionable advancements. This period was called the winter of the AI era. The British government ceased funding except in the major universities, soon to be followed by the US government. The creation of Deep Blue, the chess playing computer by IBM which defeated the reigning Russian chess champion of that time Garry Kasparov in 1997, was a great comeback. This achievement reopened the blocked road and paved the way for further advancements in the world of AI, including the accomplishments of Kismet, AIBO, Roomba, and Siri.

The introduction of AI in the medical field was quite late because of certain imperfections and limitations in the early years. In the late 1970s and 1960s, various computer scientists, researchers, and scientific philosophers like Bruce Buchanan and Edward Feigenbaum came together and in association explored the application of AI in the life sciences, mostly in DENDRAL experiments. This project was intended to apply AI to illuminate structures and automate inferences, such as interpretations of mass spectrometry data. The researchers were fascinated by the application of AI in solving biomedical problems in the 1970s. This approach was accelerated by the development of the SUMEX–AIM computer resource at Stanford University [16].

In the early 1970s plenty of scientists and working groups were researching computational paradigms and models directed towards clinical decision making and problem solving. This research led to the development of various AI programs including MYCIN (1975), an expert system which assists doctors in choosing the correct therapy for patients with varied bacterial infections as well as for diagnoses. There are a certain number of rules encoded in the system that helps it to justify its advice. CASNET (Causal Associational NETwork) in 1975 was developed at Rutgers and was another tool for aiding decision making in disease diagnosis. The information encoded in the system contained patient observations, pathophysiological states, and classifications of diseases. It was first used for glaucoma. DIALOG (INTERNIST) (1976) was a similar computer assisted diagnostic tool developed at the University of Pittsburgh for the diagnosis of various conditions of internal medicine by structuring or building the behavior of the clinicians so as they can take the appropriate decision. Over the next decade of the 1980s, the community of scientists working on AI grew exponentially and led to the formation of the American Association of Artificial Intelligence with a sub-division for its application in the medical field (AAAI-M) [17].

The early 1980s marked the proliferation of various expert systems. These systems consisted of four major entities: a knowledge base (the encoded information that can be used by the system, including human and learning systems); a problem solver (algorithms for using the knowledge base); a communicator (for facilitating effective communication between the expert system, developers, and users); explanation and help for explaining the functioning as it solves a problem. One of these systems was ABEL (Acid Base and Electrolyte Program) which was developed in the Department of Computer Science at MIT and which provided the reasoning for the management of acid base and electrolyte disorders. Another system was ONCOCIN, developed by the Department of Medicine and Computer Science at Stanford University in 1980; it was specially developed to assist oncologists in the management of cancer patients and protocols and was designed to answer basic scientific questions using excellent knowledge. Quick Medical Record (QMR) was a similar system which assisted in the diagnosis of various diseases and used the knowledge base INTERNIST. The decade continued to experience the creation of many such medical diagnostic expert systems including MED 1 and MED 2 developed in 1983 and 1985 respectively. In 1986, DXplain, a computer-based decision support system developed by the University of Massachusetts, enabled users to enter certain symptoms and listed the possible diagnostic conditions that may relate to them. It also acted as an e-medical textbook providing details about diseases; starting with 500 diseases it later expanded to about 2400 diseases. The period from the late 1980s to the late 1990s was an AI winter, with no significant developments being made during this time. Despite this phase, the community of scientists, logicians, mathematicians, and computer scientists interested in AI continued to grow and worked on the current limitations and failures of AI [18]. In the 1990s various concepts like Markov models and Bayesian networks were incorporated into AI thinking, leading to the development of machine learning. Previously computers had only been able to read instructions and provide output; later computers were required to extract information and rules from given large sets of data by themselves and utilize them for predictions, which was achieved by ML, also called statistical learning. The machine learning algorithms were utilized for assessing medical datasets. Certain limitations led to the development of artificial neural networks (ANNs) which were first developed by Frank Rosenblatt in 1958. These are a set of computational algorithms inspired by the central nervous system of animals. In other words it is a data or information processing technique which mimics the human brain. Earlier, the application of machine learning in medicine had been hindered, as it could only focus on a limited set of data due to insufficient computing capacity. To overcome this problem, a convolutional neural network (CNN), which is a class of deep learning, was invented. This was able to solve more complex problems and focus on large amounts of data. It had potential for lesion detection, classification, image reconstruction, and natural language processing [19].

Since 2000 until now technology has boomed and the utilization of AI in medicine has grown rapidly. In 2007 IBM developed an open domain question-answer system named Watson with technology called DeepQA, which was capable of competing with two excellent contestants in a quiz show called *Jeopardy!* and win. This creation has vast applications in the healthcare system, mainly in diagnosis and treatment, in assisting practitioners in providing appropriate knowledge from large databases, and helping in the collection of proper evidence to support diagnosis and treatment so that practitioners don't have to go through excessive information and waste time. Later in 2017, Watson was utilized for the identification of new RNA-binding proteins altered in amyotrophic lateral sclerosis. Computer aided diagnosis (CAD) in 2010 was used in endoscopy and further enhanced colon detection.

The increasing potential of computer software and hardware over time has led to the digitization of healthcare very quickly. The natural language processing in AI has enhanced the quality of interfaces and allowed more complex conversations instead of superficial ones. This technology aided the creation of Apple's virtual assistant Siri in 2011, which was integrated in the iPhone, followed by Amazon's virtual assistant Alexa in 2014. The year 2015 was marked by the development of Pharmabot, a pediatric generic medicine consultant chatbot that assists in the prescription and suggestion of generic medicines for children. Arterys, a cloud-based deep learning technology, in 2017 received Food & Drug Administration(FDA) clearance for its application in the healthcare sector; it can be used for the measurement of blood flow, detection of tumors and potential cancer cells, along with easy application to radiological standards [20]. Since then the use of Deep Learning has continued to increase for various purposes including detection of lesions, screening of diabetic retinopathy, identification of melanoma and non-melanoma skin cancers, prediction of cardiovascular risk in a population, prediction of the progression of Alzheimer's disease, as well as drug therapy response. Various clinical trials are going on for the application of DL in gastroenterology and endoscopy as well.

AI has faced a lot of dead ends and setbacks since its advent. But now this technological boom is at its peak, though there is still a lot of scope to be unfurled and a lot of trials to be carried out. As far as the healthcare sector is concerned, the potential of AI seems to be endless. The aim is ultimately to actualize the highest potential of AI to improve medical proceedings and enhance the healthcare system by its application. The time profile for AI in healthcare is represented in Table 5.1

TABLE 5.1
AI in Healthcare: Timeline Profile

Time Period	Events
1950–1970	Alan Turing develops the "Turing test"
	Advent of basic Machine Learning
	John McCarthy coins the term "artificial intelligence"
	"Unimate" is first ever industrial robot
	"Shakey" is first electronic person
	"ELIZA" is first chatbot
	DENDRAL experiments
1970–1980	MYCIN expert system for diagnostic aid
	Creation of SUMEX-AIM
	Development of CASNET
	Development of INTERNIST
	Development of Present Illness expert system by MIT for diagnosis of kidney diseases
	Establishment of American Association of AI in Medicine (AAA-M)
	Development of EMYCIN

(Continued)

TABLE 5.1 (*Continued*)
AI in Healthcare: Timeline Profile

Time Period	Events
1980–2000	Development of ABEL expert system for diagnosis of acid base and electrolyte disorders
	Development of MED 1 and MED2 expert systems
	Release of DXplain decision support system
	Development of machine learning
	Last decade experienced AI winter
2000–present	Deep learning
	Development of DeepQA technology by IBM (Watson)
	Apple introduces the virtual assistant "Siri"
	CAD application to endoscopy
	Amazon's virtual assistant "Alexa"
	Development of Pharma Bot and Mandy
	Approval of Aterys cloud-based system based on DL for application in healthcare
	Continuous research in gastroenterology and endoscopy

5.4 AI TECHNOLOGIES USED IN HEALTHCARE

Today, AI is employed in all sorts of services and products including the healthcare sector and it is evident that it holds the potential to completely transmute patient care and even outstrip humans in certain areas like disease diagnosis. AI is not a single technology but a cluster of different technologies that can be combined together or used one at a time to automate the various facets of patient monitoring and the overall healthcare system. Some basic technologies used in medicine are machine learning, deep learning, neural networks, expert systems, and robotics.

5.4.1 MACHINE LEARNING

The term "machine learning" was proposed by Arthur Samuel, a computer scientist at IBM in 1959. It is basically a class or subset of AI. Machine learning involves a set of algorithms (encoding information), which enables a system to learn from data and previous experience and utilize that learning for prediction. Patterns within the data are identified or in other words important knowledge and useful information from the data is withdrawn and can be applied to create intelligent systems. The major areas in medicine which have benefited from ML are diagnosis and outcome prediction (disease identification and relapse). There are various machine learning techniques or algorithms; the main four are supervised learning, unsupervised learning, semi-supervised learning, and reinforcement learning. These different algorithms are also known as models; the type of model to employ depends upon the data type. In supervised machine learning, the output is preset along with the input; the system then identifies or predicts the predetermined attributes, and the performance is tested on the basis of the number of correctly predicted attributes [21]. Supervised learning involves educating the system with the data that already consists of desired outputs associated with it. Supervised learning can be further divided into classification and regression algorithms. On the other hand, unsupervised machine learning educates itself on data. It doesn't involve any target aspect, that is all the attributes used are the input variables, thus this algorithm is useful for cluster and association mining techniques. Hoffman stated that these algorithms are useful for label creation in data which is utilized for the enforcement of supervised machine learning tasks. Unsupervised algorithms recognize certain groups in the unlabeled data and ultimately assign all values with certain labels. Semi-supervised learning involves the combination of both supervised and unsupervised learning algorithms; it can be used on both labeled and unlabeled data types. The aim of using the semi-supervised learning model is to obtain better prediction than was obtained from the labeled data. The reinforcement machine algorithm is a model where the agent or the machine has to work and take action intelligently in an environment or in a certain provided situation to maximize the reward and minimize the risk. These types of models can be used for enhancing the activity of systems such as robotics and for increasing automation [22].

5.4.2 Deep Learning

There is another division of machine learning known as "deep learning" (DL). DL is a class of machine learning which comprises ANNs along with representation learning and helps in dealing with a large amount of data. This class of algorithm involves various layers of network and extracts the best output or attributes from the provided set of input data; one example is image processing. Deep learning in the healthcare sector offers a variety of applications like clinical imaging. It supports the prediction of Alzheimer's disease and its variation by analysis of Magnetic Resonance Imaging; it is also helpful in spotting benign and malignant tumors in the breast by ultrasound imaging. The other applications of DL in healthcare include electronic health records (prediction of diseases and disease progression from the clinical data of patients) and genomics (DNA sequencing, RNA measurements). DL provides improved performance and helps in discovering high level attributes as compared to traditional models, though there are many challenges that hinder the way, such as continuously increasing data volume, interpretability, temporality (as diseases are changing rapidly over time), and incorporating expert knowledge. Deep learning is highly potent when it comes to the future of predictive healthcare systems. [23,24].

5.4.3 Machine Vision

It is well known that computers are capable of continuous improvement. Systems have undergone drastic changes in a short span of time, due to enhanced access to large volumes of data and the inclusion of many more new technologies in AI. One of the AI technologies is computer vision. This is a field where patterns, images, and vision are used for extracting sense from data. It involves the capability of the computer to see and process images in pixel forms and make sense of the data, as a human tends to do. In the healthcare sector, computer vision has a number of applications such as screening, disease diagnosis, prediction of outcomes, clinical research, and digital monitoring of disease. Recently the research regarding the application of computer vision in certain areas like ophthalmology, radiology, pathology, and dermatology have been enhanced drastically. Computer vision aids therapists to obtain detailed conditions of patients via medical imaging and also supports the timely detection of illness [25].

5.4.4 Natural Language Processing

One of the major linguistic components of AI is natural language processing (NLP). This enables the computer program to recognize the natural language that humans use. The foundation of NLP comprises various disciplines including information technology, mathematics, linguistics, AI, and robotics. Making a system understand natural language is a typical task but which faces a lot of challenges such as thought processes, analyzing the meaning and representation of the linguistic input, and world knowledge. The process of understanding goes on step by step: first the words, then sentences, analyzing meaning, word order, and grammatical contexts. Certain areas of NLP are of great interest to researchers who strive to improve them, such as lexical and morphological analysis, noun phrase generation, word segmentation, semantic and disclosure analysis, word meaning and knowledge representation, along with various knowledge based tools and techniques. One of the main facets of NLP is the processing of texts for the extraction of important information, indexing, and abstracting. This involves structuring large bodies of text so that particular required information can be obtained or in other words converting the unstructured text into structured, to ease analysis; this process is also called text mining [26].

Humans possess the ability to analyze certain things like different linguistic patterns, contextual meanings, and spelling variations which computers often fails to do; on the other hand humans are not able to get through the large amount of data which can be easily done by computers. However, there are certain technologies employed to bridge this gap [27]. The techniques for effective text extraction include:

1. Information extraction: the collection of useful information from a large set of unstructured data.
2. Information retrieval: information is withdrawn by identification of various patterns and phrases, for example search engines like Google.
3. Text categorization: this involves the division of the acquired text into a variety of predetermined categories.
4. Text summarization: the aim is to cut short lengthy data as per the user's requirements.

NLP aids in the creation of various models that can be utilized efficiently in the healthcare sector. The major requirement is effective quantification of disease risk factors, disease burden over a specific population, identification of best practices, and measurement of outcomes which are currently represented by the PICO (patient/population, intervention, comparison and outcomes.)model, involving patient/problem, intervention/exposure, and comparison and outcome. This NLP-based concept helps in answering specific clinical or public healthcare questions. NLP has also paved the way for data or text-based research and evidence-based decision making. One study has highlighted that with the help of NLP-based models, depression can be diagnosed prior to its appearance in the medical records. The major applications of NLP includes patient experience and value-based care, root cause analysis and predictive analysis, and patient feedback management. During the recent pandemic, NLP supported the analysis of huge amounts of COVID information and helped researchers and scientists in finding answers to important questions, question answering, and summarizing evidence.

5.4.5　Robotics in Healthcare

Along with NLP, the advancements in AI and robotics are grooming the healthcare sector too. The use of robots in medicine is not new. In 1985 a robotic arm was utilized in association with the Computed Tomography (CT) scanner for brain tumor biopsy. Robot applications are actively used in the healthcare sector, mostly backstage, such as in drug development, drug production, drug dispensing, patient monitoring and care, and hospital administration. Robots in pharmaceutical industries aid in meeting the required specifications and performing repetitive tasks with ease and accuracy; in manufacturing units they are mostly involved in filling, labeling, packaging, and assembling areas [28]. They are also used in the discovery of vital treatments and in stages of drug development. Robots can be differentiated on the basis of their applications, such as surgical robots, telemedicine robots, serving robots in hospitals, radiologist robots, rehabilitation robots, and cleaning and disinfecting robots [29]:

- Surgical robots: these robots assist surgeons and specialists in complicated surgery, and they provide minimal invasive surgery with a lot more accuracy than humans. The most prominent one is the Da Vinci robotic surgery system, whose fourth generation is currently in use.
- Radiologist robots: these robots help in resolving protection concerns as large amounts of radiation are involved. The Twin Robotic X-ray system by Siemens allows therapists to see

real time 3D images, as the system is mobile and the patient doesn't have to move. It allows for fluoroscopy and angiography as well.

- Rehabilitation robots: one of the popular ones is the Kinova assistive robot that helps patients with the picking and placing of objects along with the use of a brain computer interface (BCI). Another one is EksoNR (exoskeleton) that is used for improving the mobility of disabled people.
- Cleaning and disinfecting robots: these are remote controlled and provide protection to humans coming in contact with hazardous chemicals and disinfectants.
- Telemedicine robots: these allow the remote checkup, diagnosis, and treatment of patients without the physical presence of the therapist by using audio visual aids. One such robot is RP-VITA (MMed Tech Boston, MA, USA) which was the first such system to be approved by the Food &Drug Administration.

The use of robotics in the healthcare sector has undoubtedly enhanced its functioning and has provided therapists and researchers with convenience, accuracy, and precision. Yet there are some factors which should be taken into account while designing robots for medical fields, such as kinematics and dynamics, control and dexterity (sufficient degrees of freedom in the required axes), operator safety (safety requirements for surgical robots as per IEC 80601-2-77, for rehabilitation robots as per IEC 80601-2-78), ease of handling and maintenance, power requirements, and cost [18,19]. Healthcare digitization enhances the quality of healthcare management in all respects. There are many systems and robots currently being researched, like RAVEN and MicroSurge (endoscopic telesurgery), Amadeus (a laparoscopic surgical robot system to compete with Da Vinci), NeuroArm, MrBot, and TraumaPod, that, with the help of technical improvements, will change the shape of the healthcare sector in the future [30].

5.5 ROLE OF AI IN PATIENT MONITORING

5.5.1 The Modern Health Care Era

AI is a proven tool for next generation healthcare technology. People believe in the power of the internet. The smallest of queries and the biggest of problems are usually pursued over the internet.

The demand for healthcare services is rising all the time. With advancements in wireless technology and smartphones, healthcare services with the help of health tracking applications and search platforms have paved the way. Also, this technological advancement has enables remote services for healthcare delivery. This nature of providing services has improved the situation in disadvantaged areas, has aided in cutting down expenses, and assisted in avoiding unnecessary exposure to infectious diseases at clinics. The AI related healthcare industry is anticipated to develop at a quick pace, and to reach up to USD6.6 billion by 2021, representing a 41 percent compound yearly growth rate [31].

5.5.2 PRECISION MEDICINE

Precision medicine allows healthcare action to be tailored to specific patients or groups of patients depending on their illness profile, diagnostic and prodiagnostic information, or therapy response. The personalized therapy will take into account genetic factors and also the medical treatment as per age, immunity, metabolic profile, gender, and family history. As the name suggest, it focuses on individual characteristic traits instead looking out for the traits of the population i.e. precise. It entails gathering data from people, such as physiological data monitoring, electronic medical records, and genetic profiles, and then customizing the therapy by use of special models [32]. It usually proves to be advantageous as it minimizes cost and adverse effects and improves drug efficacy.

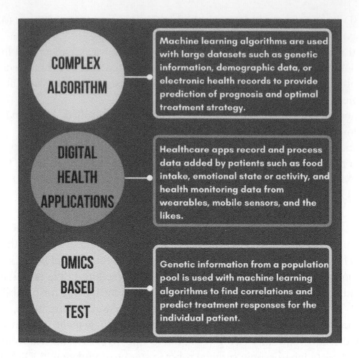

FIGURE 5.2 Types of clinical areas.

Precision medicine projects come in a variety of forms. There are basically three sorts of clinical areas, which are shown in Figure 5.2.

Applications of precision medicine include:

- Providing a solution based on genetics: this takes into account the full genome sequencing of an individual. The genome sequence of an individual will link to Electronic Medical Record (EMR) that will aid in precision medicine. Deep Genomics, a healthcare company, is already working on this. The company keeps an eye on new therapeutic targets or new sets of populations with a disease. Many genetic features contribute to a possible or predicted illness which can be prevented or reported, even without diagnosis [33].
- Drug discovery and development: discovering a new drug has always been a very hectic, time consuming, and expensive process. To accelerate healthcare services it is important to design and market a formulation to safeguard the health of individuals. AI here plays a major role. It uses molecular network descriptors, fingerprints of molecules, and a simplified molecular input line entry system (SMILES) and convolutional neural networks (CNNs). AI simplifies the action by working on:
  - (i). drug property and activity prediction;
  - (ii). deep learning aided de novo design;
  - (iii). drug target interaction; and
  - (iv). AI and medical visualization.

It might be difficult to interpret data that is presented in the form of a picture or a video. This task requires skills. AI can be efficiently utilized for the task. It comprises machine vision, medical image recognition, augmented reality, and virtual reality.

Machine vision diagnosis for surgery is the interpretation of pictures and videos by machines beyond the skills of a human. It includes image-based diagnosis and image-guided surgery. Computer vision for the diagnosis of a disease and also for surgery is used. Computer vision algorithms are designed to classify images of lesions on tissues. The data from the video has more than 20 times the data in comparison to high resolution diagnostic images such as CT. Deep learning is also the most promising technique for medical image recognition [34,35].

5.5.3 INTELLIGENT PERSONAL HEALTH RECORDS

Personal health records have always been restricted to physicians and may lack many patient related features. A patient specific and centric record gives scope to self-involvement and customization and helps the engagement of patients in their healthcare monitoring. This always assists patients to manage their own minor illnesses and give physicians the time to deal with emergencies. It includes health monitoring wearables, natural language processing, and personal record integration [36].

With the change in trends of lifestyle, there has been a sudden increase in lifestyle-related disorders in people. There has been a tragic increase in chronic illness caused by lifestyle disorders over the past decade. People with developing mindsets want to live freely and independently until they die. They aspire to maintain their autonomy over their life decisions. Assistive technologies have increased patient's self-reliance with their involvement in information and communication technology [37]. They boost self-reliance and productivity in people regarding their health management and also for their idea of a healthy lifestyle.

5.5.4 ROBOTICS AND AI POWERED DEVICES

Robots are the new advancements of the healthcare system. They are quicker, more skilled, and more consistent and accurate than humans. A single robot can work as efficiently as an entire staff of people. They can be programmed for any operation which is required. The use of robots is seen in minimally invasive surgery and neuroprosthetics [38].

5.6 AI IN CANCER TREATMENT

AI is utilized to forecast anticancer medication action or to aid in the discovery of anticancer drugs. Various malignancies and medicines may respond in different ways, and results from rising screening techniques frequently indicate a link between cancer cell genetic diversity and therapeutic activity. The major functions it provides are lesion detection, outlining the target area, 3D localization of the tumor, clinical and pathological analysis, quantitative analysis of the tumor, and tumor image segmentation [39,40].

5.6.1 APPLICATIONS OF AI IN ONCOLOGY ARE

1. Improved screening and diagnosis;
2. Characterization of genome;
3. AI in chemotherapy;
4. AI in radiotherapy;
5. AI in immunotherapy;
6. AI in clinical decision making and support;
7. Deep learning and image datasets;
8. Machine learning and deep learning for anticancer drugs.

5.6.2 BENEFITS OF USING AI IN CANCER THERAPY

1. Predictive diagnosis based on genomic sequence;
2. Understanding type and severity better than the conventional diagnosis;
3. Personalized therapy;

4. Minimizing the side effects caused by chemotherapy;
5. Predicting the body's response to the treatment more efficiently;
6. Tracing the drug's pharmacokinetic and pharmacodynamics measures;
7. Efficient and accurate surgical measures can be taken when required;
8. Data monitoring and healthcare record management becomes easy for patient and physician with the help of AI;
9. Easy tracing of any side effects or adverse effects.

5.6.3 CANCER GENOMICS

AI has aided the collection of widespread data on genome sequencing related to cancer, called "cancer genomics." The mutation in the genomic sequence of a cancer affected person is traced and recorded. Google's DeepVariant, ExPecto, Oncomine Dx target test, MSK-IMPACT, and so on are used as AI tools in cancer genomics [41] (Table 5.2).

5.7 AI IN HEALTHCARE: CURRENT CHALLENGES

AI has the potential to transform everything, be it sectors like communication and media, business and finance, and now even the healthcare and patient monitoring system.

This comes with many challenges. A current operational AI platform holds several potential challenges as stumbling blocks that delay its progress. AI often has many ethical issues too, especially in fields like healthcare and patient monitoring. The following are some of the challenges affecting the momentum of AI in the current healthcare system [42,43]:

5.7.1 ETHICAL CHALLENGES

• Data privacy. The privacy of personal data can be seen as a bedrock to the whole concept of AI introduced into healthcare. For a machine to work in parallel with a human brain, it must have access to the human brain; thus fetching the personal data of patients or customers is essential to produce effective output. Apps and devices must assure consumers about the privacy of their data, which must be protected by law [44]. As of now, patients or consumers have given the benefit of the doubt to companies and researchers, but there are still people concerned about the use of modern applications because of the fear of losing the privacy of their personal data or the data being misused by the company.
• Transparency to consumers. Transparency and fairness of the AI algorithms to patients are very essential. A consumer must know and understand how the application processes their data. Patients, as data owners, have the right to know how and to what extent their individual health information along with their personal details are stored and utilized.

TABLE 5.2
Some of the Image Datasets for Cancer

Serial no	Type of Cancer	Dataset
1.	Breast	BreakHis
2.	Cervix	CCSD
3.	Skin	ISIC 2018
4.	Prostate	PROMISE12
5.	Liver	PAIP
6.	Miscellaneous	TCIA

5.7.2 CHALLENGES TO DOCTORS UNDER CLINICAL PRACTICE

AI may claim to bring about a revolution to current healthcare, and at first it may seem trustworthy, but right now in reality a medical practitioner is more reliable when experience is required in complex medical conditions and not just the input fed in. Even with machines the doctor must be present as an active operator rather than just being a passive user [45]. This is implemented in the joint statements on AI ethics in countries like Canada, the whole continent of Europe, and the USA.

5.7.3 SOCIOCULTURAL IMPACTS OF AI

Patients must assent to the use of AI in their routine healthcare in order for it to be effective and successful. As already mentioned AI has the potential to transform the way diagnosis and treatment regimens are presented to patients. There are several questions with regards to the patient's consent for the use of AI driven apps, and many marketing and research companies are also focusing on surveys to reach a conclusion on the overall response of the patient or general user. Perhaps the relevance of the incorporation of AI into healthcare is still unclear to many, and thus can be seen as a challenge to the app developers and software companies to get their proposed emerging technology accepted by the masses [46]. As humans are half-built of emotions, accepting a machine in the form of a doctor is not that easy, for it cannot provide the compassion they often seek.

5.7.4 AI SECURITY

If researchers are thinking of incorporating AI into healthcare and medicine then there will always be a security threat.

Hardware security issues. Currently almost every healthcare application requires hardware for it to function, for example, smart phones or fit bands (used to record daily physical activities of an individual who carries it, in order to motivate him/her to stay fit and active. Utilization of such hardware comes with some security issues. Although these devices have mathematical unclonability they may still be affected by external factors like temperature and cost, thus affecting the overall result they are meant to deliver to users [47]. Also these devices use a mix of multiple technologies and data, both from medical practitioners and AI engineers, so it becomes difficult for stakeholders to have an understanding of each other's fields, causing technological error and workflow disruption.

Software security issues. There is always a possibility of design attack, even with applications with powerful algorithms and functions. The initial inspection of a design may remain excellent, but each and every stage of the design algorithm of AI can be attacked, if we assume that the attacker knows everything from the training data to model weights.

Human factors causing security issues. The emergence of AI is totally dependent on code generated by human engineers alone. And making errors while coding is normal, yet dangerous when output is related to healthcare and patient monitoring. These errors turn out to be inevitable and life threatening [48].

5.8 THE FUTURE OF AI IN PATIENT MONITORING AND HEALTHCARE

AI is having a great impact on the healthcare system, and its thorough study reveals it has the greatest potential to transform this system and medicine. According to many studies, in the current healthcare system professionals are more focused and involved in administrative formalities than performing their fundamental duty which is managing and treating the patient. Through the incorporation of AI

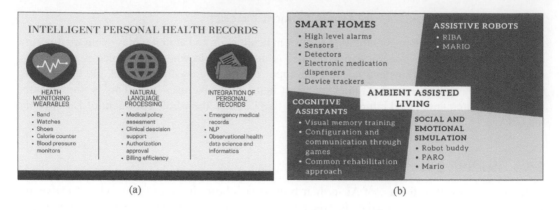

FIGURE 5.3   Intelligent personal health records and ambient assisted living.

in the healthcare system, researchers are looking forward to creating a balance between automation and the capabilities or functionalities of a professional human mind. Scientists aspire to free up the energy and time of healthcare professionals via AI [49,50]. This comprises image-guided surgery and image-based diagnostics. Intelligent personal health records and ambient assisted living are also products of AI which has made life easier as shown in Figure 5.3.

The future of AI in healthcare can be seen as aggregating and resolving abundant data, and detecting complex diseases. In the coming 30 years AI may come to predict and analyze the various factors influencing our day-to-day health. The whole system of diagnosis will be factor driven—factors which are not only related to our medical condition but others too, such as an individual's eating habits, his or her work culture, income, and native place, which are in the dictionary of the World Health Organization (WHO) as "the social determinants of health" (SDOH). This can definitely advance the early detection process [51].

Alongside this, the coming years will be those of "medical selfies," as stated by Eric Topol, who is a noted cardiologist and researcher. There will be a wide variety of new applications to assist patients to monitor their own health conditions through their lives, such as by smart devices and phones that detect skin malignancies, which means that just by taking a picture, you will receive the diagnosis result. Researchers are also looking forward to realizing the idea of chained or network hospitals, where there will be one digitally handled centralized platform which commands various centers. These centers will be designed to monitor different levels of healthcare issues, similar to present day emergency wards, ICUs, and outpatient departments. The AI system will be utilized to monitor the supply and demand, to direct patients to specific centers as per their urgency, and to provide them with the required healthcare services. In this way, AI will remove the bottlenecks and improve workflows.

Back in reality, all these future plans are hypothetical and still under development. A single organization cannot bring the change that the healthcare system demands of the governing bodies; however, private startups and individuals together can open the doors of possibilities for the AI system to reach its presumed heights. However, amongst all the advancements, the objective of AI should remain the same: to ease things for humans, and not to replace them. After all, AI is for the people and by the people only; it is not meant to demean the people [52].

5.9   CONCLUSION

Due to growing data quantities, algorithm advances, and improved computer power and storage, AI has become highly popular today. AI has seen the most progress in technology-driven sectors and, according to many studies, it will be of critical benefit to the fourth industrial and technological revolution. AI is now being used in a variety of fields. In the era of technological advancements there is still more to be learned and much more testing to be done in order to progress AI further. In terms of the healthcare industry, AI appears to have limitless potential. The ultimate goal is to identify AI's greatest potential for improving medical procedures and enhancing the healthcare system through its use.

With its skills and functions, AI can go beyond human intelligence. In general, the idea of AI may be comprehended by categorizing it into two: the first is based on its capability, and the second is based on the role it will have. AI is being used in nearly all types of services and goods, including healthcare, and it is clear that it has the ability to fundamentally transform patient care and even out-perform humans in some areas, such as illness diagnosis. AI is a collection of technologies that may be employed together or separately to automate various aspects of patient monitoring and the entire healthcare system. Machine learning, deep learning, neural networks, expert systems, robotics, and other fundamental technologies are employed in medicine.

Machine learning is a part of AI. It involves a set of algorithms (which encode information), which enables the system to learn from data and previous experience and utilize that learning for prediction. The patterns within the data are identified, or in other words important knowledge and useful information from the data is withdrawn and applied to create intelligent systems. The major areas in medicine that have benefited from ML are diagnosis and outcome prediction (disease identification and relapse). There are various machine learning techniques or algorithms; four main ones are supervised learning, unsupervised learning, semi-supervised learning, and reinforcement learning. Deep learning is another subset of machine learning. DL is a type of machine learning that includes both artificial neural networks and representation learning, and it aids in the handling of enormous amounts of data. Image processing is an example of this type of method, which uses multiple layers of a network to extract the best output or characteristics from a collection of input data. Clinical imaging is one of the many uses of deep learning in the healthcare industry. Other than this, machine vision and natural language processing are also technological aspects of AI.

The need for healthcare services is always increasing and these services with the assistance of health tracking software and search platforms have advanced thanks to developments in wireless technology and smartphones. Furthermore, technology advancements have enabled remote healthcare delivery. Precision medicine is an AI-based tool that allows healthcare actions to be customized to particular patients or groups of patients based on their illness profile, diagnostic and prognostic data, and therapeutic response. Machine vision diagnosis is another AI technique. It is a surgical tool and assists machines in interpreting images and videos beyond the capabilities of a person. AI is a boon in the field of oncology too. Anticancer drug activity is predicted using AI, and AI is used to help in the development of anticancer medicines. Various cancers and medications may react differently, and recent screening tools have repeatedly revealed a connection between cancer cell genetic variety and therapeutic efficacy. Its main features are lesion recognition, target area delineation, 3D tumor localization, clinical and pathological analysis, quantitative tumor analysis, and tumor picture segmentation.

AI has had a significant influence on the healthcare system, with a thorough investigation revealing the greatest potential for it to alter the system and medication in the future. The future of AI in healthcare may be seen in the aggregation and resolution of massive amounts of data, as well as the detection of complicated illnesses.

As people and technology advance hand in hand, the future will prove the success of mankind in collaboration with technology.

ACKNOWLEDGMENT

I would like to thank my Co-Authors for contributing their knowledge and time and giving their support in compiling the work.

REFERENCES

1. Mahajan, A., Vaidya, T., Gupta, A., Rane, S., & Gupta, S. Artificial intelligence in healthcare in developing nations: The beginning of a transformative journey. *Cancer Research, Statistics, and Treatment, 2*(2), 182, 2019.

2. Reddy, S., Fox, J., & Purohit, M. P. Artificial intelligence-enabled healthcare delivery. *Journal of the Royal Society of Medicine, 112*(1), 22–28, 2019.

3. Panigrahi, C. M. A. Use of artificial intelligence in education. *Management Accountant, SSRN, 55,* 64–67, 2020.

4. Bohr, A., & Memarzadeh, K. The rise of artificial intelligence in healthcare applications in: *Artificial Intelligence in healthcare*, pp. 25–60, Denmark, 2020.

5. Transforming healthcare with AI: The impact on the workforce and organizations, https://www.mckinsey.com/industries/healthcare-systems-and-services/our-insights/transforming-healthcare-with-ai, McKinsey & Company, 2020

6. Brady, M. Artificial intelligence and robotics in: *Robotics and Artificial Intelligence*, pp. 47–63. Springer, Berlin, Heidelberg, 1984.

7. Wang, Z., Srinivasan R. S. A review of artificial intelligence based building energy use prediction: Contrasting the capabilities of single and ensemble prediction models. *Renewable and Sustainable Energy Reviews, 75,* 796–808, 2017.

8. Kibria, M. G., Nguyen, K., Villardi, G. P., Zhao, O., Ishizu, K., & Kojima, F. Big data analytics, machine learning, and artificial intelligence in next-generation wireless networks. *IEEE Access, 6,* 32328–32338, 2018.

9. Baum, S., Barrett, A., & Yampolskiy, R. V. Modeling and interpreting expert disagreement about artificial superintelligence. *Informatica, 41*(7), 419–428, 2017.

10. Topol, E. *Deep medicine: how artificial intelligence can make healthcare human again*. Hachette UK, 2019.

11. Randhawa, G. K., & Jackson, M. The role of artificial intelligence in learning and professional development for healthcare professionals. In *Healthcare Management Forum* (Vol. 33, No. 1). Sage CA: Los Angeles, CA: SAGE Publications, 2020.

12. Deng, Z., Chen, Y., Liu, Y., & Kim, K. C. Time-resolved turbulent velocity field reconstruction using a long short-term memory (LSTM)-based artificial intelligence framework. *Physics of Fluids, 31*(7), 075108, 2019.

13. Roziere, B., Teytaud, F., Hosu, V., Lin, H., Rapin, J., Zameshina, M., & Teytaud, O. Evolgan: Evolutionary generative adversarial networks. *Proceedings of the Asian Conference on Computer Vision*, 2020.

14. Important types of AI to watch out for in 2021 https://www.jigsawacademy.com/what-are-the-different-types-of-ai/, Jigsaw Academy, 2021

15. Stanfill, M. H., & Marc, D. T. Health information management: Implications of artificial intelligence on healthcare data and information management in: *Yearbook of Medical Informatics, 28*(1), pp. 056–064, 2019.

16. Davenport, T., & Kalakota, R. The potential for artificial intelligence in healthcare. *Future Healthcare Journal, 6*(2), 94, 2019.

17. Chen, M., & Decary, M. Artificial intelligence in healthcare: An essential guide for health leaders. In *Healthcare Management Forum* (Vol. 33, No. 1). Sage CA: Los Angeles, CA: SAGE Publications, 2020.

18. Esmaeilzadeh, P. Use of AI-based tools for healthcare purposes: A survey study from consumers' perspectives. *BMC Medical Informatics and Decision Making, 20*(1), 1–19, 2020.

19. Blasch, E., Kadar, I., Grewe, L. L., Stevenson, G., Majumder, U. K., & Chong, C. Y. Deep learning in AI and information fusion panel discussion. In *Signal Processing, Sensor/Information Fusion, and Target Recognition XXVIII* (Vol. 11018, p. 110180Q). International Society for Optics and Photonics, 2019.

20. Al-Ghadhban, D., & Al-Twairesh, N. Nabiha: An Arabic dialect chatbot. *International Journal of Advanced Computer Science and Applications, 11*(3), 1–8, 2020.

21. Park, C., Took, C. C., & Seong, J. K. *Machine Learning in Biomedical Engineering*. Springer, 2018.

22. Luger, G. F. Modern AI and how we got here. In *Knowing Our World: An Artificial Intelligence Perspective*, pp. 49–74. Springer, Cham, 2021.

23. Shorten, C., Khoshgoftaar, T. M., & Furht, B. Deep Learning applications for COVID-19. *Journal of Big Data*, *8*(1), 1–54, 2021.

24. Zhang, C., Bengio, S., Hardt, M., Recht, B., & Vinyals, O. Understanding deep learning (still) requires rethinking generalization. *Communications of the ACM*, *64*(3), 107–115, 2021.

25. Hyatt, Y. The role of adaptive vision AI in autonomous machine vision: Leveraging sophisticated AI to create the ultimate user friendly technology. *PhotonicsViews*, *18*(2), 45–47, 2021.

26. Juhn, Y., & Liu, H. Artificial intelligence approaches using natural language processing to advance EHR-based clinical research. *Journal of Allergy and Clinical Immunology*, *145*(2), 463–469, 2020.

27. Danilevsky, M., Qian, K., Aharonov, R., Katsis, Y., Kawas, B., & Sen, P. A survey of the state of explainable AI for natural language processing. *arXiv preprint arXiv:2010.00711*, 2020.

28. Pradhan, B., Bharti, D., Chakravarty, S., Ray, S. S., Voinova, V. V., Bonartsev, A. P., & Pal, K. Internet of things and robotics in transforming current-day healthcare services. *Journal of Healthcare Engineering*, 2021.

29. Kyrarini, M., Lygerakis, F., Rajavenkatanarayanan, A., Sevastopoulos, C., Nambiappan, H. R., Chaitanya, K. K., & Makedon, F. A survey of robots in healthcare. *Technologies*, *9*(1), 8, 2021.

30. Dixit, P., Payal, M., Goyal, N., & Dutt, V. Robotics, AI and IoT in Medical and Healthcare Applications, in: *AI and IoT Based Intelligent Automation in Robotics*, pp. 53–73, 2021.

31. Rajendran, S., Vakil, M., Kallur, R., Shree, V., Gupta, P. K., & Hiremat, L. A review on patient monitoring and diagnosis assistance by artificial intelligence tools, in: *Handbook of Artificial Intelligence in Biomedical Engineering*, pp. 195–216. Apple Academic Press, 2021.

32. Spiga, O., Cicaloni, V., Visibelli, A., Davoli, A., Paparo, M. A., Orlandini, M., … Santucci, A. Towards a precision medicine approach based on machine learning for tailoring medical treatment in alkaptonuria. *International Journal of Molecular Sciences*, *22*(3), 1187, 2021.

33. Mathur, S., & Sutton, J. Personalized medicine could transform healthcare. *Biomedical Reports*, *7*(1), 3–5, 2017.

34. Samek, W., Wiegand, T., & Müller, K. R. Explainable artificial intelligence: Understanding, visualizing and interpreting deep learning models. *arXiv preprint arXiv:1708.08296*, 2017.

35. Chittaro, L. Information visualization and its application to medicine. *Artificial Intelligence in Medicine*, *22*(2), 81–88, 2001.

36. Roehrs, A., Da Costa, C. A., da Rosa Righi, R., & De Oliveira, K. S. F. Personal health records: A systematic literature review. *Journal of Medical Internet Research*, *19*(1), e13, 2017.

37. Gams, M., Gu, I. Y. H., Härmä, A., Muñoz, A., & Tam, V. Artificial intelligence and ambient intelligence. *Journal of Ambient Intelligence and Smart Environments*, *11*(1), 71–86, 2019.

38. Andreu-Perez, J., Deligianni, F., Ravi, D., & Yang, G. Z. Artificial intelligence and robotics. *arXiv preprint arXiv:1803.10813*, 2018.

39. Leatherdale, S. T., & Lee, J. Artificial intelligence (AI) and cancer prevention: the potential application of AI in cancer control programming needs to be explored in population laboratories such as COMPASS. *Cancer Causes & Control*, *30*(7), 671–675, 2019.

40. Yu, C., & Helwig, E. J. The role of AI technology in prediction, diagnosis and treatment of colorectal cancer. *Artificial Intelligence Review*, *1–21*, 2021.

41. Shimizu, H., & Nakayama, K. I. Artificial intelligence in oncology. *Cancer Science*, *111*(5), 1452, 2020.

42. Bartoletti, I. AI in healthcare: Ethical and privacy challenges, in: *Conference on Artificial Intelligence in Medicine in Europe*, pp. 7–10. Springer, Cham, 2019.

43. Kelly, C. J., Karthikesalingam, A., Suleyman, M., Corrado, G., & King, D. Key challenges for delivering clinical impact with artificial intelligence. *BMC Medicine*, *17*(1), 1–9, 2019.

44. Singh, R. P., Hom, G. L., Abramoff, M. D., Campbell, J. P., & Chiang, M. F. Current challenges and barriers to real-world artificial intelligence adoption for the healthcare system, provider, and the patient. *Translational Vision Science & Technology*, *9*(2), 45–45, 2020.

45. Gerke, S., Minssen, T., & Cohen, G. Ethical and legal challenges of artificial intelligence- driven healthcare, in: *Artificial Intelligence in Healthcare*, pp. 295–336. Academic Press, 2020.

46. Racine, E., Boehlen, W., & Sample, M. Healthcare uses of artificial intelligence: Challenges and opportunities for growth, in: *Healthcare Management Forum* (Vol. 32, No. 5). Sage CA: Los Angeles, CA: SAGE Publications, 2019.

47. Chen, T., Liu, J., Xiang, Y., Niu, W., Tong, E., & Han, Z. Adversarial attack and defense in reinforcement learning-from AI security view. *Cybersecurity*, *2*(1), 1–22, 2019.

48. Bertino, E., Kantarcioglu, M., Akcora, C. G., Samtani, S., Mittal, S., & Gupta, M. AI for Security and Security for AI, in: *Proceedings of the Eleventh ACM Conference on Data and Application Security and Privacy*, 2021.

49. Fouad, H., Hassanein, A. S., Soliman, A. M., & Al-Feel, H. Analyzing patient health information based on IoT sensor with AI for improving patient assistance in the future direction. *Measurement*, *159*, 107757, 2020.

50. Panesar, A. Future of Healthcare. In *Machine Learning and AI for Healthcare*, pp. 255–304. Apress, Berkeley, CA, 2019.

51. Fadhil, A. Beyond patient monitoring: Conversational agents role in telemedicine & healthcare support for home-living elderly individuals. *arXiv preprint arXiv:1803.06000*, 2018.

52. Siyal, A. A., Junejo, A. Z., Zawish, M., Ahmed, K., Khalil, A., & Soursou, G. Applications of blockchain technology in medicine and healthcare: Challenges and future perspectives. *Cryptography*, *3*(1), 3, 2019.

6 Artificial Intelligence in Healthcare and Its Application in Brain Stroke Diagnosis

Ambarish Kumar Sinha and Gaurav Kumar
Galgotias University, Greater Noida, India

CONTENTS

6.1 INTRODUCTION

Artificial intelligence (AI) is the use of data-driven algorithms in machines to mimic human cognitive processes such as learning and reasoning. The algorithms depend on the number of inputs provided to the machine, the type of analysis performed on the inputs, and the complexity of the outcome required [1]. Currently, the most popular algorithmic method is machine learning (ML) whereby a model is trained on a dataset to independently analyze and categorize new datasets. The cognitive reasoning ability of the ML-based models depends on the complexity and the volume of data [2]. The most established method of ML is supervised ML which trains the model based on known categories in the data to predict those categories on novel datasets. Supervised ML has been successfully used for risk prediction and disease classification in cancer. Unsupervised ML assumes no prior categorization of data and trains the model based only on input data [3]. The model uses clustering methods to find inherent groups or patterns within the dataset, thus enabling the discovery of novel or previously unknown groups within a dataset [4]. As a result, the larger the volume of data and the more complex the data used, the more enhanced the cognitive reasoning ability of the model. in the prediction of cardiovascular disease using electronic health records. Deep learning is a branch of unsupervised ML and uses neural networks to account for associations between data points leading to more sophisticated detection and categorization. The growth of big data and computational processing power has rapidly expanded the development of deep learning algorithms enabling the detection of complex patterns in large datasets [5]. This method is commonly used in image and speech recognition and has been successfully used in the detection of disease.

AI is defined as an emulation of human intelligence by machines. Computers, for example, can simulate the functions of human intelligence using AI.

These processes consist of learning by collecting information, comprehending the rules for utilizing that information, applying arguments to generate insights, and self-rectification.

Another definition sees AI as "the ability of a machine to understand a problem and act like a human being in the same situation" [6]. However, there is no limit to the shape that AI can take. AI may appear invisible when solving advanced problems: it could be present in self-driving cars, parts of factories, or even in some advanced robotics in the future. The important thing is that there are no restrictions on the formats that AI can or may use to interact with us, now or in the near future. Optimistically, AI is being looked at as the next industrial revolution, with disruptive potential for healthcare solutions. It is considered as one of the most powerful and fascinating innovations that is likely to influence us in the near future. Its potential to offer breakthrough social and industrial transformation is comparable with the invention of the steam engine, electricity, and the personal computer [7].

In 2018, the global AI market was worth approximately $20.7 billion; however, it is expected to reach over $200 billion by 2026 [8]. As PricewaterhouseCoopers (PwC) estimates, by 2030, AI is going to add more than $15.7 trillion to the global economy [9]. As per a Fortune Insights forecast, the North American AI market is set to grow at 33.1 percent compound annual growth rate (CAGR) to 2026 with global AI revenues set to increase 12-fold to $118 billion [10] in the North American market. Growth will be driven by: increased prevalence of vascular diseases, rising diagnoses, and treatment rates with the wider use of imaging technologies; increased patient affordability; better access to vascular therapies; and continued innovation leading to new product launches [11]. Business process automation such as robotic process automation, natural language processing, and ML are going to be the major areas that will witness major investment and growth. Other growth drivers will be the utilization of big data and the use of robotics in manufacturing processes, the Internet of Things (IoT), inter-industry collaboration, and increased capital investment. According to another report, AI's growth in the manufacturing sector will be driven by bigger players on the market such as IBM, Oracle, Microsoft, NVIDIA, and Intel. The report also states that the AI manufacturing sector will be dominated by North America until 2024; however, the Asia Pacific region will be the fastest-growing due to continued investment in AI-enabled solutions [12] (Figure 6.1).

In the last 20 years since the inception of the Human Genome Project, a lot of progress has been made in electronic medical records, clinical trials, biomarkers, and CRISPR gene editing. However, progress in systems biology is much lower, that is, the understanding of the interactions of pathways in response to pathogens or drugs has been slow, which has retarded research in personalized medicine. To put it simply, while the understanding of genome tools has progressed, disease mechanism prediction has made limited progress, due to which therapeutic development hasn't been sufficient [13].

Currently, doctors spend a disproportionate amount of time on diagnostics, prescriptions, and monitoring. AI aims to reverse this so that doctors can focus on higher-order issues. In this scenario, complex diagnoses, treatment, and monitoring will be assisted by machines to complement (and not replace) human judgment. This will allow even an average physician or nurse to perform better across multiple domains. AI can significantly reduce administrative tasks. It can be applied in these contexts to capture paper documents and automate paperwork processing like data entry, filling in forms, invoicing, and automated reports. Paper-based medical charts and clinical notes can be captured and classified, providing further information and insight. It is forecast that the annual revenue for converting paperwork into digital assets in healthcare was worth $138 million worldwide in 2015 and is projected to expand at a CAGR of 10.2 percent through 2025 [10]. An AI system can trawl through thousands of databases and clinical trials of existing molecules and thus predict how these molecules will behave and how likely they are to make a useful drug. This can save time and money on unnecessary tests [14].

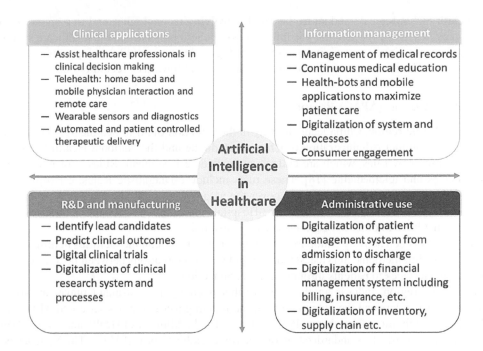

FIGURE 6.1 AI in healthcare: AI/ML plays a pivotal role in digital health space. It helps healthcare professionals in making clinical decisions. It is exclusively used in hospital settings for information management and administrative purposes such as the digitalization of finance, inventories, and supply chains. In R&D, AI helps in identifying lead candidates, designing clinical trials, and predicting clinical outcomes.

6.2 REGULATORY FRAMEWORK FOR AI IN HEALTHCARE

The regulatory framework provides guidelines, a code of practice, and requirements for the adoption and use of AI in the healthcare space. Concerns for sustainable development have considerably grown over the past few years. On account of this, several companies are investing in AI technology to cater to the associated benefits in healthcare. In the next sections, we discuss government regulations around AI in the healthcare space at the regional level [15].

6.2.1 NORTH AMERICA

North America is one of the fastest-growing regions in terms of integration of AI in healthcare. Because of this, the region has developed one of the best regulatory frameworks for AI in the healthcare space. The new and emerging medical technologies and devices are generally evaluated for safety and efficacy by the Food and Drug Administration (FDA). The FDA has set forward and has issued new guidance implementing legislation called the 21st Century Cures Act which was enacted in December 2016 [16]. Under the Act, software or tools that support administrative functions, serve as electronic patient records, provide clinical decision support (CDS), assist in displaying or storing data, or promote a healthy lifestyle are no longer considered to be, and regulated as, medical devices. AI and ML-based products will come in this category when they are used for clinical benefit. Recent FDA actions indicate that the regulatory framework for AI-based products is evolving and it seems open to input on software regulation. Similar to the USA, Canada is also putting in efforts and resources for the development of regulation for the use of AI in the healthcare space. Under the Regulatory Review of Drugs and Devices initiative, Health Canada has established a new division within the Therapeutic Products Directorate's Medical Devices Bureau for a thorough evaluation of digital health technologies, to adapt to the rapidly evolving technologies, and to respond to faster innovation cycles. It is expected that this initiative will benefit patients and the healthcare system by improving access to innovative digital health technologies that have rapid development cycles while reducing costs. The formation of this division is the first step towards a regulatory approach [17].

6.2.2   Asia–Pacific (APAC) Region

In the Asia–Pacific region, China leads the way in the direction of AI in healthcare. On September 14, 2018, the National Administration of Chinese Medicine and the National Health Commission announced three new rules, which are collectively called "e-Healthcare Rules," for internet-based health services and telemedicine [18]. These rules include e-Diagnostic Rules, e-Hospital Rules, and a Telemedicine Service Standard and cover the areas of internet-based hospitals, e-diagnosis, and telemedicine services respectively. The e-Hospital rules stipulate the qualifications a medical institution must have in order to become a certified hospital.

China has also been actively endorsing the integration of telemedicine facilities in hospitals since 2014 [18]. The Telemedicine Service Standard regulates collaborations between hospitals by offering healthcare services to patients through remote connection.

In the APAC region, India is another country that is emerging as a major player in AI-related development. To understand the potential of AI, the Indian government has set up an AI task force, which includes individuals from the medical field as well. The Ministry of Health and Family Welfare is also working towards the standardization of electronic health records (EHRs). The Ministry is also working on the establishment of a National eHealth Authority (NeHA) to promote, regulate, and standardize the medical field [19]. The Department of Science & Technology and the Department of Biotechnology have been instrumental in funding AI and health startups. India has come up with a number of policies that regulate different aspects of the development and use of AI in healthcare. These include regulations on the use of health data, digital medical device certification, digital medical device standards, and patient/relationship framework conditions. To incentivize the development of AI-enabled health solutions, the Indian government has also put forward a number of policy initiatives. Some of the existing rules and policies are the Open Data Policy and Medical Devices Rules, 2017, the Electronic Health Records Standards, 2016, the Information Technology (Reasonable Security Practices & Procedures and Sensitive Personal Data or Information) Rules, 2011, and The Indian Medical Council (Professional Conduct, Etiquette and Ethics) Regulations, 2002 [20].

6.3   APPLICATIONS OF AI IN THE HEALTHCARE SPACE

After continued efforts at digitization, the transformation of the MedTech industry is meaningfully underway. AI, ML, remote patient monitoring, and cloud-based and other disruptive technologies provide the opportunity to enhance healthcare by driving new insights from the vast amount of data generated. Medical device companies are investing heavily in these technologies to create new products in order to assist healthcare professionals and improve diagnosis and care. While these technologies are not new, they appear powerful and potentially disruptive to the traditional healthcare space. It seems that such technologies are going to be key drivers since a number of companies are investing in these programs and providing added clinical evidence to support the adoption of these technologies [21].

AI and ML are among the most discussed topics in MedTech because of their potential to create the most differentiated solutions. The ability of AI/ML to absorb real-world data and translate these into meaningful insights is unparalleled. With constant healthcare shortages and an aging population, healthcare companies are gradually looking at AI/ML-enabled technologies as a solution to a number of problems. It seems that MedTech markets are going to be driven by AI and ML. AI-enabled robots can be used to analyze the data from pre-op medical documents to generate meaningful insights as well as in assisting the surgeon during surgery, which will ultimately lead to a shorter hospital stay and improved patient care. Medical imaging companies are also integrating AI-enabled tools in order to improve image clarity and assist the technicians in reporting the results [22]. AI-enabled imaging tools can also be used to support rural areas with limited access to healthcare services. Companies are also using AI/ML to monitor patients remotely through wearables and are automating the treatment via mobile applications. These remote patient monitoring (RPM) tools use AI/ML to collect the data of patients even when they are out of the healthcare facility and then utilize the data to fill the gap in inpatient care. The utility of RPM was evident during COVID-19 when most patients' deferred hospital visits were due to lockdowns and stay-home restrictions [23].

In primary care, some progress has been made with AI. The UK firm Babylon Health's intelligent health companion assesses symptoms reported by users to offer a diagnosis that is based on an account of the patient's history, monitors health, follows up on past symptoms, gives medication reminders, and can set up a live video GP consultation if necessary [24]. While blood pressure and sugar monitoring have been around for several years, AI has steadily advanced to allow remote monitoring by physicians. AliveCor has developed an AI-based platform for patients and clinicians to detect early atrial fibrillation and reduce the risk of stroke [25]. The aim is to work on a platform that can predict disease outbreaks in advance of their occurrence. The Dengue Outbreak Prediction platform uses ML to provide users with the exact geolocation and date of a potential dengue outbreak up to three months in advance [26] (Figure 6.2).

6.3.1 MEDICAL IMAGING

Research suggests that medical image analysis and virtual assistants for patients are likely to be the biggest users of AI. Medical images like MRIs, X-rays, CT scans, and other diagnostic images are likely to see advancement. Enlitic uses deep learning enabled technology for analysis of imaging reports, such as MRI/CT scans and X-rays to identify even the smallest suspicious sightings like tumors and hairline fractures [27]. It now focuses on chest scans and has exhibited 50 percent greater accuracy than a panel of four radiologists in determining the nature of a disease in the lung. It works to expand functionality to include a focus on breast, thyroid, prostate, and liver cancer [27].

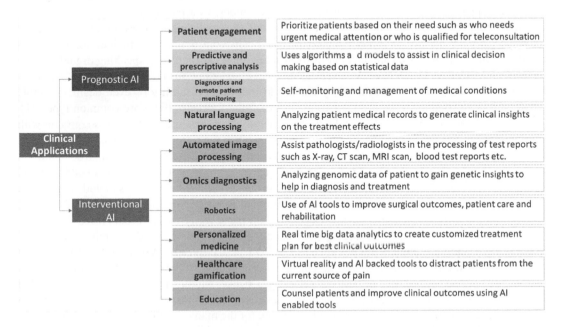

FIGURE 6.2 Clinical applications of AI: Prognostic AI is used to improve patient engagement, clinical decision making, self-monitoring at the patient level, and analyzing treatment effectiveness. Interventional AI finds its uses in medical image processing, omics, robotics, creating personalized medicines, and so on.

6.3.2 Virtual Patient Assistants

Distance to the clinic, costs, time constraints, and difficulty in getting an appointment in some cases are a few of the impediments in a doctor–patient relationship. AI, while not replacing doctors, can scale up their ability to provide guidance. Virtual assistants can be used to address multiple conditions and can be tied into a smartphone, tablet, or existing virtual assistant device. Ada offers a mobile app-based virtual assistant to support patients' understanding of symptoms. Here patients interact with it like a nurse answering questions in conversational language. It is also integrated with Amazon Alexa and can capture details doctors don't ask or patients forget to mention in person. The app has diagnosed both common and rare conditions, and since its continuous training includes real doctors, it pools shared expertise [28].

6.3.3 Other Real-world Applications

Besides the applications mentioned above, we may note that AI has gained acceptance among regulatory authorities too. For e.g., Arterys's Deep Learning Image Recognition for the Heart (lung and liver are in process). On average it takes only 15 seconds for Arterys to generate results for a case, whereas a professional will take around 30 minutes to an hour [29].

6.3.4 Google's Deep Mind Instant Alerting Tool for Acute Kidney Injury

The Streams app monitors patients' blood test results, which is combined with Electric Health. The record sends an instant alert to the relevant doctor when it identifies deterioration in the body. Thus, detection happens at a fairly early stage [30] (Table 6.1).

6.4 WHAT AI CAN DO FOR STROKE PATIENTS

A stroke happens when the movement of oxygenated blood to a part of the brain is obstructed. Consequently, brain cells become deprived of oxygen and start to die within a few minutes. Symptoms may appear in any part of the body which these brain cells control and may include weakness and numbness in the arms, legs, face, and paralysis in severe cases, difficulty in speaking or understanding speech as well as vision loss. As a serious medical emergency, stroke warrants urgent attention because it causes permanent brain injury leading to long-term disability or even death. Ischemic stroke and hemorrhagic stroke are the two main forms; the former is the more common type [31]. Eighty-seven percent of all stroke incidents are ischemic. Hemorrhagic stroke is less common with an incidence of only 13 percent. Ischemic stroke occurs when the artery supplying oxygenated blood is blocked by a clot that leads to ischemia [32]. On the other hand, a hemorrhagic stroke occurs when the artery breaks open or ruptures due to external factors, and the pressure from the leaking blood damages brain cells. The common conditions that can cause hemorrhagic strokes include high blood pressure and aneurysms. An IV injection of recombinant tissue plasminogen activator (IPA) is the typical treatment for an ischemic stroke. Depending on the severity of the stroke, it requires either clot-dissolving medicine (tPA) or surgery (mechanical thrombectomy) in order to return blood flow to the brain. Landmark clinical studies such as ESCAPE, EXTEND-IA, MR CLEAN, SWIFT, and PRIME have demonstrated that the addition of stent thrombectomy to restore blood flow to the brain significantly reduces disability in patients suffering a stroke. Studies have also demonstrated that patients treated with mechanical thrombectomy have improved functional outcomes compared to pharmaceutical treatment. The current standard of care for the management of stroke has been modified to include stent thrombectomy as a first-line treatment in addition to tPA. As per the Centers for Disease Control and Prevention (CDC), stroke is the leading cause of long-term disability and lays a substantial load on the healthcare system, and accounts for $34 billion per year for care, delivery

TABLE 6.1
US FDA-Approved AI-Based Devices/Algorithms

Device/Algorithm	Company	AI Platform	Description	Approval Pathway	Approval Date	Application	510(k) Pre-market Notification number
Genius AI Detection	Hologic	Machine Learning	Software that identifies abnormalities in breast tomosynthesis images	510(k) premarket notification	Nov-20	Radiology	K201019
AVA (Augmented Vascular Analysis)	See-Mode Technologies	Artificial Intelligence	Vascular ultrasound: analysis and reporting	510(k) premarket notification	Aug-20	Radiology	K201369
EyeArt	Eyenuk, Inc.	Artificial Intelligence	Automatically detects diabetic retinopathy	510(k) premarket notification	Jun-20	Ophthalmology	K200667
qER	Qure.ai Technologies	Artificial Intelligence	Computer assisted triaging and notification software for CT scans	510(k) premarket notification	Jun-20	Radiology	K200921
AIMI-Triage CXR PTX	RADLogics Inc.	Artificial Intelligence	Chest X-ray prioritization service	510(k) premarket notification	Mar-20	Radiology	K193300
QuantX	Quantitative Insights Inc.	Artificial Intelligence	Radiological software for cancer detection	denovo pathway	Jan-20	Oncology	DEN170022
Eko Analysis Software	Eko Devices Inc.	Artificial Neural Network	Cardiac monitoring	510(k) premarket notification	Jan-20	Cardiology	K192004
TransparaTM	Screenpoint Medical B.V.	Machine Learning	Mammogram	510(k) premarket notification	Dec-19	Oncology	K192287
EchoGo Core	Ultromics Ltd	Machine Learning	Quantification/reporting of cardiovascular function	510(k) premarket notification	Nov-19	Cardiology	K191171
AI-Rad Companion (Cardiovascular)	Siemens Medical Solutions USA, Inc.	Deep Learning	Cardiovascular-CTscan analysis	510(k) premarket notification	Sep-19	Radiology	K183268
BrainScope TBI	BrainScope Company, Inc.	Not Available	EEG scan analysis	510(k) premarket notification	Sep-19	Neurology	K190815
Critical Care Suite	GE Medical Systems, LLC	Artificial Intelligence	Assessment of chest X-rays	510(k) premarket notification	Aug-19	Radiology	K183182
Biovitals Analytics Engine	Biofourmis Singapore Pte. Ltd	Not Available	Cardiac monitor	510(k) premarket notification	Aug-19	Cardiology	K183282

(Continued)

TABLE 6.1 (Continued)
US FDA-Approved AI-Based Devices/Algorithms

Device/Algorithm	Company	AI Platform	Description	Approval Pathway	Approval Date	Application	510(k) Pre-market Notification number
Caption Guidance	Caption Health, Inc.	Artificial Intelligence	Software to assist medical professionals in the acquisition of cardiac ultrasound images	de novo pathway	Aug-19	Radiology	DEN190040
SubtleMR	Subtle Medical, Inc.	Convolutional Neural Network	Radiology image processing software	510(k) premarket notification	Jul-19	Radiology	K191688
AI-Rad Companion (Pulmonary)	Siemens Medical Solutions USA, Inc.	Deep Learning	CT image reconstruction: pulmonary	510(k) premarket notification	Jul-19	Radiology	K183271
ACR I LAB Urine Analysis Test System	Healthy.io Ltd	Not Available	Urinary tract infection diagnosis	510(k) premarket notification	Jul-19	Urology / General practice	K18238
Current Wearable Health Monitoring System	Current Health Ltd	Not Available	Monitoring vital signs	510(k) premarket notification	Jul-19	Hospital monitoring	K191272
physIQ Heart Rhythm and Respiratory Module	physIQ, Inc.	Not Available	Detection of atrial fibrillation	510(k) premarket notification	Jul-19	Cardiology	K183322
RayCare 2.3	RaySearch Laboratories AB	Not Available	Medical charged-particle radiation therapy system	510(k) premarket notification	Jul-19	Radiology	K191384
Advanced Intelligent Clear-IQ Engine (AiCE)	Canon Medical Systems Corporation	Deep Convolutional Neural Network	Noise reduction algorithm	510(k) premarket notification	Jun-19	Radiology	K183046
Koios DS for Breast	Koios Medical, Inc.	Machine Learning	Diagnostic software for lesions suspicious of cancer	510(k) premarket notification	Jun-19		K190442
HealthPNX	Zebra Medical Vision	Artificial Intelligence	Assessment of chest X-rays	510(k) premarket notification	May-19	Radiology	K190362
ReSET-O	Pear Therapeutics, Inc.	Not Available	Adjuvant treatment of substance abuse disorder	510(k) premarket notification	May-19	Psychiatry	K173681
Deep Learning Image Reconstruction	GE Medical Systems, LLC	Deep Learning	CT image restoration	510(k) premarket notification	Apr-19	Radiology	K183202
eMurmur ID	CSD Labs GmbH	Not Available	Heart murmur detection	510(k) premarket notification	Apr-19	Cardiology	K181988

Product	Company	Technology	Description	Regulatory Pathway	Date	Specialty	Number
cmTriage	CureMetrix, Inc.	Artificial Intelligence	Mammogram workflow	510(k) premarket notification	Mar-19	Oncology	K183285
KardiaAI	AliveCor, Inc.	Not Available	Six-lead smartphone ECG	510(k) premarket notification	Mar-19	Cardiology	K181823
Loop System	Spry Health, Inc.	Not Available	Monitoring vital signs	510(k) premarket notification	Mar-19	Hospital monitoring	K181352
RhythmAnalytics	Biofourmis Singapore Pte. Ltd	Not Available	Monitoring cardiac arrhythmias	510(k) premarket notification	Mar-19	Cardiology	K182344
Study Watch	Verily Life Sciences LLC	Not Available	ECG feature of the study watch	510(k) premarket notification	Jan-19	Cardiology	K182456
iSchemaView RAPID	iSchemaView, Inc.	Not Available	Stroke detection on CT and MRI	510(k) premarket notification	Dec-18	Radiology	K182130
Quantib ND	Quantib BV	Not Available	Neurodegenerative disease MRI brain reading	510(k) premarket notification	Dec-18	Radiology	K182564
FerriSmart Analysis System	Resonance Health Analysis Service Pty Ltd	Artificial Intelligence	Measure liver iron concentration	510(k) premarket notification	Nov-18	Internal Medicine	K182218
Embrace	EmpaticaSrl	Not Available	Wearable for seizure monitoring	510(k) premarket notification	Nov-18	Neurology	K181861
Accipiolx	MaxQ-AI Ltd	Artificial Intelligence	Acute intracranial hemorrhage triage algorithm	510(k) premarket notification	Oct-18	Neurology	K182177
icobrain	icometrix NV	Machine Learning and Deep Learning	MRI brain interpretation	510(k) premarket notification	Oct-18	Neurology	K181939
FluoroShield™	Omega Medical Imaging, LLC	Not Available	Radiation dosage reduction	510(k) premarket notification	Oct-18	Radiology	K191713
SubtlePET	Subtle Medical, Inc.	Deep Neural Network-Based Algorithm	Radiology image processing software	510(k) premarket notification	Sep-18	Radiology	K182336
AI-ECG Platform	Shenzhen Carewell Electronics, Ltd	Artificial Intelligence	Analysis of ECG reports	510(k) premarket notification	Sep-18	Cardiology	K180432
FibriCheck	Qompium NV	Not Available	Cardiac monitor	510(k) premarket notification	Sep-18	Cardiology	K173872
Irregular Rhythm Notification Feature	Apple Inc.	Not Available	Detection of atrial fibrillation	de novo pathway	Sep-18	Cardiology	DEN180042
RightEye Vision System	RightEye, LLC	Not Available	Identifying visual tracking impairment	510(k) premarket notification	Sep-18	Ophthalmology	K181771

(Continued)

TABLE 6.1 (Continued)
US FDA-Approved AI-Based Devices/Algorithms

Device/Algorithm	Company	AI Platform	Description	Approval Pathway	Approval Date	Application	510(k) Pre-market Notification number
Arterys MICA	Arterys Inc.	Artificial Intelligence	Diagnosis of liver and lung cancer	510(k) premarket notification	Aug-18	Oncology	K182034
ECG App	Apple, Inc.	Not Available	Detection of atrial fibrillation	de novo pathway	Aug-18	Cardiology	DEN180044
BriefCase	Aidoc Medical, Ltd	Deep Learning	Triage and diagnosis of time sensitive patients	510(k) premarket notification	Jul-18	Radiology	K180647
ProFound™ AI Software V2.1	iCAD, Inc.	Deep Learning	Mammography (breast density)	510(k) premarket notification	Jul-18	Oncology	K191994
DreaMed	DreaMed Diabetes, Ltd	Artificial Intelligence	Managing type 1 diabetes	de novo pathway	Jun-18	Endocrinology	DEN170043
LungQ	Thirona Corporation	Not Available	Quantitative analysis of chest CT scans	510(k) premarket notification	Jun-18	Pulmonology	chestct
HealthCCS	Zebra Medical Vision Ltd	Not Available	Coronary artery calcification algorithm	510(k) premarket notification	May-18	Cardiology	K172983
MindMotion GO	MindMaze SA	Not Available	Software with rehabilitation exercises for the elderly	510(k) premarket notification	May-18	Orthopedics	K173931
EchoMD Automated Ejection Fraction Software	Bay Labs, Inc.	Machine Learning	ECG analysis	510(k) premarket notification	May-18	Cardiology	K173780
NeuralBot	Neural Analytics, Inc.	Not Available	Transcranial doppler probe positioning	510(k) premarket notification	Apr-18	Radiology	K180455
Guardian Connect System	Medtronic	Artificial Intelligence	Blood glucose monitoring	PMA	Mar-18	Endocrinology	P160007
DM-Density	Densitas, Inc.	Not Available	Breast density via mammography	510(k) premarket notification	Feb-18	Radiology	K170540
ContaCT	Viz.AI	Artificial Intelligence	Stroke detection through CT scans	de novo pathway	Feb-18	Neurology	DEN170073
OsteoDetect	Imagen Technologies, Inc.	Deep Learning	Diagnosis of wrist fracture by X-ray	de novo pathway	Feb-18	Emergency medicine	DEN180005
WAVE Clinical Platform	Excel Medical Electronics, LLC	Not Available	Vital sign monitoring	510(k) premarket notification	Jan-18	Hospital monitoring	K171056
Idx	IDx LLC	Artificial Intelligence	Detection of diabetic retinopathy	De novo pathway	Jan-18	Ophthalmology	DEN180001

Product	Company	Technology	Description	Pathway	Date	Specialty	ID
BioFlux	Biotricity Inc.	Not Available	Detecting arrhythmias	510(k) premarket notification	Dec-17	Cardiology	K172311
Rooti Rx System ECG Event Recorder, Rooti Link APP Software	Rooti Labs Ltd	Not Available	Wearable continuous ECG monitor	510(k) premarket notification	Nov-17	Cardiology	K163694
Arterys Oncology DL	Arterys Inc.	Deep Learning	Medical diagnostics software	510(k) premarket notification	Nov-17	Oncology	K173542
AmCAD-US	AmCad BioMed Corporation	Not Available	Analysis of thyroid nodules	510(k) premarket notification	May-17	Endocrinology	K162574
EnsoSleep	EnsoData, Inc.	Automated Algorithm	Diagnosis of sleep disorders	510(k) premarket notification	Mar-17	Neurology	K162627
Cantab Mobile	Cambridge Cognition Ltd	Not Available	Memory assessment for the elderly	510(k) premarket notification	Jan-17	Neurology	K161328
Arterys Cardio DL	Arterys Inc.	Deep Learning	Software analyzing of cardiovascular images from MRI	510(k) premarket notification	Nov-16	Cardiology	K163253
Steth IO	Stratoscientific, Inc.	Not Available	Acoustic device to collect heart and lung sounds	510(k) premarket notification	Jul-16	General medicine	K160016
PixelShine	AlgoMedica	Not Available	Algorithm used to denoise CT datasets to increase image quality at reduced dose levels	510(k) premarket notification	Jun-16	Radiology	K161625
QbCheck	QbTech AB	Not Available	Diagnosis and treatment of ADHD	510(k) premarket notification	Mar-16	Psychiatry	K143468
Ahead 100	BrainScope	Not Available	Device to interpret the structural condition of the patient's brain after head injury	de novo pathway	Aug-14	Neurology	DEN140025
AliveCor	AliveCor	Not Available	Detection of atrial fibrillation	510(k) premarket notification	Aug-14	Cardiology	K140933
Temporal Comparison	Riverain Technologies	Not Available	Chest X-ray scanning software	510(k) premarket notification	Dec-12	Radiology	K123526
BodyGuardian Remote Monitoring System	Preventice	Not Available	Remote monitoring device for patients with cardiac arrhythmias	510(k) premarket notification	Aug-12	Cardiology	K121197
Pathwork Tissue of Origin Test Kit-FFPE	Pathwork Diagnostics, Inc.	Machine Learning	MI test to aid diagnosis of difficult-to-diagnose tumors using formalin-fixed, paraffin-embedded samples	510(k) premarket notification	Jun-10	Oncology	K092967

of medications, and lost workdays in the USA. The main stroke-related expenses arise from the lengthy rehabilitation period. In the management of stroke, the ideal case scenario might be to prevent patients from getting a stroke or reduce the time to diagnose it in order to curtail the brain damage. AI has the potential to offer several opportunities in the diagnosis and management of stroke, from detection of underlying risk factors to alerting healthcare professionals about abnormalities in medical test records. Scientists at Imperial College London and the University of Edinburgh have developed software based on ML which is able to identify the markers of small vessel disease (SVD) in patients with stroke or memory impairment undergoing CT scans [33]. Results show that the software is able to achieve high accuracy compared to an MRI scan, which is the current gold standard tool for the diagnosis of stroke. Another study from Google's research team demonstrated that applying deep learning to images of the retinal fundus can predict several cardiovascular risk factors such as age, gender, and systolic blood pressure (SBP). The fact that these variables are main variables used by several cardiovascular risk calculators, indicates that the model may be able to directly predict cardiovascular risk. In the case of general diseases, once a patient is discharged from hospital, the patient has completely recovered from the disease. However, in the case of stroke, discharge is just the beginning of the recovery phase. Stroke rehabilitation is an important but often ignored aspect. Rehabilitation helps patients more effectively recover their motor functions and independence. It drives neuroplasticity, which is the brain's ability to reorganize itself by forming new connections. In an effort to increase accessibility, Penumbra launched Real Immersive System, a "virtual-reality" based tool with a head-mounted display that helps patients in recovering from stroke and other neurological injuries. In addition, other companies have embarked on a similar journey, including Ceregate, which looks to develop a stroke rehabilitation program. However, it is estimated that only 30 percent of patients go for rehabilitation [34]. The severity of stroke complications and each person's ability to recover vary widely; however, there are many approaches to rehabilitation including motor skill exercise, mobility training, constraint-induced therapy, range of motion, and technology-assisted physician activities. In July 2019, Medtronic made a deal with Viz.ai, whose technology leverages AI to quickly identify suspected large vessel occlusions (LVOs) from CT angiogram images. The technology also automatically notifies specialists to facilitate synchronization of stroke care, reducing door-to-needle time and improving patient outcomes. As part of the agreement, Medtronics is expected to commercialize Viz.ai's current LVO detection and triaging software solution to all the stroke centers in the USA [35]. While it's early days, we expect AI to be increasingly leveraged and adopted in the treatment of atrial fibrillation (Afib), especially in the areas of mapping and diagnosis. Advances in imaging technology have improved the visualization of the intravascular environment and improved the detection rate of vascular disease. For example, the development of ischemic penumbra has facilitated early detection and prevention of stroke and increased the pool of coping patients. Increasing the use of AI as a new trend, in our opinion, will enable a more efficient diagnosis of vascular disease [36].

6.5 DISCUSSION

The adoption of AI is likely to usher in a new regime in the field of pharma, diagnostics, and healthcare services. AI holds tremendous potential across the broad spectrum of healthcare—aiding doctors in diagnosis, the advent of faster and non-invasive diagnostic tests, personalized medicine, operational efficiencies, supply chain management, cost savings in developing medicines, and disease management. While the translation of science to the lab has been slower than anticipated, we note some success in AI which can potentially drive growth, namely (i) a higher number of personalized medicines, the success of which can act as a precursor to further growth; (ii) governments chipping in by allocating funds; (iii) approval for AI-based medical imaging platforms; and (iv) virtual medical assistants designed to streamline clinical workflows which have improved efficiency. In a nutshell, what AI can give is personalized, participatory, preventive, predictive, precision, and stratified medicines.

6.6 CONCLUSION

The emergence and rapid development of AI-enabled solutions have important implications for the healthcare industry which is facing the continued pressure of demand which is outgrowing the limited resources available. Also, the increasing costs continue to put substantial pressure on the economy. AI has the potential to provide solutions to various healthcare problems by offering better accuracy, efficiency, and sensitivity compared to human intelligence. With the proliferation and spread of digital health around the world, AI-enabled technologies have the potential to revolutionize healthcare, including the processing of large and complex data and the automation of routine, labor-intensive processes. AI-enabled healthcare tools will save on costs, shortages of resources, and expand the reach of healthcare in the future. In stroke patients, timely detection and treatment are very important in order to reduce morbidity and mortality. Currently available AI platforms for stroke find multiple applications in stroke management ranging from treatment selection to improving clinical outcomes by helping in the various steps of diagnosis and treatment pathways, including detection, triaging, and prediction of outcomes. In the future, AI solutions that can be used in clinical settings are needed for the better care of stroke patients.

REFERENCES

[1] Ryszard Stanisław Michalski, *Machine Learning A Multistrategy Approach, Volume IV*. Elsevier Science Publishing Co Inc., 1994.

[2] H. J. Kulik, "Making machine learning a useful tool in the accelerated discovery of transition metal complexes," *Wiley Interdiscip. Rev. Comput. Mol. Sci.*, 2020.

[3] D. I. F. Konstantina Kourou, Themis P. Exarchos, Konstantinos P. Exarchos, Michalis V. Karamouzis, "Machine learning applications in cancer prognosis and prediction," *Comput. Struct. Biotechnol. J.*, vol. 13, pp. 8–17, 2015.

[4] G. Dandy, H. Maier, R. May, "Review of input variable selection methods for artificial neural networks," in *Artifical Neural Networks*, K. Suzuki, Ed. InTech.

[5] R. Wason, "Deep learning: Evolution and expansion," in *Cognitive Systems Research*, Elsevier Science Publishing Co Inc, 2018, pp. 701–708.

[6] J.-M. Hoc, "Towards a cognitive approach to human–machine cooperation in dynamic situations," *Int. J. Hum. Comput. Stud.*, vol. 54, no. 4, pp. 509–540, 2001.

[7] R. Kurt, "Industry 4.0 in terms of industrial relations and its impacts on labour life," *Procedia Comput. Sci.*, vol. 158, pp. 590–601, 2019.

[8] "2026, Global Artificial Intelligence (AI) Market to Reach US$291.5 Billion by the Year," *ReportLinker*, 2021. [Online]. Available: https://www.globenewswire.com/news-release/2021/10/27/2321714/0/en/Global-Artificial-Intelligence-AI-Market-to-Reach-US-291-5-Billion-by-the-Year-2026.html

[9] A. Rao, "PwC's global artificial intelligence study: Exploiting the AI revolution."

[10] R. (Rick) Mills, "The Promise Of AI," 2019. [Online]. Available: https://www.fnarena.com/index.php/2019/12/04/the-promise-of-ai/.

[11] C. Kreatsoulas and S. S. Anand, "The impact of social determinants on cardiovascular disease," *Can. J. Cardiol.*, vol. 26, Suppl C, pp. 8C–13C.

[12] "United Nations Conference on Trade and Development."

[13] A. Pasipoularides, "Genomic translational research: Paving the way to individualized cardiac functional analyses and personalized cardiology," *Int. J. Cardiol.*, vol. 230, pp. 384–401, 2017.

[14] E. Viceconti, A. Henney, E. Morley-Fletcher, "in silico Clinical Trials: How Computer Simulation will Transform the Biomedical Industry," in 2016.

[15] K. Sagara, & H. Das, "Crisis in Technical Education in India: Evolving Contours of the Computer and Information Sciences Discipline," in *The Digitalization Conundrum in India: Applications, Access and Aberrations, 263*, Springer, 2020.

[16] A. S. Kesselheim and J. Avorn, "New '21st century cures' legislation," *JAMA*, vol. 317, no. 6, p. 581, 2017.

[17] B. Hutchison, J.-F. Levesque, E. Strumpf, and N. Coyle, "Primary health care in Canada: Systems in motion," *Milbank Q.*, vol. 89, no. 2, pp. 256–88, 2011.

[18] J. B. Christopher Chen, "China expands regulations on e-healthcare issues," *Covignton*, 2018. [Online]. Available: https://www.covingtondigitalhealth.com/2018/10/china-expands-regulations-on-e-healthcare-issues/.

[19] E. C. Schiza, T. C. Kyprianou, N. Petkov, and C. N. Schizas, "Proposal for an eHealth based ecosystem serving national healthcare," *IEEE J. Biomed. Heal. Informatics*, vol. 23, no. 3, pp. 1346–1357, 2019.

[20] U. T. Yesha Paul, Elonnai Hickok, Amber Sinha, "Artificial Intelligence in the Healthcare Industry in India," 2017.

[21] A. Panesar, *Machine Learning and AI for Healthcare*. Apress, 2021.

[22] T. Davenport, R. Kalakota, "The potential for artificial intelligence in healthcare," *Futur. Healthc. J.*, vol. 6, no. 2, pp. 94–98, 2019.

[23] N. El-Rashidy, S. El-Sappagh, S. M. R. Islam, H. M. El-Bakry, S. Abdelrazek, "Mobile health in remote patient monitoring for chronic diseases: Principles, trends, and challenges," *Diagnostics* (Basel, Switzerland), vol. 11, no. 4, 2021.

[24] "Revolutionising healthcare by empowering doctors with artificial intelligence." [Online]. Available: https://www.babylonhealth.com/en-gb/ai

[25] D. A. Greenwood, H. M. Young, and C. C. Quinn, "Telehealth remote monitoring systematic review: Structured self-monitoring of blood glucose and impact on A1C," *J. Diabetes Sci. Technol.*, vol. 8, no. 2, pp. 378–389, 2014.

[26] S. K. Sood, V. Sood, I. Mahajan, and Sahil, "An intelligent healthcare system for predicting and preventing dengue virus infection," *Computing*. 2021.

[27] Sachchidanand Singh and Nirmala Singh, "Object classification to analyze medical imaging data using deep learning," 2017.

[28] J. F. Ha and N. Longnecker, "Doctor-patient communication: A review," *Ochsner J.*, vol. 10, no. 1, pp. 38–43, 2010.

[29] "The future of precision medicine that only human + AI can achieve," 2021. [Online]. Available: https://www.arterys.com/

[30] S. Majumder, T. Mondal, M. J. Deen, "Wearable sensors for remote health monitoring," *Sensors (Basel).*, vol. 17, no. 1, 2017.

[31] C. D. A. Wolfe, "The impact of stroke," *Br. Med. Bull.*, vol. 56, no. 2, pp. 275–286, 2000.

[32] M. V. Malfertheiner et al., "Incidence of early intra-cranial bleeding and ischaemia in adult veno-arterial extracorporeal membrane oxygenation and extracorporeal cardiopulmonary resuscitation patients: a retrospective analysis of risk factors," *Perfusion*, vol. 35, no. 1_suppl, pp. 8–17, 2020.

[33] M. Fatahzadeh and M. Glick, "Stroke: epidemiology, classification, risk factors, complications, diagnosis, prevention, and medical and dental management," *Oral Surgery, Oral Med. Oral Pathol. Oral Radiol. Endodontology*, vol. 102, no. 2, pp. 180–191, 2006.

[34] M. Slater and M. V. Sanchez-Vives, "Enhancing our lives with immersive virtual reality," *Front. Robot. AI*, vol. 3, 2016.

[35] Medtronic, "Medtronic Partners with Viz.ai to Accelerate Adoption of New Artificial Intelligence Software in U.S. Stroke Centers," *Global Newswire*. [Online]. Available: https://www.globenewswire.com/news-release/2019/07/22/1885725/0/en/Medtronic-Partners-with-Viz-ai-to-Accelerate-Adoption-of-New-Artificial-Intelligence-Software-in-U-S-Stroke-Centers.html

[36] N. M. Murray, M. Unberath, G. D. Hager, and F. K. Hui, "Artificial intelligence to diagnose ischemic stroke and identify large vessel occlusions: A systematic review," *J. Neurointerv. Surg.*, vol. 12, no. 2, pp. 156–164, 2020.

7 Computational Cloud Infrastructure for Patient Care

Urvashi Sharma
Medi-Caps University, Indore, India

Deepika Bairagee, Nitu Singh, and Neelam Jain
Oriental University, Indore, India

CONTENTS

DOI: 10.1201/9781003226949-7

7.1   INTRODUCTION

Patient care comprises the support that is given by healthcare providers to the patients in terms of diagnosis, prevention, treatment, and management of disease or illness, to preserve physical and mental well-being [1]. All over the world, healthcare systems are facing problems concerning rising costs, increasing numbers of aged populations, a growing burden of chronic diseases, and shortages of necessary equipment and healthcare workers [2].

Being a lifelong required service, patient care systems also require improvement and systemic innovation with modern resources, and this should be the topmost priority of all healthcare professionals so as to enable patient satisfaction. The other major contributing factors behind this are enhanced awareness, increased demand, market competition, strict regulatory requirements, concerns about poor outcomes, and so on [3].

Personnel competence, efficiency of operational systems, and the quality of infrastructure and training are the key determinants for evaluation of patient care quality, hence the adopted system must be "patient oriented." The major challenge in patient care for developing countries is to maintain the balance between quality and cost recovery. To resolve this, a comprehensive system should be implemented that is applicable for both medical and non-medical factors [4].

As a response to the challenges, from the 1960s healthcare systems started implementing information technology (IT) to extend patient care services so as to have a direct impact on people's health. Technically, the digitalization of services (IT) has brought up the concept of electronic health records (EHRs) [5,6].

EHRs enhance the productivity of workflow and provide a safer way for patient care, but transforming from manual to EHR is not enough alone, as EHRs require maintenance, integration, resources, and high-cost implementation. Thus, moving the patient care sector to a cloud computing system will be a one-stop solution to solve all the problems [7,8].

Cloud computing is one such technology that is receiving interest on a daily basis. As the service offers numerous benefits, the healthcare system has also started implementing cloud-based software for patient care to reduce investment and minimize the support requirements, in terms of technology. Easy accessibility and high-volume storage capacity also favor the market of cloud computing. This evolution is occurring at such a rate that in a short time most parts of the healthcare system will switch to cloud computing to provide cost-effective and efficient patient care services [9].

According to market analysis, the global healthcare cloud computing market is projected to reach up to US$84.56 billion by 2026, with a Compound Annual Growth Rate (CAGR) of about 19.18 percent during the forecast period [10].

We aim to provide a good depth review on the implementation of cloud computing in the patient care system. As the concept of cloud computing is evolving as a faster-growing technology, every field is taking it in hand and trying to take advantage of web applications and huge data affordably and reliably for the improvement of modern management and health-related services needful of patient care. Along with the applications of cloud computing in healthcare, some crucial issues that rise during implementation have also been discussed.

7.2   CLOUD COMPUTING

Cloud computing has recently emerged as a newer technology to deliver IT services through the internet by utilizing both hardware and software resources. This technology provides an on-demand service on a pay-per-use basis, any time and anywhere, with the advantage that the person does not need themselves to own the resources. This service reduces the heavy burden of buying software, hardware, and so on, hence relieving organizations of extra investment [11].

As per the definition framed by the National Institute of Standards and Technology (NIST), cloud computing is a model that enables the convenient, on-demand, ubiquitous, and cost-effective access to a shared band of configurable computing resources such as servers, storage, applications, and services that can be delivered and released quickly with minimal management effort or interaction with the service provider [12].

7.2.1 BASIC MODELS OF CLOUD COMPUTING: DEPLOYMENT MODELS

A deployment model of the cloud can be defined on the basis of the infrastructure in which the deployment resides and who has regulation and control over that infrastructure. According to NIST, four cloud deployment models have been discussed:

- *Public cloud.* As its names indicates a "public cloud" is open and conveniently accessible to the general public or large industrial groups. These are economical and off-premises clouds, owned and managed by a service provider. Generally, small organizations make use of such clouds to fulfill their demands.
- *Private cloud.* These clouds are solely operated for a person or organization as they are usually on-premises, secured, well configured, but a little expensive. Generally bigger ventures utilize such clouds to satisfy their business-related needs.
- *Community cloud.* Like a public cloud, this is shared by organizations, but here it concerns those having similar requirements and business targets, hence it supports a specific community. A community cloud can be placed on-premises or off-premises, providing enhanced security and privacy.
- *Hybrid cloud.* This type of cloud is usually a combination of two or more clouds, distinctive as entities, but connected together via technology that facilitates application and data portability. This single cloud can be situated on the user's premises or at the provider's place, enabling a combination of shared services (Figure 7.1). The main issue with this cloud is data protection, security and control [13–15].

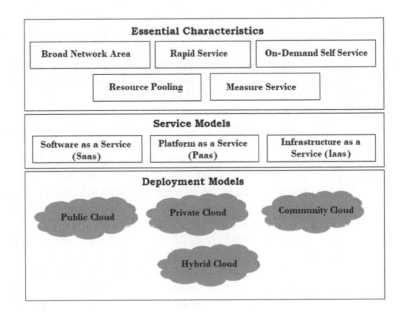

FIGURE 7.1   Overview of NIST definition of cloud computing.

7.2.2　Basic Models of Cloud Computing: Service Models

These models indicate that the services being provided relate to hardware/software infrastructure, application development, testing and deployment platforms, or business software pre-configured with a subscription. Service models are available in three types:

- *Infrastructure as a Service (IaaS)*. Another name for this service is Hardware as a Service (HaaS). The main advantage is that it provides the resources, such as processing, storage, network hardware, associated software, and other computing infrastructure to users, by avoiding a purchasing and managing cost. The well-known provider of this service is Amazon EC2.
- *Platform as a Service (PaaS)*. This platform has been created to deliver a cloud-based environment where users can develop and deliver application and deployment platforms, such as application servers and databases, without installing and working with integrated development environments (IDEs). The major providers in this field are Amazon Elastic Compute Cloud (EC2) and Savvis.
- *Software as a Service (SaaS)*. This is the earliest model of cloud computing technology available as on-demand software, enabling the user to access applications provided on the web. These are managed by the software provider and not by the company using them. Prominent providers of this model are Google with its Google Apps, Oracle along with its CRM on-demand solution, and Salesforce.com [16–18].

7.3　CLOUD COMPUTING IN PATIENT CARE

In the healthcare industry, a quantum of heterogeneous data is generated regarding the patient's background, imaging, video data, and so on. To store these numerous data, high-tech computers are required which demand a lot of investment and ultimately will impose a financial burden on patients. Cloud computing is the practice of employing a network of remote servers hosted on the internet for the storage, management, and processing of data. This does not require a local server, thereby reducing the entire infrastructural, setup, and maintenance costs [19].

In recent years, cloud technologies have been on the rise as they allow storage for a massive quantity of data. Cloud computing provides on-demand calculations using the latest technology to interactively access, distribute, and use information as a useful resource. This technology believes in sharing resources to achieve consistency and financial benefits. Reports about the entire evolution and advancement of cloud computing are based on the availability of computer systems, high-capacity networks, storage facilities, service-centric architecture, wide acceptance, and useful computation at a reasonable cost [20,21].

With the ongoing trend for cloud computing, a new application has been fabricated, namely "cloud health care." This refers to the services of health or patient care that allows diagnosis and treatment more effectively by employing medical resources via technologies like IoT and cloud computing [22]. Some other serious problems related to the health industry, such as the lack of availability of medical experts and skilled teams in all regions all the time, could be better addressed through the use of cloud services. Cloud computing services could be helpful to multiple healthcare organizations (HCOs) in working as a chain of efficient healthcare providers, allowing the sharing of health-related data with each other to build expert advice by ensuring patient care [23].

The most important companies, like Google and IBM, are using this idea of cloud computing to keep their marketing and services ongoing, which has finally highlighted this approach. According to the guidelines given by Health Information Technology for Economic and Clinical Health (HITECH) and the American Recovery & Reinvestment Act, the concept has already been practiced by healthcare institutions to store and use medical information in the form of EHRs and has proven effective to some extent. In simple words, the concept of cloud computing is an amenity along with other web facilities for users [24].

The following are a few essential healthcare requirements that are successfully met by cloud-based healthcare systems:

- The cloud provides on-demand access with huge storage facilities, which is not possible in traditional healthcare providing systems.
- Large volumes of data generated in genomics, radiology imaging, and EHRs can be easily supported.
- It is possible to exchange EHRs between licensed medical practitioners, hospitals, and institutions furnishing care in different regions worldwide.
- They allow on-time access to information stored on clouds irrespective of location especially when required in the case of life-threatening disease, hence minimizing the need for duplicate tests.
- They allow for better analysis and data monitoring for diagnosis, treatment, cost, and performance data [25].

Several developed countries have already begun the implementation of cloud services to provide collaborative healthcare and are also transforming their medical records and paper files into electronic format to secure them in a cloud environment. They are heavily investing in advanced technologies to improve patient care. Similarly, Canada has created several diagnostic imaging repositories across the country representing the level of improvement in patient healthcare [26].

The American Occupational Network is raising healthcare standards using the cloud-based software of the IBM Business Partner MedTrak System to digitize medical data and update its clinical processes. After executing the cloud-based system, the company is now able to provide quicker and more accurate billing to individuals and insurance companies by reducing the average time needed to generate an invoice, which previously was seven days, to less than 24 hours, and hence decreasing the cost of medical subscriptions by up to 80 percent [27].

In the USA, cloud computing has been employed in several patient care sectors for maintaining patients' health records and for management. Recently, the Office of the National Coordinator for Health Information Technology within the U.S. Department of Health and Human Services selected the cloud-based customer relationship and project management software from Acumen Solutions to start the use of EHR systems in the USA. This software helps regional extension centers (RECs) to track and regulate interactions more efficiently with medical service providers while implementing the EHR systems [28,29].

In Europe, an agreement between IBM, Portuguese energy and solution providers (Energias de Portugal & EFACEC), Sirrix AG security technologies, San Raffaele Hospital in Italy, and various other European academic and business research organizations has resulted in the announcement of Trustworthy Clouds that can deliver better healthcare facilities and more patient-oriented healthcare services at home using remote monitoring, diagnosing, and assisting patients outside the hospital premises. The entire process, starting from prescription to delivery, from hospitalization to reimbursement, will be reserved in the cloud and be easily accessible by patients, physicians, and pharmacy persons [28,30].

The Royal Australian College of General Practitioners and Telstra have also declared their collaboration in building an eHealth cloud. Telstra is a well-known Australian telecommunications provider, while the College is Australia's largest representative body in general practice with 20,000 members, together with 7,000 in its National Rural Facility. The applications hosted by the eHealth cloud will include clinical software, care plans, decision support tools for diagnosis and management, reference tools, prescriptions, training, and other administrative and clinical services [28,31].

Despite the benefits that cloud computing offers, there is a continuous tradeoff between profitable and inexpensive health services and the issues which arise after storing data on clouds. Some common public concerns are mostly about data privacy and lack of security while sharing their sensitive information (Figure 7.2).

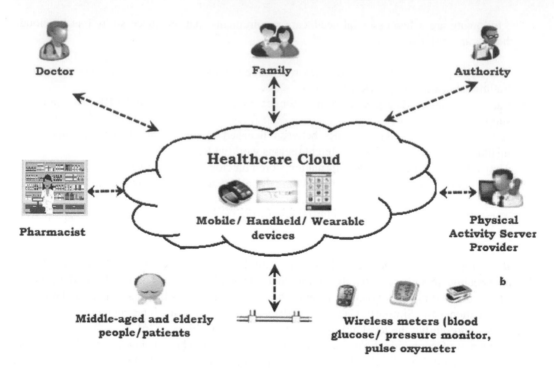

FIGURE 7.2   Healthcare cloud architecture [32].

7.3.1 Features of Cloud Computing in Healthcare

Nowadays, the new technology of cloud computing is constantly being implemented by healthcare systems to streamline the various processes of patient care and to provide better health-related services. Some of the characteristic features of cloud computing that has enabled the application of this IT-based technology for patient care are described as follows:

1. *Self-service model.* The most fascinating feature of cloud computing is its on-demand availability to the user. With this, a user can monitor the allotted network storage, computing capabilities, and server period. All the resources are provided spontaneously by the service provider without any human intervention.

2. *Scale-up elasticity.* For futuristically required technology, it becomes important that the technique provides a margin for modifications and development; this essential character has been provided by cloud computing as it allows rapid and easy moderation or scaling up, as per company requirements. Cloud computing enables the incorporation or deletion of required data storage, processing speed, and bandwidth over a minimum time frame.

3. *Large network access.* Cloud computing allows access to the broad network using the internet from any available device at any time and anywhere.

4. *Shared resources.* This service permits multiple customers to use resources such as memory, software, networks, and server, using a multi-tenant model simultaneously. These physical or virtual resources are allocated as per customer need, can be fluctuated with demand, and the client can have no idea about the exact geographical location of the provided resources except for a higher level of abstraction.

5. *Security.* Security and privacy of data are the utmost desired characteristics and which has been delivered well by cloud computing. As the data are stored within devices and managed by experts, they remain secure from system failure and hacking.

6. *Easy maintenance.* This is an essential aspect with respect to storage. The cloud computing servers can be maintained with ease and with no, or minimal, downtime. Maintenance keeps them updated, enabling the device to perform better and faster.

7. *Measured service.* Cloud computing resources are monitored by the provider using several metrics and a detailed report of usage is prepared to preserve consumer rights and transparency.

8. *Pay as you go.* Cloud computing offers the advantage of paying only for the space or service that the user has utilized, without any additional or hidden charges. Consumption-based billing allows the estimation of the exact cost on the basis of actual consumption, making the service economical.

9. *Availability.* Based on the usage, cloud capability can be changed and extended significantly to the desired capacity. The service permits the user to purchase extra storage whenever desired.

10. *Economic.* The service requires only one-time investment for buying the storage and the host company can then provide it to multiple users, thereby providing saving of yearly or monthly expenses. [33–36]

Before the arrival of cloud computing, a few problems were often noticed by the patient care sector (see Table 7.1).

7.3.2 BENEFITS OF CLOUD COMPUTING IN PATIENT CARE

In the healthcare sector, cloud computing is usually of two types:

- The distribution model. This model is based on a hardware/software perspective and can either be Software as a Service, Infrastructure as a Service, or Platform as a Service.
- The deployment model. This is based on who owns the cloud and hence can be private, community, public, or hybrid [38].

TABLE 7.1

Problems of Patient Care [37]

Uncertainty of Records	The enormous amount of patient care data present in the healthcare industry is mostly unstructured because of its obtainability from various diverse sources. Dealing with such data becomes critical at times as one cannot access it, so it becomes important to segregate and arrange it for easy accessibility. Most of the facilities lack the technology which could sort out the data; however, a cloud healthcare service would help provide easy dealing, maintenance, and storage of patient care data.
Slow Speed	Old data management technologies often create speed issues, and in patient care this occurs frequently due to the vast volumes of available data, making the system work more slowly. Being an emergency service, this technological error generates serious outcomes. Moreover, as the data keeps on building daily, the pace keeps on decreasing, which leads to system failure and data loss. Healthcare cloud computing can increase the system speed, making it work faster.
Flaws in Data Transfer	Hospitals working as chains at different locations suffer a lot during data transfer, since a large amount of data may take a longer time than usual to process, which could become problematic for any medical facility requiring emergency medical situations. Here also cloud computing allows data storage on the central cloud that is reachable from different locations at the same time.
Inventory Issues	Medical facilities are always required to update their inventories on a regular basis. But in multi-specialty hospitals, the number of inventories is so massive that the chances of missing out on some products are very common. This may result in a shortage of the desired medicines and medical equipment during the time of the medical emergency. With the application of cloud computing, such issues might never be generated as the technology can handle such vital data in a well-organized manner.

Cloud computing offers benefits to almost every aspect of the healthcare industry and can provide actual solutions to the difficulties discussed in Table 7.1. Several advantages that cloud computing renders in the patient care sector are:

1. *Mobility of records*. In this decade of digital health, connectivity between patients and the healthcare professional is foremost. Cloud computing technology enables easy and anytime availability of patient information even from remote areas. This increases the reach of patient care to every individual, ensuring the dispersal of better services. In some instances, such as the study of any critical illness, a patient's information may be required by more than one healthcare organization. In this case, by implementing cloud computing technology, information can be easily shared without any waste of time. Even in healthcare organizations, health information exchanges (HIEs) are used for sharing the data available in proprietary EHR systems. Here also cloud computing systems can be developed for HIEs, to prevent the security of the healthcare data from being breached and to keep it safe [39].

2. *Excessive storage facility*. Today, most healthcare facilities have started the practice of maintaining EHRs, where cloud computing can help by providing sufficient storage and enabling the timely upgrades of this data by healthcare personnel. The widespread use of cloud storage for patient care makes collaborative working on patient information much easier for physicians. Even in other hospital facilities like pharmacies or pathology departments, the larger quantity of generated data regarding medical equipment, medications, and purchased stocks need to be managed properly and must include essential entries such as purchase date, expiry date, and vendor details. The gathered information can easily be shifted onto clouds and recovered immediately during an emergency. With cloud computing, it becomes smoother to track available stock and get timely updates via the cloud on equipment and drugs that are close to expiring and require immediate refilling or exchange.

3. *Speed*. According to a survey by the Internap Corporation (INAP) in 2019, network performance has become the most important reason cited by companies for moving to the cloud. The cloud-based solution provides unbeaten speed and faster access to patient information, which is often needed in an hour. The availability of such a huge amount of patient care data at any one time can avoid serious consequences during emergency conditions or surgical procedures. This futuristic technology has also transformed the scope of clinical research; the cloud can even facilitate clinical trial management and knowledge sharing [40].

4. *Data security*. In the healthcare industry, a significant concern while storing patient information on the computer is data protection and ensuring its security in the face of unauthorized sources. Shifting patient care data to the cloud can furnish adequate protection to health information (PHI) and HIEs. Cloud computing is most useful for the online storage of medical records or patient information that requires extreme security and privacy. Cloud healthcare-based service provider companies evaluate and then apply the measures required for secured hosting. They also need to comply with the updated Health Insurance Portability and Accountability Act (HIPAA), ensuring the complete security, backup, and encryption of patient-related information. Security can be further enhanced by using secured and permission-based databases [41].

5. *Cost reduction*. Through cloud computing technology, hospitals are freed from buying resources like hardware and servers for computing purposes, leading to huge cost savings. According to a recent survey by Healthcare Financial Management, the implementation of EHRs in the healthcare industry will lift savings to $37 million over a five-year period. This massive cost saving will allow healthcare providers to reduce service charges levied on

patients. In the healthcare industry, cloud computing also provides improved assistance in human resource, administrative, and other operational activities. It provides facilities in terms of scheduling, sourcing files, inventory management, and referrals to make the whole process more competent and profitable. Hence, resource allocation of a high grade is achievable at a low cost using cloud services [42].

6. *Extensive research*. Patient care providers, physicians, and medical personnel finance a very long period of research aimed at ameliorating their practice of gathering and storing pivotal information obtained during surgery and treatment. This segregated information is then analyzed and proper research is done to well establish them as case studies and theses. Using cloud computing technology, concise and easy to reference data can be prepared in the form of case studies or theses that will later help new doctors during their research or surgery. With the help of the cloud, data can be easily accessed from multiple sites and analytics can also be performed on patient data, paving the way to personalized care plans for individual patients [43].

7. *Centralized access to digital health records*. Previously, every patient used to keep different medical files or records for each doctor's visit, and these were updated by medical professionals themselves. This much paperwork becomes unmanageable for doctors and staff during rushes; so to overcome the process and make it more manageable, all patient data is now migrated onto clouds. Because of cloud services, entire medical data are stored at one central location which remains available through health center web portals and can be easily retrieved when needed. A completely secured cloud platform assures storage facilities for data, along with hosting solutions and virtual machines to quickly access medical information and thus allow rapid disease diagnosis and patient treatment [44].

8. *Access to high powered analytics*. Data storage and manipulation is a crucial part of analytics, and cloud-based tools are becoming more functional in analytical tasks. Healthcare data, whether structured or unstructured, serve as an enormous asset, not only for the organization but also for society. The cloud makes it feasible to assemble patient-relevant data from various sources; by implementing big data analytics and artificial intelligence algorithms on this cloud-stored patient record, medical research activities can be boosted. With advanced cloud computing, large datasets can be quickly processed, confirming the on-record presence of entire patient details and assuring that nothing gets left out while prescribing the treatments.

9. *Ownership of data*. Cloud computing produces much patient-centric data, giving patients control of their health and thereby emphasizing individual patient care. It improves the participation of the patient in making decisions about their health and serves as a tool for their education. Retrieval of medical records and images becomes easier when data is stored in the cloud. Though cloud security remains an issue, the reliability of the cloud for data storage is far superior. Data redundancy also decreases with increased system uptime. Since backups are automated and data is stored at a centralized cloud, recovery of data becomes effective and easier.

10. *Collaborative interoperability*. Transitioning healthcare data onto clouds not only promotes easy accessibility but also improves collaboration. Cloud computing technology enables physicians and healthcare professionals to collaborate for the improvement of patient health outcomes. Accessibility of all data from a single point helps in the formation of a collaborative unit of stakeholders required to prepare plans, trace the progress of treatment, and provide constant focused care for better results. Patient histories, diagnostics, testament plans, and other medical records can be shared immediately via the cloud with multiple medical experts. Additionally, partnering and working with health insurance companies becomes far easier for healthcare facilities, resulting in hassle-free payments [45].

7.4 APPLICATIONS OF CLOUD COMPUTING IN PATIENT CARE

The ecosystem in healthcare is highly complex, multifarious, and vast, as it includes hospitals, patients, a physician network, pharmacies, laboratories, health insurance companies, and other entities. For better patient care, these all should perform in collaboration with each other and must comply with the laid down government regulations.

In the current scenario, the rising demand for patient care services with continuously rising patient service charges, data security and integrity, and disaster recovery are top of the priority list. Some inherent features present in cloud computing technology can address these priorities to benefit the healthcare industry. For this system to work efficiently and at a faster pace, timely information sharing between entities are of utmost importance along with keeping it confidential. This major concern of data security can also be easily solved by implementing private cloud computing [46].

Cloud computing has emerged as a novel and influential technology for the medical sector that is continuously being adopted by organizations in patient care to provide better healthcare services at a minimal cost. Cloud computing offers several services in patient care, covering a wide range of capabilities. Various applications of cloud computing in patient care have been elaborated, which are essential to driving an advanced tech-led healthcare system.

7.4.1 INFORMATION SYSTEMS

An information system has multiple users in the healthcare industry. The physician uses the system to deliver better patient care while the patients or customers use this service to get their health-related queries resolved. Administrators use the system to manage resources, finances, and so on, and higher management personnel use it for decision making and forecasting. A computing-based management information system (CMiS) is capable of providing accurate information at all levels, handling numerous management related issues in an organization, as well as being capable of generating reports automatically with data analysis. Therefore, the healthcare industry has begun the use of management information systems for streaming the information flow inside an organization.

The cloud-based health information system functions as a SaaS application, where the service provider employs cloud-based platform services to prepare, test, and deploy this system. These health information systems are reachable through desktop apps or web browsers and give access to all infrastructure information systems. Cloud computing-based healthcare information systems eliminate the issues related to data storage, transmission, high setup costs, and software mainte-nance, with the optimization of resources.

Exemplary work done in such a field is the cloud-based medical service delivery framework (CMSDF) developed for sharing resources between a general hospital and affiliated healthcare institutions. A prototype CMSDF has also been tested in which the cloud-based virtual desktop infrastructure (VDI) of a large hospital was allowed to share its medical software (as SaaS) with healthcare institutions [47,48] (Figure 7.3).

7.4.2 TELEMEDICINE PRACTICES

Today, the blending of information and communication technologies has been utilized in the form of telemedicine technology to provide and support patient care services. Cloud computing has been the prominent player in conferring such types of services.

Telemedicine service can be defined as the procedure of delivering and receiving medical and clinical data anytime from anywhere in the world by using advanced technologies. The primary use of telemedicine in the patient care sector is for providing health care services not only to urban but also to rural and remote areas. The service is imparted on the basis of gathered information about patients' health. Cloud computing makes it possible to access the required data easily. This system is a convenient way to deliver healthcare services as the patient doesn't hesitate to discuss their

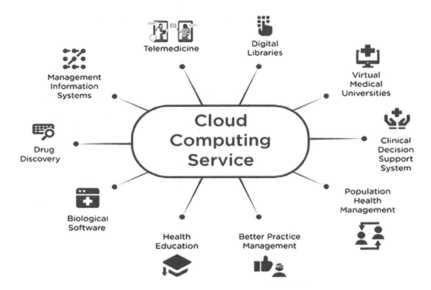

FIGURE 7.3 Cloud computing service-based patient care applications [46].

problems with the consultant who is far away. Several advanced technologies such as teleradiology, telesurgery, and audio/video conferencing have made the communication and collaboration between healthcare stakeholders necessary. Cloud-based software allows doctor–patient and doctor–doctor interaction easier with the transmission and archiving of medical images. This telemedicine technology also enables medical professionals to share their opinion on their expert field so as to deal with complex medical cases appropriately.

In telemedicine practice, cloud-based solutions are applicable for:

- Exchanging real-time patient medical data without any geographical boundaries;
- Cutting off unnecessary visits to doctors, thereby saving the time, expenses, and consequent hardship of traveling;
- Retrieving information at the inquirer's place and time. [49–51]

7.4.3 Digital Libraries

The primary purpose of the library is to serve as a source of knowledge among practitioners, researchers, and medical students. Paper-based libraries are usually unable to satisfy the demands of society due to financial barriers, especially in developing countries. In such places, a cloud-based library provides an opportunity for every individual to access the available information. Cloud computing technology is used to create digital libraries by providing sufficient file storage, query languages, an indexing service, a hosting service, library management systems, and so on. This provides librarians with a pathway to exchange the dispersed resources and services belonging to various organizations or sites with one another.

Cloud-based digital libraries have the following advantages:

- Allow on-demand facilities to individuals and institutions;
- The semantic-based query approach makes the finding or searching process easier for information seekers;
- Permit information seekers to access several literature pieces, simultaneously;
- Hassle free and readily available information to researchers without going through any files or books;

- Physicians can easily get to know about ongoing progress and trends in the medical domain, which helps them to enhance their knowledge and improve their work practice.

Some examples of digital health libraries are:

1. *Online Computer Library Center (OCLC)*. This library employs cloud computing technology to supply online cataloging tools and share its resources, data, and innovation with ease.
2. *Ex-Libris*. This is a USA-based leading library software provider which offers a private cloud for the use of customers. It provides cloud-based solutions to upscale mobile campus services, student engagement, library management, and research outcomes. The world's only library service platform which manages electronic, print, and digital materials in a single interface is Ex Libris Alma.
3. *Duraspace's DuraCloud*. DuraCloud is another service provider, mainly imparting services to participating libraries by utilizing their own remote computers or servers, which saves the libraries from the expenditure of device management [52,53].

7.4.4 VIRTUAL MEDICAL UNIVERSITIES

Today's education and teaching patterns need to be modified innovatively to grab the attention of students and to make them concentrate for a longer time. Teaching-learning must incorporate the practical and intellectual use of graphics, more than ever before. This can be achieved by forming a university cloud that shares the available resources digitally and worldwide. Cloud computing, because of its modifiable and pay-per-use model, is building roots in the academic sector too. For learning in the academic sector, several on-campus and off-campus support facilities have been developed by renowned IT companies like Google, Microsoft, Amazon, and HP. Universities imparting medical education can take advantage of these cloud-based models to effectively conduct online conferences, webinars, deliver lectures, and for greater collaboration across academia. This technology can be extremely useful for emerging nations in reaching the maximum number of students with little effort and low cost. Cloud computing service models that are being implemented effectively in academia are shown in Table 7.2 [52,54].

7.4.5 CLINICAL DECISION SUPPORT SYSTEM

The healthcare industry faces the problem of huge operational data costs, data integrity, and confidentiality. Hence there is a serious requirement for adopting the cloud-based clinical decision support system (CCDSS) to manage and maintain EHRs which can be easily accessed by healthcare professionals and patients from different geographical locations.

A clinical decision support system (CDSS) has been designed to upgrade health and patient care services by incorporating the expertise of clinicians, patient records, and several health-related

---

TABLE 7.2

Cloud Computing for Academic Purposes [52]

Cloud Service	Users	Applications
SaaS	Student, faculty and administrative staff	Teaching and learning software, collaboration tools
PaaS	Developers	Software development, deployment, and testing
IaaS	Researcher, faculty, administrative staff, students	Storage, computation, I/O, network

information, to improve medical decisions. Conventional CDSS contained the software prepared for making the clinical decision directly by comparing the clinical database available in the computer with features of a particular patient; patient-focused advice was then given to the physician for a final decision. Nowadays, such CDSSs are being utilized for patient care where physicians blend their expertise with the data or recommendations given by the CDSS. Recently CDSSs have also been designed with the capacity to interpret their information or data which is uninterpretable by human beings [55,56].

Physicians use the CDSS for the purpose of disease diagnosis and medication as it offers a wide range of functions such as prescription (Rx), diagnostics, alarm systems, disease management, drug control, and medication errors. Cloud computing can also help design the system as needed for patient care. For example, the arrival of cellphones with smart technology and in-built sensors to trace the heart rate, blood pressure, and so on allowed these cloud-based systems to do real-time diagnoses. By adopting cloud services, the patient can share actual diagnosed information with the system and receive suitable health suggestions or treatment on time in the case of emergency or when the doctor is unavailable [55,56].

7.4.6 Population Health Management

The application of cloud computing solutions in health information management is known throughout the world as cloud computing technology can bring massive changes to healthcare agencies and organizations. This can provide numerous benefits for the enhancement of health status, in eliminating health disparities, and reducing overall healthcare costs. For instance, American Occupational Network and HyGen Pharmaceuticals are using cloud-based software for the digitalization of health records and the renovation of clinical processes, hence improving patient care services. Other examples are the Canadian government and Mount Sinai Hospital of Toronto, both of which are working in collaboration to build a community cloud that will allow 14 hospitals of their community to access a fetal ultrasound application and stored patient information [57].

Cloud-based services help in tracking diseases, mapping them geospatially, and informing the high-risk population about it. Organizations utilizing cloud computing can foster the sharing of all the stored and gathered information among public health and healthcare organizations for real-time use, hence freeing up healthcare staff to deal with more crucial and difficult duties in an organized and economical manner. Today the service employing cloud computing technology is the Centers for Disease Control and Prevention (CDC), which mainly focus on improving public health data by gathering the buried information of EHRs, upgrading data collection capabilities, and playing a major role in the surveillance of public health [58].

7.4.7 Patient Management Practices

To improve patient care services and patient satisfaction, healthcare providers are utilizing cloud computing technology for patient management activities like patient billing and claims. By employing cloud technology, patient care activities can be smoothly tracked, finances can be easily managed, and administrative processes can also be optimized. Such practices also boost productivity and save time in day-to-day work. Cloud-based medical billing software works on a remote server and is attainable from any authorized computer having an internet connection. Billing software automates the whole process, starting from the payment done during scheduling an appointment to final billing, enabling the healthcare providers and family to spend more time on patient care and less time on keeping track of billing [59]. Revenue cycle management (RCM) is one such financial process, using the billing software to track finances engaged in patient care activities from registration to final payment. This unites the clinical aspects of healthcare with administrative data—like the name of the patient, an insurance provider with the treatment plan, and healthcare data—allowing ease at the time of applying for a claim with the insurance company. Smart Hospital, Halemind, and eClinic Systems are some examples [60].

The technology enables the practitioner to access broad information for constructing an effective treatment plan. Patients can also take advantage of such services for online collaboration with the treatment provider, to resolve their medical issues. For instance, cloud-based Flatiron oncology is an end-to-end technology prepared for the value-based supervision of cancer patients. This healthcare technology mainly focuses on accelerating research in the field of cancer to provide better care services to cancer patients [61].

7.4.8 HEALTH EDUCATION

The learning environment can be easily modified using technological skills. Information and communication technology is an efficient support tool to upgrade the quality of health education by providing the content through multiple modalities. In today's world of online teaching and learning, the demand for cloud computing is spreading at a faster rate in the education sector too. In this time, where information is available at one click, the web serves as a knowledge source to spread awareness among the masses about health, dietary, fitness, disease, and sanitation issues. All this health-related information or data regarding specific disease types can be easily acquired from numerous trusted sources such as blogs, helper organizations, and websites. Patients who have suffered in the past from any specific or uncommon disease can also share their experience, knowledge, dietary plans, treatment procedures, and medication taken with a dosing schedule to newer patients for appropriate self-care. Several cloud-based services such as PaaS and SaaS provide self-care training to people. Helpers can also rent cloud applications to start their group using chat tools to extend health advocacy.

Medical organizations must finance cloud-based learning management systems (LMSs) to facilitate online training programs and e-learning courses which should be accessible by healthcare personnel, irrespective of geographical location and time. LMSs are software platforms where e-learning content can be created, stored, and managed in an organized way. With the right LMS tool, the training process can be made automatic by reducing training costs. Modified training materials can also be updated as per the industrial regulations laid down by the Health Insurance Portability and Accountability Act and the American Society for Testing and Materials (ASTM) for learning management systems. The most popular LMS apps for the patient care sector are SkillPort, Medical Lab LMS, and Blackboard LMS [62,63].

7.4.9 BIOLOGICAL SOFTWARE

Advancement in biomedical research from genome sequencing to patient monitoring gadgets, from image collections to the evolution of EHR platforms, produces larger and more complex data that will continuously rise with the passage of time, leading to more obstacles in the storage, maintenance, and preservation of data. Moreover, biomedical research is now regulated through the insights obtained during the analysis and interpretation of vigorous datasets. High-throughput technologies have made the ability to create and test hypotheses more feasible and even common, therefore the task of acquiring valuable information has switched from the testing towards the computer [64].

The evolution of biomedical research has occurred now in an automated data-intensive process that relies upon a secured and extensible storage, computing, and networking infrastructure, which was previously purchased and managed locally. The growing number of cloud-based tools and platforms can benefit biomedical research and, with growing big data concerns, researchers are moving towards cloud computing platforms. Hence, for a variety of applications in the field of biomedicals, cloud computing models come out as a substitute for conventional cloud computing concerns and big data approaches.

TABLE 7.3
Cloud-Enabled Bioinformatics Platform [67]

Name	Year	Description	Application tools
CloudBLAST	2008	Combining MapReduce and virtualization on distributed resources for bioinformatics application	Hadoop, ViNe, BLAST
CloudBurst	2009	Highly sensitive read mapping with MapReduce	MapReduce, AmazonEC2
Galaxy	2010	A comprehensive approach for supporting accessible, reproducible, and transparent computational research in life sciences	Python, web server, SQL database
Galaxy Cloudman	2010	Delivering cloud computing clusters	Amazon EC2, Bio-Linux, Galaxy
AzureBlast	2010	A case study for developing science applications on the cloud	Azure, BLAST
CloudAligner	2011	A fast and full-featured MapReduce-based tool for sequence mapping	CloudBurst, MapReduce, Amazon EMR
CloVR	2011	Pre-configured and on-demand bioinformatics computing for the genomic community	VM, VirtualBox, VMWare
FX	2012	An RNA-Seq analysis tool on the cloud	Hadoop, Amazon EC2
Rainbow	2013	Tool for large-scale whole-genome sequencing data analysis using cloud computing	Crossbow, bowtie SOAPsnp, Picard, Perl, MapReduce
SeqPig	2014	Simple and scalable scripting for large sequencing data sets in Hadoop	Hadoop, Apache Pig

An example of one such application of a cloud-based model in biological research is Bioinformatics. This is that branch of science that integrates information technology and computational science with the biological world. The data obtained while sequencing, such as nanopore sequencing, pyrosequencing, and non-optical ion chip techniques, creates petabytes of data every day and creates a challenge to analyze such a huge amount of data efficiently. The cloud computing technology used to resolve the problem mentioned is called a "bioinformatics cloud." In biological research, cloud computing has also found utility in genome informatics and biomedical information, comparative genomics, metagenomics, the neurosciences, RNA analysis, and so on [65,66]. Some examples of cloud-enabled models for biological research are shown in Table 7.3.

7.4.10 DRUG DISCOVERY

Drug discovery is a process of discovering novel chemical entities that have proved therapeutic effectiveness, thereby highlighting its efficacy and adverse effects if any. The drug discovery concept usually brings the image of chemistry experimentation, biological assay, and large-scale automation inside the laboratory premises. Now, over the last few years, organizations are using a virtual mode for drug discovery processes by utilizing the software and taking advantage of cloud computing technology [68].

Cloud computing has proven to be a game-changer for the drug discovery process, otherwise ample computing resources are required during discovery to find the lead compounds among several chemical structures. Many pharmaceutical companies are using cloud computing and artificial intelligence to speed up the drug development process. Hyperscale cloud providers like Amazon Web Services (AWS), Microsoft, and Google are major service providers for this approach.

To promote this new approach of drug development, AWS, Microsoft, and Alphabet (Google) provide services not only for established drug companies but also for startups. For example, at Moderna, AWS is imparting services for drug production, and the research and development process. The company is formulating a newer treatment class by utilizing messenger RNA or mRNA that will make use of DNA instructions and help in building proteins in human cells.

Drugs prepared with mRNA will signalize the body to produce the proteins necessary for the treatment of particular illnesses. To develop drugs for the cure of infectious diseases, funding is being provided to Moderna by the military, while Merck and AstraZeneca are helping financially to formulate cancer vaccines [69].

Several cloud-based IaaS services are coming forward to reduce the cost and time needed for drug discovery. An example is Molplex Clouds against Disease, which is a joint venture started by a small drug discovery company Molplex, Newcastle University, and Microsoft Research [70].

Another example is SCYNEXIS, which is an innovative biotechnology-based company producing medicines to prevent and treat infectious diseases, mainly drug-resistant fungal infections. The company collaborated with Norak Biosciences and has entered into drug research through a cloud-based software system known as Hit Explorer Operating System (HEOS) [71].

7.5   ISSUES IN EMPLOYING CLOUD COMPUTING IN HEALTHCARE

Within patient care, cloud-based applications can resolve so many problems in the field, but it is still a developing paradigm. Despite the advantages that cloud computing offers, its adoption rate is quite low [72]. As per the data, the retail industry has adopted the technology at a much faster rate (57 percent) than healthcare (31 percent) [73]. Hence like any other innovation, cloud computing must be thoroughly evaluated before its widespread adoption. Several issues that exist while implementing cloud computing in patient care are discussed below.

7.5.1   TECHNOLOGICAL ISSUES

One of the major disadvantages of cloud computing is the lack of reliable service delivery models. Many times, customers are drawn to aspects like storage capacity and applications; however, as demand increases, cloud service providers (CSPs) frequently suffer from network congestion and are unable to fulfil consumers requirements. Because of this, the company reduces the value either through restricting access or by not upgrading its infrastructure. Since CSPs are rarely controlled by regulatory authorities, this results in poor service quality leading to unfulfillment of customers' expectations.

Data transfer is another important aspect that needs to be investigated. Whenever a CSP fails or shuts its venture, companies will either move services to another CSP or will adopt an internal IT environment. For instance, when on January 1, 2012, Google stopped hosting the Google Health service, a one-year period was given to service users to download their data and store it somewhere else. During these incidents, significant data transfer challenges occurred. Likewise, biomedical research laboratories also need regular and faster uploads and downloads from clouds for their enormous datasets; however, this may also lead to overcrowding [74].

Two other elements of technology are complexity and compatibility, which impact cloud adoption and deployment in the industry. Employing cloud services and applications becomes more critical when combined with healthcare. Hence for better compatibility, it is necessary to first verify how many applications and infrastructures of the cloud are compatible with existing IT systems present in the hospital. For the successful implementation of cloud healthcare, the cost of technology needs to be addressed carefully to avoid future discrepancies. Like any other investment, implementing the cloud also requires major funding in hardware, software, and systems integration. Hence the health administrator needs to think about this before migrating to the cloud [75].

7.5.2   SECURITY AND PRIVACY ISSUES

Despite the infinite advantages that cloud computing has in e-health services, privacy and security of information is still a problem, and this becomes more complex in the cloud model, requiring implementation of data management policies and thereby raising the investment cost.

Within the IT sector, major security and privacy concerns include hacker attacks, data misuse, and network failures. As in a cloud virtualized environment, the stored data can be accessed by numerous customers, giving rise to issues in data transmission, confidentiality, access control, integrity, and so on. In such an environment, the absence of resources for separate storage, reputation, and routing are major privacy concerns, leaving users vulnerable to privacy breaching from external parties [76]. During data storage and transfer on the cloud, data protection integrity and issues relevant to the transfer of healthcare data is another challenging task. Various security aspects that must be taken care of are:

- Software security which involves personnel identification.
- Platform safety, involving interfaces and aspects of the framework.
- The concept of accountability, in terms of data practice, which also applies to cloud computing services that require rigorous security and privacy, particularly for those involving sensitive health-related aspects or medical data.
- Infrastructure security is required for online privacy and storage settings.

The provision of cloud computing services is more vulnerable to poor encryption key management, separation failure, a public management interface, and privilege abuse. Besides this, several other security threats like viruses and malware are more difficult to resolve than conventional in-house IT systems, especially if using the public cloud. Various studies have confirmed that most users have cited data privacy and security as one of the major barriers in adopting cloud computing. Highly sensitive information and applications are the major concerns, while switching data onto a cloud model is still seen as doubtful and remains an active area of investigation because of privacy controls and their effectiveness. Therefore, security must be offered at affordable prices by CSPs to customers for better adoption of the service [74].

Apart from this, the healthcare sector also has stricter regulatory requirements for the security and privacy of patient rights regarding sensitive medical and health data. The confidentiality of data is a recurring theme precisely from the point of unapproved persons trying to access medical records. The transfer of these voluminous and confidential data is especially troublesome, and hence greater measures for security must be taken. Establishing a safe environment for patient data sharing and integrating is even more challenging and requires much effort to resolve the issue [77].

7.5.3 LEGAL ISSUES

Cloud computing applications can generate numerous legal problems, like disputes over contractual laws, data jurisdiction, intellectual property rights, and data privacy. Between them, the main issues are privacy and data jurisdiction.

In the cloud, physical depositories could be spread under multiple jurisdictions, each having different regulations concerning security, data privacy, intellectual property rights, and data usage. For instance, the HIPAA limits an organization from revealing its data to unapproved third parties. But the Providing Appropriate Tools Required to Intercept and Obstruct Terrorism (PATRIOT) Act gives the US government the right to request data in emergency conditions or when it is important for national security [78].

Likewise, the Canadian Personal Information Protection and Electronic Documents Act (PIPEDA) restricts organizational rights in collecting, using, or disclosing any personal information for commercial or business activities. However, the provider may have the right to shift data from one jurisdiction to another without any consent of the user. Sometimes, cloud data can have more than one registered location at the same time, with different legal consequences [78,79].

But as cloud computing is a shared resource and provides the multi-user environment for capacity, storage, and network, there is a higher risk of privacy infringement. The failure of the mechanism to separate the memory, storage, routing, and even reputation among the various users of the shared infrastructure are some of the risks present in such an environment. Centralized storage and joint physical storage ownership simply mean that cloud users are at greater risk of their sensitive data (e.g., medical records) being disclosed to unwanted parties [78,80].

Another significant privacy concern is poor breach notification. PIPEDA has put forward the latest regulation for companies where they are required to disclose data breaches to the Canadian Privacy Commissioner along with information to individuals, whether there is any potential harm or not. However, breach notification doesn't ensure consumer privacy. In a recent study, it was found that users receiving breach notifications of data over the last few years were at higher risk of fraudulent activity than other consumers. Legal solutions to address these issues are still awaited and are major blocks in the wider adoption of cloud computing technology for the health and patient care sector, especially when it is concerned with government patient care services [78].

7.5.4 MANAGEMENT ISSUES

Management issues while adopting cloud computing are insufficient trust in data privacy and security, the inertia of companies, uncertain vendor compliance, and loss of governance. Many customers still don't trust the utility of cloud computing, and prime concerns emerge while switching sensitive data and critical applications to a cloud computing paradigm where vendors are unable to guarantee the efficiency of their privacy and security controls. Another administrative challenge in adoption is cultural resistance, that is, organizational inertia to share data and modify traditional working patterns [78].

Sometimes, service level agreements might not render any assurance to the consumer to inspect cloud data. This data governance loss could severely affect the user's strategy and hence their ability to achieve their targets. Hence, when a supplier is unable to satisfy the required compliance standards, such as applicable laws, regulations, and standards, investment made by the consumer will be in danger [78,81].

7.5.5 ORGANIZATIONAL ISSUES

The implementation of cloud computing in healthcare is vastly influenced by several organizational factors. As per the study by Borgman et al, the size of the company/organization is a major concern while adopting cloud technology. Bigger firms need to spend much more on incorporating cloud services, exposing them to a greater risk of health cloud deployment failures. Mid and small size organizations, being dynamic, can easily and quickly adapt to a cloud setup. Plus, they will not require much expenditure because of their small size.

Another important required element with respect to implementing the cloud in an organization is support from senior management. As cloud computing will directly affect the implementation process, budget, and responsibility, support from the administrators is always required. Moreover, it is the responsibility of senior managers to assign the appropriate resources for support and implementation of new technologies. The success rate of health cloud deployment would be very low without the support of top management. The presence of IT skills or cloud expertise in non-technical employees has a huge effect on cloud adoption. The availability of sufficient employees with IT skills in any organization increases the chances of efficient and successful implementation of cloud technology. An IT savvy employee could help the organization in switching to the healthcare cloud more easily [82,83].

7.5.6 ENVIRONMENTAL ISSUES

Environmental problems are a major challenge as they are generally connected with the company's basic profile, such as "where a company conducts its business: its sector, competitors, approach to various resources provided by others and its relationship with government." From the environmental aspect, the two crucial factors are market competition and regulatory restrictions.

As competition is rising in the healthcare sector and even the smaller clinics are switching to cloud services, this will pressure the remaining hospitals to implement new IT technologies faster. Furthermore, regulatory constraints are usually relevant to safety and patients' privacy. Hence hospitals must first confirm that a chosen cloud infrastructure is secure and reliable. This becomes more difficult when physical and virtual cloud infrastructure is completely owned and operated by outsourced service providers. The data must be processed by prescribed means laid by the HIPAA, as the healthcare providers are asked to ensure the user's approach is monitored in a controlled way. Moreover, it is not easy to prove that cloud infrastructures comply with the HIPAA [83].

7.5.7 HUMAN ISSUES

It is very essential in healthcare to focus on several human-related aspects before employing cloud technology because end-users, like healthcare personnel, patients, insurance staff, and administrators, all must be ready to implement and work with newly enforced cloud applications. Every individual varies in behavior and attitude, though most of them have resistance to new technologies. Before implementing cloud technology, users' knowledge related to information technology must be assessed. Few users have good IT skills, therefore administrators must take care of this issue also. Proper training sessions must be conducted before the implementation of the cloud in the patient care sector [83].

7.6 REGULATORY ASPECTS FOR CLOUD COMPUTING IN PATIENT CARE

Generally, standards are constructed to express acceptable product or service characteristics laid down by experts from various institutions and organizations. These are the documented standards and represent consent on parameters such as quality, safety, reliability, and security, which should remain relevant over a long period of time. The aim of doing so is to help people and support businesses in the acquisition of goods and services. Service providers of cloud technology can improve their market image by meeting the laid down standards. Several nations have established numerous standards to ensure cloud data security and privacy. In this section, US regulatory standards (e.g., HIPAA and HITECH) and several other international standards like ISO/IEC 27000 and General Data Protection Regulations (GDPR) are elaborated [84].

7.6.1 US STANDARDS

1. **HIPAA:** The Health Insurance Portability and Accountability Act is a federal law, laid down to protect the health and patient care systems. The Health and Human Services (HHS) Secretary is required by the HIPAA to establish the guidelines, acts, and rules for the security and privacy of health data. Therefore, the HIPAA Security and Privacy Rules were issued by the HSS. The primary purpose of security rules is to secure patient healthcare data by enabling bodies to accept information technology for the betterment of health services and to provide the services to individuals and healthcare professionals in a qualitative manner. In particular, the security rules require technological bodies to utilize administrative, physical, and technical safeguards for the protection of patients' health data and also to provide security against all expected threats, thereby confirming confidentiality, integrity, and compliance.

   The HIPAA Privacy Rule focuses on establishing the guidelines and standards to save patients' medical data. The rule imparts adequate safeguards to secure patient health records and also imposes restrictions on data usage without the patient's authorization, thereby reducing the chances of health or patient data misuse. These rules give patients the right to inspect and obtain a copy of their medical records, hence giving them a chance to rectify incorrect information [84–86].

2. **HITECH:** The Health Information Technology for Economic and Clinical Health Act is health legislation created by the HHS, aimed at expanding and accelerating the adoption of EHRs to upgrade the performance of healthcare systems. This act inspires and facilitates healthcare professionals by giving them rewards, granting their programs, along with establishing adequate privacy and security measures, and hence encouraging trust in EHRs. It also motivates funding for the development of healthcare systems. The regulations of the HITECH act were inspired by the lack of a secure infrastructure, the scarcity of economic resources, and insufficient technical understanding. For example, for becoming the user of electronic health records from 2011 to 2021, the healthcare professionals might receive up to $63,750 as an additional incentive to survive the financial hurdles. The US government has also allocated approximately $650 million under the HITECH Act to design an infrastructure for health information exchange, termed the National Health Information Network, and to set some policies and standards to assure the secured transfer of health information via the internet [84,87].

7.6.2 International Standards

1. **ISO/IEC 27000-Series:** The series is a set of standards for directing information safety issues. The is the joint publication of the International Organization for Standardization (ISO) and the International Electrotechnical Commission (IEC). The series offers standards on information security management within an information security management system (ISMS). The connectivity among various standards of the ISO and IEC 27000 series shows that on the basis of purpose and scope, the standards can be broadly subdivided into four categories:

    (a) The vocaulary and terminology category gives a briefing about ISMS fundamentals and explains relevant terminologies.

    (b) The requirement standards category specifies the guidelines for ISMS development and its operation.

    (c) The guideline standards category issues guidance on practical implementation to protect information from several corners.

    (d) The sector-specific guideline standards comprise rules that address several industrial sectors such as telecommunications and finance.

The other mentioned standards provide guidance and support for ISO/IEC 27001/27002 audits and the certification process [84]:

• ISO/IEC 27001 defines the requirements for developing, implementing, maintaining, and monitoring with continuous improvement in the information security management system and its alignment with the objectives of the organization. This certification protects information assets and helps in the restoration of patient assurance in cloud service providers. The Plan-Do-Check-Act (PDCA) model is adopted by standards to design information security management system processes which also confirms that the ISMS is developed implemented, measured, evaluated, and upgraded continuously. The current standard cites 1400 controls divided into 14 control objectives, each objective comprising communication security, encryption, and information security incident management. Normally, an accredited registrar reports a rise in the requirements for ISO/IEC 27001 certification from service providers [88].

- The ISO/IEC 27002 emphasizes safety parameters throughout the system's planning and development phases. This mainly provides guidelines on the information security standards of organization and information security management practices, along with the selection, implementation, and management of controls, taking into account the information security risk environment of the organization. The purpose of designing this is for the use of organizations that want to:
  (a) Choose controls during the process of adopting an ISMS on the basis of ISO/IEC 27001;
  (b) Implement widely accepted information security controls;
  (c) Design information security management guidelines for themselves [89].
2. **EU General Data Protection Regulation (GDPR):** The GDPR is a regulation in the European Union (EU), which manages the protection of individual health data of EU citizens. The current law improves people's privacy rights and empowers authorities to take action against non-compliant organizations. This new rule provides personal data protection to citizens of the EU in the 28 member states and is intended to coordinate the privacy laws for local data throughout Europe. The regulations will help to gain customers' trust in several digital facilities by putting aside fears, which will result in an economic upswing.

   The GDPR was launched on May 25, 2018, and thereafter replaced the previous regulations on data protection. It offers numerous services like greater control over a user's data, protection from a free flow of personal data within EU boundaries, and also controls data export outside the EU. This law is relevant all over the world and applies to each organization handling EU citizens' data such as data controllers and processors who gather or process private data of residents and also to those who are providing data-related goods and services to EU residents [84,90].

7.7 SERVICE PROVIDERS FOR THE HEALTHCARE SECTOR

Many IT companies provide cloud computing services for a longer time in the patient care sector. Healthcare cloud storage solutions allow the expansion and scale-up of IT infrastructures in patient care to satisfy overall needs with ease. A few well-known companies providing the services in this area are:

- **Amazon Web Services (AWS):** AWS mainly focuses on supporting healthcare professionals by offering them efficient and standard services for patient care, reducing the unnecessary waste of time needed to perform existing tasks and allowing access to analytical facilities. AWS also prioritizes compliance with all security and privacy requirements.
- **Microsoft Azure:** This is another recognized healthcare cloud service provider, delivering solutions over an entire range, starting from the Internet of Things (IoT) to big data and analytics. This provides all the tools required to strengthen the care teams, engage patients, and optimize clinical as well as operational effectiveness. This also allows facilities regarding clinical analysis, remote patient monitoring, and care coordination.
- **Google Cloud Platform:** This provides an upgraded infrastructure with analytics and big data capabilities with an emphasis on code development rather than server configuration. Google Cloud Platform is committed to meeting strict security and complying with regulatory controls like HIPAA, enabling healthcare organizations to trust them. This supplies a variety of products like cloud virtual networks, cloud storage and databases, and a cloud machine learning engine [91].

Some other leading market players in healthcare cloud computing are summarized in Table 7.4.

TABLE 7.4

Cloud-Based Healthcare Service Providers with Details

Name of Service Provider	Company Type	Address of Headquarters and Website	Concerned Areas of Healthcare
IBM healthcare	Public Company	Armonk, New York www.ibm.com [92]	Disease Diagnosis and Treatment, Medical Imaging, Healthcare Operations, Clinical Research [93]
ClearDATA	Privately Held	Austin, Texas www.cleardata.com [94]	Data Privacy Risks, Data Management Services, Healthcare IT Infrastructure [95]
Athenahealth	Privately Held	Watertown, Massachusetts www.athenahealth.com [96]	Electronic Health Records, Revenue Cycle Management, Patient Engagement, Mobile Capabilities, Telehealth [97]
Siemens Healthineers	Public Company	Erlangen, Germany http://siemenshealthineers.com [98]	Medical Imaging, Laboratory Diagnosis, Digital Health Solutions and Consulting, Clinical Field Educational Programs, Laboratory Management Software Tools [99]
Philips HealthSuite	Privately Held	Los Angeles, California www.healthsuite.com/	Claim Processing & Audit, Revenue Cycle Management, Healthcare Financial Inclusion, Maintenance Services, Software Development for Healthcare Organization [100]
Allscripts Healthcare	Public Company	Chicago, United States of America www.allscripts.com [101]	Electronic Health Records (EHR), Financial Management Solutions, Population Health Management Solutions, Precision Medicine, Consumer Solutions, Entering Prescription Information, Managing Orders for Lab Tests and Medical Workflows [102]
Fujifilm Holdings	Public Company	Tokyo, Japan www.fujifilm.com [103]	X-ray Imaging, Diagnostics, Endoscopes, Ultrasound Diagnostics, Medical IT, *in vitro* Diagnostic System [104]
GE Healthcare	Public Company	Chicago, United States of America www.gehealthcare.com [105]	Advanced Visualization, Dose Management, Hemodynamic Recording, Medical Affairs and Medical Information Center, Imaging Patient Monitoring, Digital Solutions, Documentation Library, Healthcare Technology Management, Service Agreements [106]
NetApp	Public Company	Sunnyvale, California www.netapp.com/	Network Storage, Cloud Computing, Storage Efficiency, Information Management, Data Storage, and Hybrid Cloud [107]
CareCloud	Public Company	Somerset, NJ www.CareCloud.com	Healthcare IT, Mobile Applications, Practice Management, Physicians' Practices, Revenue Cycle Management, EHR, Electronic Health Records, and Patient Portal [108]

7.8   CONCLUSION

Cloud computing is being adopted continuously in every part of the world. It is a rapidly growing and developing technology that supports better use of IT infrastructure, services, and applications. In the patient care industry, cloud-based technologies are modifying the scenario in many ways and at a much faster pace. In healthcare, starting from hospitalization to filling out insurance documents, the implementation of the cloud is making the entire process easy and smooth. It offers several other benefits that have been discussed above and which resolve issues related to storage, bandwidth, mobility, and record accessibility. Most important among the benefits are deductions in patient care charges and resource optimization, which became possible due to the reduced need for separate infrastructure, software, and hardware requirements for every individual hospital. Standardized cloud-based applications allow the sharing of software, hardware, and information, hence providing advantages not only to patients but also to doctors, pharmacies, insurance companies, imagining centers, and all healthcare personnel. As the shared information is readily accessible from anywhere at any time, this additional gain helps the individual to retrieve their data in case of any loss and also to assist medical organizations in yielding better patient care results.

Information systems, telemedicine, drug discovery, bioinformatics, and hospital management systems are a few fields of healthcare that are gaining benefit from cloud computing, as renowned IT companies serve in this area, such as AWS, Microsoft Azure, Netapp, and Cloudcare. Certain challenges like security and privacy concerns, and legal, technical, and management issues, also arise during implementation, but the need of the hour is to make use of the new cloud technology for the welfare of patients. The remaining problems will be easily resolved over a period of time by imposing stricter regulatory requirements, such as those laid down by HIPAA, HITECH, and other organizations. Although the adoption of the computational cloud infrastructure in patient care is advancing slowly despite all the obstacles, the application of best practices to design, implement, and use cloud computing will bring continuous growth in cloud-based hospital and patient care systems.

ACKNOWLEDGMENT

The authors are grateful to Dean Pharmacy and the management of Medi-caps University, Indore for providing kind cooperation and support for the completion of this work.

REFERENCES

[1] Duger, A., Leaning, J et al., How is patient care a human rights issue?, *Health and human rights resource guide*, FXB Center for Health and Human Rights and Open Society Foundations, 5th Ed., pp. 42, 2013.

[2] Joshi, G.P., Acharya, S., Kim, C.S., Kim, B.S., Kim, S.W., Smart solutions in elderly care facilities with RFID system and its integration with wireless sensor networks. *International Journal of Distributed Sensor Networks*, 10, 1–11, 2014.

[3] Chatman, C., How cloud computing is changing the face of health care information technology. *Journal of Health Care Compliance*, 12, 37–70, 2010.

[4] Rao, G.N., How can we improve patient care. *Community Eye Health*, 15, 1–3, 2002.

[5] Atasoy, H., Greenwood, B.N., McCullough, J. S., The digitization of patient care: A review of the effects of electronic health records on health care quality and utilization. *Annual Review of Public Health*, 40, 487–500, 2019.

[6] Malik, G.S., Health cloud implementation using smart analytics features. *International Journal of Technical Research & Science*, 14–23, 2020.

[7] Aguirre, R.R., Suarez, O., Fuentes, M., Gonzalez, M.A.S., Electronic health record implementation: A review of resources and tools monitoring. *Cureus*, 11, e5649, 2019.

[8] Bamiah, M., Brohi, S., Chuprat, S., Ab Manan, J.L., A study on significance of adopting cloud computing paradigm in healthcare sector. *International Conference on Cloud Computing Technologies, Applications and Management*, 65–68, 2012.

[9] Erfannia, L., Sadoughi. F., Sheikhtaheri, A., The advantages of implementing cloud computing in the health industry of Iran: A qualitative study. *International Journal of Computer Science and Network Security*, 18, 198–206, 2018.

[10] MarketsWatch, Healthcare Cloud Computing Market Research Report (2021 to 2026), https://www.marketwatch.com/press-release/healthcare-cloud-computing-market-research-report-2021-to-2026-hy-technology-product-distribution-channel-application-and-region-2021-12-17, 2021

[11] Masrom, M., Rahimli, A., Cloud computing adoption in the healthcare sector: A SWOT analysis. *Asian Social Science*, 11, 12–18, 2015.

[12] Mell, P., Grance, T., The NIST definition of cloud computing. *National Institute of Standards and Technology Special Publication 800-145*, 1–7, 2011.

[13] Rountree, D., Castrillo, I., *The Basics of Cloud Computing Understanding the Fundamentals of Cloud Computing in Theory and Practice*, pp. 1–17, Syngress 2014.

[14] Mekawiea, N., Yehia, K., Challenges of deploying cloud computing in ehealth, *Procedia Computer Science*, 181,1049–1057, 2021.

[15] Joshi, M., Tewari, N., Budhani, S.K., Security challenges in implementing a secured hybrid cloud model for e-health services. *9th International Conference System Modeling and Advancement in Research Trends (SMART)*, 3–7, 2020.

[16] Laszewski, T., Nauduri, P., *Migrating to the Cloud: Oracle Client/Server Modernization*, pp. 1–19, Syngress 2011.

[17] Bhandayker, Y.R., A study on the research challenges and trends of cloud computing. *International Journal of Multidisciplinary Research Review*, 4, 441–447, 2019.

[18] Rosy, M.A., Muthu, M.F.X., Shyamala, D., Challenges, service models and deployment models of cloud computing. *Journal of Emerging Technologies and Innovative Research*, 6, 81–86, 2019.

[19] WBOC Delmarva's News Leader, https://www.wboc.com/story/44146067/global-healthcare-cloud-computing-market-2021-is-expected-to-register-a-cagr-of-18-with-top-countries-data-industry-size-share-business-growth, 2021

[20] Mesbahi, M.R., Rahmani, A.M., Hosseinzadeh, M., Reliability and high availability in cloud computing environments: A reference roadmap. *Human-centric Computing and Information Sciences*, 8, 1–31, 2018.

[21] Maniah, S.B., Gaol, F.L., Abdurachman, E., A systematic literature review: Risk analysis in cloud migration. *Journal of King Saud University – Computer and Information Sciences*, 1–10, 2021.

[22] Gu, D., Yang, X., Deng, S., Liang, C., Wang, X., Wu, J., Guo, J., Tracking knowledge evolution in cloud health care research: Knowledge map and common word analysis. *Journal of Medical Internet Research*, 22, e15142, 2020.

[23] Misra, S.C., Kumar, A., Munnangi, A.K., Cloud-based healthcare management: identifying the privacy concerns and their moderating effect on the cloud-based health-care services. *Security and Privacy*, 2, e63, 2019.

[24] Singh, R.P., Haleem, A., Javaid, M., Kataria, R., Singhal, S., Cloud computing in solving problems of covid-19 pandemic. *Journal of Industrial Integration and Management*, 6, 209–219, 2021.

[25] Shad, G., Healthcare information technology & cloud evolution, status and future. *International Journal of Engineering Research & Technology*, 6, 445–459, 2017.

[26] Hitachi Data Systems, How to improve healthcare with cloud computing, http://docs.media.bitpipe.com/io_10x/io_108673/item_650544/cloud%20computing%20wp.pdf, 2012

[27] Equity Bulls, IBM Business Partner MedTrak Systems provides cloud-based service to healthcare clients, https://www.equitybulls.com/admin/news2006/news_det.asp?id=47172, 2009

[28] Joseph, A., Ndaba, A.Z., The assessment of cloud computing technology in health care records management: Opportunities and challenges. *International Journal of Science and Research*, 6, 700–770, 2017.

[29] HHS.gov Health Information Privacy, Health Information Technology, https://www.hhs.gov/hipaa/for-professionals/special-topics/health-information-technology/index.html, 2020

[30] IBM Press Room, European Union consortium launches advanced cloud computing project with hospital and smart power grid provider, https://newsroom.ibm.com/2010-11-22-European-Union-Consortium-Launches-Advanced-Cloud-Computing-Project-With-Hospital-and-Smart-Power-Grid-Provider, 2010

[31] Korea IT Times IT Times, Telstra Plans launch of e-health cloud services, tip of the iceberg for opportunity, http://www.koreaittimes.com/news/articleView.html?idxno=9826, 2010

[32] Geetha, K., Impact of cloud database in medical healthcare records based on secure access. *International Journal of Engineering and Advanced Technology*, 8, 652–654, 2019.

[33] Sharmila, K., A review paper on cloud computing models. *Journal of Analysis and Computation*, ICAIMI 2020, 1–5, 2020.

[34] Devadass, L., Sekaran, S.S., Thinakaran, R., Cloud computing in healthcare. *International Journal of Students' Research in Technology & Management*, 5, 25–31, 2017.

[35] Rashid, A., Chaturvedi, A., Cloud computing characteristics and services: A brief review. *International Journal of Computer Sciences and Engineering*, 7, 421–426, 2019.

[36] Data Flair, Features of Cloud Computing – 10 Major Characteristics of Cloud Computing, https://data-flair.training/blogs/features-of-cloud-computing/, 2019

[37] Chapter 247, Cloud computing in healthcare, https://www.chapter247.com/blog/cloud-computing-healthcare/, 2019

[38] Intellectsoft, Cloud computing in healthcare as the future of the industry, https://www.intellectsoft.net/blog/cloud-computing-in-healthcare/, 2021

[39] Fernandez, G., Torre-Diez, I.D.L., Rodrigues, J.J.P.C., Analysis of the cloud computing paradigm on mobile health records systems. *Sixth International Conference on Innovative Mobile and Internet Services in Ubiquitous Computing*, 927–932, 2012.

[40] Reddy, G.N., Reddy, G.J.U., Study of cloud computing in healthcare industry. *International Journal of Scientific & Engineering Research*, 4, 68–71, 2013.

[41] Ahmadi, M., Aslani, N., Capabilities and advantages of cloud computing in the implementation of electronic health record. *Acta Informatica Medica*, 26, 24–28, 2018.

[42] EHRINPRACTICE, Cloud EHR: A complete buyers' guide, https://www.ehrinpractice.com/cloud-ehr-buyers-guide.html, 2020.

[43] Galen Data, 9 Key benefits of cloud computing in healthcare, https://www.galendata.com/9-benefits-cloud-computing-healthcare/, 2019

[44] IoT for All, How does cloud computing benefit the healthcare industry?, https://www.iotforall.com/how-does-cloud-computing-benefit-healthcare-industry, 2020

[45] Ahuja, S. P., Mani, S., Zambrano, J., A survey of the state of cloud computing in healthcare. *Network and Communication Technologies*, 1, 12–19, 2012.

[46] LeewayHertz, How does cloud computing impact healthcare industry?, https://www.leewayhertz.com/cloud-computing-in-healthcare/

[47] Yao, Q., Han, X., Ma, X.K., Xue, Y.F., Chen, Y.J., Li, J.S., Cloud-based hospital information system as a service for grassroots healthcare institutions. *Journal of Medical Systems*, 38, 1–7, 2014.

[48] HIT Infrastructure, Benefits of cloud-based health information management systems, https://hitinfrastructure.com/news/benefits-of-cloud-based-health-information-management-system-s, 2016

[49] Sharma, N., Anand, A., Husain, A., Cloud based healthcare services for telemedicine practices using internet of things. *Journal of Critical Reviews*, 7, 2605–2610, 2020.

[50] Kissi, J., Dai, B., Dogbe, C.S.K., Banahene, J., Predictive factors of physicians' satisfaction with telemedicine services acceptance. *Health Informatics Journal*, 26, 1–15, 2019.

[51] Bahl, S., Singh, R. P., Javaid, M., Khan, I. H., Vaishya, R., Suman, R., Telemedicine technologies for confronting covid-19 pandemic: A review. *Journal of Industrial Integration and Management*, 5, 547–561, 2020.

[52] Nigam, V. K., Bhatia, S., Impact of cloud computing on health care. *International Research Journal of Engineering and Technology*, 3, 2804–2810, 2016.

[53] The Scientific World, Application of cloud computing technology in library services, https://www.scientificworldinfo.com/2021/03/application-of-cloud-computing-in-libraries.html, 2021

[54] Al-Ani, M.S., Ibrahim, M.S., Efficient virtual universities via cloud computing environment. *Journal of Emerging Trends in Computing and Information Sciences*, 3, 1553–1561, 2012.

[55] Sutton, R.T., Pincock, D., Baumgart, D.C., Sadowski, D.C., Fedorak, R.N., Kroeke, K.I., An overview of clinical decision support systems: Benefits, risks, and strategies for success. *NPJ Digital Medicine*, 3, 1–10, 2020.

[56] Oh, S., Cha, J., Ji, M., Kang, H., Kim, S., Heo, E., Han, J.S., Kang, H., Chae, H., Hwang, H., Yoo, S., Architecture design of healthcare software-as-a-service platform for cloud-based clinical decision support service. *Healthcare Informatics Research*, 21, 102–110, 2015.

[57] Kuo, M.H., Kushniruk, A., Borycki, E., Cloud computing for health information management. *Health Management*, 13, 1–5, 2013.

[58] Cloud Standards Customer Council, Impact of cloud computing on healthcare version 2.0, https://www.omg.org/cloud/deliverables/CSCC-Impact-of-Cloud-Computing-on-Healthcare.pdf, 2017

[59] SelectHub, The best cloud medical billing software solutions, https://www.selecthub.com/medical-billing/cloud-medical-billing-software/, 2021

[60] SearchHealthIT, Revenue cycle management, https://searchhealthit.techtarget.com/definition/revenue-cycle-management-RCM, 2017

[61] Businesswire, Flatiron Health Ranked the Top End-to-End Oncology Technology Solution by Black Book Research, https://www.businesswire.com/news/home/20190402005833/en/Flatiron-Health-Ranked-the-Top-End-to-End-Oncology-Technology-Solution-by-Black-Book-Research, 2019

[62] Buber, M., Sucu, F., Bulut, I., Kursun, R., Cloud computing environments which can be used in health education. *International Journal of Intelligent Systems and Applications in Engineering*, 3, 124–126, 2015.

[63] Capterra, 3 Best LMS (Learning Management Systems) software for healthcare, https://blog.capterra.com/top-rated-learning-management-systems-for-healthcare/, 2019

[64] Navale, V., Bourne, P.E., Cloud computing applications for biomedical Science: A perspective. *PLOS Computational Biology*, 14, e1006144, 2018.

[65] Thakur, R.S., Bandopadhyay, R., Role of cloud computing in bioinformatics research for handling the huge biological data, *Biology of Useful Plants And Microbes*, pp. 321–329, Narosa Publishing House, 2013.

[66] Moghaddasi, H., Tabrizi, A.T., Applications of cloud computing in health systems. *Global Journal of Health Science*, 9, 33–39, 2017.

[67] Lee, H., Using bioinformatics applications on the cloud, http://dsc.soic.indiana.edu/publications/bioinformatics.pdf, 2013

[68] McCarthy, A., Drug discovery in the clouds. *Chemistry & Biology*, 19, 1–2, 2019.

[69] ZDNet, Pharma companies are counting on cloud computing and AI to make drug development faster and cheaper, https://www.zdnet.com/article/pharma-companies-are-counting-on-cloud-computing-and-ai-to-make-drug-development-faster-and-cheaper/, 2019

[70] Microsoft Research Blog, Cloud computing unlocks drug discovery, https://www.microsoft.com/en-us/research/blog/cloud-computing-unlocks-drug-discovery/, 2012

[71] Bost, F., Jacobs, R.T., Kowalczyk, P., Informatics for neglected diseases collaborations. *Current Opinion in Drug Discovery & Development*, 13, 286–296, 2010.

[72] Griebel, L., Prokosch, H.U., Köpcke, F., Toddenroth, D., Christoph, J., Leb, I., Engel, I., Sedlmayr, M., A scoping review of cloud computing in healthcare. *BMC Medical Informatics and Decision Making*, 15, 1–16, 2015.

[73] The Economist Intelligence Unit, Ascending cloud: The adoption of cloud computing in five industries executive summary, https://eiuperspectives.economist.com/technology-innovation/ascending-cloud-adoption-cloud-computing-five-industries-0, 2016

[74] Ali, O., Shrestha, A., Soar, J., Wamba, S. F., Cloud computing-enabled healthcare opportunities, issues and applications: A systematic review. *International Journal of Information Management*, 43, 146–158, 2018.

[75] Lian, J.W., Yen, D.C., Wang, Y.T., An exploratory study to understand the critical factors affecting the decision to adopt cloud computing in Taiwan hospital. *International Journal of Information Management*, 34, 28–36, 2013.

[76] Mehraeen, E., Ghazisaeedi, M., Farzi, J., Mirshekari, S., Security challenges in healthcare cloud computing: A systematic review. *Global Journal of Health Science*, 9, 157–166, 2017.

[77] Rodrigues, J.J.P.C., Torre, I.D.L., Fernández, G., López-Coronado, M., Analysis of the security and privacy requirements of cloud-based electronic health records systems. *Journal of Medical Internet Research*, 15, e186, 2013.

[78] Kuo, M., Opportunities and challenges of cloud computing to improve health care services. *Journal of Medical Internet Research*, 13, e67, 2011.

[79] Minister of Justice, Canada, Personal Information Protection and Electronic Documents Act (PIPEDA), http://laws.justice.gc.ca/PDF/Readability/P-8.6.pdf, 2011

[80] European Network and Information Security Agency ENISA, Cloud Computing: Benefits, Risks and Recommendations for Information Security, http://www.enisa.europa.eu/act/rm/files/deliverables/cloud-computing-risk-assessment 2009

[81] Guo, Y., Kuo, M.H., Sahama, T., Cloud computing for healthcare research information sharing. *4th IEEE International Conference on Cloud Computing Technology and Science Proceedings*, 889–894, 2012.

[82] Borgman, H.P., Bahli, B., Heier, H., Schewski, F., Cloudrise: Exploring cloud computing adoption and governance with the TOE framework. *46th Hawaii International Conference on System Science*, 4425–4435, 2013.

[83] Ashtari, S., Eydgahi, A., Lee, H., Exploring cloud computing implementation issues in healthcare industry. *Transactions of the International Conference on Health Information Technology Advancement*, 3, 122–129, 2015.

[84] Issa, Y.A., Ottom, M.A., Tamrawi, A., eHealth cloud security challenges: A survey. *Journal of Healthcare Engineering*, 1–15, 2019.

[85] HHS.gov Health Information Privacy, Summary of the HIPAA Security Rule, vol. 5, US Department of Health & Human Services (HHS), Washington, DC, https://www.hhs.gov/hipaa/for-professionals/security/laws-regulations/index.html

[86] HHS.gov Health Information Privacy, Summary of the HIPAA Privacy Rule, vol. 5, US Department of Health & Human Services (HHS), Washington, DC, https://www.hhs.gov/hipaa/for-professionals/privacy/laws-regulations/index.html

[87] Blumenthal, D., Launching HITECH. *New England Journal of Medicine*, 362, 382–385, 2010.

[88] ISO/IEC 27001:2013, Information Technology-Security Techniques-Information security management systems-Requirements, https://www.iso.org/standard/54534.html, 2013

[89] ISO/IEC 27002:2013, Information Technology- Security Techniques – Code of Practice for Information Security Control, http://www.iso27001security.com/html/27002.html, 2013

[90] EU General Data Protection Regulation (GDPR), https://gdpr.eu/what-is-gdpr/, 2017

[91] Thavamani, S., Rajakumar, M., Privacy preserving healthcare data using cloud computing. *International Journal of Innovative Technology and Exploring Engineering*, 8, 118–124, 2019.

[92] IBMInformationTechnology&Services,https://www.linkedin.com/company/ibm/?originalSubdomain=in

[93] IBM, What is healthcare technology?, https://www.ibm.com/topics/healthcare-technology

[94] ClearDATA, https://www.linkedin.com/company/cleardata-networks/

[95] ClearDATA, http://www.cleardata.com

[96] Athena Health Care Systems, https://www.linkedin.com/company/athenahealth/about/

[97] Athenahealth, http://www.athenahealth.com

[98] Siemens Healthineers, https://www.linkedin.com/company/siemens-healthineers/?originalSubdomain=in

[99] Siemens Healthineers, http://siemens-healthineers.com

[100] HealthSuite LLC, https://www.linkedin.com/company/healthsuite/about/

[101] Allscripts, https://www.linkedin.com/company/allscripts/

[102] Allscripts, www.allscripts.com.

[103] FUJIFILM Corporation, https://www.linkedin.com/company/fujifilmcorporation/about/

[104] FUJIFILM Healthcare, https://www.fujifilm.com/jp/en/about/corporate/field/healthcare

[105] GE Healthcare, https://www.linkedin.com/company/gehealthcare/

[106] GE Healthcare, https://www.gehealthcare.com/

[107] NetApp, https://www.linkedin.com/company/netapp/about/

[108] CareCloud, https://www.linkedin.com/company/carecloud/about/

8 Advancement in Gene Delivery

The Role of Bioinformatics

Shilpa Rawat, Akash Chauhan, Rishabha Malviya,
Md. Aftab Alam, and Swati Verma
Galgotias University, Greater Noida, India

Shivkanya Fuloria
AIMST University, Bedong, Malaysia

CONTENTS

DOI: 10.1201/9781003226949-8

8.1   INTRODUCTION

Leroy Hood and Marvin Carruthers (MC) identified the genomes of 579 humans, not only mapping *in situ* hybridization but also inventing an automated procedure of DNA sequencing; this project and related organization were founded in 1988. Huang et al. used the above principle in molecular biology investigations in 2000. Thus, this software is a fusion of evaluating biological signals (BS) and generating databases relating to the structures and protein sequencing set-up of the European Molecular Biology Laboratory and GenBank (GB). According to recent research, this program is to target and enclose every detailed study of protein structure analysis with the functional detail of the protein or gene [1, 2]. In 1970, Paulein Hogewag and Bew Heasper coined the term "bioinformatics." Bioinformatics was described as 'the science of informatics phenomena in biology." Bioinformatics is a mix of two terms: bio + information technology, implying that there is an application for biological information. Computational systems aid in the understanding of biological data in bioinformatics. Examples of biological data include DNA and proteins. Bioinformatics is an interdisciplinary area that incorporates biology, mathematics, computer science, chemistry, physics, and information engineering. This field of research is capable of comprehending biological facts. This technology assists in the storage, retrieval, manipulation, and sharing of biological data [3].

Bioinformatics is a statistical approach used to direct clear biological inquiry. Bioinformatics solves the entire query with the assistance of computational and mathematical equations (as shown in Figure 8.1). So, to comprehend bioinformatics tools, the following is a list of some of the most popular bioinformatics tools. Phylogenetic and evolutionary research. The primary focus of medication design and discovery. Analysis of the entire genome, Restrictions on searches, Gene expression, Designing epitopes, conducting research on protein-protein interactions, and locating mutation hotspots [3].

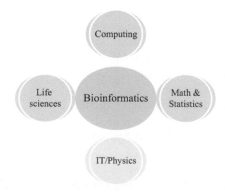

FIGURE 8.1   Composition of bioinformatics.

Bioinformatics is a branch of science that studies computational methods for investigating biological problems. This is the science of database computing, which involves inventing and calculating algorithms to speed up biological research and statistical methodologies. Bioinformatics is software that is used to tackle various biological problems depending on current data. It is the study of how to address biotic problems based on current research findings. The development of software and algorithms, as well as the analysis and interpretation of biological data using specific algorithms and various software tools, are the two main components of bioinformatics [4]. It establishes a path for collecting all data related to a study. It will assist researchers in getting an idea of which process they will use to conduct experiments and will provide them with good results from the investigation. Bioinformatics is a research-based field that encompasses all aspects of biotic acquisition. The data's clarity, reporting, deposition, and evaluation, as well as interpolation, incorporate numerous new biological research, computational, and mathematical methodologies. Bioinformatics has grown to be a worldwide endeavor, with networks capable of gaining access to genetic information and continuing to allow the application of new software for quick analysis. Several large projects focused on making gene and protein datasets available are easily accessible online to the entire fraternity of scientists [5]. Bioinformatics is crucial in the discovery of new biological relationships. It is quite beneficial in managing a large amount of data, and providing valid responses. Bioinformatics has made significant contributions to genetic biology in the modern era. It is the approach used to determine biotic findings and is hence regarded as the best source of biological data. Bioinformatics software plays an important role in creating or predicting scientific findings for exploratory purposes [6]. To analyze data, a combination of science is required, including chemistry, biology, genetics/genomics, statistics, and computer science. Signaling and imaging techniques in bioinformatics, which are essential components of biology and experimental molecular biology, enable the extraction of results from massive amounts of raw data. It sequences genomes, monitors mutations, and analyzes genetic and genomic data. G-DOC Plus (*software) is a bioinformatics platform with integrated data and tools that organizes and analyzes clinical data using cloud computing [7–9].

Bioinformatics applications for future cancer medicines and treatments must be discovered.

Many molecular targeting drugs, like cancer therapies, only function on subsets of people. As a result, many people receive unsatisfactory therapy responses, which are frequently costly. On the other hand, the Human Genome Project (HGP), expanded and advanced in 2003, exerted a demand on computational technology to be applied in the treatment of cancer. Researchers and specialists have used bioinformatics to conduct an extensive and speedy study on bioinformatics tools, which have been identified as an important tool in the treatment and cure of neoplastic diseases/cancer [8].

In 2003, the HGP supplied a tremendous quantity of information and genomic data to the scientific world. Bioinformatics is used in a variety of fields:

1. Examination of a gene expression picture;
2. Detecting the protein DNA sequence to ascertain its location inside the cell in gene therapy;
3. Observing and reporting hereditary disorders such as cancer, sickle cell disease, and cystic fibrosis;
4. In the creation of a new medicine or drug delivery technology to improve therapeutic response;
5. Examining the protein DNA sequence array to identify the exact gene location;
6. Defining the RNA array for their assumed models. [10].

In the field of biomedical informatics, the volume of data is rapidly and exponentially expanding, as illustrated in Figure 8.2. ProteomicsDB8, which has a data volume of around 5.17 TB, according to the Swiss-Prot database of human genes, covers approximately 92 percent of the human gene. Many patients' data have already been electronically saved, and the scan generated from this data improves and increases medical facilities as well as research opportunities. Medical imaging is an example of this, as technology can extract or generate vast amounts of data, even with complex properties [11]. By making extensive use of Quantative Structure-Activity Relationship (QSAR)

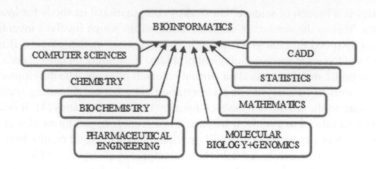

FIGURE 8.2 Multidisciplinary sectors in bioinformatics.

TABLE 8.1

Bioinformatics Tools and Advantages for a General-Purpose Programming Language

Bioinformatics Tools	Era	Application	Reference
Gene quiz (GQ)	1994 (earliest)	Protein processing bench (sets of new standards for bioinformatics software)	[12]
Lab base (LB)	1998	Dataset mapping for data sequencing	[13]
Phred-Phrap consed (PPC)	1998	Assembly and completion of the genome	[14]
Swiss knife (SW)	1999	SWISS-PROT protein sequence data bank	[15]
MuMmer (MM)	1999	Whole genome sequencing (WGS)	[16]

and computational chemistry, bioinformatics has revolutionized drug discovery and delivery development. The advancement of genomics has made it easier to hold a vast number of datasets, including computational tools like MAFT, Mauve, Jaligner, HMMER, BioEdit, SeWeR, VeeScreen, ORF Finder, Genome Workbench, Pepinfo/Pep window/Pepstats, SAPS, T-Coffee, TRansseq, BLAST, and FASTA. Table 8.1 shows some useful tools with their advantages. This facilitates the examination of enormous amounts of data using bioinformatics. Using bioinformatics, we can extract all of the critical data for each organism, particularly genetics and related disciplines of interest. Because of the medication's specific and localized impact on the cell, this was a novel delivery strategy that resulted in improved characteristic qualities such as drug effectiveness, efficiency, potency, lowered adverse responses, other side effects, and reduced possible secondary facts. Many computational measures, including the unlocking of complex methodologies and procedures, are used to accelerate the identification and selected election processes [17]. Computational technologies are gradually becoming a key component of research, hastening the scientific research process, which is the primary goal of computational technology and bioinformatics, because it contains a database of information from several disciplines such as chemistry and biological biotechnology. It also helps to explain drug target binds, such as proteins and enzymes involved in target delivery [18]. The initial step in updating and modernizing the technique is to target a specific site in the desired genome at a certain sequence in the nucleic chain for better screening analysis using different models such as Hughes, Rees, and others. Because of the further phenotypic screening results, it was considered to be premature [17–19].

Bioinformatics, by merging knowledge from several fields, can help with a variety of issues at a particular level. Bioinformatics has become a multidisciplinary source that reproduces different methods and computational tools and technologies for evaluating biological and genomic data as

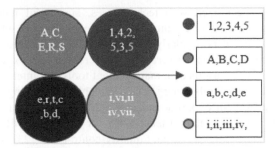

FIGURE 8.3 How bioinformatics can help us achieve our goals.

a result of this perfect mix and from the gathering of data from all of the aforementioned fields (as shown in Figure 8.3) [20].

Bioinformatics has made significant progress in improving society's health and safety, despite an increase in death and morbidity rates. Because of its broad scope of operations, it has played a critical role in restoring equilibrium by improving the safety and effectiveness of pharmaceuticals, and it can handle both pre-clinical and post-clinical responsibilities. Bioinformatics aids in the analysis and determination of novel drugs and improved ways of diagnosis by combining verified information from genetics, biotechnology, computer technology, and statistics. Various contemporary technologies, including docking, molecular dynamic simulations, and QSAR, are helpful in this research procedure for obtaining fast results. One of the most significant achievements of bioinformatics is the analysis of genetic data, especially the assessment of the HGP. The future of bioinformatics involves its commitment to the fundamental aspects of human genetics, which will contribute to improved therapeutic target identification and personalized therapy [21].

Software that incorporates databases and assists in the elimination of bias and the conduct of structural design studies includes electronic data capture (EDC), remote data capture (RDC), and electronic case report (ECR) forms. Oracle and e-clinical are two examples of software that have been regarded as useful for statistical analysis and marketing monitoring. There are two types of genetic data: nucleotide databases and protein databases. These two databases work together to build a library, which is represented and kept in a bioinformatics warehouse.

The nucleotide database is sourced from the following websites:

- The National Centre for Biotechnology Information (www.ncbi.nlm.gov.in)
- The European Molecular Biology Laboratories (EMBL) (www.ebi.ac.uk)
- Japan's DNA Data Bank (JDDB) (www.ddbj.nig.ac.jp)
- Protein Information Resources (www.pir.georgetown.edu)
- "SWISS-PROT" (SP) (www.expasy.ch/sprot/)
- Protein Data Base (www.pdb.org)

The following are some other protein databases: Pfams, PRINTS, BLOCKS, POROSITY, and Interpro. The combination of biology and computer science has resulted in bioinformatics. As a result, it is used to enhance the use of drug attributes for target identification. It is also an excellent resource for predicting protein activity and sequencing sites for altering drug activity and making medicines more target-specific with acceptable protein binds [18, 22].

The span of bioinformatics encompasses several powerful databases holding the greatest possible knowledge in biology, genetics, genomics, computer sciences, and technology using statistical data.

This database aids in the discovery and improvement of medications and medicines, in addition to the development of newer software and technology, procedures, and processing facilities.

Additionally, by utilizing specialized web technologies, successful medicine distribution and discovery can be accomplished. It is essentially a platform through which the general public may access research work, and it is regularly updated to give more efficient work processes and pharmaceutical creation or distribution. As scrutiny has increased over experimental research, most of researchers and scientists use various data management tools and internet technology for simple data filtering. As a result, it has recently emerged as a valuable time-saving and quality-control tool. As scrutiny has increased over an experimental research, most of researchers and scientists use various data management tools and internet technology for simple data filtering. As a result, it has recently emerged as a valuable time-saving and quality-control tool [23]. Internet Depot is a shop that provides easy access to any data. This facilitates the collecting of the vast majority of critical data required for analysis or other research endeavors. The data is organized in such a way that the researcher or reader is encouraged to examine and comprehend it thoroughlySynthesized data saves time when selecting the appropriate data for analysis, a task, or operations because there is no duplication [24].

The major purpose of this bifunctional bioinformatics approach is to improve public health. This combines the processed analytical data, which satisfies all of the requirements for researchers to continue in this area. This could be a management change, a technological update or enhancement, or a functional change in a pharmaceutical or delivery mechanism. The database of this model provides a systematic structure of data that is suited for gathering information for various disorders and proteomics, allowing them to be linked to the healthcare industry. Healthcare is an essential component of any regulatory management system; it also symbolizes a long-term vision of society's physical and mental well-being. The World Health Organization (WHO) defines health as a condition of entire physical, mental, and social well-being, rather than the lack of sickness and infirmity [25].

Because the health of a country's population is closely tied to its growth, and because it is a well-known saying that "a healthy mind lives in a healthy body," concern for public healthcare should be prioritized for productive output. As a result, bioinformatics is focused more on societal healthcare by emphasizing bioinformatics technologies, methods, and systems that are tailored to faster growth in healthcare systems that are simply accepted and stressed in line with public wants and requirements. Genetics is used as a mother source in many research endeavors [26]. Some initiatives, such as the HGP, have been completed to chart a better course forward in the field of healthcare. Bioinformatics has become crucial for this strategy since it includes verified data, detailed analyses, and other results that may be used to complete the process and research work more quickly and reliably [27]. This new approach to development with new technologies provides a better means to detect and treat various aspects of healthcare as technology improves. This bi-domain bio-healthcare informatics depot platform provides all informatory data that aid in several areas such as illness prevention, prediction, and tailored health therapy. These strategies have a direct impact on a country's healthcare development. This bioinformatics technology has been acknowledged as the most effective information and resource platform for promoting public health and scientific study. This informatics is a blend of computer information and biological sciences that aid in healthcare delivery [28]. Healthcare informatics is best understood as an advanced approach or component of a healthcare program that offers professionals informatory data about the patients' health status, making treatment easier and more successful. Healthcare informatics fosters collaboration and the exchange of critical data between patients and healthcare professionals, as well as the management of other healthcare services. According to the US Department of Health, "healthcare informatics is defined as the knowledge, skills, and technologies that enable information to be obtained, managed, utilized, and shared to improve the delivery of health care and accelerate healthcare" [29]. Traditional healthcare delivery systems may be viewed as the foundation for the advancement of healthcare informatics. Healthcare informatics has many synonyms, including eHealth and telehealth, both of which are well-known. Today's research is strongly embedded in the triangle of biological research, healthcare administration and management, and computing technology [30]. Genetics has evolved into the mother of medical research, and it now plays an important role in public health. It investigates the most unusual genetic issues as well as other syndromes and disorders, as well as assisting in diagnosis and therapy. Next-generation sequencing has evolved into a means for the cost-effective examination of enormous amounts of genomic data.

Bioinformatics also works as a guiding hand by providing appropriate and precise data to achieve goals. It acts as a storehouse for a multitude of verifiable and relevant data, making it easy to manage and ensure a healthy outcome for the entire public health sector. This is a one-of-a-kind combination of bioinformatics and genetic biology that has grown into a significant area of biological research.

It also guides the recommendations given regarding the healthcare procedure [25]. It treats ailments in a more complex, accurate, and validated manner, with more sophisticated, accurate, and verified diagnosis and therapy. This mutual integration of bioinformatics and genetic biology yields guidance that is accepted not just by professionals but also by patients. The present approach is known as "the Sanger chain-termination" and was developed by the renowned scientists Paul Berg, Frederick Sanger, and Walter Gilbert. It is a novel sequencing technology for DNA analysis and was followed by single-base alteration. Then, as the research matured, nanotechnology and informatics took over and replaced Sanger sequencing. Next-generation sequencing, or NGS, has the potential to reproduce a vast quantity of data in a single run of equipment, which is why it is in high demand throughout the world and praised by many prominent firms such as Ion Torrent, Oxford Nanopore Technologies, and PacBio. Above all, many action plans have been suggested in response to the same challenge, namely the massification of sequencing data [31].

Bioinformatics is a component of the triangle of health information, data, and knowledge – where information is defined as the particular arrangement of things or the sequence of information, data is defined as a statistical collection of raw facts and figures for reference and analysis, and knowledge is defined as a specific understanding of a subject. This is helped by many computing approaches for analyzing biological databases. There are certain ideal characteristics for healthcare analysis. It needs to be acceptable for all public health, be of low-cost, and be effective across all economic systems. Bioinformatics is a multidisciplinary science that develops methods and tools for displaying distinctive kinds of biological data. Informatics spans many fields, including Alexa software engineering, computational technologies, and statistics, all of which contribute to the extraction of meaningful data.

Informatics is also concerned with diagnosing and treating patients by analyzing data obtained from molecular analysis, qualifying medical imaging, and analyzing information from customers' prescription regimes, as well as Medicare bioinformatics. It is presently being used in selective gene determination for advanced genomic research and a better understanding of problems and demographic disparities. The fundamental purpose of bioinformatics is to offer a home for the information generated by molecular biological technology, which aids in the focusing of a society's healthcare. Healthcare informatics is a synthesis of data and information acquired from several medical fields, such as preclinical, clinical, post-clinical, and healthcare administration management.

With the arrival of a new era, information technology has advanced, assisting various analysts, experimenters, and investigators in improving the health sector and healthcare system, with the primary goal of medical informatics being to make all available data about a patient's health available to healthcare providers. This collected database makes it easier for specialists to choose the best therapy and diagnose illnesses at the right moment [32].

8.2 THE CONCEPTUAL VISION OF BIOINFORMATICS

Bioinformatics is the study of how to examine biological information and genetic information by employing conceptual concepts and statistical approaches, as well as the development of computational tools for huge volumes of biological databases and algorithms to speed up and enhance biological research. The primary goal of creating bioinformatics is to organize enormous amounts of molecular biology data systematically to develop mechanisms to aid in the investigation

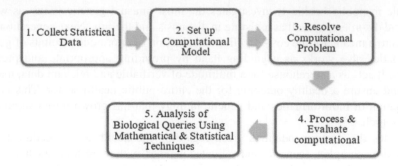

FIGURE 8.4   Concept of bioinformatics.

of such data to ascertain accurate and valid results. Bioinformatics has been the most influential form of data analysis, data searching, integration, and simulation instrument in molecular or genetic biology [2].

The unparalleled rise of information technology, as well as the long-term expansion of cell genetics, genetic research, and new genetic technologies are playing a vital role in healthcare. Principally, it has been related to data storage and genetic sequence analysis. Computational biology is a reductive science that sprang from the unanticipated expansion of information technology, as well as the impressive growth of genetic analysis and DNA sequencing technologies, and their linked research. Bioinformatics is sometimes known as bio-computing or computational biology. In recent years, genomics has grown in importance in bioinformatics or the study of fundamental biological processes [33] (Figure 8.4).

8.3   THE GOALS OF BIOINFORMATICS

As a result, bioinformatics is also known as bio-computational biology. We can now grasp genomic research and gene delivery thanks to bioinformatics [34]. The following are the basic five goals of bioinformatics:

1. Arranging biotic data in such a way that researchers or biologists can access the current data.
2. Creating and developing a software application to help researchers organize and analyze data.
3. Analyzing the results using existing or collected biological data.
4. In the pharmaceutical industry, aiding researchers in identifying and comprehending protein structures, which aids in drug development.
5. Assisting clinicians in understanding gene structure, which aids in the detection and diagnosis of cancer-like disorders [35].

Bioinformatics is the application of mathematical and information programs to determine and simplify genetic information at various levels of interaction within molecular pathways and cellular bodies. Current bioinformatics encompasses a considerable proportion of scientific study, demonstrating a broad spectrum of information for biological investigation.

Bioinformatics includes sequence analysis, which includes parts such as sequence alignment, gene detection, phylogenetics, gene delivery, the three-dimensional protein structure of DNA and RNA, structural determination, visualization, gene replacement, reconstruction, modeling, and molecular process stimulation. Construction genomes enable the locating of the optimal delivery site, statistical analysis of practical data, and the establishment of a data storage system that collects all information about genetic studies [8].

8.4   BIOLOGICAL DATABASES

Biological data is a type of data in which a collection of biological information is stored electronically. This is referred to as a biological data bank. In biological databases, information is stored in an easily retrievable format that may be accessed using search criteria. NCBI, GenBank (GB), and PDB are some illustrations of databases. They are collaborative databases that have been specifically designed for quick accessing and skimming across desktop or laptop computers [36]. They successfully work with a large amount of DNA sequencing data and contain additional practical reports (connected to the bodily function of living things, requiring computer files full of information) that have been established and are continuously updated. These are methods and approaches designed to search for specific information about genetic arrays, genetic models, and genetic changes [37].

8.5   DATABASE SEQUENCE FILTERING

A filtering database sequence is a database in which the sequences are the result of filtered data containing an array of DNA and peptide chains containing sites with specifically selective restricted nucleic acid (NA) and amino acid (AA) as well as a large number of recurrent short alignments. The goal of filtering data is to make sure that the data being searched for is still in the database after filtering, that the filtered data is much smaller, and that the filtering process is very fast. In terms of outcomes, there are a few genetic arrays that provide ascending result configurations that directly highlight the bias. This is unnecessary for many applications (clearly linked or related) and may hide other important information (where things are barely distinguishable). As a result, these arrays filter out less-complex regions of difficulty by raising inquiries; and array becomes worthless for searching critical one. As a result, these NCBI, BLAST providers successfully use (segmented data) SEG to filter these peptide chain divides. Although this docket filter avoids the vast majority of matching problems, certain issues will always exist due to self-regulation. As a result, there is difficulty in masking limitations/guidelines and data fractions. The amount of knowledge available on the functions of database sequence filtering is rising fast, necessitating the development and maintenance of databases to serve the research community [38].

8.6   SEARCHING A DATABASE

It gives effect to the data source, which we're looking for, and represents them in a simple way. A question order is generated that covers all orders in the data source with the written order in the acceptance state, and is calculated using the right array. Regardless, the order contrast technique necessitates a legitimate request. The elevated bursting blow data source model looks for information that may be used to construct an interesting inquiry order. [39].

The constraining force for data source searching describes the data for similarity and may not make evident the purpose or utilization. The critical force for restricting data source searching specifies the data for similarity and may not make the purpose obvious (e.g., comparing the 3D structures of different peptide chains together) [40]. As a result, we prefer 3D models to first-order models, which were kept throughout the natural development process. However, the information presented in different circumstances will only constitute the first order [38].

The purpose of searching is to determine the relationship between the query and the database records. The relatedness of nucleic acids and proteins is characterized by "homology." A 'Query' sequence is used to search a database for each entry, or 'subject'. When two sequences have a sequence identity over a specific threshold, they are said to be homologous. Depending on the purpose, thresholds can be specified by length, % identity, E-value, Bit-score, r.m.s.d. (for structures), or a combination of one or more of these.

DNA: Some facts were investigated during differentiation of DNA:

- During structural alterations at every tertiary site in each sequence;
- Through the correspondence of non-sequential arrays.

Moreover, the chemical properties of AA establish analogue for the value ascribed instead of state forward wide approval of research. [41]. DNA in opposition to DNA comparison (BLASTN work roadmap) is commonly utilized to discover similarities in all manner of fields, and across ranges of order in a fact base. This search should be requested as a way to discover RNA sequencing or regulating fields; ranges also test the redundancy of peptide sequencing, or has splice joints in it [42]. In summary, a long peptide-position acts to make discoveries that are of significant value for detecting sophisticated allied genetic code; DNA investigations have DNA analysis has been shown to be the most successful in delivering more relevant facts in a systematic order [43]. When constructing a database with the aim of making discoveries, the following factors should be considered:

- Look for a contemporary database with a large number of records (e.g., swiss 10 – Prot, Embl, gene bank);
- Make a comparison of relevant facts;
- Use liquid-cleaning apparatus for low-complexity divisions and nearby portions;
- Consider having a specific reason written in an order with e values [18, 44–50].

8.7   DATABASES OF PROTEIN STRUCTURE

The intricacies and complexity of biological molecular interactions are incredible. In this context, developing bioinformatics tools capable of reliably predicting protein structure is critical, as structure dictates how a protein interacts with a set of different molecules (substrates, activators, repressors, and drugs) and other proteins (either specifically as in natural multi-protein complexes or nonspecifically), thereby disclosing the cell's role. Representative structures for the vast majority of water-soluble protein domains will be accessible soon, allowing for the modeling and classification of comparable sequences to yield structures for all gene products. However, defining the function of all gene products *in vivo* will be a long-term task for scientists. The emphasis will move to biological function and regulatory principles, as well as molecular interactions. A 3D protein model may help in grasping the "docking" between ligands and proteins, which is critical for the rational design or modification of therapeutic targets or novel medicines addressing both pathogenic protein and genetic disorder in human proteins [51–53].

8.7.1   CLASSIFICATION OF PROTEIN STRUCTURE

The Protein Data Bank (PDB), also referred to as the "Brookhaven National Laboratory Protein Data Bank" (BNL PDB), was founded in 1977 as a computer-based repository for macromolecular structural data. The PDB library presently has around 22,053 items in a consistent file format that can be read and accessed on the internet. PDB data is being used for further research in many initiatives. The SCOP database seeks to give a complete and detailed description of all the known structural and evolutionary links of proteins, including all PDB entries. It is provided as a collection of neatly connected hypertext pages that make the vast database understandable and accessible. SCOP employs three fundamental hierarchical levels: family (clear evolutionary link), superfamily (possible common evolutionary origin), and fold (major structural similarity). The CATH dataset, which is a hierarchical domain classification of protein complexes in the PDB, employs a similar method, although it is limited to crystal structures with a resolution greater than 3.0 and nuclear magnetic resonance (NMR) structures. CATH includes four key levels in this hierarchy: class, architectural, topological (fold family), and homologous recombination superfamily.

8.7.2 MODELING OF STRUCTURE

Only the "homology modeling" technique, which normally consists of four phases, produces solid findings in the prediction of 3D protein complexes (modeling):

- Data banks are used to detect structural homologs;
- Alignment of the target and the template;
- Model development and optimization;
- Model evaluation.

SWISS-MODEL is a 3D protein structure comparative homology modeling tool. In 1993, it pioneered the field of automated modeling, and it is today the most widely used free web-based automated modeling tool. In 2002, the service processed 120,000 user queries for 3D protein models. The SWISS-Internet MODEL interface allows for varying levels of user involvement. In "first approach mode," only an amino acid sequence of a protein is supplied to build a 3D model. The server handles all template selection, alignment, and model creation. In "alignment mode," the modeling approach is based on a user-defined target–template alignment. In "project mode," Deep View, an integrated sequence-to-structure workbench (available for PC, Macintosh, Linux, and SGI at https://www.expasy.org/spdbv), can perform sophisticated modeling jobs. All models are returned via email, along with a detailed modeling report. The What Check and ANOLEA assessments are entirely optional. CPHmodels, Geno3D, and ESyPred3D are examples of homonymy modelers [54].

8.8 SOURCE OF PROTEIN STRUCTURE DATA

Protein–protein interactions play a crucial role in practically all cellular activities. BIND is an expression for the Bimolecular Interaction Network Database, which is a database that contains detailed descriptions of interactions, molecular combinations, and processes. An interaction record is produced when two items interact with one another. Objects include proteins, DNA, RNA, ligands, and chemical complexes. The description of interaction includes the cellular location, the experimental values used to examine the interaction, the conserved sequence, the molecular location of the interaction, chemical action, kinetics, thermodynamics, and chemical state, and it can be accessed by running a BLAST search against the database to gather information on the interactions of the query sequence stored in BIND. The DIP database is a compilation of scientifically found protein interactions. It combines data from several sources to create a single, consistent database of protein–protein interactions.

Almost 30 years ago, biophysical chemists and computational biologists were attracted by the topic of protein–protein or protein–ligand docking. A docking technique determines a complex's 3D shape since the proteins are rotated and translated, producing a huge amount of potential complexes on the computer, and selecting the most favored ones. The PDB is used to put docking techniques to the test on protein–protein complexes, specifically protease–inhibitor and antigen–antibody complexes. CAPRI, a method inspired by Critical Assessment of Structure Prediction (CASP), provided molecular dimensions to the protein components of several target assemblies. When the anticipated interactions were compared to X-ray patterns, they were shown to be particularly effective on several of the targets.

However, the prediction failed in some situations, showing that further research is needed while large-scale protein–protein interactions can be predicted continuously [54].

The classification of the biological databases are as follows:

- Primary database;
- Supplementary database;
- Database structure;
- Database type;
- Database quality.

8.9   CLASSIFICATION OF DATABASES

Bioinformatics are the biotic investigation which propagates huge load of information (including molecular array, structure, etc.) (Figure 8.5).

8.10   FEATURES OF BIOINFORMATICS

- Systematically organized information;
- Data can be approached computationally;
- Various tools and technologies like BLAST and NCBI (online);
- Effective filtration of the complex used in drug advancement;
- Big data (next generation sequence) analysis;
- Targeted identification of molecules.

8.11   INITIATIVE FOR PARALLEL BIOINFORMATICS (IPAB)

- Organizer: Tokyo Institute of technology;
- Target: cKyes kinase;
- Library: Enamine (2.2 million compounds);
- Identification: 120 compounds;
- Test: 50 compounds;
- Inhibition: 4 compounds;

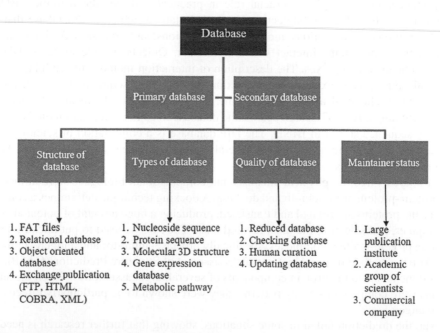

FIGURE 8.5   Flow chart showing database classification.

- Probable hit: 1 compound;
- 2015: 200 compounds; inhibition: 5; hits 2 [55, 56]

8.12   SOFTWARE TOOLS FOR BIOINFORMATICS

The first type of software tool is for creating or mending items that rely mostly on mathematics and are dependent on: extremely short sequence comparisons; physical or chemical characteristics of small, complicated components; or statistics. The second type of software, which is strongly reliant on databases, will be discussed further below. As so-called "mix techniques" become more popular, it is becoming more difficult to categorize programs into these two categories. There are numerous programs that are used regularly to generate connecting DNA orders from in-natural facts obtained from power to put large amounts through sequencers, to give quality written order to each base, to remove the incorrect orders, and to prepare the means to connect orders having in its applications. Some programs are not completely detailed here.

Any DNA field, range, or usage that can be attributed to a purpose or use is critical. They contain: one starting company and multiple record-writing factor-binding sites on the internet; ribosome-binding sites; and start and stop codon splice sites. According to what is mentioned, these are referred to as signals. Methods of locating them include signal output sensors. What it refers to are stretched and variable-length divisions, as well as neighboring components such as exons and introns. These are ingested in methods that may be referred to as sensors. A major difficulty is the capacity to use sections critical for protein sequences, modulation, expression, and record-writing. Bioinformatics techniques for detecting genes and other usable sections in genomic DNA have gained relevance in recent years [57–74].

8.12.1   THE VARIOUS TYPES OF TOOLS USED IN BIOINFORMATICS

- Databases;
- Swiss-Protection;
- EMBL;
- Entrez;
- GDB;
- GenBank;
- GSDB;
- PDB.

8.12.2   TRADITIONAL INSTRUMENT BIOINFORMATICS

- Database curiosity;
- Sequence Alignment GB (GenBank)/EMBL/DDBL, Medline, Swissprot, PDB;
- BLAST, FASTA, Clustal, Multalin, and Dialign Structure Prediction;
- Identifying Genes Genscan, Genomescan, Denmark, and GRAIL. [75]

8.12.3   TOOLS FOR ANALYZING AT DIFFERENT LEVELS

Unprocessed RNA happens in transitions by utilizing initial gene prediction, which is followed by mRNA, which changes it into a Gm3 polypeptide chain via a translation process that uses a comparative gene. This is then followed by the nascent polypeptide in the translation process. It first creates the three-dimensional structure for the protein, which is required for its activity, and then uses the functional identification function to transform the active enzyme into a round-folding chain. So, the entire process from gene to protein is reversed over a huge number of steps, and each step can be analyzed using bioinformatics tools. For example, at the sequencing level, we employ tools that are used at different levels of the process of turning a gene into a protein [76].

8.12.4   GENE PREDICTION SOFTWARE

8.12.4.1   GRAIL

- Identifies coding areas;
- Makes use of the neuro-synaptic framework, which holds a plethora of genetically encoded information;
- Recognizes the strength of coded data within absolute size (100 bases) structures;
- Assesses coding potential without the need for additional capabilities;
- Later versions include more information about humans and other creatures.

8.12.4.2   A Genetic Marker

- Uses inhomogeneous Markov models;
- Uses statistical trends in Dinucleotide Frequencies to predict coding and noncoding areas. [77]

8.13   GENE FINDING METHODS

The rapid development automated Di-Ribonucleic acid progression methods that are very good at making an impact have sped up the process of getting genetic data. This led to the strong conclusion of the human genome in 2001. A vast amount of DNA order information is ready for use, and databases are growing in size and power. Proteomics equipment for producing or mending things has quickly grown to find genes that can use proteins or RNA. This is significant research when considering the best-produced tiny life forms of enterobacteria. More than 30 percent of microorganisms and germs are assumed to be wide perusal figures, constituting ideas-based genetic code with no practical function or application. Following that, questions about genetic data order observers include viewpoints, disease awareness, genetic code command, and assimilation. Furthermore, the method for observing proteins, known as proteomics, has a lot of unexplored promise in medical and biotechnology. The wide range of bioinformatics tools for generating or putting the right information ready (to be used) for researchers includes complicated issues that can be used to achieve scientific solutions.

In this section, we will introduce a roadmap for the ideal way to produce an impact of way to get detailed information of a specified sequence or to maintain appropriate data by trying to make a recommendation of current publicly ready (to be used) software tools and database set that mainly use the Web [78].

8.13.1   METHOD OF SEQUENCING ALIGNMENT

Alignment is the way of evaluating two or more patterns by finding a succession of specific characters or character sequences that exist in almost the same position in both sequences To align chains, similar or identical sequences are placed in the same column, resulting in mismatch, while no identical characters may be placed in the same column, resulting in mismatch, or facing a gap in one of the other sequences, causing a mismatch. Mismatches and gaps are scattered in an optimum alignment to optimize matches [79]. Two forms of sequence alignment have been discovered. A global alignment makes every effort to match the entire sequence with as many characters as possible. The sequence lengths with the highest density of matches are favored in a local alignment, resulting in one or more islands of matches and completely mismatching regions in the aligned sequences. Alignments are the fundamental concept underpinning programs (such as BLAST) that search for similar sequences by gradually aligning an inquiry with a large database of sequences; they are also useful for determining the genetic gap between homologous genes of various sources [80].

8.13.2   MULTIPLE SEQUENCE ALIGNMENT

Multiple sequence comparisons can uncover gene activity that would not be visible from simple sequence homologies. New sequences are commonly revealed to be connected to numerous previously uncharacterized sequences as a consequence of genome-sequencing research, leading in the formation of entire families of gene mutations with no obvious function. Having such a family, on the other hand, allows for the use of more efficient similarity search algorithms. Software techniques from multiple-sequence alignments can now be used to construct profiles. Position-specific score information derived from the occurrence of a certain residue in a column that has been aligned is contained in profiles. Because certain essential residues and patterns are preferentially retained by sequence families, this knowledge should enable more sensitive database searches. The majority of modern profile software makes use of statistical Hidden Markov Model (HMMs). Other websites provide far more in-depth evaluations of the literature on profile HMM approaches. When compared to other alignment approaches, ClustalW is a very well and commonly used free application that can handle large volumes of sequences at high processing rates. It is compatible with Macintosh, Windows, and a variety of UNIX systems. There is also a graphical user interface (ClustalX) available. The programmable T-COFFEE, which is more accurate but slower than ClustalW, may be employed for sequences with less than 30 percent identity [81].

Once the family has been recognized, obtaining a good multiple-sequence alignment is usually simple. Multiple alignments can be made using FASTA format data (through a ClustalW supported website) or DbClustal, which generates a BLAST output from which family members can be selected and the multiple alignments built. Check the alignment in ClustalX's graphical representation for correctness.

The alignment can also be saved as a Multiple Sequence Format (MSF) file, which other programs can read for additional analysis (e.g., careful editing, trimming, coloring, shading, and printing). Many of these editing tools are available in the Windows version of GeneDoc (http://www.psc.edu/biomed/genedoc)[82].

8.13.3   PHYLOGENETIC INVESTIGATION

A high number of alignments can be used to build phylogenetic trees. The tree extends or bifurcates until it reaches the terminal branches, tips, or leaves at the top, depicting the ancestral condition of the species or genes under investigation at the base. The concept of an uprooted tree is hazier. Uprooted trees show the branching sequence but do not include the position of the last common ancestor's root. Although rooted trees are preferred in theory, practically every phylogenetic reconstruction technique includes an uprooted tree [31].

Molecular sequence analysis is a young discipline with limited analytical tools based on broad mathematics and statistical concepts. As a result, many phylogenetic trees based on the sequencing of molecules are inaccurate. The following are the primary reasons:

- The sequences are not properly aligned.
- Failure to account for a variance from site to site (all sites within sequences may evolve at varying rates).
- Inequitable interest rate consequences (the inability of most tree-building algorithms to produce good phylogenic noetic trees when genes from different taxa in the tree have evolved at different rates).

The most serious of the three possible hazards is the alignment of artefacts. The fourth stumbling issue is potentially overcome by employing a novel method called paralinear (logged) distances. Before constructing evolutionary trees, sequence alignments should be double-checked [2]. There are numerous tools available to assist in tree calculation using genetic data. The most well-known software for tree reconstruction is the Phylogenetic Analysis Using Parsimony (PAUP) tool, which is part of the GCG sequence analysis package that enables logdet analysis. PAUP is simple to use and contains a wealth of information. PHYLIP/Phylodendron are two more well-known packages that offer a varied collection of techniques, including those that incorporate the most recent theoretical advances. Tree View is a stand-alone program that allows you to view, edit, rearrange, and print trees on a variety of computer systems [83, 84].

8.13.4 PROTEIN STRUCTURE AND PROPERTY PREDICTION

Protein sequences allow for detailed computations that aid in function assignment, topology prediction (subcellular localization, membrane-spanning), and identification of locations that are likely to be cleaved or changed; interaction and catalytic activities can also be modeled. The ExPASy proteomic website has a plethora of tools. Many of these individual utilities have been combined into a single interface due to the enormous number of programs accessible. META PP and Predict Protein are two examples. NetOglyc identifies mucin-type O-glycosylation sites in human proteins; NetPhos predicts probable phosphorylation sites in protein sequences at serine, threonine, or tyrosine residues; and NetPico predicts picornaviral protease cleavage sites. Transmembrane helices are detected using TMHMM, TopPred, and DAS, whereas secondary structure is predicted using JPRED. FRSVR and SAM-T02 search structural databases for parallels between distant homolog proteins that are too subtle to be inferred using standard techniques for aligning sequences.

Detecting distant homologs, on the other hand, is a problem that must be addressed because the majority of the findings supplied are supposedly incorrect. The results must be double-checked. META PP also supports homology modeling, which may be accomplished with both the SWISS-MODEL and the CPHmodels, as mentioned further below [85] (Figure 8.6).

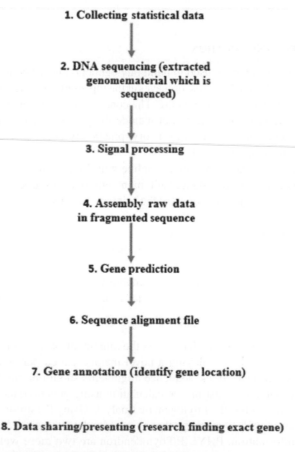

1. Collecting statistical data

2. DNA sequencing (extracted genomematerial which is sequenced)

3. Signal processing

4. Assembly raw data in fragmented sequence

5. Gene prediction

6. Sequence alignment file

7. Gene annotation (identify gene location)

8. Data sharing/presenting (research finding exact gene)

FIGURE 8.6   Flow chart showing mechanisms of bioinformatics tools.

8.14 BIOINFORMATICS METHODOLOGIES

Biological data as a large-scale omics tool refers to the collection of technologies used to investigate the roles, interacytions, and activities of the numerous kinds of molecules that comprse an organism's cells. Omics may be used to study enormous collections of biological molecules using modern algorithms, statistical software, computational and systems biology to coordinate the interactions of numerous ecosystem components and emergent characteristics. Bioinformatics is a relatively new innovation that bridges the gap between two fundamental concepts: biological systems and informatics technology. These technologies include a wide range of topics, including genomics, transcriptomics, and proteomics, as well as epigenomics, pharmacogenomics, met genomics, and metabolism. As a result, the primary technique in system bioinformatics improves computational therapies and diagnostics, and advances studies in systems biology and system medicine, gene therapy, and gene delivery [86].

8.15 GENOMICS AND BIOINFORMATICS MEDICAL APPLICATIONS

Genetic code assessment indexes:Almost all the tools and information given will be employed in conjunction with any sort of DNA or AA cycle. Access to the whole genetic data index of many related entities (mainly biogenesis) allows for further advancements towards the primary work objective, making concealed genetic codes and AA unachievable along with fair group genetic codes. There is also a wealth of medically narrated material available, such as online mandolin inheritance in man, which includes databases about the treatment of various illnesses. Furthermore, venture agreements containing certain illnesses are introduced, such as the cancer genetic code analysis predict, which assesses recognizable changes in genetic inheritance occur precisely.

Bioinformatics and statistics are concerned with the analysis and interpretation of large amounts of genomic data, as well as its collection, improvement, and enhancement. The construction of extensive data centers is enabled by the transformation in computing competency, which presents the idea of electronic health records (EHRs). To identify disease, many statistical tools are utilized to examine and evaluate vast genomic databases, and the predictions are valuable for associating clinical information. Presently, researchers and scholars in this field are working on developing novel models and algorithms for interpreting genomic data that is used in a variety of sectors including drug development, pharmacy, and other related professions [2, 87, 88].

8.16 COMPARATIVE GENOMICS

As a result, these small chemical assembly instructions within living things provide intriguing targets for explicitly stated/specific medications against danger/disease system. Comparisons of full whole sets of small chemical assembly instructions of a living thing show groupings that are used to protect inherent properties. . The last described method is useful for identifying small chemical assembly instructions inside living things that may convey a message of identification of danger/disease toward people or plants. The comparison can only be performed utilizing a detailed probable future occurrence of cells; when we compare expression profiles or use proteomics, we get more accurate results. Orthologous groups of proteins called COGs were found by comparing protein sequences, translated in full, which are the total sets of the microscopic chemical assembly instructions of a living thing. COGs are important evolutionary families.. This process produces candidates who are most likely accountable for B's disease-causing phenotype. As a result, it is of particular importance to medical science, the pharmaceutical sector, and agriculture. Anthrax might be used as a disease-preventing treatment. The COG (computer file containing information) provides a phylogenic correlation-based website to aid in the building of an explicitly expressed filter that, when applied to the COGs, may filter out a COG set that will obey the criteria specified in the query [84, 89–93]. So, here we will concentrate on the bioinformatics tools used in gene delivery. Gene delivery is essentially a sophisticated method of targeting gene systems. So, by employing bioinformatics tools, illness diagnostics will be advanced, as will gene delivery to the target region. This is extremely beneficial in diagnosis and cancer therapy and other chronic disorders, immunological issues, cardiovascular disorders, heart failure, and so on. The emphasis here is on how bioinformatics is being used in gene delivery. Because of advancements in medical treatment, the therapeutic impact has increased, hastening growth into new domains that are offered as advanced therapy. This advancement focuses on diagnosis techniques to eliminate the highlighted component rather than healing the disease's presentation. As a result, more research is being conducted on the subject of genetics, as well as the advancement of genetic research. Gene delivery for targeted medicine delivery is the result of genetic research. By using smart delivery to target the gene for delivery, it is possible to identify both hereditary and non-hereditary diseases. Gene therapy is an interesting experimental research area in molecular medicine that has the opportunity to profoundly alter human health soon. Gene therapy has seen a considerable surge in utilization in recent years. In it, gene delivery vectors are increasingly employed. It has developed and is now positioned to revolutionize approaches [94, 95].

The use of bioinformatics technologies for flawless gene prediction therapy is being used to address inherited genetic disorders. Gene delivery has the potential to help the vast majority of newborns suffering from illness. As a result, it is a promising method for delivering the gene in a safe, effective, and profit-only manner [96]. The act of delivering foreign genetic material, such as DNA or RNA, into a living cell is known as gene delivery. Gene delivery is a critical step in gene therapy for initiating the gene's therapeutic function in patients. A gene can be delivered in a variety of ways. Microinjections and electro-portion are two common physical techniques. In general, the rate of plasma lemma permeation must be increased to perforate the cell membrane and introduce exogenous nucleic acids into the cell [97].

Gene delivery strategies are follows:

- Gene enhancement;
- Replacement of a faulty gene;
- Gene correction;
- Gene transmission;
- Introduction into a target tissue;
- The mutated gene that still functions
- Inserting a healthy copy of the gene.

Through homologous recombination, the faulty gene might be replaced with a normal healthy gene. The damaged gene might be restored using a selective gene by a reverse mutation procedure, which would transport the gene directly to the target tissue and restore its normal function. Gene targeting to the proper tissue at the right time might help increase gene delivery [98, 99].

8.17   GENE DELIVERY OBJECTIVES

Gene delivery objectives are to extend, localize, target, and safeguard gene interactions with sick tissue. Gene delivery systems are frequently employed to treat a wide range of disorders and diseases, including inherited disorders, toxic chemicals, viral and bacterial infections, and hazardous tumors. Nowadays, gene delivery systems are strongly applicable for cancer therapy, since viral genes may be transferred to the cytoplasm of a cell which then restores the function of a protein [100].

8.17.1   THE GENE DELIVERY PROCESS USING BIOINFORMATICS TOOLS

A foreign DNA gene sequence is obtained and directed to the tissue/cell of the organ where the gene is to be delivered. The foreign DNA sequence is fed into the bioinformatics tools. The gene of foreign DNA is investigated and evaluated. Furthermore, the sequence of protein expression is completed, which occurs immediately after the sequence of the interpreting gene. From a database of bioinformatics tools, the DNA sequence of the faulty gene may be rectified. This study is carried out with the use of bioinformatics tools that employ computational approaches and statistical calculations. After the repaired gene is delivered, it has a therapeutic impact by rectifying the ailment. An appropriate approach is used to convey the foreign gene sequence. This is carried out at the intended site of action. As a result, the aim of gene delivery achieved via the use of bioinformatics tools is accomplished, efficiently and effectively. Mooney et al. have reported that the prediction of gene candidates for the gene delivery process is selected by bioinformatics software from the biological database [101].

8.17.2 Using Bioinformatics Techniques to Modify Genes

Infective genes are modified to contribute to the normalized gene's performance.

8.17.2.1 Gene Substitution

A gene sequence that has been transmuted and metamorphosed is replaced by an exact regular functioning gene. Here, bioinformatics techniques use a biological database to fix the mutation and assess gene expression, which is then followed by interpreting the protein structure of the gene DNA. Computational algorithms are used to solve the question of the faulty gene.

This leads to the replacement of a healthy gene. This kind of modification is used to treat disorders that cause enzyme and protein deficiencies. The downside of this strategy is that it is a somewhat difficult process to complete.

8.17.2.2 Genetic Alteration

It is only associated with the infective portion of the transmuted gene, which is rendered to provide the gene without returning it to its original function.. Find a mutant gene region using these bioinformatics tools. Then, using gene tool prediction, change the sequence of a mutant gene.

8.17.2.3 Genetic Augmentation

The goal is to provide altered copies of the infected gene; this approach is typically used for gene-based products that have lost their regular function or reflect their unique protein expression. Transmuted gene expression is a faulty gene that has been changed by inserting a normal gene sequence via gene targeting [102].

8.18 GENE DELIVERY SYSTEM

The design of a gene delivery system is based on a group of viruses known as viral-based, a group of non-viruses known as non-viral, and others are hybridized combinations. Gene-mediated delivery is a feature of viral-based delivery systems. It is made up of a set of viruses that have been altered to be deficient duplications and which may be delivered as the foreign gene for effect. Adenoviruses (Adv), retroviruses (RV), and lentiviruses (LV) are employed in viral-based vectors. As an alternative for a viral-based method, non-viral gene delivery technologies were devised. This is one of the most significant advantages of the increased transferring of these systems. The physical mechanism is ascribed to gene transfer via physical attraction for increasing plasma lemma penetration. Gene gum, microinjection, electroporation, ultrasounds, and hydrodynamic applications are popular physical methods of delivery. In contrast to chemical approaches, naturalistic or artificial transporters of a gene towards a cellular mass are used. For genetic transportation systems, DNA molecular conjugates, lipoplexes, human artificial chromosomes, polymers, dendrimers, and positively charged lipid systems are used. Nanoparticles are being tested as a potential DNA carrying system. They should have a high slot of circulation, low immunogenicity, and be mostly physiologically equivalent, as well as be extremely appealing to concentrating on barrier penetration [103, 104]. Bioinformatics software aids in the delivery of the targeted gene by utilizing a biological

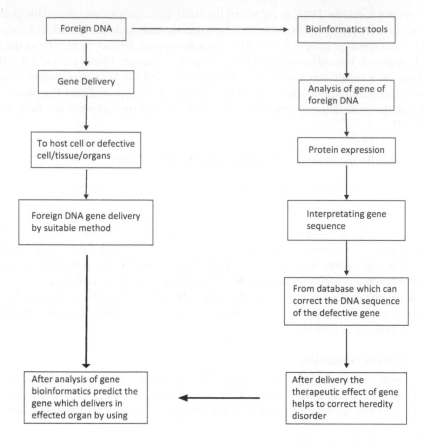

FIGURE 8.7   Schematic representation of the process of gene delivery by using a bioinformatics tool.

database that associates chemical and pharmacological data with various gene targets and provides comprehensive information about the sequence, structure, and pathway information, as well as recommending a method of a specific gene delivery system.

Bioinformatics methods are useful in gene delivery systems for identifying genes in specific areas and validating toxicogenomic and biological indicators, as well as pharmaco-genomics. These programs are used to increase the therapeutic action of genes (Figure 8.7).

8.19   USING BIOINFORMATICS TECHNOLOGIES TO DEVELOP A GENE DELIVERY SYSTEM FOR THERAPY

In a gene delivery system, bioinformatics software is used. This technology has demonstrated many qualities that are particularly beneficial in the targeting of gene delivery at the location of the action. As a result, the whole sequencing of the human genome system has aided in the discovery of genetic donations for a variety of illnesses. This application includes drugs for individuals (personalized medicines), drug discovery, design, and medicines for the prevention of many ailments, as well as gene therapy in the delivery of genes.

8.19.1   Cancer

If the gene is connected to cell division and aberrant growth, it is a carcinogenic gene where mutations in it cause cancer. There are two sorts of groups that are accountable for gene mutations that cause cancer. Gene therapy's effects can be extended to a wide range of disorders that are not exclusively inherited, such as cancer and cardiovascular disease. Furthermore, cell therapy techniques can go much further: inserting disease-modifying genes into existing malfunctioning organs may change the course of illness. The first gene is in charge of oncogenes, whereas the second is a tumor suppressor gene. As a result, gene delivery is a phenomenon in which a foreign DNA gene is transported to the host cell by replacing the host gene at the targeted spot. The gene will be transported to the desired location. The technique of gene delivery is based on the mechanism of replacing a faulty gene in a diseased cell by sending a healthy gene created outside the body in the laboratory. Following the successful delivery of that gene in that particular organ or cell in the body, current technology, such as a bioinformatics tool, has simplified the process of creating healthy genes and delivering genes to a specific cell. Bioinformatics uses statistical data to collect all of the facts about the malfunctioning gene in a malignant cell and set up a computational program for replacing the gene with computational methods. After fixing the faulty gene issue bioinformatics analyzes biological issues using mathematical and statistical tools to get the best possible answer for a gene that will be delivered. Furthermore, it gives information of the tumor gene, as well as an oncogene suppressor, including cancer therapy and gene therapy. The tumor suppression gene, cancer gene antagonist, and suicide gene all attack cancer cells at the molecular level. As a result, this gene encrypts cytokines, which restores the immune response against malignant cells. Cancer bioinformatics is a significant approach to the early and accurate identification and treatment of cancer using gene delivery systems. In the detection section, bioinformatics analysis of morphological masses and other behavioral alterations in medical scanning images is obtained by particular filtration of genetic databases [105, 106].

8.19.2 IMMUNOLOGICAL STRATEGY

The human immune system contains two types of pathways that recognize an antigen from a foreign gene. One of the initial pathways for antibody release by B cells, lymphocytes begin their lives in the bone marrow. This is related to the immunoglobulin activity of the B cell receptor–antigen interrelationship. Immunoglobulins are hydrophilic proteins that travel through the bloodstream to reach the target antigen. The second pathway responds to antibodies generated by T cells, which go to the thymus gland and result in the development of T-lymphocytes. T cells are classified into two categories. The first contains T helper cells, which have a higher affinity for T cells or phagocytes, and the second contains killer cells (cytotoxic T-lymphocytes), which act by identifying a little bit of the virus on the extracellular region of the infected cells, resulting in lysis of the discovered infectious cells. As a result, preclinical investigations rapidly reveal that the recipient's immune technique plays a crucial role in gene expression following gene delivery.

As a result, bioinformatics has advanced algorithms that improve the treatment and prediction of immunological disorders by efficiently merging aggregate clinical data with genetic data [107].

8.19.3 CARDIOVASCULAR DISORDERS

The promise of cardiovascular gene delivery is becoming increasingly apparent. The gene would be delivered intra-arterially via endovascular catheter technology. In the past, hyperlipidemia has been treated by delivering the gene to the target site. In addition, in-stent restenosis, stenosis, cardiac arrest, vein graft, arrhythmia, angina, and vascular peripheral disease were accepted as conditions for gene-targeted delivery, which has been proven to be exceptional in terms of catheter-based strategies and their targeted action power. a focus for delivering the gene to the target site; some circumstances involved in-stent restenosis, stenosis, cardiac arrest, vein graft, arrhythmia, angina, and vascular peripheral disease were accepted as the efficient ability for gene target the delivering of the gene is the technique which has been extra ordinary concerning catheter-based strategies and their power of targeting in the site power full new therapy. The future of gene delivery will involve meticulously recorded approaches with specifications such as flow in the heart and activity, which is dependent on metabolic pathways and cardio vascular disorders [108].

8.20   CONCLUSION

Gene delivery is a required step in gene therapy for the introduction or silencing of a gene to promote a therapeutic outcome in patients; it also has an important role in the genetic alterations of a gene. Nanoparticles, which will carry genes to numerous types of cells and tissues, are the next form of gene delivery. Bioinformatics plays an important part in finding gene expression by using a biological database to fix the damaged gene. Computational approaches and statistical estimates provide excellent results.

REFERENCES

1. Hogeweg P. The roots of bioinformatics in theoretical biology. *PLoS Computational Biology* 2011;7(3):e1002021.
2. Majhi V, Paul S, Jain R. Bioinformatics for healthcare applications. *2019 Amity international conference on artificial intelligence (AICAI)* 2019 February 4 (pp. 204–207). IEEE.
3. Gauthier J, Vincent AT, Charette SJ, Derome N. A brief history of bioinformatics. *Briefings in Bioinformatics* 2019;20(6):1981–1996.
4. Zhang S-Y, Liu S-L. *Bioinformatics. Brenner's Encyclopedia of Genetics.* 2013. 338–340. doi:10.1016/b978-0-12-374984-0.00155-8.2.
5. Bayat A. Science, medicine, and the future: Bioinformatics. *BMJ: British Medical Journal.* 2002;324(7344):1018.
6. Sharma MK, Dhar MK, Kaul S. Bioinformatics: An introduction and overview. *2012 International Journal of Engineering Research and Development* 2012;3(8):88–99.
7. https://en.wikipedia.org/wiki/Bioinformatics
8. Chowdhary M, Rani A, Parkash J, Shahnaz M, Dev D. Bioinformatics: an overview for cancer research. *Journal of Drug Delivery and Therapeutics* 2016;6(4):69–72.
9. Bhuvaneshwar K, Belouali A, Singh V, Johnson RM, Song L, Alaoui A, Harris MA, Clarke R, Weiner LM, Gusev Y, Madhavan S. G-DOC Plus–an integrative bioinformatics platform for precision medicine. *BMC Bioinformatics* 2016;17(1):1–3.
10. Simon R. Bioinformatics in cancer therapeutics—hype or hope? *Nature Clinical Practice Oncology* 2005; 2(5):223.
11. Luo J, Wu M, Gopukumar D, Zhao Y. Big data application in biomedical research and health care: a literature review. *Biomedical Informatics Insights* 2016;8:BII-S31559.
12. Scharf M, Schneider R, Casari G, Bork P, Valencia A, Ouzounis C, Sander C. GeneQuiz: a workbench for sequence analysis. In *Proceedings of the Second International Conference on Intelligent Systems for Molecular Biology.* 1994 (pp. 348–353). AAAI Press.
13. Goodman N, Rozen S, Stein LD, Smith AG. The LabBase system for data management in large scale biology research laboratories. *Bioinformatics.* 1998;14(7):562–574.
14. Gordon D, Abajian C, Green P. Consed: a graphical tool for sequence finishing. *Genome Research.* 1998;8(3):195–202.
15. Hermjakob H, Fleischmann W, Apweiler R. Swissknife-'lazy parsing'of SWISS-PROT entries. *Bioinformatics.* 1999;15(9):771–772.
16. Kurtz S, Phillippy A, Delcher AL, Smoot M, Shumway M, Antonescu C, Salzberg SL. Versatile and open software for comparing large genomes. *Genome Biology* 2004;5(2):1–9.
17. Duarte Y, Márquez-Miranda V, Miossec MJ, González-Nilo F. Integration of target discovery, drug discovery and drug delivery: a review on computational strategies. *Wiley Interdisciplinary Reviews: Nanomedicine and Nano Biotechnology* 2019;11(4):e1554.
18. Anil R, Jyotika B, Lal SB. Software tools and resources for bioinformatics research. Indian agriculture statistics research institute library avenue. 2012. pp. 1–17.
19. https://databricks.com/glossary/bioinformatics
20. https://microbenotes.com/bioinformatics-introduction-and-applications/
21. Benton D. Bioinformatics—principles and potential of a new multidisciplinary tool. *Trends in Biotechnology* 1996;14(8):261–272.

22. Gill SK, Christopher AF, Gupta V, Bansal P. Emerging role of bioinformatics tools and software in evolution of clinical research. *Perspectives in Clinical Research* 2016;7(3):115.

23. Henry Stewart.bioinformatics software resources. *Software Review* 2004;5(3)300–304.

24. Khandelwal I, Sharma A, Agrawal PK, Shrivastava R. Bioinformatics database resources. In *Biotechnology: Concepts, Methodologies, Tools, and Applications* 2019 (pp. 84–119). IGI Global.

25. Milanowska K, Rother K, Bujnicki JM. Databases and bioinformatics tools for the study of DNA repair. *Molecular Biology International* 2011.

26. Wood RD, Mitchell M, Lindahl T. Human DNA repair genes, 2005. *Mutation Research/Fundamental and Molecular Mechanisms of Mutagenesis* 2005;577(1–2):275–283.

27. Wen L, Feng JA. Repair-FunMap: a functional database of proteins of the DNA repair systems. *Bioinformatics* 2004;20(13):2135–2137.

28. Safran M, Dalah I, Alexander J, Rosen N, Iny Stein T, Shmoish M, Nativ N, Bahir I, Doniger T, Krug H, Sirota-Madi A. GeneCards Version 3: the human gene integrator. *Database* 2010;2010.

29. Why Health Informatics Is Its Own Discipline, October 7, 2021. https://online.shrs.pitt.edu/blog/why-health-informatics-is-its-own-discipline/

30. Sayers E, Barrett W, Benson T, Bryant DA, Canese SH, Chetvernin K, Church V, DiCuccio DM, Edgar M, Federhen R, Feolo S, Geer M, Helmberg LY, Kapustin W, Landsman Y, Lipman D, Madden DJ, Maglott TL, Miller DR, Mizrachi V, Ostell I, Pruitt J, Schuler KD, Sequeira GD, Sherry E, Shumway ST, Sirotkin M, Souvorov K, Starchenko A, Tatusova G, Wagner TA, Yaschenko L, Ye E. Database resources of the National Center for Biotechnology Information. *Nucleic Acids Research.* 2009;37(Database):D5–D15.

31. Oyelade J, Soyemi J, Isewon I, Obembe O. Bioinformatics, healthcare informatics and analytics: an imperative for improved healthcare system. *International Journal of Applied Information System* 2015;13(5):1–6.

32. Pereira R, Oliveira J, Sousa M. Bioinformatics and computational tools for next-generation sequencing analysis in clinical genetics. *Journal of Clinical Medicine* 2020;9(1):132–. doi:10.3390/jcm9010132.

33. Sakharkar MK, Yu Y, Kangueane P. Bioinformatics analysis: Gene fusion. In *Bioinformatics: A Concept-Based Introduction* 2009 (pp. 175–181). Springer, Boston, MA.

34. https://www.biologydiscussion.com/biodiversity/bioinformatics/bioinformatics-concept-and-development-genetics/72309

35. Luscombe NM, Greenbaum D, Gerstein M. What is bioinformatics? An introduction and overview. *Yearbook of Medical Informatics.* 2001;10(01):83–100.

36. Van Kamper AH, Horrevoets AJG. *The Role of Bioinformatics in Genomic Medicine; Cardiovascular Research: New Technologies, Methods and Applications.* New York 2005.

37. Gromiha MM, Ou YY. Bioinformatics approaches for functional annotation of membrane proteins. *Briefings in Bioinformatics* 2014;15(2):155–168.

38. Bateman AP, Stein WR, Stormo LD, Gary D, Yates JR. Current protocols in bioinformatics. *The Importance of Biological Databases in Biological Discovery.* 2002;1.1.1–1.1.8. doi:10.1002/0471250953.bi0101s50.

39. https://www.researchgate.net/publication/344759763_Biological_Databases

40. Cannataro M, Guzzi PH, Tradigo G, Veltri P. Biological databases. In *Springer Handbook of Bio-/Neuroinformatics* 2014 (pp. 431–440). Springer, Berlin, Heidelberg.

41. Benson DA, Cavanaugh M, Clark K, Karsch-Mizrachi I, Lipman DJ, Ostell J, Sayers EW. GenBank. *Nucleic Acids Research*, 2013;41(D1):D36–D42. doi:10.1093/nar/gks1195.

42. Kulikova T, Akhtar R, Aldebert P, Althorpe N, Andersson M, Baldwin A, Bates K, Bhattacharyya S, Bower L, Browne P, Castro M. EMBL nucleotide sequence database in 2006. *Nucleic Acids Research.* 2007;35(suppl_1):D16–D20.

43. Robbins RJ. Biological databases: A new scientific literature. *Publishing Research Quarterly.* 1994;10(1):3–27.

44 Krane DE. *Fundamental concepts of bioinformatics.* Pearson Education India; 2002.

45. Gromiha MM. *Protein Bioinformatics: From Sequence to Function.* Academic Press; 2010 September 22.

46. Yanofsky C, Horn V, Thorpe D. Protein structure relationships revealed by mutational analysis. *Science* 1964;146(3651):1593–1594.

47. Altschuh DA, Lesk AM, Bloomer AC, Klug A. Correlation of co-ordinated amino acid substitutions with function in viruses related to tobacco mosaic virus. *Journal of Molecular Biology* 1987;193(4):693–707.

48. Altschuh D, Vernet T, Berti P, Moras D, Nagai K. Coordinated amino acid changes in homologous protein families. *Protein Engineering, Design and Selection* 1988;2(3):193–199. doi:10.1093/protein/2.3.193.

49. Göbel U, Sander C, Schneider R, Valencia A. Correlated mutations and residue contacts in proteins. *Proteins: Structure, Function, and Bioinformatics* 1994;18(4):309–317.
50. Devlin J, Chang MW, Lee K, Toutanova K. Bert: Pre-training of deep bidirectional transformers for language understanding. arXiv preprint arXiv:1810.04805. 2018 Oct 11.
51. Collobert R, Weston J. A unified architecture for natural language processing: Deep neural networks with multitask learning. In *Proceedings of the 25th International Conference on Machine Learning* 2008 July 5 (pp. 160–167).
52. Dai AM, Le QV. Semi-supervised sequence learning. *Advances in Neural Information Processing Systems* 2015;28:3079–3087.
53. Walker M, Ji H, Stent A. Proceedings of the 2018 Conference of the North American Chapter of the Association for Computational Linguistics: Human Language Technologies, Volume 1 (Long Papers). In *Proceedings of the 2018 Conference of the North American Chapter of the Association for Computational Linguistics: Human Language Technologies*, 2018 June.
54. Baevski A, Edunov S, Liu Y, Zettlemoyer L, Auli M. Cloze-driven pretraining of self-attention networks. arXiv preprint arXiv:1903.07785. 2019 Mar 19.
55. Radford A, Wu J, Child R, Luan D, Amodei D, Sutskever I. Language models are unsupervised multitask learners. *OpenAI Blog*. 2019;1(8):9.
56. https://www.pnas.org/content/suppl/2021/04/05/2016239118.DCSupplemental
57. Roumpeka DD, Wallace RJ, Escalettes F, Fotheringham I, Watson M. A review of bioinformatics tools for bio-prospecting from metagenomic sequence data. *Frontiers in Genetics* 2017;8:23.
58. Suarez CG, Burbano ME, Guerrero VA, Tovar PA. Bioinformatics software for genomic: a systematic review on GitHub; 2018.
59. Zou D, Ma L, Yu J, Zhang Z. Biological databases for human research. *Genomics, Proteomics & Bioinformatics* 2015;13(1):55–63.
60. Diniz WJ, Canduri F. Bioinformatics: an overview and its applications. *Genetics and Molecular Research* 2017;16(1):10–4238.
61. Rehm BH, Reinecke F. Bioinformatic tools for gene and protein sequence analysis. In *Medical Biomethods Handbook* 2005 (pp. 387–407). Humana Press.
62. http://www.ncbi.nlm.nih.gov.in
63. http://www.ebi.ac.uk
64. http://www.biochemfusion.com/
65. http://www.rasmol.org/
66. http://qutemol.sourceforge.net
67. http://pymol.org/
68. http://biomolecular-modeling.com/Ascalaph/Ascalaph_Designer.html
69. http://www.gromacs.org/
70. http://www.fos.su.se/~sasha/mdynamix/
71. http://dasher.wustl.edu/tinker/
72. http://www.nvidia.com/object/namd_on_tesla.html
73. www.jmol.org
74. http://spdbv.vital-it.ch/
75. http://gel.ahabs.wisc.edu/mauve/
76. http://jaligner.sourceforge.net/
77. http://hmmer.janelia.org/
78. http://www.mbio.ncsu.edu/BioEdit/bioedit.html
79. http://www.bioinformatics.org/sewer/
80. Clark T, Martin S, Liefeld T. Globally distributed object identification for biological knowledgebases. *Briefings in Bioinformatics* 2004;5(1):59–70.
81. Rai A, Bhati J, Lal SB. Software Tools and Resources for Bioinformatics Research.
82. Ahamed ME. Use of bioinformatics tools in different spheres of life sciences. *Journal of Data Mining Genomics Proteomics* 2014;5:158.
83. Xia X. Bioinformatics and drug discovery. *Current Topics in Medicinal Chemistry* 2017;17(15):1709–26.
84. Thompson JD, Higgins DG, Gibson TJ. CLUSTAL W: improving the sensitivity of progressive multiple sequence alignment through sequence weighting, position-specific gap penalties and weight matrix choice. *Nucleic Acids Research* 1994;22(22):4673–4680.

85. Daugelaite J, O'Driscoll A, Sleator RD. An Overview of Multiple Sequence Alignments and Cloud Computing in Bioinformatics. *ISRN Biomathematics*, 2013:1–14. doi:10.1155/2013/615630.

86. Khan FA, Phillips CD, Baker RJ. Timeframes of speciation, reticulation, and hybridization in the bulldog bat explained through phylogenetic analyses of all genetic transmission elements. *Systematic Biology* 2014;63(1):96–110.

87. Phylogenetic analysis and comparative data: a test and review of evidence. *The American Naturalist* 2002;160(6):712–726. doi:10.1086/343873.

88. Price MN, Dehal PS, Arkin AP. FastTree 2–approximately maximum-likelihood trees for large alignments. *PloS One* 2010;5(3):e9490.

89. Prestridge DS. Predicting Pol II promoter sequences using transcription factor binding sites. *Journal of Molecular Biology* 1995;249(5):923–932.

90. Eddy SR. Profile hidden Markov models. *Bioinformatics*. 1998;14(9):755–763.

91. Baldi P, Brunak S. *Bioinformatics: The Machine Learning Approach*, MIT Press, Cambridge, MA; 1998.

92. Korenberg MJ, David R, Hunter IW, Solomon JE. Automatic classification of protein sequences into structure/function groups via parallel cascade identification: a feasibility study. *Annals of Biomedical Engineering*. 2000;28(7):803–811.

93. Thonpson J. The CLUSTAL X windows interface: flexible strategies for multiple sequence alignment aided by quality analysis tools. *Nucleic Acids Research* 1997;24:4876–4882.

94. Nicholas KB. GeneDoc: Analysis and visualization of genetic variation. *Embnew News* 1997;4:14.

95. Arjmand B, Larijani B, Hosseini MS, Payab M, Gilany K, Goodarzi P, Roudsari PP, Baharvand MA. The horizon of gene therapy in modern medicine: advances and challenges. *Cell Biology and Translational Medicine* 2019;8:33–64.

96. Sung YK, Kim SW. Recent advances in the development of gene delivery systems. *Biomaterials Research* 2019;23(1), 8. doi:10.1186/s40824-019-0156-z

97. Patil PM, Chaudhari PD, Sahu M, Duragkar NJ. Review article on gene therapy. *Research Journal of Pharmacology and Pharmacodynamics* 2012;4(2):77–83.

98. Sagar M, Singh G, Singh B, Pandey N. Bioinformatics advances genetic engineering applications in gene therapy. *International Journal of Advanced Research* 2016; 2(1):37–43.

99. Kuo YC, Wang CC. Colloidal drug delivery system for brain-targeting therapy. *Colloid and Interface Science in Pharmaceutical Research and Development*. 2014:389–410.

100. Gonçalves GA, Paiva RD. Gene therapy: advances, challenges and perspectives. *Einstein* (Sao Paulo). 2017;15:369–375.

101. Mooney SD, Krishnan VG, Evani US. Bioinformatic tools for identifying disease gene and SNP candidates. *Genetic Variation* 2010;307–319.

102. Wivel NA, Wilson JM. Method of gene delivery. *Hematology/Oncology Clinics of North America* 1997;12(3):483–501.

103. Wu D, Rice CM, Wang X. Cancer bioinformatics: A new approach to systems clinical medicine. *BMC Bioinformatics* 2012;13(1):1–4.

104. Douglas JT. Cancer gene therapy. *Technology in Cancer Research & Treatment* 2003;2(1):51–64.

105. Nimesh S, Halappanavar S, Kaushik NK, Kumar P. Advances in gene delivery systems. *BioMed Research International* 2015;2015.

106. Singh G. Treatment options for osteoarthritis. *Surgical Technology International* 2003;11:287–292.

107. Nayerossadat N, Maedeh T, Ali PA. Viral and nonviral delivery systems for gene delivery. *Advanced Biomedical Research* 2012;1.

108. Ylä-Herttuala S, Baker AH. Cardiovascular gene therapy: past, present, and future. *Molecular Therapy* 2017;25(5):1095–1106.

9 Drug Development Using Cloud Application

Shilpa Singh, Sonali Sundram, and Rishabha Malviya
Galgotias University, Greater Noida, India

Mahendran Sekar
University Kuala Lumpur, Ipoh, Perak, Malaysia

CONTENTS

DOI: 10.1201/9781003226949-9

9.1   HISTORY OF CLOUD COMPUTING

Amazon, a prominent e-commerce company, created cloud computing in 2002 after investing in a fleet of massive servers that were designed to deal with the tremendous load of orders placed at the site during the Christmas season, which instead, were left idle for the rest of the year. Amazon has made significant investments in this field to keep growing their network and solutions. Other IT firms, such as Google and Microsoft, have also begun to provide comparable services [1].

Their objective was to standardize data exchange procedures throughout an informatics-enabled investigation, innovation, and clinical genomes that will increase the speed of R&D collaboration [2–4]. Nevertheless, due to the absence of subscriptions financing from the pharmaceutical industry, the initial sector cloud-based research strategy was not realized [2, 4]. Bioscience's research academics, especially, have started seeing the advantages of cooperation and interdisciplinary abilities because of the constant flow of high-throughput datasets. For example, in 2005, two worldwide grid-computing efforts, WISDOM and DIANE, concentrated on discovering enzyme inhibitors and therapeutic targets for malaria parasites and bird flu (H1N1 virus) [4–6].

Cost–benefit analysis (CBA) of the grid systems – a collection of networked computers that collaborate as a virtual supercomputer to handle enormous tasks like data analysis and weather forecasting - though, found that total grid effectiveness didn't exceed 50 percent due to network failures and work burden management issues. Unlike many other industry sectors, in which cloud computing requirements are described by cost-efficiency concerns, bioscience's ecosystem cloud execution is best acknowledged through the light of the biochemist and his or her study requirements, which are prominent due to the data-intensive essence of bioscience studies [4].

9.2   AIM OF CLOUD COMPUTING

Cloud computing's primary purpose is the delivery to customers of hardware as well as software assets via network connections. The benefits of cloud computing can differ from one cloud to the next. Memory, CPU, storage, explicit programmers, operating systems, and so on are examples of these assets [7].

9.3   DRUG DEVELOPMENT USING CLOUD COMPUTING

Drug development companies can no longer manage to use old, expensive, and time consuming techniques for drug discovery. They also can't cling to obsolete ideas that rely on prior computer drug development flops. A variety of modern ways are producing outcomes that are faster, more precise, and less expensive. Cloud computing, paired with Moore's Law, has created a once-in-a-lifetime chance to employ the low-cost high-performance computer to drug development. As a result of this mix, the cloud has emerged as one of the most powerful locations for drug development, with novel methodologies that may be used to gain greater success. Conventional drug development costs and timetables are far too expensive, exacerbated by exorbitant system failures, developing extremely high expenses that are passed on to the customer, and jeopardizing our medical system's economic viability [8, 9]. The production of new medicines with possible interactions with targeted therapies is critical in the drug discovery procedure. Investigational high-throughput screening (HTS) was used to identify potential leads in the past; however, it is costly and time consuming [10]. A common drug research process might take 14 years to complete from target identification to FDA approval, with an estimated cost of $800 million. However, losses in various rounds of drug testing has lately resulted in a drop in the number of new pharmaceuticals on the market. Research done in November 2018 to determine the overall price of crucial studies for the production of new FDA-approved medications showed that in the 2015 to 2016 timeframe, the average price of studies conducted for 59 novel medications was $19 million. As a result, it is critical to replace the inefficient, low-price, and broad-spectrum computing methodologies used in traditional drug development with more efficient, low-cost, and wide computing options [11].

Cloud computing allows for more complex computational methods to be combined with quick production and evaluation, allowing corporations to find molecules that are better suited for development from the start. Choosing molecules with a better likelihood of succeeding can then be used to lower total costs, which is necessary if customized treatment or "nichebuster" medications are to be achieved. Cloud computing allows for greater computational methods, which addresses two of the key issues with conventional drug development. It aids in increasing productivity by selecting chemicals that attach to target antigens and also have excellent drug-like qualities. However, the objective isn't just to save costs and enhance speed. It's all about developing significantly better chemicals for extremely difficult-to-drug targets [12]. Cloud computing aids in the development of molecules for such targets by supplying large amounts of computer capacity, allowing for the use of high time-consuming approaches, but which have designs that are atomic structurally exact and in silico. Cloud computing finds compounds in new chemical regions, rather than using old screening decks that have previously failed. Drug targets that were difficult to achieve are now becoming easy because of cloud computing. Traditional algorithms, for instance, are inadequate when dealing with targets with little structural information, like G-protein-coupled receptors (GPCRs). Nevertheless, using comprehensive homology modeling with molecular modeling approaches can assist in the acquisition of information about the structure, when paired with quantum chemistry in the cloud and when exploring molecular space for new compounds, which may lead to viable molecules for traditionally unsolvable targets [13]. Cloud computing is widely utilized for creating computation-intensive concurrent programs in computer servers across the globe. The computational requirements of many complicated applications are met by operational scheduling algorithms that take into consideration a variety of criteria such as resource price and power, and execution time (makespan). When it comes to meeting client needs and providing a better end-user experience, cloud networks provide an atmosphere with appropriate scheduling algorithms to gain greater task-to-processor mappings [14].

9.4   DEFINITION OF CLOUD COMPUTING

Cloud computing (CC) is a way of looking at the world that enables "utility computing," such as the gradual rental of computation tools like computer processing capacity, memory, and tools related to networking in which there is little or no collaboration with the supplier. The plan of these systems was focused on security and privacy perspectives, which are both considered as basic [15]. CC also alleviates the need for a huge amount of storage to deal with complex kinetic data, which is required by this method [16].

CC is a collection of business-driven services that provide on-demand, flexible, QoS-assured, often customized, cost-effective computing that can be accessed simply [17]. Whether an organization chooses to purchase and operate its cloud or procure cloud services from a third party, the management, pricing, and security of the cloud are all affected [18]. Clients have access to their apps and data at any time and from any location. They can use any computer connected to the internet to access the CC system. Data is not restricted to a single user's hard disk or even a company's internal network [19]. Pharmaceutical production can be improved by using automated equipment, cloud-based smart apps, and cyber-security technologies. This is beneficial to the manufacture of pharmaceuticals. This sector is focused on supplying safe, certified, and high-quality products to meet market demands [20]. There are three elements in CC: the cloud service provider (CSP), the data owner (DO), and the client. The data owners at the cloud server share their information or keep track of their records. The cloud facilities are available from the CSP to both the DO and the client [21].

- **Cloud Service Provider (CSP):** the focal authority or general administrator of every cloud system which is responsible for maintaining the foundation and providing cloud services by utilizing several servers with sufficient processing power and memory.
- **Data Owner (DO):** the device that saves private and ordinary statistics as well as larger statistics; in a cloud environment the CSP regulates the statistics.
- **User:** approved elements or groups of people who are able to use the data or services available in the cloud server [22].

9.5 CLOUD COMPUTING CLASSIFICATIONS

The deployment model and the service model are the two paradigms that describe CC. There are three types of service models [23]. The service models are explained below with examples (see also Table 9.1).

To begin, SaaS is known as the uppermost part of the arrangement, and is easily defined as the client employing some apps of the service provided by the cloud platform [23].

9.5.1 SAAS (Software as a Service)

This provides clients with an opportunity to make use of software on demand. Clients are given the software on a rental basis and are only charged for what they use [25–27].

A few instances of SaaS techniques for drug development involve Swiss Target Prediction for predicting proteomics for small molecules [28], SwissADME for assessing pharmacokinetic profile, drug-likeness, pharmaceutical chemistry affability of small molecules [29], and numerous application programming interfaces (APIs) and graphical user interfaces (GUIs) for predicting structural parameters like partition coefficients [30, 31].

9.5.2 PAAS (Platform-as-a-Service)

This layer is called the middleware part of the service architecture, in which software engineers may install more commands and operate packages and software resources to develop applications [23].

TABLE 9.1

Cloud Computing Technologies with Applications [24]

	Cloud Computing Platforms	Cloud Applications (Examples)
1	Software as a Service (SaaS)	Facebook, YouTube, Google Apps
2	Platform as a Service (PaaS)	Amazon SimpleDB, Microsoft Azure, Google App Engine
3	Infrastructure as a Service (IaaS)	Amazon Elastic Compute Cloud (Amazon EC2), FlexiScale, GoGrid

For executing an application in the cloud, this service must be run in a certain environment. As a result, the vendors provide the stage which has the operating system, web server, and programming language [27].

9.5.3 IAAS (INFRASTRUCTURE-AS-A-SERVICE)

Finally, IaaS is the lowest part of the service level in which customers have command of hardware resources such as storage, a disk part, and a central processor, which they may use based on how they pay [23]. Customers who utilize the IaaS cloud directly employ IT infrastructures (processing, storage, organizations, and other important computer resources) [32]. The deployment arrangement is known as the second type of CC [23] (Figure 9.1, Table 9.2).

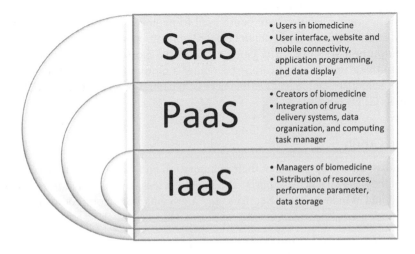

FIGURE 9.1 Cloud computing models used in biomedicine research.

TABLE 9.2
Three Service Models of Cloud Computing [31]

		Infrastructure as a Service (IAAS)	Platform as a Service	Software as Service
1	Application	User Managed	Provider Managed	Provider Managed
2	Data	User Managed	Provider Managed	Provider Managed
3	Runtime	User Managed	Provider Managed	Provider Managed
4	Middleware	User Managed	Provider Managed	Provider Managed
5	Operating System	User Managed	Provider Managed	Provider Managed
6	Virtualization	Provider Managed	Provider Managed	Provider Managed
7	Networking	Provider Managed	Provider Managed	Provider Managed
8	Storage	Provider Managed	Provider Managed	Provider Managed
9	Servers	Provider Managed	Provider Managed	Provider Managed

9.6 FOUR CATEGORIES OF CLOUD TRANSMITTING MODELS

- Private cloud;
- Public cloud;
- Community cloud;
- Hybrid cloud [21] (Figure 9.2).

9.6.1 PRIVATE CLOUD

In private CC, the cloud merchant's adaptive resources and virtual applications are kept jointly for making it accessible to CC customers for using and sharing. This is different from the public cloud in which all of the cloud services and implementation, such as intranet functionality, are managed by the real organization. Because of its established inner openness, private CC usage has more security compared to public cloud usage [33]. CC is managed and controlled within an organization's server farm, referred to as a private cloud [34].

Container-orchestration solutions are being used to manage the installation and administration of a huge proportion of this kind of container-based apps in operation. K8s (Kubernetes), initially created and non-proprietary software by Google, is now the most extensively utilized system today. A K8s cluster running on local hardware is becoming a more popular option for the private cloud platform, giving scientists simple and flexible access to central processing units (CPU) and graphic processing units (GPU) [28, 29].

9.6.2 PUBLIC CLOUD

Customers that use the cloud outsource their computation and storage to public providers and pay for the services they use on a per-use basis. The main services in public clouds are Amazon Elastic Compute Cloud and Windows Azure Services, and a growing number of companies are riding this

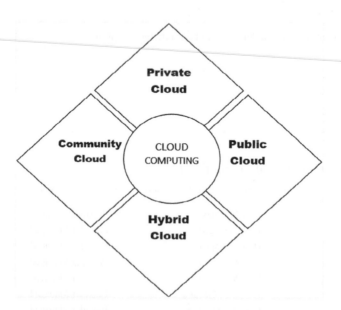

FIGURE 9.2 Types of cloud computing.

wave to provide public computing services. These cloud providers offer a diverse range of cost, good performance, and functionality options [35, 36].

Most public cloud services, like Google Cloud Platform, Microsoft Azure, Amazon Elastic Computing (EC2), and Aliyun, all have substantial and expandable catalogs of the virtual appliance (VA) and the virtual machine image (VMI) with preloaded software platforms that are ready for deployment and use. These VMIs can considerably ease tool deployment in the drug development process and aid repeatability [37].

9.6.3 COMMUNITY CLOUD

This alludes to a one-of-a-kind cloud environment that is distributed and regulated by the group that linked organizations interested in a certain sector or for a vertical market. This deployment paradigm brings together resources from a variety of organizations in a community that shares common issues (like security, administration, and consistency). It usually refers to specific purpose cloud computing systems that are distributed and taken care of by many linked organizations operating around a certain area or a vertical market [38].

9.6.4 HYBRID CLOUD

A hybrid cloud is one type of private CC that is connected with at least one outer cloud service, is operated in the middle, is functioned as a single unit, and is defined with the help of a secured organization. It provides digital information technology services by combining public and private clouds [33].

9.7 CONCEPT OF THE DRUG DEVELOPMENT PROCESS

It is currently well accepted that the use of computational drug revelation (CDD) methodologies may help with the revealing of novel pharmaceuticals, and several endorsed medications have reached and passed clinical preliminaries with their help. The majority of drug disclosure studies focus on improving certain aspects of the drug development cycle, which may be divided into three stages:

1. A stage of revelation in which a large number of candidate compounds are tested.
2. A selection step, during which the prospective medications are tested in a preclinical setting.
3. A stage of assessment, during which the medicine is developed and wide clinical preliminaries are carried out [39].

9.8 DRUG DISCOVERY

Drug development is a difficult task that requires many boundaries that are enhanced for designs that have already been created for different pharmacological properties. Adequate bonding affinities among the medicine and its main purpose is the explanation given to the drug's intensifying consequences when it targets certain biological molecules. As a result, the fundamental simplification of the results obtained in the process of the drug development levels of hit ID improves the initial stage which is also called a hit to lead and enhances the binding affinity. For hit distinguishing evidence, a collection of mixes is linked to confirmed movement for the biological results, generally by high throughput screening and virtual screening, and this is followed by exploratory approval from a bundle of various combinations [40].

9.8.1 Drug Discovery Pathway

Generally, the current drug discovery procedure is divided into three stages: drug discovery, drug designing assessment, and drug development.

- **Stage 1:** Drug discovery is the process of identifying and synthesizing drugs from plant origin and compounds. It includes some tests to determine the efficacy.
- **Stage 2:** A study of drug design might concentrate on ways to improve the selectivity and efficacy of potential drugs.
- **Stage 3:** Pre-clinical research, clinical development, drug authorization, and recalls are all part of drug development. It stresses more drug knowledge, such as possible advantages, safety issues, optimal dosage, the best method of preparation, and the mode of delivery selected. It also includes human tests for efficacy, safety, as well as many other critical factors.

The drug development method eventually switches to the following six methods that have previously been validated by experts [41].

9.8.2 Pathophysiology of Diseases

This offers superior suitable solutions to drug discovery concerns, such as the precise diagnosis and management of patients and disease areas.

- **Target identification:** This phase entails determining the precise mechanisms in a given disease region.
- **Development and screening of assays:** This will look into what type of test to perform. The very first step is to determine if it is target-dependent or phenotypic.
- **Hit to lead:** You'll get the hit triage in this stage. The findings will divide into three categories: highly fascinating, informative, and nonfactor.
- **Lead optimization:** This entails classic pharmaceutical science, and each will begin to increase efficacy, specificity, hazardous adverse effects, and bioavailability. The applicants are reduced to a maximum of three clinical applicants.
- **Preclinical development:** In this phase, the typical scalable issues with each novel drug must be addressed.
- **Clinical trial drug development:** This is the stage at which actual investment is made. It is also the pivotal step for the entire procedure. To avoid wasting effort and money, ensure all is in order when proceeding with this phase [41, 42] (Figure 9.3).

9.9 ROLE OF CLOUD COMPUTING IN DRUG DEVELOPMENT

CC is an attractive tool in the contribution of computational resources for drug research conducted with a variety of purposes. To begin, you simply require a little hardware if you utilize the public cloud service. Other customers pay only if they use assets throughout the research and if the quantity of the asset is adjusted as per requirement. This is useful in the prediction of modeling since the majority of the computational power is only required for a smaller duration, and the cost for developing a model can be simply calculated. Model builders without access to computer clusters may find cloud computing to be an interesting tool for speeding up their work. When a large number of services (known as cloud sourcing) and the administration of IT infrastructure and the organization of cloud providers are outsourced, it becomes less difficult in research and development to follow in their footsteps since the formal and legal frameworks are already in place. In drug development, data

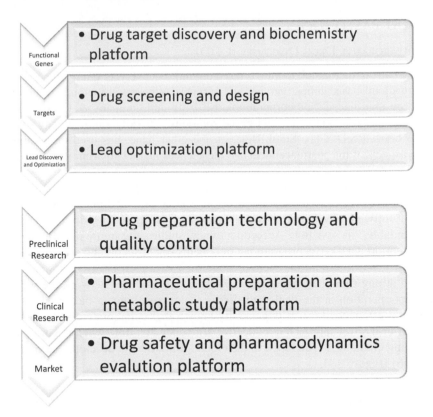

FIGURE 9.3   Discovery and development process.

TABLE 9.3
Drug Development Using Cloud Computing

R & D (Step 1)	Clinical Trial Phases (Step 2)	Production and Distribution (Step 3)	Postmarketing Surveillance (PMS) (Step 4)
Computation and model construction	Clinical research analytics	Sales and marketing analytics	Process safety
Partnerships and collaborative investigation	Clinical partnerships	Campaign analysis	Clinical data management (CDM)
Converting research	Clinical research partnership	Supply chain management	Tools for connecting patients with healthcare providers
Computer-assisted biology	–	Contract administration	–
Biometry	–	–	–

security is crucial and using a cloud provider which is external needs a proper-thought-out security policy and encrypted data to transfer with suitable authority/authenticity. On the other side, cloud providers are fully aware of this, and most of them adhere to stringent security procedures [36].

CC is a disrupting factor in the pharmaceutical and biotech business model [4]. The steps of drug development using CC are shown in Table 9.3.

9.10   CLOUD-BASED TOOLS

9.10.1   COLLABORATIVE DRUG DISCOVERY (CDD)

In the pharmaceutical sector, collaborative research and discovery is one of the most prominent applications of cloud-based infrastructures and services. Whereas the cloud's effect on R&D is rising, two large pharmaceuticals corporations, Eli Lilly and company & GlaxoSmithKline, are acknowledged as early adopters of cloud-based solutions. Eli Lilly and company only use cloud technology to boost R&D. GlaxoSmithKline, on the other hand, has used cloud applications to tackle several aspects of the pharmaceutical and biosciences market environment, such as R&D and worldwide sales [4, 43].

"There are almost no borders in a cloud-based world," explains Barry Bunin, CDD's CEO and founder. CDD's service is more than just a data facilitator or storage solution. It also contains restricted software developed in-house to aid and work on drug discovery and make the data "understandable," he says [44]. According to new studies, the future paradigm of biomedical research will be more CDD. The program not only helps scientists organize and analyze their data more successfully, but it also allows them to share their data in any way they want, with anyone they want, and at any time they want. The CDD software and user network are well-positioned to strengthen cooperation in the neglected illness sector, resulting in increased drug discovery and development efficiency [45]. It is generally known that collaborative technologies for drug development offer a novel approach to collective efficiency at a time when the drug development industry is facing challenges. The move to the cloud allows for the development of a solution for the industry [46] (Figure 9.4).

9.10.2   IN SILICO DRUG DISCOVERY

In silico drug discovery—in silico meaning "computer-aided"—is a cost-effective way to lower the price of the creation and invention of modern medications in the future. Virtual screening is used for this purpose to find the most effective drugs for *in vitro* study from a massive number of chemical ingredients (millions of compounds) [47].

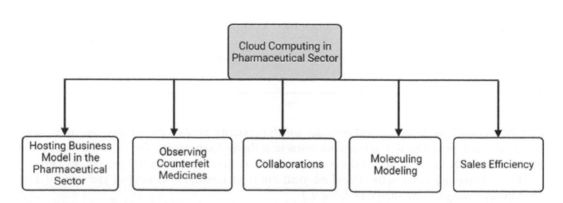

FIGURE 9.4   Cloud computing in the pharmaceutical industry.

9.10.3 FREE ENERGY PERTURBATION (FEP)

The free energy perturbation (FEP) method, which is based on statistical concepts, has been getting a lot of interest for predicting the binding affinities between candidate compounds and their biological targets because of its consistency in terms of effectiveness. The initial state is interpolated between two distinct physical states when performing FEP computations, and the final (target) stage is gradually altered by a coupling parameter. The binding free energy of a ligand can be calculated in two ways: relative binding free energy (RBFE) and absolute binding free energy (ABFE) [40].

9.11 CLOUD COMPUTING ROLE IN DRUG REPOSITIONING

The examination of preclinical and toxicological evaluation in the previous phases accounts for a substantial percentage of the expense of medication growth. An acceptable practical advantage can be established by discovering a unique capacity for an all-around existing medicament. CC can assist in drug repositioning by speeding up virtual computers being used to predict ligand-protein binding that performs the same computations. By utilizing CC, researchers may investigate the site of 3D ligand binding faster by employing tools like cloud protein-ligand binding sites (C-PLBS). These are capable of performing many investigations concurrently, thereby speeding up the cycle without monopolizing important local resources.

9.12 DRUG MONITORING WITH INTEGRATED CLOUD COMPUTING

Every collaborator in the drug development process can benefit from guidelines that handle data formats where the issue of organization discontinuity might be addressed. As a result, experts will want to use the resource of CC to integrate a huge amount of data collection to address available drug disclosure issues, like drug security after sale. The program, as well as CC SMAP (which is a set of software tools for analyzing and comparing data and similarity searches for 3D protein themes), provide the opportunity to conduct this kind of data-mining study as well as, to elucidate its findings, combine databases for detecting off-target medicines by using the genomic sequence. Furthermore, SMAP operating in Cloud-PLBS may operate in several equal assignment modes, speeding up the cycle [48].

9.13 HIGH THROUGHPUT SCREENING (HTS)

Approval, target selection, high throughput, and hits for lead change absorption, distribution, metabolism, excretion, and toxicity (ADMET) studies are all performed using HTS, among other things. Even though innovation has aided us in identifying a variety of new targets and a large number of candidate molecules, and with an enormous expansion in the disclosure cycle and development cost, the pace of transformation from "hit-to-drug" is still problematic. Two methodological studies on ensuring DNA arrangement were published by Fred Sanger and Alen R. Coulson in 1977, which revolutionized biology by creating a technology that can translate the complete genome [49, 50]. Even medium-sized experimental labs had never anticipated providing terabytes of sequencing data. Advances in high-throughput technology have simplified the process of obtaining patient genetic profiles. The cost of sequencing genomes has dropped to new lows because of cutting-edge sequencing technology. In pharmacogenomics and genomics research, these kinds of sequencing techniques are increasingly often employed. When these tools are used in large-scale clinical research, they create a data storm. Scientists face many challenges as a result of the abundance of data and the promising conditions. To begin with, storing such data demands a lot of room due to its constant increase, and arranging space for this expanding data is becoming ever more burdensome. Second, analyzing omics data necessitates the use of particular bioinformatics software and tools, which necessitate a large number of computer resources, which is a difficult task [51].

9.14 INTRODUCTION TO HIGH-PERFORMANCE COMPUTING (HPC)

Biological data cannot be randomly divided because of its complexity. Also, this makes it difficult for the next generation high-performing computing technologies to find accuracy and scalability [52]. HOC and cloud computing are very different. In HPC, the architecture is designed for parallel execution and there is a fast interconnection between nodes. Cloud computing, on the other hand, is better at scalability, and for doing multiple things at the same time [36].

9.15 MAIN APPLICATION OF CLOUD COMPUTING IN DRUG DEVELOPMENT

9.15.1 VIRTUAL SCREENING AND DOCKING USING CLOUD COMPUTING

Virtual screening has recently gained traction as a dynamic and useful innovation in the pharmaceutical business for exploring new drug-like chemicals or alleged hits. Virtual screening based on construction comprises the computerized as well as the docking in a hurry of a huge number of chemical substances in opposition to a protein-binding or rather a dynamic area, directing a plan for using the rapidly increasing quantity of protein three-dimensional structures. Virtual screening based on primary data starts with a well-known confirmation of a target molecule's probable ligand-binding area [53].

Kang et al. in 2012 built the computational biology community cloud (CBCC), which is a service-oriented cloud computing architecture (SOCCA). Cloud users, cloud services, and the community cloud platform (CCP) are the three key aspects, CBCC fundamental architecture consists of cloud services. CCP's user-friendly software platform interface makes obtaining and configuring bandwidth a breeze. It gives customers complete power over their computational services and allows it to run on a CBCC computing environment, enabling them to scale capacity up or down quickly as their computation requires. Cloud users can start working as soon as they sign into a CCP. Then it's up to the CCP to schedule services and fulfill the requirements of the user quickly and properly. In CBCC, users may now use DOCK, FlexGAsDock, and AGAsDock for molecular docking and virtual screening.

The CBCC will send certain http tasks to computers as part of the cloud task. Each http task finds certain potential molecules for such screening inside the compound's database, which has a nearly comparable number of small molecules. The task comprises numerous activities which will complete the hunt for a molecule's best configuration. When a CBCC's services (virtual servers) receive an http task, each one of the tiny molecules provided to the task is evaluated separately; also the best conformational finding for every molecule is recirculated to the CBCC for evaluation [54]. Computing in cloud virtualization is the backbone of CC because it employs virtual machine monitor (VMM) technologies to hide, partition, and distribute essential hardware functions as virtual machines (VMs). CC integrates virtual services such as network and memory and enables users to swiftly scale resources up or down with little input from the service provider. Because of its widespread adoption, CC is currently used in almost all types of drug research [31, 55]. In actuality, drug research is a dynamic process, and cloud-based solutions enable a company or laboratory to adapt and reuse underlying hardware assets to meet changing demands [31, 56] (Figure 9.5).

9.15.2 STRUCTURE-BASED DRUG DISCOVERY WITH VIRTUAL SCREENING

Test information like X-beams, nuclear magnetic resonance (NMR), neutron scattering spectroscopy (NSS), molecular dynamics (MD), or homology modeling recreations can all be used to obtain an objective design. The receptor's drug capability, the binding location chosen, the most appropriate protein structure chosen, the receptor's incorporation adaptability, and protonation states all have a job to do. Considering whether in a binding site there are water particles is another important factor to consider regarding a biological objective for Structure-based virtual screening (SBVS).

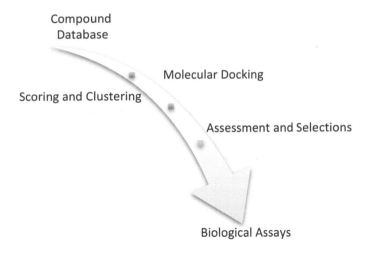

FIGURE 9.5 Workflow of molecular docking-based virtual screening.

It is becoming increasingly crucial to find the sites of ligand binding on biological targets [57]. There are two main types of virtual screening: structure-based virtual screening (SBVS) and ligand-based virtual screening (LBVS) [58].

9.15.3 SMALL MOLECULE VIRTUAL SCREENING

Here, we present a free online protocol for small-molecule virtual screening that integrates three recently released web servers and incorporates three key advances: ADME-Tox is filtered using the FAF-Drugs4 through the network server; virtual screening based on docking using network server MTiOpenScreen, Molecular echanics (MM) optimization through the network server Automatic Molecular Mechanics Optimization for in silico screening (AMMO). There are three web servers hosted by Ressource Parisienne in Bioinformatique Structurale (RPBS). There is a step dedicated to bioinformatics computations at their most basic level (around 60,000 associations each year). Work execution, storage, asset standards, and other functions are all controlled by the RPBS computer system. All clients' data is kept confidential [59].

9.15.3.1 New Trends in Virtual Screening

The scale on which trials are conducted is one component of virtual screening that has altered dramatically in recent years. Previously, it was assumed that a virtual screen was made up of ranging from a few hundred thousand to a few million molecules. Firms can supply databases comprising more than a billion molecules due to a combination of known chemistry and easily available reagents. Virtual screening is no longer limited to local computer clusters due to these billion-molecule datasets. However, the expansion of low-cost cloud computing capabilities has paralleled the expansion of available chemical libraries. With the right computing infrastructure, virtual displays with low-cost access to tens of thousands of CPUs are possible [60].

9.16 HIGH CONTENT SCREENING (HCS)

HCS is a powerful logical invention that yields physiologically relevant, truly vigorous data that is amenable to high throughput, which is a common requirement. Furthermore, HCS allows for the testing of new types of measures, including morphological examinations, like movement assessments, neuronal growth, and cylinder design, as well as tests that focus on only a subpopulation of cells. Cell cycle tests, infection tests, and cell separation are all common models [61]. It is difficult to pinpoint a pivotal moment in the development of HCS technology, although Giuliano and colleagues coined the term "high content screening" for the first time in 1997. The availability of enhanced disease-relevant cell models, reagents, open-source image inspection tools, and, most importantly, increasingly complicated and acceptable HCS stages has aided the spread of HCS in pharmaceutical companies and academia. Along with the biological model, HCS innovation is heavily reliant on the availability of atomic tools (antibodies, fluorescent colors, assays, fluorescent proteins, and so on), apparatus, and image analysis software [62]. Whether "blasting" HTS hits against a battery of HCS analyses, or analyzing the most current novel lead arrangement in a single cell-based screen, knowing what impact on cell homeostasis has occurred is critical for all pharmacological targets. This can address both the desired and unfavorable outcomes (or the off-target impacts) [63]. HCS includes two major examination systems: fluorescence-based reagents along with fluorescence microscopy using auto-electronic pictorials. For more than 20 years, imaging fluorescence microscopy has been a useful human-interaction research technology. Test preparation, examination improvement and advancement, and a high-efficiency magnifier to take images, as well as subsequent image development and investigation, are all part of the overall work procedure in high-content imaging. Regardless, the largest challenge in current picture-based drug discovery is assessing and selecting the relevant highlights from a noisy data collection and then interpreting the HCS findings [63].

9.17 NEXT GENERATION SEQUENCING (NGS)

Success (known length), arrangement quality, high throughput, and low cost are all important estimates for the success of cutting-edge technology. Because of their short lengths, NGS methods are useful for discovering noncoding RNA. NGS can also help by detecting recent genomic biomarkers, the recognition of variations, pharmacogenetics, self-treatment, object identification, drug resistance research and approval, clinical diagnostics, vaccine development, and other things [64]. Clinical diagnostics has a lot of promise as well. The drug research and development sector has many issues, including rising R&D costs and the coordination of diverse medications to meet the needs of patients, regulators, and payers. NGS has also been shown to be an effective approach for identifying therapeutically relevant variants in mice. This can frequently provide useful information for target approval [65]. Massively parallel sequencing can be used on germline DNA for quality affiliation reads and cancer genome research, and it might lead to a paradigm shift in how mutations that cause rare diseases are identified.

Largely equitable sequencing will need access to advanced computational and bioinformatics assistance much beyond that of most research labs [66]. While we recognize that several kinds of genomic techniques based on NGS (transcriptome and methylation portraying are among the techniques used) are used in drug manufacturing, they only look at how DNA sequencing is utilized for identifying the object in the medication sector for drug targeting and hereditarily defined preliminaries in medicine in this audit. NGS has a plethora of applications that can reveal a slew of variations associated with gene disorders, as well as differentiate target features for future drug development efforts [67]. NGS approaches, such as pharmacogenetics and genomics, have transformed the recognition of differences in a variety of genome studies and portrayals.

The next aspect to consider is the ability of NGS technology to detect PGx (pharmacogenomics) differences in clinical practice. There is no denying that NGS methods help to identify PGx mutants in drug testing, as well as projecting medication reactions or toxic effects, resulting in the computation or evaluation of appropriate medication measurements for patients. The drug result could be classified as proficient, inefficient, toxic, or safe, based on the patient's reactions. Although many techniques based on NGS in genomics are used in clinical trials, (including transcriptome and methylation profiling), we will only look at how DNA sequencing is utilized for the medication sector for drug targeting to recognize the main points and the hereditarily defined medication preliminary in this audit [68].

9.18 CLOUD COMPUTING FOR COMPARATIVE GENOMICS

The cloud has been widely used in the financial sector, fitness, and the amusement sector. However, it still has little influence on related comparative genomics. Certain parameters, such as "- - jobconf mapred.task.timeout," need trial and error to get the ideal value for optimal compute cloud performance and cost effectiveness. The greatest amount of time is estimated for conducting reciprocal smallest distance (RSD) cloud computation from the set of two genomes. This is determined using this threshold [69]. In this case, CC services have emerged as a cost-effective option for privately installed computer clusters. They provide computational resources and data storage that are effectively limitless, unaffected by other clients' applications or system maintenance, and charged on a per-user basis. As a result, comparative genomics is a powerful and growing subject that is becoming ever more insightful as genetic grouping data accumulates. In comparative genomics, the arrangement of DNA successions is the central interaction. A mapping of the nucleotides in one grouping onto the nucleotides in the other grouping is called an arrangement. To enhance the number of places with matching nucleotides, holes are added into either sequence. To alter at least two successions, several strong arranging algorithms have been developed. Regardless, the computing power required to alter billions of nucleotides between at least two species is much beyond what is generally available in individual laboratories. As a result, a few research groups make pre-computed genome succession arrangements available via servers or software [70]. The genomics community is steadily moving to CC, resulting in the creation of a new genome informatics ecosystem that is reliant on CC. Data and computational resources are stored in the cloud, which is managed by a cloud service provider in cloud-based genomic informatics systems.

RSD is a method of determining orthologous groupings between sets of genomes by examining the entire genome. The calculation achieves the goal through a work process that includes a few other programs. It is evaluated to look at 1000 genomes with constant access to 300 processing centers [71]. Cloudburst and Cloud Aligner are parallel read mapping algorithms that are designed to map NGS information to the genetic code and the scientific research is used for other standard genomes such as genotyping, personal genomics, and Single Nucleotide Polymorphism (SNP) discovery. Hadoop MapReduce technology, which is open source, is hired by them to virtualize the computations across several multiple processors. A lengthy series was specifically developed by Cloud Aligner. Crossbow, a Hadoop alignment and SNP identification tool, combines the speed of the short read aligner Bowtie with the accuracy of SOAPsnp to execute several human-parts datasets per day. This is another tool that is part of Hadoop[72].

9.19 CLOUD PLATFORMS FOR GENOMICS

- Microsoft, Google, and Amazon all provide CC services for genomics, which is a cost-effective solution for experts.
- Amazon Web Services is now the most popular cloud service provider.
- They provide a variety of tools for storing and analyzing the data generated by whole genome sequencing. Amazon S3 is used to store data in a secure, encrypted, and repeatable environment, while EC2 provides a flexible, agile, and robust computing environment.

9.19.1 GOOGLE GENOMICS

Google Genomics seems to be a CC service that allows you to save, analyze, examine, and share genomics information. Plan and diminish are the two primary steps of the MapReduce computation. The operations are carried out simultaneously throughout the cluster's vast number of nodes [73]. MapReduce assesses genomic applications, whereas the guide interaction generates a large amount of intermediate data, which may be saved on disk or sent to reducer hubs around the company [74]. MapReduce is a significant improvement in CC because it can quickly and safely handle large datasets on commodity hardware [75].

9.19.2 DNANEXUS

DNAnexus provides solutions for DNA sequencing as well as for professionals who work with the data generated by sequencing [73]. Mercury was created in the cloud using the DNAnexus platform (using Amazon Web Services' EC2 and S3). On a cloud architecture, DNAnexus works on a monitor, and collaborates, develops, and executes by supplying a certain amount of reflection. In the organization of the DNAnexus platform, Mercury pipeline's constituent steps appear as individual "applets," which are subsequently interconnected to form a work process. In DNAnexus, the Mercury computing consists of commands, hence it is used in the DNAnexus command-line interface and starts the pipeline in the cloud. On a neighboring terminal, the Mercury code for DNAnexus is run. For example, Mercury might be provided with a set of test FASTQ documents and metadata areas, and will transmit the data and start the predetermined work process within DNAnexus [76].

9.19.3 MICROARRAYS

The pharmaceutical sector is being crushed by the increasing costs of bringing a medicine to market and lower profits. To stay profitable, pharmaceutical companies need to expand the number of medications they create by reducing development time, lowering clinical costs, reducing the rate of disappointment, and promoting better medication launches. In pharmaceutical development, microarrays are expected to be the dominating innovation for articulation and hereditary exploration. Microarrays are two-dimensional tiny surfaces to which a large number of tests are attached. They provide nearly identical results when it comes to hybridization-based sequencing or articulation quality evaluation [77]. Microarray technology consists of two types of chips:

1. Expression microarrays, which are used to research gene activity under various conditions;
2. Genomic microarrays (such as Drug Metabolism Enzymes and Transporters (DMET) arrays), which are used to explore differences in genome sequences [78].

Although microarrays have been used for a long time, the advent of genome sequencing has sparked interest in multi-quality inquiries at the same time. Microarrays have been used in the drug development and treatment sector for the articulation assessment of tissues or cells in numerous illness conditions, pharmacogenomics, toxicogenomics, and SNP analysis. However, alternative technologies are improving the DNA microarray, which is currently employed in many drug development domains and will continue to develop. The influence of DNA microarrays in our study on the natural chemistry of common and unusual cells is substantial, along with therapeutic target selection. However, their application is not limited to the biology of human cells: this is also being worked on in many other medication fields [79]. Microarrays can aid in assessing a compound's therapeutic index by identifying its possible hazardous liabilities. One of the most challenging aspects of medication development is avoiding toxicity, and despite extensive research, the key instruments of toxicity are still poorly understood. The use of microarrays to improve our understanding of disease will allow for the selection of people for clinical trials and the selection of appropriate medicines in the clinic, resulting in significant cost savings for the industry and medical benefits for patients [80]. The use of large datasets has transformed the processes in solving lengthy drug discovery challenges, which are still long-running, along with difficult procedures and a significant degree of unpredictability about whether or not a treatment will function. More complicated ways could also create a blank area in a combination of information and standardization, covering a variety of people, specimens, and methods as big data and CC become more frequent analytic practices [81].

9.20 AMAZON ELASTIC CLOUD COMPUTING

According to Proffitt, previous CC users included Eli Lilly, Johnson and Johnson, Pfizer, Amazon Elastic Compute Cloud (EC2), and AWS (Amazon Web Services). These drug companies make use of the cloud for R&D. Afgan demonstrated how to use the Amazon EC2 cloud and Galaxy CloudMan to set up a computing cluster. Bowers further on these points, claiming that CC assists in the streamlining of highly regulated clinical trials by transforming labor-intensive operations into controlled, secure, and efficient operations [82].

9.21   DISCOVERY CLOUD

We propose the Discovery Cloud by leveraging recent commercial IT breakthroughs, particularly the cloud server SaaS (software as a service) and PaaS (platform as a service) [83].

9.22   BIG DATA

This explosion in big data, as well as the need to use big data technologies, has created a significant demand for data researchers, computer researchers, and mathematicians who are experts in big data, scientific tactics, insights, data mining, and computer programming. CC provides a flexible and cost-effective solution to the big data dilemma; nevertheless, it is mostly undefined and used to address anything that is online. The National Institute of Standards and Technology (NIST) defines cloud computing as a "pay-per-use system for clarifying on-demand network admission control to a shared pool of configurable computing resources, such as networks, storage, servers, tools, and services that can be rapidly provisioned and released with service provider interaction or minimum effort management". It is easy to miss the distinction in CC and big data technologies, as CC is frequently utilized to work with the intelligent storage of massive datasets [84]. Data from the 1000 Genomes Project, for example, is available in Amazon Web Services' cloud big data collections [36].

9.23   PRECLINICAL CLINICAL DEVELOPMENT USING CLOUD COMPUTING

When activity in the cloud is completed, the fully validated hit list is prepared for future pre-clinical study. Because a lot of applications that have a higher risk of failing have already been weeded out, this round should move much faster. Because all standard pre-clinical development methods must be completed, they are deployed to a substantially more competent candidate list, resulting in a significantly higher outcome, faster development, lower costs, and innovative and challenging therapeutic targets. Cloud Pharma conducts the majority of these stages in conjunction with clinical research companies (CROs) and risk-sharing partnerships (RSPs).

The cloud's value stems from its capacity to generate new compounds for complex pharmacological targets while simultaneously offering high performance, which lowers pricing and shortens time to market. Furthermore, as provided by Cloud Pharma, collaborative drug research and development may be safely maintained across several collaborators through clouds. In contrast to employing the cloud for computing resources in conceptual design, the business efficiently conducts a substantial chunk of drug research, drug designing, and drug development by combining the contributions of its network of partners [12]. CC is gaining popularity due to its potential to expedite clinical trial operations, shorten timescales, and minimize IT costs. However, numerous new clinical study methods are emerging in the biological sciences, first focusing on the more effective management of dataset amounts produced by research and development. A primary aim is to maximize the collecting, transmission, and preservation of data from various sources. Due to stringent security measures, it is possible to combine and manage data processes involving several collaborators in the cloud. Conventional journal articles or basic personal computer methods of documentation are currently becoming unsustainable as research and development, complex processes, and compliance needs activities create massive amounts of data, making the cloud an appealing solution [85].

9.24 BENEFITS OF CLOUD COMPUTING

The CC model has numerous important aspects:

1. **Quick elasticity:** Simply distribute supplies as they are required, then adjust up or down as the demands change; after a while, you need to adjust your permitted resources.
2. **Pay-as-you-go:** Just pay for computer resources only when you use them, and only for the amount you need.
3. **Self-service on-demand:** Without the assistance of service providers, the user may request and manage computer resources.
4. **Economically viable:** Data is processed by technology that has been in use for a long time but which may be useless and tough to adjust up or down; however, the cloud provides a feasible solution and for large amounts of data processing, there is a cheaper option [75].

9.25 LIMITATIONS

The key hazards associated with CC are:

- There may be some issues with the technology;
- Sometimes there is insufficient support;
- It is inflexible [86];
- It is necessary to have a continuous internet connection;
- Slow connections don't work well;
- It can take a long time;
- Some features may be restricted;
- It is possible that the data you've saved isn't safe;
- It is disastrous if your data is lost in the cloud [87].

9.26 FUTURE PROSPECTS FOR CLOUD COMPUTING IN DRUG DEVELOPMENT

There are many useful applications of this technology in different industries like pharmaceuticals, healthcare, and academia. The availability of worldwide datasets via CC, the implementation of cheap modeling trials, the supply of large and adaptable computer capacity for drug development, and real-time health monitoring are all examples of this possibility. CC may start channel coordination by allowing for quick prototyping, collaborative design, and the enhancement of production methods. In addition, technology may serve as the foundation for highly participatory, collaborative learning [24].

9.27 CONCLUSION

CC has a wide range of applications in today's technologically evolved environment. It has changed the way services are delivered via the internet by lowering the amount of hardware required. Most crucially, programs do not require certain computer specifications to be executed. Cloud infrastructures will undoubtedly play an important role in the ever-increasing complexity of the healthcare and pharmaceutical industries. Pharmaceutical organizations can get the most out of cloud technology by optimizing and cutting costs throughout their whole value chain. As new innovation models are deployed, the demands of life sciences organizations for product and process innovation will determine how much money is spent on cloud infrastructure in the future, which has evolved into a significant component of much research when it comes to drug development. You don't have to maintain any infrastructure with public cloud providers, but there are certain negatives, such as greater costs and a lack of data security. The majority of drug research companies will have to use both local and public cloud infrastructure in their operations. From the perspectives of information technology, high-end computing, biomedicine uses, and drug development, this chapter has established the fundamental applications of CC in drug development.

REFERENCES

1. Nayak S, Yassir A. Cloud computing as an emerging paradigm. *International Journal of Computer Science and Network Security*. 2012 Jan;12(1):61–65.
2. Bio IT-World. I3C missing in action. 2005 October; http://www.bio-itworld.com/newsitems/2005/oct2005/10-27-05-news-i3c (2005, accessed 15 October, 2011)
3. Neumann EK, Miller E, Wilbanks J. What the semantic web could do for the life sciences. *Drug Discovery Today: BIOSILICO*. 2004 Nov 1;2(6):228–236.
4. Subramanian B. The disruptive influence of cloud computing and its implications for adoption in the pharmaceutical and life sciences industry. *Journal of Medical Marketing*. 2012 Aug;12(3):192–203.
5. Breton V, Kasam V, Jacq N. High throughput grid enabled virtual screening. In *Proceedings of the NETTAB 2006: Santa Margherita* 2006 Jul (pp. 14–18).
6. Lee HC, Salzemann J, Jacq N, Chen HY, Ho LY, Merelli I, Milanesi L, Breton V, Lin SC, Wu YT. Grid-enabled high-throughput in silico screening against influenza A neuraminidase. *IEEE Transactions on Nanobioscience*. 2006 Nov 30;5(4):288–295.
7. Rehman HU, Khan A, Habib U. Fog computing for bioinformatics applications. *Fog Computing: Theory and Practice*. 2020 May 5:529–546.
8. Morgan S, Grootendorst P, Lexchin J, Cunningham C, Greyson D. The cost of drug development: a systematic review. *Health Policy*. 2011 Apr 1;100(1):4–17.
9. Mullin R. Cost to develop new pharmaceutical drug now exceeds $2.5 B. *Scientific American*. 2014 Nov 20;24.
10. Cheng T, Li Q, Zhou Z, Wang Y, Bryant SH. Structure-based virtual screening for drug discovery: a problem-centric review. *The AAPS Journal*. 2012 Mar;14(1):133–141.
11. Batool M, Ahmad B, Choi S. A structure-based drug discovery paradigm. *International Journal of Molecular Sciences*. 2019 Jan;20(11):2783.
12. Addison E, Keinan S. Cloud computing. *Drug Development & Delivery*. 2016;16(2):62–66.
13. Sekharan S, Wei JN, Batista VS. The active site of melanopsin: the biological clock photoreceptor. *Journal of the American Chemical Society*. 2012 Dec 5;134(48):19536–19539.
14. Nicholas PE, Sofia AS. ESCC-RPE: effective scheduling in cloud computing to reduce price and energy. *European Journal of Molecular & Clinical Medicine*. 2020 Dec 28;7(3):5533–5543.
15. Aceto G, Persico V, Pescapé A. Industry 4.0 and health: Internet of things, big data, and cloud computing for healthcare 4.0. *Journal of Industrial Information Integration*. 2020 Jun 1; 18:100129.
16. Hsu CH, Lin CY, Ouyang M, Guo YK. Biocloud: cloud computing for biological, genomics, and drug design. *BioMed Research International*. 2013 Jan 1;2013.
17. Wang L, Von Laszewski G, Younge A, He X, Kunze M, Tao J, Fu C. Cloud computing: a perspective study. *New Generation Computing*. 2010 Apr;28(2):137–146.
18. Grossman RL. The case for cloud computing. *IT Professional*. 2009 Mar 21;11(2):23–27.
19. Sareen P. Cloud computing: types, architecture, applications, concerns, virtualization and role of it governance in cloud. *International Journal of Advanced Research in Computer Science and Software Engineering*. 2013 Mar;3(3).
20. Asha P, Reddy PH, Manikanta PV, Sai KS. Cloud computing based drug delivery system in the manufacturing of drugs and online purchase. In *2020 4th International Conference on Trends in Electronics and Informatics (ICOEI)* (48184) 2020 Jun 15 (pp. 847–851). IEEE.
21. Namasudra S. Data access control in the cloud computing environment for bioinformatics. *International Journal of Applied Research in Bioinformatics (IJARB)*. 2021 Jan 1;11(1):40–50.
22. Namasudra S, Devi D, Kadry S, Sundarasekar R, Shanthini A. Towards DNA based data security in the cloud computing environment. *Computer Communications*. 2020 Feb 1; 151:539–547.
23. Taufiq-Hail GA, Alanzi AR, Yusof SA, Alruwaili M. Software as a service (SAAS) Cloud computing: an empirical investigation on university students' perception. *Interdisciplinary Journal of Information, Knowledge & Management*. 2021 Jan 1;16(2021).

24. Domdouzis K. Sustainable cloud computing. In *Green Information Technology* 2015 Jan 1 (pp. 95–110). Morgan Kaufmann.

25. Daina A, Michielin O, Zoete V. SwissADME: a free web tool to evaluate pharmacokinetics, drug-likeness and medicinal chemistry friendliness of small molecules. *Scientific Reports*. 2017 Mar 3;7(1):1–3.

26. Daina A, Michielin O, Zoete V. SwissTargetPrediction: updated data and new features for efficient prediction of protein targets of small molecules. *Nucleic Acids Research*. 2019 Jul 2;47(W1):W357–W364.

27. Hans A, Kalra S. Comparitive analysis of various cloud based biomedcial services. In *2014 International Conference on Medical Imaging, m-Health and Emerging Communication Systems (MedCom)* 2014 Nov 7 (pp. 386–390). IEEE.

28. Peters K, Bradbury J, Bergmann S, Capuccini M, Cascante M, de Atauri P, Ebbels TM, Foguet C, Glen R, Gonzalez-Beltran A, Günther UL. PhenoMeNal: processing and analysis of metabolomics data in the cloud. *Gigascience*. 2019 Feb;8(2):giy149.

29. Emami Khoonsari P, Moreno P, Bergmann S, Burman J, Capuccini M, Carone M, Cascante M, de Atauri P, Foguet C, Gonzalez-Beltran AN, Hankemeier T. Interoperable and scalable data analysis with microservices: applications in metabolomics. *Bioinformatics*. 2019 Oct 1;35(19):3752–3760.

30. Lapins M, Arvidsson S, Lampa S, Berg A, Schaal W, Alvarsson J, Spjuth O. A confidence predictor for logD using conformal regression and a support-vector machine. *Journal of Cheminformatics*. 2018 Dec;10(1):1.

31. Spjuth O, Frid J, Hellander A. The machine learning life cycle and the cloud: implications for drug discovery. *Expert Opinion on Drug Discovery*. 2021 May 30:1–9.

32. Dillon T, Wu C, Chang E. Cloud computing: issues and challenges. In *2010 24th IEEE International Conference on Advanced Information Networking and Applications* 2010 Apr 20 (pp. 27–33). IEEE.

33. Kuyoro SO, Ibikunle F, Awodele O. Cloud computing security issues and challenges. *International Journal of Computer Networks (IJCN)*. 2011;3(5):247–255.

34. Sun P. Security and privacy protection in cloud computing: discussions and challenges. *Journal of Network and Computer Applications*. 2020 Jun 15;160:102642.

35. Li A, Yang X, Kandula S, Zhang M. Comparing public-cloud providers. *IEEE Internet Computing*. 2011 Mar 17;15(2):50–53.

36. Moghadam BT, Alvarsson J, Holm M, Eklund M, Carlsson L, Spjuth O. Scaling predictive modeling in drug development with cloud computing. *Journal of Chemical Information and Modeling*. 2015 Jan 26;55(1):19–25.

37. Schaduangrat N, Lampa S, Simeon S, Gleeson MP, Spjuth O, Nantasenamat C. Towards reproducible computational drug discovery. *Journal of Cheminformatics*. 2020 Dec;12(1):1–30.

38. Rani D, Ranjan RK. A comparative study of SaaS, PaaS and IaaS in cloud computing. *International Journal of Advanced Research in Computer Science and Software Engineering*. 2014 Jun;4(6).

39. Banegas-Luna AJ, Imbernón B, Llanes Castro A, Pérez-Garrido A, Cerón-Carrasco JP, Gesing S, Merelli I, D'Agostino D, Pérez-Sánchez H. Advances in distributed computing with modern drug discovery. *Expert Opinion on Drug Discovery*. 2019 Jan 2;14(1):9–22.

40. Lin Z, Zou J, Liu S, Peng C, Li Z, Wan X, Fang D, Yin J, Gobbo G, Chen Y, Ma J. A cloud computing platform for scalable relative and absolute binding free energy predictions: new opportunities and challenges for drug discovery. *Journal of Chemical Information and Modeling*. 2021 Jun 4;61(6):2720–2732.

41. Masuda Y, Zimmermann A, Viswanathan M, Bass M, Nakamura O, Yamamoto S. Adaptive enterprise architecture for the digital healthcare industry: a digital platform for drug development. *Information*. 2021 Feb;12(2):67.

42. Food US. Drug Administration. The Drug Development Process, Step 3. Clinical Research. 2018.

43. Bio IT World. Cloud computing for life sciences. 2009 November–December; http://www.bio-itworld.com/issues/2009/nov-dec/cloud-report.html

44. McCarthy A. Drug discovery in the clouds. *Chemistry & Biology*. 2012 Jan 27;19(1):1–2.

45. Ekins S, Bunin BA. The collaborative drug discovery (CDD) database. In *In silico models for drug discovery* 2013 (pp. 139–154). Humana Press, Totowa, NJ.

46. Bunin BA, Ekins S. Alternative business models for drug discovery. *Drug Discovery Today*. 2011 Aug 1;16(15–16):643–645.

47. Quang BT, Kim JS, Rho S, Kim S, Kim S, Hwang S, Medernach E, Breton V. A comparative analysis of scheduling mechanisms for virtual screening workflow in a shared resource environment. In *2015 15th IEEE/ACM International Symposium on Cluster, Cloud and Grid Computing* 2015 May 4 (pp. 853–862). IEEE.

48. Dalpé G, Joly Y. Opportunities and challenges provided by cloud repositories for bioinformatics-enabled drug discovery. *Drug Development Research.* 2014 Sep;75(6):393–401.

49. Sanger F, Air GM, Barrell BG, Brown NL, Coulson AR, Fiddes CA, Hutchinson CA, Slocombe PM, Smith M. Nucleotide sequence of bacteriophage X174 DNA. *Nature* 1977 Feb; 265 (5596):687–695.

50. Sanger F, Nicklen S, Coulson AR. DNA sequencing with chain-terminating inhibitors. *Proceedings of the National Academy Sciences* 1977 Dec 1; 74 (12):5463–5467.

51. Garg V, Arora S, Gupta C. Cloud computing approaches to accelerate drug discovery value chain. *Combinatorial Chemistry & High Throughput Screening.* 2011 Dec 1;14(10):861–871.

52. Ikram AA, Ibrahim S, Sardaraz M, Tahir M, Bajwa H, Bach C. Neural network based cloud computing platform for bioinformatics. In *2013 IEEE Long Island Systems, Applications and Technology Conference (LISAT)* 2013 May 3 (pp. 1–6). IEEE.

53. Reddy AS, Pati SP, Kumar PP, Pradeep HN, Sastry GN. Virtual screening in drug discovery-a computational perspective. *Current Protein and Peptide Science.* 2007 Aug 1;8(4):329–351.

54. Kang L, Guo Q, Wang X. A hierarchical method for molecular docking using cloud computing. *Bioorganic & Medicinal Chemistry Letters.* 2012 Nov 1;22(21):6568–6572.

55. Sobeslav V, Maresova P, Krejcar O, Franca TC, Kuca K. Use of cloud computing in biomedicine. *Journal of Biomolecular Structure and Dynamics.* 2016 Dec 1;34(12):2688–2697.

56. D'Agostino D, Clematis A, Quarati A, Cesini D, Chiappori F, Milanesi L, Merelli I. Cloud infrastructures for in silico drug discovery: economic and practical aspects. *BioMed Research International.* 2013 Jan 1;2013.

57. Lionta E, Spyrou G, Vassilatis DK, Cournia Z. Structure-based virtual screening for drug discovery: principles, applications and recent advances. *Current Topics in Medicinal Chemistry.* 2014 Aug 1;14(16):1923–1938.

58. Stumpfe D, Bajorath J. Current trends, overlooked issues, and unmet challenges in virtual screening. *Journal of Chemical Information and Modeling.* 2020 Feb 3;60(9):4112–4115.

59. Lagarde N, Goldwaser E, Pencheva T, Jereva D, Pajeva I, Rey J, Tuffery P, Villoutreix BO, Miteva MA. A free web-based protocol to assist structure-based virtual screening experiments. *International Journal of Molecular Sciences* 2019 Jan;20(18):4648.

60. Walters WP, Wang R. New trends in virtual screening. *Journal of Chemical Information and Modeling* 2019 Sep 10;59(9):3603–3604.

61. Bickle M. The beautiful cell: high-content screening in drug discovery. *Analytical and Bioanalytical Chemistry* 2010 Sep;398(1):219–226.

62. Fraietta I, Gasparri F. The development of high-content screening (HCS) technology and its importance to drug discovery. *Expert Opinion on Drug Discovery* 2016 May 3;11(5):501–514.

63. Lin S, Schorpp K, Rothenaigner I, Hadian K. Image-based high-content screening in drug discovery. *Drug Discovery Today* 2020 Aug 1;25(8):1348–1361.

64. Yadav NK, Shukla P, Omer A, Pareek S, Singh RK. Next generation sequencing: potential and application in drug discovery. *The Scientific World Journal* 2014 Jan 1;2014.

65. Woollard PM, Mehta NA, Vamathevan JJ, Van Horn S, Bonde BK, Dow DJ. The application of next-generation sequencing technologies to drug discovery and development. *Drug Discovery Today* 2011 Jun 1;16(11–12):512–519.

66. Reis-Filho JS. Next-generation sequencing. *Breast Cancer Research* 2009 Dec;11(3):1–7.

67. Torshizi AD, Wang K. Next-generation sequencing in drug development: target identification and genetically stratified clinical trials. *Drug Discovery Today* 2018 Oct 1;23(10):1776–1783.

68. Tafazoli A, Wawrusiewicz-Kurylonek N, Posmyk R, Miltyk W. Pharmacogenomics, how to deal with different types of variants in next generation sequencing data in the personalized medicine area. *Journal of Clinical Medicine* 2021 Jan;10(1):34.

69. Wall DP, Kudtarkar P, Fusaro VA, Pivovarov R, Patil P, Tonellato PJ. Cloud computing for comparative genomics. *BMC Bioinformatics* 2010 Dec;11(1):1 2.

70. Hardison RC. Comparative genomics. *PLoS Biology* 2003 Nov;1(2): e58.

71. Shanker A. Genome research in the cloud. *Omics: A Journal of Integrative Biology* 2012 Jul 1;16(7–8):422–428.

72. Calabrese B, Cannataro M. Bioinformatics and microarray data analysis on the cloud. *Microarray Data Analysis* 2015:25–39.

73. Kaur S, Kaur S. Genomics with cloud computing. *International Journal of Scientific and Technology Research* 2015;4(4).

74. Yeo H, Crawford CH. Big data: cloud computing in genomics applications. In *2015 IEEE International Conference on Big Data (Big Data)* 2015 Oct 1 (pp. 2904–2906). IEEE.

75. Zhao S, Watrous K, Zhang C, Zhang B. Cloud computing for next-generation sequencing data analysis. *Cloud Computing-Architecture and Applications* 2017 Jun 14:29–51.

76. Reid JG, Carroll A, Veeraraghavan N, Dahdouli M, Sundquist A, English A, Bainbridge M, White S, Salerno W, Buhay C, Yu F. Launching genomics into the cloud: deployment of Mercury, a next generation sequence analysis pipeline. *BMC Bioinformatics* 2014 Dec;15(1):1–1.

77. Braxton S, Bedilion T. The integration of microarray information in the drug development process. *Current Opinion in Biotechnology* 1998 Dec 1;9(6):643–649.

78. Agapito G, Cannataro M, Guzzi PH, Marozzo F, Talia D, Trunfio P. Cloud4SNP: distributed analysis of SNP microarray data on the cloud. In *Proceedings of the International Conference on Bioinformatics, Computational Biology and Biomedical Informatics* 2013 Sep 22 (pp. 468–475).

79. Howbrook DN, van der Valk AM, O'Shaughnessy MC, Sarker DK, Baker SC, Lloyd AW. Developments in microarray technologies. *Drug Discovery Today* 2003 Jul 15;8(14):642–651.

80. Crowther DJ. Applications of microarrays in the pharmaceutical industry. *Current Opinion in Pharmacology* 2002 Oct 1;2(5):551–554.

81. Qian T, Zhu S, Hoshida Y. Use of big data in drug development for precision medicine: an update. *Expert Review of Precision Medicine and Drug Development* 2019 May 4;4(3):189–200.

82. Sommer T. Cloud computing in emerging biotech and pharmaceutical companies. *Communications of the IIMA* 2013;13(3):3.

83. Foster I, Chard K, Tuecke S. The discovery cloud: accelerating and democratizing research on a global scale. In *2016 IEEE International Conference on Cloud Engineering (IC2E)* 2016 Apr 4 (pp. 68–77). IEEE.

84. O'Driscoll A, Daugelaite J, Sleator RD. 'Big data', Hadoop and cloud computing in genomics. *Journal of Biomedical Informatics* 2013 Oct 1;46(5):774–781.

85. Bowers L. Cloud computing efficiency. *Applied Clinical Trials* 2011 Jul 1;20(7):45.

86. Apostu A, Puican F, Ularu G, Suciu G, Todoran G. Study on advantages and disadvantages of Cloud Computing–the advantages of Telemetry Applications in the Cloud. *Recent Advances in Applied Computer Science and Digital Services* 2013;2103.

87. Mirashe SP, Kalyankar NV. Cloud computing. *Journal of Computing* 2010 Mar 22;2(3):1–12.

88. Giuliano KA, Haskins JR, Taylor DL. Advances in high content screening for drug discovery. *Assay and Drug Development Technologies* 2003 Aug 1;1(4):565–577.

10 Cloud Application in Drug Development

Nitu Singh
Oriental University, Indore, India

Urvashi Sharma
Medi-caps University, Indore, India

Deepika Bairagee and Neelam Jain
Oriental University, Indore, India

CONTENTS

10.1 INTRODUCTION

Drug discovery is a time-consuming and costly process that takes 12–15 years and costs between US$1 billion and $2 billion [1]. After finding a lead chemical through the drug discovery process, drug development is the process of bringing a new pharmaceutical medicine to market. The first phase in the drug research and development process is to identify and confirm targets. A target might be a protein, DNA, or RNA that causes or contributes to illness. Validation requires demonstrating that changing the target has a therapeutic effect. Assay development is an objective technique for screening potential medications to identify target interaction and/or modification after target validation. The next step after developing an assay is to find compounds that actively interact with the target. From a pool of potential compounds, a few chosen leads are developed that show a relationship between chemical structure and target-based activity in a biochemical or cell-based test.

Potential compounds can be created using binding/functional, biochemical, and cellular or cytotoxicity experiments, for example. Using high-throughput screening of a vast chemical library, several medicines can be discovered. To get to a lead molecule, researchers can utilise complex cellular tests, toxicological surrogate assays, bio-pharmacological surrogates, and absorption, distribution, metabolism, and excretion (ADME) surrogates [2].

It may also include the step of obtaining regulatory approval with a new drug application to market the drug, as well as preclinical research on microorganisms and animals, as well as filing for regulatory status, such as an investigational new drug application with the US Food and Drug Administration (FDA) to begin human clinical trials. Animals are used to study the pharmacological and toxicological properties of the lead compounds. Many workshop attendees emphasise that efficacy studies, rather than safety tests, are often not necessary prior to first-in-human testing. Following the development of a lead medication, it undergoes further testing to optimise its physico-chemical and pharmacological qualities, notably potency and selectivity. Optimization is a difficult, time-consuming, and costly procedure, despite the time, manpower, and financial resources spent on lead compound research [3,4]. Following optimization, a Phase Ia clinical research in which healthy volunteers are given a single dosage of the drug can begin. The next step is to performPhase Ib trials, which comprise a series of escalating doses to establish safety, steady-state pharmacokinetics, and the maximum tolerated dose. Proof of concept (POC) and effectiveness evidence are increasingly being sought in Phase Ib studies. A typical POC clinical trial consists of a small controlled study with less than 100 subjects/patients done at fewer than four locations. If the drug is shown to be safe and effective at POC, larger Phase II and Phase III studies with randomised, often placebo-controlled arms are done to ensure safety and effectiveness. After successfully completing Phase III and submitting a new drug application (NDA) to the FDA, a pharmaceutical becomes eligible for commercialization, as indicated in Table 10.1. Even after a drug has been licensed for use, post-marketing surveillance is conducted to ensure its safety [2]. From idea through preclinical testing in the lab to clinical trial development, including Phase I–III trials, to an authorised vaccine or drug, the complete process takes more than a decade [5]. To deliver safe and effective novel therapeutic compounds, the process of finding new active pharmaceutical ingredients (APIs) begins with target identification and validation and continues with hit identification, lead discovery, and lead optimization in the preclinical stage [6,7].

As the first phase in the drug discovery process, pharmacological evaluation is utilised to categorise potential targets of a knockout molecule as a developable therapeutic contender. Until the nineteenth century, drug research and development relied on a trial-and-error technique to diagnose and treat ailments. Natural products (NPs) were entirely responsible for the therapeutic effect [8]. The active medicinal component was extracted from the full or a subset of the NPs [9]. Natural chemicals

TABLE 10.1
Stages of Drug Development [2]

Stage	Methods	Purpose
Preclinical	Animal *in vitro* and laboratory studies	Testing toxicity, efficacy, pharmacokinetics, and pharmacodynamics
Investigational New Drug Application		
Phase I	Healthy human volunteers (20–100)	Testing the safety of a single dose (Phase Ia) and multiple doses (Phase Ib) of a drug, also includes pharmacokinetics and maximum tolerated dose
Phase II	Patients (100–300)	Assessing safety and efficacy
Phase III	Patients (100–300)	Assessing safety and efficacy
New Drug Application		
Phase IV	Varies	Post marketing surveillance

are a valuable source of pharmaceuticals, thanks to enhanced sensitivity and better biochemical separation methods [10]. The whole cost of bringing a new drug (i.e., novel chemical entity) to market is difficult and disputed [11–13]. From discovery to clinical trials to approval, the entire cost of bringing a new medicine (i.e., unique chemical entity) to market is complicated and problematic. The total capital investment for a company getting a medicine authorised through successful Phase III studies was $2.6 billion (in 2013) in a 2016 evaluation of 106 drug candidates examined through clinical trials, a sum growing at an annual rate of 8.5 percent. The cost per medicine might grow to $5.5 billion for businesses that authorised 8–13 products between 2003 and 2013, owing to international geographic expansion for marketing and continued expenses for Phase IV studies for incessant safety investigation [14].

One of the most essential aims for pharmaceutical companies is to identify novel and effective medicinal compounds that will reach the market quickly, as well as those that will fail. Furthermore, regulatory compliance criteria have become more onerous as the creation of new therapeutic items has become more sophisticated. As medication pipelines shorten and regulations get more complicated, companies are investing in more cooperation, standardisation, and analytical tools to increase R&D efficiency as well as sales and marketing processes.

As the market for novel pharmaceuticals grows, so does the need for effective communication and collaboration methods among partners. Meeting compliance standards, on the other hand, may take precedence over incorporating new technologies in order to protect patient safety. To adopt business software platforms that allow researchers in laboratories all around the world to interact, companies have had to look to other sectors [15].

A few marketable corporations are already delivering cloud-based drug discovery software services to address the needs of pharmaceutical and biotech corporations, as well as a much broader cast of supportive and cooperating partners. The goal is to boost collaborative power while preserving the greatest levels of security, all the while reducing the requirement for often large amounts of internal computer power and IT overheads [16].

10.2 WHAT IS CLOUD?

The term "cloud" in cloud computing refers to an assembly of nets, similar to how real clouds are made up of water molecules. The user has unrestricted access to cloud computing modalities at any time. Users typically prefer a middleman provider for an internet service in cloud computing rather than setting up their own physical infrastructure. Operators have to only recompense for the services that they have utilised [17]. In cloud computing, the workload can be transferred to lessen the workload. The networks that make up the cloud carry a lot of the service burden, which is why the pressure on local PCs isn't very high when running an application. Cloud computing offers three services:

- **PaaS (Platform as a Service):** This service provides an environment for designing, testing, delivering, and managing software applications on demand. The application is the developer's responsibility, and the PaaS vendor provides the capacity to deploy and run it. The flexibility of PaaS is reduced, but the administration of the environment is handled by cloud vendors.
- **SaaS (Software as a Service):** This provides end users with centrally hosted and managed software services. It provides on-demand software over the internet, usually on a subscription basis. Microsoft One Drive, Dropbox, WordPress, Office 365, and Amazon Kindle are just a few examples. SaaS is utilised to reduce operational costs as much as possible.
- **IaaS (Infrastructure as a Service):** This is a service software for providing on-demand remote access to a client-specified computer environment. Apart from challenging virtualisation arrangements with numerous users sharing a single processor, High Tech Computer (HTC) also offers "bare metal" systems [18,19]. Facebook, YouTube, Dropbox, and Gmail are just a few instances of cloud computing that people utilise on a regular basis.

"Cloud computing" refers to anything that includes delivering services via the internet; it is taken from the symbol that is widely used in flowcharts and diagrams to represent the internet. Cloud services are sold on a per-hour basis; they are elastic, meaning that a user may have as much or as little of a service as they want at any one moment; and they are totally managed by the provider. All that is required of the user is a personal computer and internet access. Cloud computing has grown in popularity as a result of significant advances in virtualising and distribution computing, as well as greater access to high-speed internet and cheaper finance. The on-demand flexibility of cloud computing resources is an attractive alternative to the massive internal resources required to meet the peak demand typical of computational chemistry.

Over and above the evolutionary advancements of Moore's Law, cloud computing acts to lift the business constraint, resulting in an immediate increase in the power available. As a result, all of those software design compromises may be questioned. Cloud computing should usher in a new era of no-compromise computer-aided drug discovery, allowing for effective virtual screening to become a reality. Because virtual screening is intrinsically parallel, it matches the cloud computing paradigm perfectly: instead of waiting 100 hours for 10 CPUs to accomplish the same job, you pay no extra for 1,000 CPUs for 1 hour.

The benefit of cloud computing is that it provides access to essentially unlimited computer resources, allowing pharmaceutical researchers to scale up or down their computing environment as needed. Companies can more easily modify solutions to their specific demands thanks to cloud computing. For example, BT's cloud computing life sciences platform may provide specific pharmaceutical applications throughout the value chain, from discovery to commercial operations, ensuring that critical applications can function across pipelines rather than forcing one application on all pipeline teams. In addition to charge reductions, cloud computing has a number of commercial benefits for pharma companies. Cloud computing has been around for a while, but it has currently received a lot of interest from companies needing to analyse and handle large volumes of data. The key benefit of cloud computing for pharmaceutical organisations is that it reduces reliance on internal infrastructures while also streamlining operations around the world. Due to compliance difficulties and data protection policies, it is sometimes preferable to undertake some initial data reduction locally [20].

10.3 KEY BENEFITS OF CLOUD COMPUTING

A few of the key benefits of cloud computing include:

- **Scalability:** As a company expands, so does the amount of data that may be stored and handled on the cloud. Given the peaks and troughs of pharmaceutical development, this is extremely crucial. Let's imagine a company completes a clinical study, and the data is being saved on overburdened devices, and the business has to add two additional clinical studies. The corporation could simply access extra storage and computational capacity via cloud computing, and complete the analysis of this data. It might also do more precise searches, such as looking at cross-clinical trials or comparing the results of two competing medications in clinical trials. Most businesses previously didn't have access to such a big computational estate since it was too expensive, and they would have had to provision it for peak practice. Companies can now access considerably more elastic and scalable data storage alternatives thanks to cloud computing.
- **Flexibility:** Instead of depending on a single app, companies can easily design their pipeline and test several apps in diverse environments at the same time, with no worries about data storage or demand. Today's laboratories can operate more quickly and smartly by releasing scientists from the limits imposed by data processing constraints. They don't have to waste time thinking about IT outlines or server space availability. As an outcome, experts can make more accurate forecasts about probable drug candidates and indicate which medications

should be ruled out of the discovery process earlier. Cloud computing also enables scientists to track which data was used in data analysis and can be utilised to solve very similar computational challenges. Firms can utilise the cloud platform to examine industry leanings, such as the impact of withdrawing a drug, on the commercial side.

- **Global connections:** Companies can communicate information more quickly, conveniently, and efficiently because of the cloud's ability to be accessed from anywhere and at any time. Regardless of where team members are situated, pharmaceutical companies may scale project teams up and down based on the number of trials they are performing. The global architecture of the cloud platform delivers the connection, visibility, agility, and collaboration necessary to succeed in a global market. If a lead pharmaceutical researcher is working on a project in France, for example, he may easily hand over his work to a scientist in the USA at the end of the day, who can pick up where he left off. As a result, a colleague in China can get the findings later using the same resources as a colleague in the USA or France. The cloud aids firms to virtually eliminate downtime by allowing them to simply continue priority work 24 hours a day, seven days a week.
- **Ease of use:** As we all know, the pharmaceutical industry can be rather solitary in terms of how it operates, how it provides information to regulatory agencies, and how it adheres to rules. Pharmaceutical companies may use the cloud platform to communicate both internally and globally, allowing for better integration of all the moving elements of data connected to a medicine's life cycle.
- **Regulatory compliance adherence:** The cloud platform can make it easier to meet certain regulatory obligations. Because cloud-based systems are created and managed—and regularly updated—to handle the current security concerns and laws, they are frequently more protected and submissive than on-premises systems [20].

10.4   MARKET SIZE AND FORECAST

According to an Environmental, Social and Governance (ESG) study, during the next 12–18 months, 65 percent of healthcare firms will boost their IT spending on public cloud infrastructure services. Furthermore, when it comes to data centre modernisation, 20 percent of pharma companies will invest the most in hybrid cloud management software. Cloud platforms are increasingly being used by some of the world's biggest pharmaceutical companies to cooperate and drive clinical trials across geographically scattered R&D teams. Whether a company is conducting drug trials (preclinical or Phase I/II/III) and needs to share data with a patient based on individual results, or highlighting how different medications or treatments affect different parts of the body, timely access to properly visualised data has a direct impact on patient satisfaction. Computational drug discovery, for example, makes the drug development process quicker and less expensive by combining cloud computing and artificial intelligence. The large pharmaceutical corporations are putting this new strategy to the test thanks to advances in AI and cloud computing capacity. This tech-driven technique is being used by pharmaceutical corporations to produce both standard drugs and wholly new categories that function at the level of DNA and RNA to prevent illness [21]. According to a research by the Healthcare Information and Management Systems Society, over 83 percent of pharmaceutical businesses are currently using cloud services. With the COVID-19 pandemic pushing innovation, the pharmaceutical sector is already making progress in producing vaccinations, repurposing medications, and discovering new treatments to limit the infection's spread. Huge expenditures are being made in R&D, with the cloud becoming a significant instrument for decreasing costs and enhancing efficiency across all IT expenses. According to a new study published by Research Reports World, the revenue for cloud computing in the pharma market was $3173 million in 2019 and is expected to reach $7021 million in 2025, with a CAGR of 14.15 percent between 2020 and 2025 as shown in Figure 10.1.

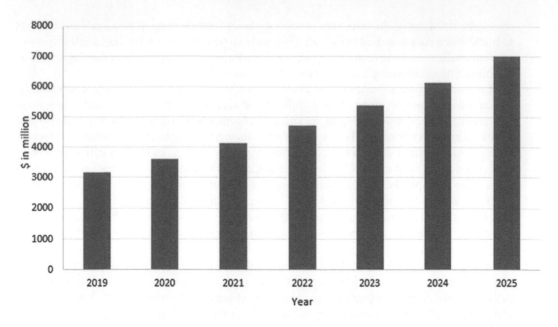

FIGURE 10.1 Pharma market revenue [22].

The market for cloud-based drug discovery platforms can be divided into two categories: type and use. It is additionally divided into pharmacy firms, hospitals, biotech suppliers, and contract research organisations based on application. The pharmaceutical sub-segment is the leading end-user sector in the worldwide cloud-based drug discovery platform market. The steady rise in drug demand from various pharmaceutical businesses is predicted to propel the cloud-based drug discovery platform market forward.

North America, Asia-Pacific, Latin America, Europe, the Middle East, and Africa make up the worldwide cloud-based drug discovery platform market. North America is expected to lead the market due to the widespread availability of cloud platforms that allow businesses to collect real-time data from all over the world. During the research and development process, these platforms provide easier access to data. North American pharmaceutical and biotech companies are researching new technologies to improve the drug development process by utilising cloud platforms [23].

10.5 MARKET SEGMENTATION

The global cloud-based drug discovery platform market is split into these segments:

1. **By type:**
   a. PaaS (Platform as a Service);
   b. SaaS (Software as a Service);
   c. IaaS (Infrastructure as a Service).
2. **By application:**
   a. Pharmaceutical companies;
   b. Hospitals
   c. Biotech vendors;
   d. Contract research organisations.
3. **By region:**
   a. **North America (USA, Canada):** Pharmaceutical and biotech companies in the region are focusing on adopting cloud platforms to speed up drug development without compromising

safety. The widespread availability and accessibility of cloud platforms enable businesses to collect real-time data from all around the world. During the R&D process, such platforms also enable improved access to data from healthcare firms and contract research groups.

b. **Latin America (Brazil, Mexico, and the rest of Latin America):** To manage their rising data traffic while lowering IT infrastructure expenses, most health science enterprises in this region are turning to cloud computing services. Healthcare firms may store and access patient data, health information, and R&D documents more efficiently thanks to the widespread adoption of SaaS. Furthermore, SaaS enables healthcare enterprises to collaborate with a variety of vendors and contract research organisations all around the world.

c. **Europe (UK, Germany, France, Spain, Italy, the Netherlands and the rest of Europe):** European pharmaceutical companies are progressively adopting cloud-based technology to help their scientists and their work, as well as research mutations in the human genome for improving the medication development process in cancer research. More areas of pharmaceutical design that are advantageous to patients are being targeted by scientists. Furthermore, to achieve optimal R&D outcomes, healthcare firms in Europe are integrating modern cloud technologies such as machine learning and artificial intelligence (AI) platforms. AI algorithms are being utilised to create bi-specific medications that can bind to multiple targets at the same time. These platforms can assist businesses to enhance the efficiency of their drug discovery optimisation by solving complicated biological problems.

d. **Asia Pacific (China, Japan, Australia, Singapore, India, South Korea, and the rest of APAC):** Clinical cloud platforms are being used by life science organisations in the APAC region to provide innovative technologies that improve operational efficiency, productivity, and clinical trial speed. Clinical cloud platforms provide improved services and provide the drug development process with a boost. Clinical cloud platforms also assist life science organisations in speeding up the delivery of innovative treatments to patients. Life science firms are looking for cutting-edge, cloud-based research solutions to meet the basic demands of their scientific staff, which are increasingly reliant on mobile communication and social networking to boost work productivity. Researchers benefit from better and efficient data and knowledge sharing thanks to cloud-based mobile-enabled information management. Life science organisations can safely migrate their essential legacy applications to the cloud by integrating on-premise systems with bi-directional clouds.

e. **MEA (Saudi Arabia, UAE, Qatar, South Africa, and the rest of MEA):** Healthcare companies in the MEA are moving their IT infrastructure to the cloud, since the growing use of cloud platforms and mobile devices allows healthcare organisations to follow patient health across many devices, providing vital information for R&D. Governments and private entities in the MEA area fund the majority of digital transformation projects [23].

10.6 GROWTH DRIVERS AND CHALLENGES

Several growth factors in the global cloud-based drug discovery market are pushing the use of cloud-based platforms in the healthcare industry to improve research efficiency. Various developing technologies, such as machine learning and AI, have made it possible to improve medication research and formulation all over the world. Various regional healthcare firms are collaborating with global players in the healthcare industry to use cloud-based technologies that will improve illness detection and diagnosis. The cloud-based drug discovery platform may be accessed from a variety of devices, including computers, laptops, and mobile phones. The market for these platforms is projected to be hampered by a number of challenges relating to application–device correlation [23].

Cloud technologies allow multiple workflows and tools to be integrated on dynamically assigned resources. In Computer Aided Drug Design (CADD) study specifications, these instances share corresponding services, and cloud computing is a developing solution for virtual screening demands. The early days of cloud computing were spent with "IaaS," or computers that were dynamically set up and launched and were invoiced on a per-use basis. Many computer centres now provide IaaS services at a cheap cost. The settings are straightforward to use for those who are accustomed to remote access through command line interfaces (CLIs) or graphical user interfaces (GUIs).

Amazon Web Services [24] and Google Cloud [25] are the most well-known cloud service providers, although there are a rising number of open source cloud alternatives that may be of interest. OpenStack middleware [26] has become the de facto standard for deploying public and private clouds. When using a web interface to access software, the server-side implementation is concealed. A sideways glance, for example, at how payments are made online with the help of a variety of service providers, reveals what clouds also imply: a scaled-up interplay of services.

10.7 CLOUD-BASED SOLUTIONS

New analyses [27,28] and the "Click2Drug" catalogue [29] paint a bright picture of numerous various sources for many different limited explanations—either as semi-automated web services or as instances that can be started at one's leisure. All of this must be described, both semantically and technically, including how information should be moved across different instruments and how these approaches should be used to obtain redundant findings with more accuracy.

In silico techniques have been combined in the drug discovery pipeline, and they are anticipated to be used often by large pharmaceutical corporations. Professionals adopt cloud environments because of the benefits they provide in terms of lowering setup expenses. In addition, for innovative new techniques to treating a disease, knowing which target to aim at is already critical to maintaining an inexpensive benefit. Individual virtual screening results, such as those from a volunteer computing initiative, may not be regarded as critical for shared aims.

10.7.1 How Cloud Computing Improves upon Traditional Methods

Cloud computing provides clarification by allowing for extra-complex computational chemistry to be combined with quick production and optimisation, allowing corporations to find molecules that are well suitable for progress from the start. Picking composites with a better chance of achievement thus acts as a control to lower total costs, which is necessary if personalised medicine or "niche buster" medications are to be achieved. Cloud computing allows for deeper computational chemistry, which addresses two of the key issues with traditional drug discovery. It aids efficiency by selecting molecules that bind to biological targets and have good "drug-like" characteristics. However, the goal isn't just to cut costs and enhance speed. It's all about developing significantly better chemicals for extremely difficult-to-drug targets. Cloud computing aids in the design of compounds for such targets by supplying large amounts of computing power, allowing for the use of more time-consuming but atomically accurate in silico design approaches. It finds molecules in new chemical spaces, rather than using the same screening decks that have previously failed. Targets that were previously difficult to drug show potential through cloud computing's increased computational capability. Traditional algorithms, for example, are unsuccessful when dealing with targets that have minimal structural information, such as G-protein-coupled receptors (GPCRs). However, combining comprehensive homology modelling with molecular dynamics approaches to acquire structural information can then be paired with quantum chemistry in the cloud to find potential compounds for hitherto unsolvable targets, as well as scanning molecular space for novel molecules [30].

10.7.1.1 Scalable, Cost-effective Clinical Research Services

Previously, industries had to buy or develop sophisticated IT infrastructures and maintain them, incurring significant expenditures and being needed to handle a wide range of applications, from online to legacy systems. SaaS computing can also be a good option, because businesses can now plug in and use software services whenever they need them, for as long as they need them [31].

A pharmaceutical company's demands are best served by a system that can supply clinical solutions as a SaaS with an on-demand approach. This technology, which can quickly and efficiently deliver the primary value of a clinical research application while also capturing, managing, and sharing data among thousands of investigators and all stakeholders, will help shorten the clinical research cycle. The SaaS model can help to save money on investments, IT resources, and other costly IT infrastructure. The following benefits can be expected as a result of the intrinsic qualities of cloud-based software solutions:

- On-demand service and across geographic areas;
- Energetic computing resources;
- Rapid scalability;
- Low operational costs;
- Increased security, such as PCI DSS, HIPAA, SOC_2;
- Fault tolerance;
- Disaster recovery and business continuity;
- Uptime.

The pharma and biotech industries can benefit from cloud computing in a variety of ways; it is just a matter of finding the perfect solution that can provide them with the correct combination of data protection, structuring, and maintenance, by integrating database, middleware, web framework, security, and virtualisation services in a seamless and transparent manner. PaaS boosts developer productivity by reducing the integration headaches that come with traditional software development. Additionally, PaaS allows for shorter software development lifecycles or faster delivery times by combining software development and testing on a single PaaS platform rather than maintaining separate development and test environments for in-house software development.

PaaS dynamically scale up or scale down computing resources to meet changing demand levels. This delivery model's capability to quickly design and scale computing, storage, and other infrastructure resources on-demand, rather than purchasing more substructure volume than is really needed in expectation of future development, is what makes it so appealing.

SaaS enables businesses to focus on what they do best: researching, developing, and manufacturing pharmaceuticals while also managing apps and data. However, SaaS cannot analyse, monitor, or hold vendors accountable for resolving issues. Electronic records must be as reliable, dependable, and generally corresponding to paper archives as most other regulated computing applications. The pharma business will profit from categorising data into IaaS, PaaS, and SaaS [32] (see Figure 10.2).

10.7.1.2 A Novel Approach to Drug Design and Discovery

On the basis of ground-breaking effort conducted at Duke University, one approach demonstrates some of the methods the cloud serves to recover medication design and discovery. The Duke University groups of Beratan and Yang created unique algorithms for searching chemical space. In its earliest application, the linear combination of atomic potentials (LCAPs) employed molecular features as a function of parameters that specified a given chemical group's contribution at a specific chemical site in a molecule [34]. This strategy allows for the creation of a potentially vast new space of chemical structures at a fraction of the value of evaluating individual structures. The LCAP approach has been published [34–36] and experimentally verified [37], and it has been demonstrated to have a number of benefits, including numerous search methods and simplicity of parallelisation.

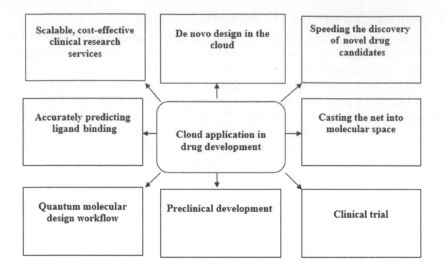

FIGURE 10.2   Various applications of cloud computing in drug development [33].

Cloud Pharmaceuticals has created more complex search algorithms for accessing novel chemical spaces, starting with the LCAP technique. With its Quantum Molecular Design technique, Cloud Pharmaceuticals has refined and amended Duke's original approach to enable for versatile, numerous, and chemically diverse compounds. The Quantum Molecular Design algorithm is a new implementation that uses a proprietary combination of chemical and vectorial space transformations, as well as integer-programming methods, to improve the identification of completely novel compounds with less medicinal chemistry effort and more operational freedom. Cloud Pharmaceuticals' mission is to create effective pharmaceuticals rather than intellectual endeavours that often lead to costly and undesirable outcomes.

10.7.1.3 Speeding the Discovery of Novel Drug Candidates

When a pharma industry seeks to progress a novel drug, the investigation team chooses a complaint and a possible chemical to investigate. The clinical trial process begins after a company isolates a promising chemical. There are four phases, and new drugs must successfully pass each phase to receive FDA clearance. The procedure is lengthy and costly. Phase II studies can cost anywhere from $7 million to $19 million, dependent on the kind of drug being examined, while Phase III trials can cost anywhere from $11.5 million to $52.9 million. Only approximately a third of the medications that begin the procedure make it to the pharmacy.

To improve their chances of success, researchers utilise computer modelling early in the drug development process to figure out which medicines are the safest and have the fewest side effects for patients. Making better decisions at the outset of the development process raises the likelihood that a new treatment will be both effective and superior to existing products.

Here the cloud enters the picture. Drug firms require the processing capacity that hyper-scale cloud providers can supply, as well as the ability to quickly scale up and down operations. To power this new approach to medication research, Amazon Web Services (AWS), Alphabet (Google), and Microsoft collaborate with major drug companies as well as startups. Moderna's drug research, development, and manufacturing operations rely heavily on AWS. By employing messenger RNA, or mRNA, the business develops a new class of medicine that uses DNA instructions to make all human cell protein. Medicines based on mRNA can instruct the body to produce specific proteins in order to treat or cure a specific condition. The military has provided financing to Moderna for the development of infectious disease medicines, as well as Merck and AstraZeneca for the development of tailored cancer vaccinations [38].

"Messenger RNA medications, like biologic software, tell the patients' bodies how to create the drugs themselves," said Dave Johnson, director of informatics at Moderna Therapeutics.

The company's mRNA platform runs multiple algorithms using cloud-based computational capability to design each mRNA sequence. Amazon Elastic Compute Cloud (EC2) with Auto Scaling, Amazon EC2 Spot Instances, Amazon Relational Database Service, and Amazon Simple Queue Service (SQS) are all used by Moderna. The jobs are pulled from Amazon EC2 instances pull the jobs, process the work, and use Amazon SQS to return results to the cluster master.

Moderna can reduce the time it takes to progress medication concepts to clinical trials and develop medicines with AWS that were previously unthinkable. Microsoft and Parexel, a worldwide biopharmaceutical services business, formed a technological development partnership in 2017.

In addition, Microsoft was an early backer in Cloud Pharmaceuticals, a drug discovery firm founded in 2011 with technology created at Duke University. Quantum Molecular Design, the company's technology platform, identifies the most promising candidates for new small-molecule medicines by combining AI, advanced quantum chemistry, and cloud computing [38].

Quantum Molecular Design, in collaboration with Genomeon, designs medication candidates and identifies companion biomarkers using molecular modelling in the cloud. In three ways, Quantum Molecular Design outperforms traditional methods. For starters, it provides a fresh method for discovering new compounds. Using a proprietary AI/"big data" technique, it detects compounds that are inferred directly from the properties of the binding site of the biological target. Second, it can predict the binding affinity of a protein to a tiny chemical with a high degree of accuracy (or peptide). The technique involves one or more of the following methods, with parametric editions: quantum mechanics/molecular mechanics (QM/MM), molecular dynamics (MD), linear interaction energy (LIE), and/or free energy perturbation (FEP). Correlations of 0.7–0.9 have been discovered on a regular basis [39,40]. It specifically depicts the protein, molecule, and aqueous environment in atomic detail. It includes a high sampling rate and properly portrays the role of water in solvation and the active site of proteins. It takes measurements of the conformation of the protein binding pocket, as well as the confirmation of tiny molecules and water molecules, and precisely envisages how they will interact. Third, it examines molecules for chemical features that are useful in the development of pharmaceuticals. Only molecules that pass all of the filters are found in the final results. You can screen compounds on the basis of their solubility, synthetic tractability, or whether or not they penetrate the blood–brain barrier, for example. Some designs may need to be filtered due to molecular weight limits. Or, for biological reasons, there can be side chains that are uneven or undesirable that can be filtered out of specific designs. Quantum Molecular Design's property-filtering methods help to produce only "excellent" molecules, reducing the medicinal chemist's effort during optimization.

Cloud Pharmaceuticals and GlaxoSmithKline (GSK) established a partnership on 30 May 2018 in. GSK identifies the ailments it wishes to focus on, while Cloud Pharmaceuticals researches and develops therapies using its technology platform.

10.7.1.4 Accurately Predicting Ligand Binding

For medications that target specific biological molecules, a high enough binding affinity between the drug and its target is required for the drug's potency to develop. As a result, throughout the drug development stages of hit identification, lead generation (hit to lead), and optimisation, binding affinity is one of the most important optimisation targets. A group of compounds with verified action to the biological target is identified for hit identification via high throughput screening or virtual screening, followed by experimental validation from a library of varied compounds. Because of its consistent accuracy and efficiency, FEP has gained traction as a computational tool for predicting binding affinities between candidate drugs and their biological targets. To move the system from one real ligand to another (the relative binding free energy approach, RBFE) or from the target-ligand complex to the separated target and ligand state, FEP uses a sequence of well-defined alchemical states (the absolute binding free energy method, ABFE).

FEP simulations can also provide time-dependent information, such as the interactions and conformational dynamics of the ligand and its target, in addition to binding affinity. FEP may use this data to optimise and validate binding posture, forecast binding affinity of different ligands, evaluate binding affinity cliffs, and generate virtual SARs, among other things. However, due to concerns with scalability, affordability, efficiency, and applicability of scenarios, there are still limitations in scaling FEP applications in drug development programmes [41].

To get around these limitations, a cloud computing platform (XFEP) for large-scale FEP simulations was created, which improves the RBFE and ABFE protocols with system-specific force fields and more sampling. The XFEP cloud computing platform was built to enable access to scalable computer resources for FEP-based simulations. RBFE, ABFE, and the associated relative hydration free energy (RHFE) and absolute hydration free energy (AHFE) simulations are all supported by the platform. As a result, XFEP promotes research into small molecule ligands, peptides, and mutant proteins' biological targets. XFEP has a graphical user interface that lets you combine perturbation pair design for RBFE and RHFE, force field parameter derivation and refinement from an existing force-field (FF) repository, enhanced sampling options for selected subsystems of interest, charge change correction schemes, decoupled and concerted electrostatic and van der Walls (vdW) interactions, and simulation settings for various tasks; 5,000 FEP pairs may be completed successfully in one week using the efficient XFEP protocol on 50–100 Graphical processing units (GPU) cards [42,43].

Modern drug design requires the discovery and classification of protein ligand binding sites as well as their interfaces with binding associates. SMAP, a software tool, was created with these objectives in mind. SMAP surpasses the majority of existing ligand binding site comparison tools; however, it lacks the scalability and availability required for large database searches.

SMAP's computing power, on the other hand, is limited. SMAP has developed a high-availability, high-performance technology that widens the comparison scale.

Cloud-PLBS is a cloud computing service that integrates the SMAP and Hadoop frameworks and runs on a virtual cloud computing platform. To handle the huge amount of experimental data on protein-ligand binding site pairs, Cloud-PLBS employs the MapReduce paradigm as a management and parallelising tool. Biologists can use Cloud-PLBS's web portal and scalability to solve a wide range of computer-intensive challenges in biology and drug discovery [44].

The master virtual machine (name node) and slave virtual machine (data node), are the master and slave VMs, respectively. SMAP jobs that are submitted are saved in a queue. The master node retrieves SMAP jobs from the job queue on a regular basis and assigns them to slave nodes; the task is completed by a slave node (or mapper). The reducer gathers the comparison outcomes from all mappers and stores them in the network file system (NFS) storage once all of the SMAP operations are completed. In NFS, a single comparison result is saved as a single file. Cloud-PLBS is endowed with three desirable features as a result of its architecture: high performance, scalability, and availability [44].

Cloud Pharmaceuticals has developed JAK3 inhibitors that do not target other family members, resulting in more focused results with fewer side effects. By adopting a multi-scale, multi-resolution approach, the methods above help increase binding accuracies. This method uses an implicit solvation term with a high sample rate, as well as a flexible protein, flexible ligand, and explicit water model. For example, this technology was used for the Janus family of kinases to find new inhibitors of the JAK3 enzyme that are selective against other Janus family proteins. Each JAK protein is targeted for distinct disorders based on its activities: JAK3 for rheumatoid arthritis, immunosuppression, and inflammation, and JAK2 for cancer [45].

10.7.1.5 Casting the Net into Molecular Space

Quantum Molecular Design looks for new space by deriving a binding pattern from the target's X-ray structure. This pattern is based on the target's binding pocket's 3D geometry. The pattern is then compared to a massive and expanding database of scaffolds, which includes all scaffolds published in the literature, many theoretical scaffolds constructed combinatorially, and the liberal hopping of those scaffolds to produce many more. After searching the database with the binding pattern, a list of molecular matches is generated. Any of those matches are scaffolds that have been stripped down to their roots. Quantum Molecular Design next extends the scaffolds by modifying the functional groups in every place where scaffolds are matched, resulting in a new chemical space with stable functional groups only. Depending on the depth of the investigation and the number of scaffolds or roots analysed, this method generates 10 million to a billion molecules. This quick and efficient algorithm runs on the cloud and generates a new, diversified, and useful virtual molecular space in a fraction of the time.

10.7.1.6 Quantum Molecular Design Workflow

This technology is used by Cloud Pharmaceuticals to pick the target and create a 3D model of it based on its X-ray structure or homology. If there is any accessible training data, it is used to improve the outcomes. The following step is chemical space creation, which is carried out using the approach described in the previous section. The system then searches the cloud for molecules that match the stated properties the best. At each level, thousands of molecules are evaluated using an ideal binding affinity and solvation method. The operation takes around a week with 3000 cloud nodes and three weeks with 1000 nodes—the process is unconsciously parallel and scales as needed. The next step is to start the preclinical optimisation process, which entails collaborating with a medicinal chemist to choose compounds to synthesise from a rank-ordered hit list of matches that have been verified for drug-like properties. Many of Cloud Pharmaceuticals' initiatives begin with the development of a limited number of compounds—perhaps ten or twenty of the most promising. This preliminary experimental effort includes synthesis, chemical characterisation and measurements, as well as binding and cell-based testing. If the initial batch's results aren't satisfactory, further molecules can be studied in a systematic, rank-ordered manner, taking variation into consideration. For *de novo* drug design, 500,000 CPU hours in the cloud are normally required; however, this might vary depending on the amount of coverage required. AWS, ProfitBricks, Cloud & Heat, Google, and Microsoft Azure are among the cloud platforms where the Quantum Molecular Design approach has been applied. Because of the method's adaptability, it can operate on almost any cloud with minimum configuration. Quantum Molecular Design is significantly more flexible than traditional high throughput screening (HTS) since it develops new compounds rather than using ones from an existing screening deck. This process has been validated by correlation with reported lab data, as well as the production of wholly novel compounds and the successful completion of activity testing. This leads to the discovery of new leads and the creation of compounds that can be further optimised by utilising biological models.

10.7.1.6.1 Preclinical Development

The properly vetted hit list is ready for further preclinical research after the work in the cloud is completed. Because you've already weeded out a lot of candidates who are likely to fail, this stage should go significantly faster. While all of the traditional preclinical development procedures must still be completed, they are being used on a far more qualified group of candidates (leading in a much greater success rate, faster advancement, and lower costs) and on novel and difficult-to-drug targets. To fulfil many of these tasks, Cloud Pharmaceuticals collaborates with contract research organisations (CROs) and risk sharing partners. The cloud's value lies in its ability to produce innovative compounds for difficult targets while also delivering enhanced results that reduce costs and shorten time to market. Furthermore, as Cloud Pharmaceuticals does, collaborative drug discovery and development can be safely maintained across several partners via the cloud. In addition to using the cloud for design work, the firm combines the efforts of its partner network to effectively complete a substantial percentage of drug discovery, design, and development.

10.7.1.6.2 *Clinical Trials*

The advantages of storing, managing, and analysing clinical data on the cloud are similar to those of other drug development tasks. On a pay-as-you-go basis, the cloud provides time on massive, scattered infrastructures. According to Erich Clementi, the Vice President of strategy and General Manager of enterprise initiatives at IBM, the necessity to transport data around among several trial locations and compare the data as it is being created accounts for 8–12 percent of clinical trial costs. Cloud computing also allows for large volumes of processing to be done at a lower cost for projects that require a lot of data crunching For example, Jeffrey T. Leek, Assistant Professor at Johns Hopkins Bloomberg School of Public Health, and colleagues used an internally built, open-source, cloud-computing platform called Myrna to quantify differential gene expression in large RNA sequencing datasets. Running an analysis for a single RNA sequence on a single laptop may take up to three weeks, according to Dr Leek. On the other hand, he also said that for $65, he could get findings in an hour and 45 minutes by renting computers for cloud computation services.

Cloud computing for clinical trials, according to Stuart Henderson, IBM's America's life sciences R&D leader, provides distinct advantages. The drug development sector can use IBM's "Clinical Cloud." The goal was to create a safe atmosphere in which partners could collaborate while having faster and easier access to data. Multi-tenant security, infrastructure, process integration and orchestration, a clinical application suite, compliance, analytics, collaboration, help and support, data sharing, and file sharing, among other things, are all part of the Clinical Cloud, according to the firm.

Several smaller corporations are entering the clinical trials area, including IBM. Drug developers, CROs, clinical sites, and regulators can use Wipro Clinical Collaboration Portal from Wipro Technologies. The goal is to "substantially increase multiregional clinical trial collaboration capabilities."

According to Wipro, the platform was developed to cut the time it takes to complete a clinical trial by 20–30 percent. The gateway allows the sponsor organisation, CRO employees, clinical site coordinators, and primary researchers to communicate and share documents more quickly.

PharmaPros is a technology company that specialises in clinical trial data and workflow management. Its Dataflow Manager™ makes use of cloud computing to allow trial administrators to make more timely and informed decisions during the course of a study.

At several levels, cloud-based computing by this time has been incorporated into pharmacological R&D. Despite security and privacy issues, drug researchers, CROs, clinical site managers, and others engaged have found the aid of utilising cloud computing in the clinical trial procedure to be intriguing. Given the transnational nature of clinical trials, the simplicity of information exchange, as well as expanded collaboration and analytical skills, are particularly appealing [46].

10.7.1.7 *De novo* Design in the Cloud

Shahar Keinan et al. presented a quantum molecular design, a novel cost-effective automated system for *de novo* computational drug design. This method not only addresses many of the challenges in the field of computer-aided medication creation, but it also substantially lowers prices by combining an AI heuristic search algorithm with a focused chemical space [47]. The importance of the technique presented here is that the hit list and early lead detection operations are entirely done in the cloud until synthesis is completed. Furthermore, the composition of matter patents that arise are more effective since they integrate several substances in the same nexus from a single procedure. The medicinal chemist will have an easier job turning the "hits" into good "leads" because good drug-like properties are already built in. Indeed, Cloud Pharmaceuticals is working with a developing life sciences data centre in Iceland to create inhibitor libraries in advance for the whole drug gable genome and known mutations, using data from the Human Proteome Initiative, a multi-year project that is predicted to disrupt HTS. This approach has been used to research kinases, allosteric proteins, GPCRs, and other receptor proteins that have a single target. The company is pursuing Aurora-A, BACE1, betaCR, DHFR, eiF4E, HDAC8, hsp90, JAK3, MetAP2, Metnase, PKCe, PKR,

PLA2, ROCK2, and Serpins, to name a few. Starting with X-ray structure or homology, Quantum Molecular Design may be utilised to tackle any of these challenges [33].

10.7.2 Cloud-Based Services

The following are the cloud-based services that explain properties of ligands or their receptors, as well as receptor-based and ligand-based services [48].

- **AceCloud:** This is a molecular dynamics simulation on-demand service. AceCloud was created to make it easier to run huge groups of replications on an exterior cloud computing provider in a secure manner (currently AWS). The AceCloud consumer, which is part of the Ace molecular dynamics (ACEMD) molecular dynamics package, provides a simple interface that abstracts all aspects of cloud interaction. AceCloud may be accessed by simply utilising three new commands included in the ACEMD molecular dynamics software package: start simulations, retrieve results, and track progress. This offers the customer the impression that all replications are screening on their own system, reducing the curve of learning that comes with switching to computing services with great results [49].
- **Bind scope:** This is a web service that uses deep convolutional neural networks to classify chemicals as active or inactive on a big scale. Performance is comparable to that of today's state-of-the-art pipelines. Users can monitor hundreds of chemicals at one click and interact with the outcomes in real time. BindScope is a web application suite by PlayMolecule.org and is available for download [50].
- **DINC:** This is a parallelized meta-docking technique for progressively docking large ligands. Instead of docking the complete ligand by exploring all of its degrees of freedom (DoFs) at once, DINC reduces issue complexity by sequentially docking larger overlapping sections of the ligand. DINC picks a small fragment of the ligand in the first round of sampling and scoring and invokes a standard molecular docking program (currently AD4) to dock this fragment. AD4 scores were calculated using a Lamarckian evolutionary method for sampling and a semi-empirical free energy force-field based on pair-wise evaluations (V) with pre-defined weights (Wi) [51].
- **DINC 2.0:** The DINC algorithm has been improved and a new website, DINC 2.0, built to dock even bigger ligands like peptides. The initial fragment is chosen and subsequent fragments are expanded using new algorithms that maximise the probability for hydrogen bonding with the receptor. DINC 2.0 also has better parallelisation management, which is critical for docking big peptides; users may increase the number of top conformations picked at each cycle, boosting sampling without increasing run time [52].
- **The Evias Virtual Screening Tool (VST):** This is a cloud-based virtual screening tool with outstanding performance. It was created to allow researchers to use our user-friendly interface to access cloud-based computational resources for computer-aided drug creation. It is connected with a chemical library management system as a scalable high performance computing (HPC) platform for structure-based VS service as a web service [53].
- **HDOCK:** This is a new web server for our template-based modelling and free hybrid docking technique, in which deceptive templates can be saved via the free docking protocol. The server, which receives both sequence and structural inputs for proteins, supports protein–protein and protein–DNA/RNA docking. The docking process is short, taking between 10 and 20 minutes for each docking run. Five docking benchmarks were used to evaluate HDOCK on samples with weakly homologous complexes with less than 30% sequence identity. On the protein–protein and protein–DNA benchmarks, the HDOCK pipeline was used in conjunction with template-based modelling. When the top 10 predictions were examined, it outscored template-based modelling on the three protein–RNA benchmarks. When more predictions were taken into account, HDOCK's performance improved [54].

- **HADDOCK (High Ambiguity Driven Protein-Protein DOCKING):** This is a flexible docking approach that uses data to model biomolecular complexes. HADDOCK varies from *ab initio* docking techniques in that it drives the docking process with ambiguous interaction restraints (AIRs), which encode information from recognised or anticipated protein interactions. HADDOCK can handle a variety of modelling issues, including protein-protein, protein-nucleic acid, and protein-ligand complexes [55].

Traditional Chinese medicine (TCM) docking and *de novo* drug design are possible with iScreen, a tiny web server. We have created a method that extracts proteins of interest from a raw input file while calculating the size of the ligand bind site. Furthermore, for those who are uncomfortable with command line systems, iScreen provides a user-friendly graphic interface. For tailored docking, a variety of docking services are available, including standard, in-water, pH environment, and flexible docking modes. Downloads of the top 200 TCM compounds with the best docking findings are available. For the user's interest in TCM *de novo* drug design, iScreen contains various molecular descriptors. Using the world's biggest TCM database, iScreen is the world's first online server for virtual screening and *de novo* drug creation [56].

- **Ligand Scout Remote:** This allows scientists to seamlessly integrate HPC resources with the Ligand Scout desktop application, which they use every day. This approach totally avoids any HPC use by transparently handling essential data conversion and network connectivity for the user, so hurdles can be overcome. We show how the developed software combines the usability of local graphical desktop programs with the performance of an HPC cluster [57]
- **M Cule:** This is a new web service that provides a quick and cost-effective approach to find and order novel medication candidates. The public can use the service, which offers a large, thoroughly maintained library of compounds that can be screened virtually right away. Several screening mechanisms have already been applied, with more being added weekly or monthly. Virtual screening workflows can be seamlessly connected with screening instruments. The calculations are carried out on cloud machines, which have a virtually infinite number of CPUs and so enable rapid access to the screening findings. The virtual displays may be used to place orders for hits [58].
- **MEDock:** Predicting ligand binding locations is an important step in the drug development process. The search for hits, the lead optimization process, the design of site-directed mutagenesis tests, and the quest for structural characteristics that alter binding selectivity in order to reduce the drug's side effects are all substantially aided by knowing the location of binding sites. In the framework of information theory, the MEDock web server includes a global search strategy that takes advantage of the maximum entropy feature of the Gaussian probability distribution. This server's objective is to offer a useful tool for predicting ligand binding locations. The optimisation technique in MEDock is substantially improved when dealing with particularly rough energy landscapes, which typically have insurmountable obstacles, thanks to the global search strategy [59].
- **MTiOpen Screen:** This offers two in-house-created drug-like chemical libraries including 150,000 PubChem compounds: the Diverse-lib, which has a wide range of molecules, and the iPPI-lib, which is enriched on molecules that inhibit protein–protein interactions. Furthermore, MTiOpen Screen allows users to screen up to 5000 small molecules from outside of our two libraries. Up to 1000 estimated binding postures and energies for the top-ranked ligands can be downloaded. In this approach, MTiOpen Screen enables researchers to do virtual screening on classic or more difficult protein targets, such as protein–protein interactions, utilising a variety of chemical libraries [60].

10.8 CONCLUSION

The term "drug discovery" conjures up thoughts of laboratory chemistry experiments, biological testing, and large-scale automation, all of which are often done in laboratories. Drug development is a lengthy, difficult, and expensive procedure that comes with a significant level of uncertainty about whether or not a drug will be successful. Traditional drug discovery costs and timetables are far too expensive, worsened by exorbitant rates of disappointment, resulting in extremely large expenses that are delivered to clients and jeopardise our healthcare system's financial stability. It is well known that only about one molecule out of every 10,000 is approved by the FDA after undergoing preclinical testing and clinical trials. Because of the high failure rate, traditional drug discovery and development costs skyrocket.

Cloud computing provides a solution by allowing for additional complex computational chemistry to be combined with quick formulation and escalation, allowing corporations to find molecules that are better adapted to growth from the beginning. Cloud computing refers to the on-demand availability of computer system resources, notably data storage (cloud storage) and processing power, without the user's direct active supervision. Large clouds commonly divide functions across several locations, each of which is a data centre. Cloud computing relies on resource sharing to achieve clarity and cost savings, cloud computing depends on resource sharing, which is often performed through a "pay-as-you-go" technique. Cloud computing can cut investment costs but also exposes consumers to unforeseen operating costs. Selecting compounds with a higher possibility of success functions as a lever to reduce total prices, which is required if tailored medicine or "niche buster" treatments are to be realised. The identification of new medication candidates is being speeded up thanks to cloud computing. Pharmaceutical industries demand processing capacity as well as the ability to scale up and down operations quickly, which hyper-scale cloud providers can deliver. Amazon Web Services, Alphabet (Google), and Microsoft are cooperating with big medical corporations as well as start-ups to fuel this innovative method to medication research. Quantum Molecular Create, in conjunction with Genome on, uses cloud-based molecular modelling to design drug candidates and identify companion biomarkers. The RBFE and ABFE protocols have been more optimised with system-specific force fields and expanded sampling using a cloud computing platform (XFEP) for large-scale free energy perturbation simulations. RBFE, ABFE, and the related RHFE and AHFE simulations are all supported by the platform. As a result, XFEP promotes research into small molecule ligands, peptides, and mutant proteins' biological targets. Depending on the depth of the investigation and the number of scaffolds or roots analysed, Quantum Molecular Design creates 10 million to 1 billion molecules. In a fraction of the time, this cloud-based tool builds a new, diverse, and useful virtual molecular environment. Cloud Pharmaceuticals develops innovative pharmaceuticals in collaboration with CROs and risk-sharing partners. The cloud's usefulness stems from its capacity to develop new compounds for difficult targets while also delivering better outcomes that reduce costs and shorten the time to market. On a variety of levels, cloud-based computing has already been employed in pharmaceutical R&D. Despite security and privacy issues, drug researchers, CROs, clinical site managers, and others participating in the clinical trial process have found the benefits of employing cloud computing in the clinical trial process to be fascinating. Cloud-based services like AceCloud, Bind Scope, DINC 2.0, Evias Virtual Screening, HDOCK, HADDOCK, and others are in high demand among pharmaceutical companies. To directly meet the demands of medicinal chemists, whole processes have been designed leveraging clouds as HPC resources. The similarity of skill enables collaboration with computational chemists in order to adapt operations to changing preclinical demands. Clouds are appealing for their ability to scale with computational demands as well as the vast array of tools that may be integrated. Using cloud-based solutions to share computing facilities and expertise is likely to be more cost effective for any isolated project. Pharmaceutical businesses can use cloud computing to exchange information in same period, execute a similar application on numerous linked computers at the same time, analyse outcomes more speedily, and connect with colleagues around the world in real time. This enables pharmaceutical businesses to increase their productivity, collaboration, and resource allocation. For the pharmaceutical business, this is an exciting opportunity to learn about the benefits of cloud computing, which alleviates the increasing challenges faced. It provides pliability and scalability for storage and analysing massive volumes of data, which is beneficial to all rising laboratories. It is a versatile platform that lets you test multiple applications at the same time. It allows employees to interact strategically in a global marketplace without being disrupted. It is inexpensive and simple to handle, therefore it lessens reliance on interior infrastructure. But the cloud does more than relieve the demands of developing pharmaceuticals more quickly and cheaply, while remaining compliant and maximising global expertise in the drug development game; it also fosters innovation and promotes efficiency.

ACKNOWLEDGMENT

The authors are grateful to the management of Oriental University, Indore, for their gracious assistance and for providing all of the required facilities and encouragement to enable them to complete their work successfully.

REFERENCES

1. U.S. Food and Drug Administration (FDA)-The Drug Development Process. https://www.fda.gov/ForPatients/Approvals/Drugs. Accessed 31 December 2018
2. Forum on Neuroscience and Nervous System Disorders; Board on Health Sciences Policy; Institute of Medicine. Improving and Accelerating Therapeutic Development for Nervous System Disorders: Workshop Summary. Washington (DC): National Academies Press (US); 2014 February 6. 2, Drug Development Challenges. Available from: https://www.ncbi.nlm.nih.gov/books/NBK195047/
3. Strovel, J., Sitta, S., Nathan, P.C., Michael, H., James, I., Andrew, K., *Early Drug Discovery and Development Guidelines: For Academic Researchers, Collaborators, and Start-up Companies*. Assay Guidance Manual. Eli Lilly & Company and the National Center for Advancing Translational Sciences. 2004.
4. Taylor, D., The Pharmaceutical Industry and the Future of Drug Development. Issues in Environmental Science and Technology. *Royal Society of Chemistry*, pp. 1–33, 2015.
5. "The Drug Development Process". U.S. Food and Drug Administration (FDA). 4 January 2018. Retrieved 21 March 2020.
6. Kopp, S., Definition of active pharmaceutical ingredient revised, 2011, pp. 1–4 https://pdf4pro.com/view/definition-of-active-pharmaceutical-ingredient-49ea44.html
7. Hughes, J. P., Rees, S., Kalindjian, S. B., Philpott, K. L., Principles of early drug discovery, *Br. J. Pharmacol.*, 162, 1239–1249, 2011.
8. Olğaç, A., Orhan, I. E., Banoglu, E., The potential role of in silico approaches to identify novel bioactive molecules from natural resources, *Future Med. Chem.*, 9, 1665–1686, 2017.
9. Kinghorn, A. D., Pan, L., Fletcher, J. N., Chai, H., The relevance of higher plants in lead compound discovery programs, *J. Nat. Prod.*, 74, 1539–1555, 2011.
10. Mueller-Kuhrt, L., Successful, but often unconventional: the continued and long-term contribution of natural products to healthcare. *Expert. Opin. Drug Discov.*, 2, 305–311, 2007.
11. http://www.worldcommunitygrid.org/research/faah/overview.do
12. Armstrong, M. S., Morris, G. M., Finn, P. W., Sharma, R., Richards, W. G., Molecular similarity including chirality. *J. Mol. Graph. Model.* 28, 368–370, 2009.
13. Ballester, P. J., Finn, P. W., Richards, W. G., Ultrafast shape recognition: Evaluating a new ligand-based virtual screening technology, *J. Mol. Graph. Model. J.*, 27, 836–845, 2009.
14. Mullin, R., The new computing pioneers, *Chem. Eng. News.*, 87, 10–14, 2009.
15. Halligan, B. D., Geiger, J. F., Vallejos, A. K., Greene, A. S., Twigger, S. N., Low cost, scalable proteomics data analysis using Amazon's cloud computing services and open source search algorithms, *J. Proteome Res.*, 8, 3148–3153, 2009.

16. McCarthy, A., Drug discovery in the clouds, *ACS. Chem. Bio.*, 119, 1–2, 2012.

17. Herhalt, J., Cochrane, K., Exploring the cloud: A global study of governments' adoption of cloud, 2012.

18. Open Whisk. https://openwhisk.apache.org/. Accessed 31 December 2018

19. Garrison, G., Kim, S., Wakefield, R. L., Success factors for deploying cloud computing, *Commun. ACM.*, 55, 62–68, 2012.

20. Shah, P., Yury, R., Cloud computing enabling better collaboration in the cloud, *Drug Dev. Deliv.*, 14, 55–57, 2014.

21. https://www.nutanix.com/blog/pharma-and-biotech-companies-are-counting-on-cloud-computing-and-ai

22. https://www.biospectrumindia.com/views/59/19153/cloud-computing-impact-on-pharma-sector.html

23. https://www.researchnester.com/reports/cloud-based-drug-discovery-platform-market/1123

24. Amazon Web Services. https://aws.amazon.com. Accessed 31 December 2018.

25. Google Cloud. https://cloud.google.com. Accessed 31 December 2018.

26. Open Stack. https://www.openstack.org/. Accessed 31 December 2018.

27. Banegas-Luna, A. J., Imbernón, B., Llanes, A., Pérez-Garrido, A., Cerón-Carrasco, J. P., Pérez-Sánchez, H., Advances in distributed computing with modern drug discovery, *Expert Opin. Drug Discov.*, 14, 9–22, 2019.

28. Potemkin, V., Potemkin, A., Grishina, M., Internet resources for drug discovery and design, *Curr. Top. Med. Chem.*, 22, 1955–1975, 2018.

29. https://www.click2drug.org/directory_Docking.html. Accessed 31 December 2018.

30. Sekharan, S., Wei, J. N., Batista, V. S., The active site of melanopsin: the biological clock photoreceptor, *J. Am. Chem. Soc.*, 134, 19536–19539, 2012.

31. Hype Cycle for Life science, Gartner report, 2013 https://www.gartner.com/doc/2570915/hype-cycle-life-sciences-

32. https://www.pharmamanufacturing.com/articles/2015/cloud-computing-in-pharma/

33. Addison, E., Shahar, K., Cloud computing using quantum molecular design & cloud computing to improve the accuracy & success probability of drug discovery, *Drug Dev. Deliv.*, 16, 62–66, 2016.

34. Wang, M., Xiangqian, H., David, N. B., Weitao, Y., Designing molecules by optimizing potentials, *J. Am. Chem. Soc.*, 128, 3228–3232, 2006.

35. Keinan, S., Hu, X. Q., Beratan, D. N., Yang, W. Designing molecules with optimal properties using the linear combination of atomic potentials approach in an AM1 semiempirical framework, *J. Phys. Chem.*, 111, 176–181, 2007.

36. Keinan, S., Therien, M. J., Beratan, D. N., Yang, W., Molecular design of porphyrin-based nonlinear optical materials, *J. Phys. Chem.*, 112, 12203–12207, 2008.

37. Keinan, S., Paquette, W. D., Skoko, J. J., Beratan, D. N., Yang, W., Shinde, S., Computational design, synthesis and biological evaluation of para-quinone-based inhibitors for redox regulation of the dual-specificity phosphatase Cdc25B, *Org. Biomol. Chem.*, 6, 3256–3263, 2008.

38. https://www.zdnet.com/article/pharma-companies-are-counting-on-cloud-computing-and-ai-to-make-drug-development-faster-and-cheaper/

39. Menikarachchi, L. C., Gascon, J. A., QM/MM approaches in medicinal chemistry research, *Curr. Top Med. Chem.*, 10, 46–54, 2010.

40. Senn, H. M., Thiel, W., QM/MM Methods for Biological Systems, In: Reiher M. (eds) *Atomistic Approaches in Modern Biology. Top Curr. Chem.*, 268, 2006.

41. Cournia, Z., Bryce, K., Allen, T. B., David, A. P., Radak B. K., Woody S., Rigorous free energy simulations in virtual screening, *J. Chem. Inf. Model*, 60, 4153–4169, 2020.

42. Peiyu, Z., Geoffrey, P. F. W., Jian, M., Mingjun, Y., Yang, L., Guangxu, S., Yide, A. J., Bruno, C. H., Shuhao, W., Harnessing cloud architecture for crystal structure prediction calculations, *Cryst. Growth Des.*, 18, 6891–6900, 2018.

43. Yang, M., Dybeck, E., Sun, G., Peng, C., Samas, B., Burger, V. M., Zeng, Q., Jin, Y., Bellucci, M. A., Liu, Y., Zhang, P., Ma, J., Hancock, B. C., Wen, S., Wood, G. P. F., Prediction of the relative free energies of drug polymorphs above zero kelvin, *Cryst. Growth Des.*, 20, 5211–5224, 2020.

44. Che-Lun, H., Guan-Jie, H., "Cloud computing for protein-ligand binding site comparison", *Biomed Res. Int.*, 2013, 1–7, 2013.

45. Thompson, J. E., JAK protein kinase inhibitors, *Drug News Perspect*, 18, 305–310, 2005.

46. https://www.genengnews.com/insights/cloud-computing-augments-clinical-trial-process/

47. Keinan, S., Hatcher-Frush, E., Shipman, W. J., Leveraging cloud computing for in-silico drug design using the Quantum Molecular Design (QMD) framework, *Comp. Sci. Eng.*, 20, 66–73, 2018.

48. Olgac, A., Aslı, T., Olgac, S., Moller, S., Cloud-based high throughput virtual screening in novel drug discovery, in: *High-Performance Modelling and Simulation for Big Data Applications*, pp. 250–278, Springer, Cham, 2009.

49. Harvey, M. J., Fabritiisg, D., AceCloud: molecular dynamics simulations in the cloud, *J. Chem. Inf. Model.*, 55, 909–914, 2015.

50. Skalic, M., Martínez-Rosell, M., Jiménez, J., Fabritiis, G. D., Play Molecule BindScope: large scale CNN-based virtual screening on the web, *Bioinform.*, 35, 1237–1238, 2019.

51. Morris, G. M., Huey, R., William, L., Michel, F., Belew, K. R., Goodsell, D. S., Arthur J. O., AutoDock4 and AutoDockTools4: Automated docking with selective receptor flexibility, *J. Comput. Chem.*, 30, 2785–2791, 2009.

52. Antunes, D. A., Moll, M., Devaurs, D., Jackson, K. R., Lizée, G., Kavraki, L.E., DINC 2.0: A new protein-peptide docking webserver using an incremental approach, *Cancer Res.*, 77, e55–e57, 2017.

53. Olgac, A., Budak, G., Cobanoglu, S., Nuti, R., Carotti, A., Banoglu, E., Evias web services: cloud-based drug discovery platform, *EuroQSAR*, 79, 2016.

54. Yan, Y., Zhang, D., Zhou, P., Li, B., Huang, S. Y., HDOCK: a web server for protein-protein and protein-DNA/RNA docking based on a hybrid strategy, *Nucleic Acids Res.*, 45, W365–W373, 2017.

55. Zundert, G. C. P. V., Rodrigues, J. P. G. L. M., Trellet, M., Schmitz, C., Kastritis, P. L., Karaca, E., Melquiond, A. S. J., Bonvin, A. M. J. J., The HADDOCK2.2 Web Server: User-friendly integrative modeling of biomolecular complexes, *J. Mol. Biol.*, 428, 720–725, 2016.

56. Tsai, T. Y., Chang, K. W., Chen, C. Y., iScreen: world's first cloud-computing web server for virtual screening and de novo drug design based on TCM database@Taiwan, *J. Comput. Aided Mol. Des.*, 25, 525–531, 2011.

57. Kainrad, T., Hunold, S., Seidel, T., & Langer, T., LigandScout remote: A new user-friendly interface for HPC and cloud resources, *J. Chem. Inf. Model.* 59, 31–37, 2019.

58. Kiss, R., Sandor, M., Szalai, F. A., http://Mcule.com: a public web service for drug discovery, *J. Cheminform.*, 4, 17, 2012

59. Chang, D. T., Oyang, Y. J., Lin, J. H., MEDock: a web server for efficient prediction of ligand binding sites based on a novel optimization algorithm, *Nucleic Acids Res.*, 1, W233–W238, 2005.

60. Labbe, C. M., Rey, J., Lagorce, D., Vavrusa, M., Becot, J., Sperandio, O., Villoutreix, B. O., Tufféry, P., Miteva, M. A., MTiOpenScreen: a web server for structure-based virtual screening, *Nucleic Acids Res.*, 1, 448–454, 2015.

11 Framework for Handling Medical Data in Research

Shashimala Tiwari

India Health Action Trust, Uttar Pradesh Technical Support Unit, Lucknow, India

CONTENTS

DOI: 10.1201/9781003226949-11

11.1   INTRODUCTION

Several legal measures, such as the implementation of the Union's General Data Protection Regulation (GDPR) are based on the protection of personal data against misuse [1,2]. Furthermore, repeated fact-gathering may be difficult and time-consuming without cause in the eyes of the patient, therefore the potential and benefits of various procedures of health information should be assessed [3].

Anticipating managing the consequences for a specific patient is sometimes made through a mixture of physical inspection, biological documents, and interaction with the patient. However, such anticipation at a group level frequently focus exclusively on readmission, mortality, and, if presented, data of similar medicinal usages as well as other usages of health services [4]. The rapid development of AI, approaching on the heels of the general adoption of electronic medical records, has unlocked electrifying possibilities in medicine.

One of the most significant impediments to the advancement of AI-based solutions is the absence of a widespread consensus on an ethical framework for the use of clinical data. Although these consequences, such as death, are unquestionably important, they are going to be unsuccessful for capturing treatment effects completely. Public relation offer (PRO) procedures are widely used to match data as a major or district distal result, or even as a substitute for unmeasured experimental data when gathering it is impossible [5]. PRO data could even be accessed at the specific patient level to notify patient care or for shared significance such as readmission and mortality rates, to notify facility delivery, and to measure the real-world usefulness of management [5].

Health informatics aims to address the cumulative challenges of data collection and distribution in order to alert single patient care and facility improvements. In a similar way, a cumulative amount of research development and creativity individually brings together health information for definite purposes. This structure is used for research and to analyze numerous health activities regarding the combined use of information, allowing for the authorized, administrative, technical, and logistical experiments that describe every data procedure.

The framework involves four data procedures—identification of the patient, collection of the data, aggregation of the data, and use of the data—further organized into two dichotomous scopes in each data process (the level: patient vs. group; unplanned: systematic vs timeframe). Though health informatics, as a correction, involves participants from a true series of specialized circumstances, parts, and benefits, it frequently does so by paying consideration to one precise single application, as demonstrated in the literature [1].

As a result, there are restricted publications on the daily use of this health data for numerous determinations. Technical, authorized, administrative, and other hurdles to the supply of information for many commitments end in the incompetent usage of assets by patients and clinicians within health care organizations and society. Where there is no other satisfaction in reciting a measurement, a portion of equivalent health information should be based on incidence.

Laboratory tests, for example, may be performed by the general practitioner before transfer to hospital; however, frequently, and in numerous cases inappropriately, this occurs after the patient reaches the hospital. Correspondingly, clinicians regularly scrap to recover desired dimensions to keep up quality registers, although they will by this time be recorded within the electronic health record (EHR) system.

In the same way, PRO measurements could even be frequently and individually collected in parallel for various uses, like medical organization, excellence investigation, and research tasks.

This would not just mean a pointless load on the patients, they also can have implications for data superiority, as reaction fatigue may cause decreased reaction rates. For successful effective usage of the health data, we have to develop a certain type of language to communicate with patients. This chapter suggests an agenda for the analysis of the application and reprocessing of health data, with precise attention to the role of specialized processes to initiate and simplify a supplementary comprehensive conversation [4].

11.2 DEFINITIONS

There is no consent on an approach to defining health data and health information [6]. Data is composed of shreds of evidence, for example from situations, individuals, occasions, etc. Data are well-defined in many ways, such as:

- Any systematized data collected through an investigator [7];
- Data or information characterized in an approximate form appropriate for improved use or processing [8];
- Data, particularly evidence & numbers, are gathered to be examined, considered, and used to aid decision-making [6].

The primary explanation considers the collecting process and eliminates purposes, apart from the investigation, though a further definition depends on the arrangement only. The third explanation recognizes three procedures related to health information: collection, examination, and use; it additionally recognizes that the character of information be well-maintained, albeit only kept and not used, at least not immediately [5]. This chapter uses the third definition and differentiates three data procedures: a collection of data, aggregation of data, and use of data. I would prefer to deliberate on a patient-identification process to determine whose information would be collected, because patients are a part of observation for health data. We will use the term "patient" to refer to those who may have a health problem or are being monitored for one, even if they don't have one [8–11]. Figure 11.1 shows the role of the data lifecycle in health information.

Four data methods within the lifecycle of patient-related health information are:

- Patient identification method: identifying the patients from whom data will be gathered.
- Data collection method: how health data is collected, including logistical operations.
- Data aggregation method: managing and organizing obtained data in preparation for utilization.
- Data usage method: using health data to complete the desired task. Each process could be repetitive or may happen at the same time as the previous processes [11].

FIGURE 11.1 Lifecycle of data in health information.

11.3   HEALTH DATA CHARACTERIZATIONS

- Health information action: an action with a health-related goal that produces health data.
- Health information procedures: any health data action includes four procedures:
  a.   Patient identification process;
  b.   Data collection process;
  c.   Data aggregation process;
  d.   Data use process [11].

Time frame: the time frame of a health information method:

- Systematic: a scheduled or recurring health information procedure;
- A non-planned procedure.

Level: the extent of a health data procedure:

- Patient-level: a single patient level;
- Group level: a level with patients gathered in line with approximately well-defined norms [11].

The patient-identification procedure relates to the characterization of the patient or the cluster of patients, which should always be confidential. Aggregation may contain logistical data processes, like a program of data, reformatting of data, and managing of data processes like uniting and amalgamation with other data [11,12]. Aggregation can be obvious during the management of data (e.g., a dedicated data manager who prepares the dataset for the researcher's usage) or implicit (e.g., in an emergency room, a clinical summary supported by patient data). Across all four data processes, two aspects are frequently recognized: level and timing [11]. A private patient or a well-defined patient group could be considered a level. The breadth of the health data action determines the timeframe, which can be unplanned or part of a scientifically planned procedure [11].

11.4   BIG DATA CHARACTERISTICS

The subsequent characteristics that describe the term "big data" are value, variety, veracity, velocity, variability, and volume, denoted as the 6 Vs [13–15] (Figure 11.2).

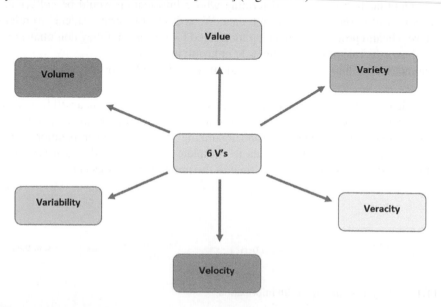

FIGURE 11.2   The 6 V's of big data.

1. **Volume:** The volume of medical and health documents is predicted to be enhanced a great deal over future years onward; it is frequently calculated in terabytes, petabytes, and zettabytes [14–18].
2. **Velocity:** This relates to the speed, motion, and frequency of information formation, processing, and analysis.
3. **Variety:** This is demanded by the complexity and variety of numerous sets of data, which might be unstructured, structured, or semi-structured.
4. **Veracity:** This term pertains to data quality, relevance, uncertainty, and predictability [14].
5. **Variability:** This refers to the data's consistency over time.
6. **Value:** The value of extensive data relates to its clear analysis, which is useful to both patients and professionals.

11.5   BIG DATA ANALYTICS

Massive information analytics may be used to improve patient-centered services by detecting illness outbreaks sooner, generating new ideas about the causes of disease, monitoring the excellence of healthcare and medical institutions, and providing better treatment options [17,19–27]. Furthermore, combining and analyzing data of various types, such as scientific and social data, can result in innovative information and intelligence, as well as the exploration of new ideas and the discovery of hidden patterns [14,28–32]. The delivery of motivational and medical counseling to patients can be replaced by mobile texts [16,33–38].

11.6   BIG DATA IN HEALTHCARE

A word is needed about the enormous volumes of data generated through the deployment of computerized technology that collects patient records and assists in the management of hospital presentation, which is then too huge and multifarious for traditional technologies [39–42].

The practice of big data analytics (BDA) in healthcare has produced lots of new benefits and even life-saving results. When used in communities, there needs to be unique health data practices to support avoiding outbreaks, preventing diseases, reducing expenditures, and so on. Doctors want to learn as much as possible because they have patients, and they want to know it as early as possible to recognize the warning signs of serious disorder as they arise. It is far easier and less expensive to treat an ailment early on [16,43,44].

In my paper, "Analytics to Spot and Accomplish High-Risk and High-Cost Patients in Health Carefulness," I propose that one way to employ prediction models is to identify and manage six convenient usage cases.—High-cost patients, decompensation, triage, readmissions, adverse events, and infection therapy optimization for different organ schemes are among them [40]. The expertise and organization that healthcare administrations require for practice cases are discussed below. I also discuss what administrations must do to advance care [39].

11.7   CHALLENGES IN BIG DATA ANALYTICS

Several difficult challenges should be considered while collecting an enormous volume of data. The value of experimental measurements is linked to the acquisition of high-throughput biological information [45]. Before integrating those heterogeneous data and utilizing information mining methods, we must examine the diversity of the information bases, the boom of the investigational–biological information, and thus the type of investigational methodologies, ambient circumstances, and natures [46].

Clustering, classification, anomaly detection, associated instructions, and summary and visualization of these large datasets are all common data processing techniques used on heterogeneous biomedical data groups. These flaws can follow the inaccuracy of a wide range of data points, such as missing standards. Despite the limitations of biological information, EHR documents are heavily predisposed by the person who collected the patient's information, which can result in absent values, erroneous data due to errors, and so on.

The addition of data from many databases, as well as calibration of research laboratory techniques and results, are ongoing challenges [10]. The high dimensionality of omics data indicates that more dimensions or traits exist than there are samples [46]. The next stage is to preprocess the data, which often includes dealing with noisy data, outliers, disappeared values, data transformation, and normalization [45].

Innovative knowledge generated by combining EHR data and omics should develop the quality of healthcare provided to patients and the ability of healthcare decision-makers to make advanced decisions [46].

Because of the exponential increase of healthcare data, the evolution of huge data poses several issues, limits, and problems. Big data is always changing, and this shift in knowledge poses numerous issues in terms of storing, analyzing, and retrieving the massive amount of data. Due to the vast size and type of knowledge, ordinary database systems cannot store, process, or extract it.

The primary issues that healthcare BDA faces are:

- Knowledge storage and quality;
- Exceptionally good data analysis;
- Data analytics expertise;
- Confidentiality and data security;
- Multiple sources of information.

The considerable data issues that healthcare professionals face is no different [46]. The most important difficulties that must be addressed are prominent data qualities. To supply and deliver medical facilities, it is critical to use big data technology. Big data technologies, on the other hand, may pose a risk to certain groups [45].

11.8 BIG DATA SECURITY AND PRIVACY

The privacy and security of patients are two critical challenges about big data in medicine and healthcare [14,23]. All health data is vulnerable, and various countries believe patients have legal ownership of this information [9]. These software solutions should enable network security and authentication for all users, as well as ensuring privacy and safety and identify sound governance rules and practices [47].

Because of the escalating dispute over the National Security Agency's gathering of information about private calls [48], there are numerous sticky concerns involving privacy. Many of us will be reluctant to have data about ourselves linked to other data, and this problem may be more sensitive in healthcare than in other areas. Patients, on the other hand, have an ethical commitment to contribute to the mutual goal of enhancing the standard and assessment of medical care, according to Ruth Faden and co-authors [48]. Policymakers are hesitant to modify the terms of the Health Insurance Portability and Accountability Act (HIPAA) of 1996, which is a milestone piece of law dealing with healthcare privacy and security. However, numerous concerns will turn crucial as additional diverse data sources that are interrelated are not addressed by the act.

11.9 EFFECT OF BIG DATA ON THE HEALTHCARE SYSTEM

Big data has the potential to change issues such as the most appropriate or accurate case determination and the best information to be employed in the health informatics system. The healthcare system needs to focus on assisting situations involving these paths, as indicated below, and to have a direct impact on the case. Right living refers to the practice of leading a better and healthier life [44].

Cases could be better managed by making the best diagnostic decisionbased on the interpretation of knowledge, mining better choices, and increasing their wealth by living correctly. Patients can take an active position by living a healthy life by adopting the correct food, preventative treatment, exercise, and other everyday activities for their diurnal health. To reduce the repetition of planning and work, this pathway guarantees that cases receive the best treatment available and that all providers secure the same data and have the same aims [43]. In the age of big data, this aspect has become increasingly feasible.

Appropriate provider: By merging data from various sources such as medical equipment, public health statistics, and socioeconomic data, healthcare workers on this pathway can get a comprehensive picture of their patient's problems.

Due to the inaccessibility of information, natural care providers can perform specialized studies and build the knowledge and skills necessary to identify and provide superior treatment alternatives for their cases [43].

Appropriate innovation: This route acknowledges that new diseases, therapies, and medical technologies will emerge in the future. Similarly, advances in the provision of care services, upgrade specifics, and the productivity of research and development activities will enable new approaches to enhance welfare and patient health through the public social insurance system [44]. For stakeholders, the inaccessibility of early trial data is critical. This information can be utilized to discover high-potential targets and strategies for improving traditional clinical treatment methods.

Exemplification, connecting and destroying data misrepresentation, manipulation, and waste, as well as increasing exchequer, are all intelligent uses of data [44].

The explosion of big data is the biggest change of the modern era. Its impact in healthcare is motivating the first steps toward improvement. Data governance used to be the most difficult challenge for the security of data-driven businesses. In the data measure, the age of enhancement is easily entering our speedy worlds. Managers in healthcare organizations are still struggling to handle big data, especially because they are dealing with a sporadic influx of information [44].

Many professionals predict that by collecting medical data through EHRs, laboratories, case experience and satisfaction rate, and medical staff that medical data will multiply at an exponential rate.

IT faces a huge task in anatomizing this massive amount of data. One response given by the cloud is to fix the root (establish) with a large medical database. IT personnel could be directed by computing systems to manage huge amounts of data. With the use of dark computing in medical care models, a new direction will be added. It is obvious that, when properly managed, big data will support the increase in the quality and intelligence of medical diligence [44]. The reception of BDA will open the way to progress in the healthcare profession.

11.10   ISSUES IN HEALTHCARE BIG DATA

Healthcare deals with significant data challenges.. Data governance includes data direction and regulation. Data governance is a critical concern as the healthcare industry progresses toward data analytics. The variety of healthcare data created necessitates standardization and governance. Economic challenges in the medical field's establishments between cases and healthcare providers during clinical visits rely on the paid service. Following that, technological advancements associated with this process place a burden on the medical community and create an unnecessary drain on human resources versus correspondent-owed services.

Concerns about security and seclusion, due to potentially sensitive information about individual healthcare stakeholders [42], the seclusion of healthcare data must be properly examined in the era of big data. Healthcare information is considered sensitive and must be safeguarded from unauthorized access to prevent it from being made widely available, as well as open to healthcare fraud. As a result, one of the most difficult responsibilities in the healthcare industry is data security [42].

11.11 RECORDING AND ANALYSIS OF BIG DATA

The funds available to collect medical data are now limited, but this will change shortly. People have previously begun to use various sorts of health-related apps and software via their smartphones and wearable gadgets [41]. These apps can monitor a variety of health issues, including calorie intake, heart rate, blood pressure, and blood sugar levels [38]. These apps can record data from monitoring processes since they can examine and watch for a variety of health issues [38]. Shortly, these apps will make cases suitable for participation in data with patients and hospitals. Medical practitioners will be able to pare them down to size and put them to good use with this information. Investigators can then construct progressive approaches with various new contrivances by combining and identifying all of the data [41].

11.12 THE FRUITFUL USE OF THE MEDICAL DATABASE

In today's society, a great amount of data is squandered because certain professionals are unable to use it or recognize its value. Data analytics with shadow-rested data – the sum of all small traces of information - knows how to apply it [37]. It makes use of its well-established tools and proclivity to remove uncertain elements and produce a calculative chunk of knowledge from a large amount of data [37]. The shadow accomplishes this in a matter of seconds, saving time.

There are more advanced approaches for combining data from millions of sources and delivering the most accessible, trustworthy, and simplified data to specialized medical specialists. Doctors and other healthcare providers will be able to design the best treatment strategy for the case in real time [37]. All of these steps will link shadow-rested analytics to healthcare experts. Medical workers and other professionals will be required to manage and use this enormous amount of data [38].

11.13 DATA ANALYSIS ASSISTANCE IN CLINICAL TRIALS

At the moment, extensive data analysis helps to build lozenges and therapy choices. Investigators were given the task of selecting informal subjects to provide informal outcomes for the participant data [36]. By combining information and data, the findings become simpler and more accessible. As an example, we can witness the discovery of desipramine's multi-functional usage [36]. Lung cancer can be cured with this physical therapy. As a result, researchers can create a distinct medicinal grammar that can combat different forms of pestilence.

11.14 SECURING MEDICAL DATA

The medical data contains the retained health data of the cases [35]. This information must be safeguarded and protected against theft or loss. Medical data is increasingly being stolen by a large number of cyber thieves. Only when information and data security can be assured can high-end big data be properly exploited [35].

11.15 HEALTHCARE AND BIG DATA SIMPATICO

Healthcare geomorphology is drenched in data, with over $30 billion in healthcare sales reclaimed at any given moment [34]. BDA in healthcare is on the verge of becoming a viable field, with solutions to some of the most common diligence issues such as cost inefficiencies and medical malpractice.

Healthcare diligence generates zettabytes of data from EHRs, medical imaging, and a slew of other sources, making big data the only way to combine, analyze, and manage the whole healthcare ecosystem [34].

Because of the large amount of data it generates, big data is suitable for providing healthcare assiduousness, providing cases that may be utilized to provide modifications to medication, knowledge, and economics, as well as other benefits to increase productivity [16].

The benefits of implementing big data have piqued the interest of healthcare executives as they seek out realistic business solutions to boost efficiency and service quality.

11.16   SMALL DATA VS. BIG DATA: WHY DO CLINICIANS PREFER SMALL DATA?

Small data investigate an individual's past data to improve models for forecasting and futuristic therapy, whereas big data examine massive volumes of data for patterns [33].

While big data has long been at the forefront of healthcare technology, doctors are increasingly depending on a small amount of data to manage patient care successfully [32]. Figure 11.3 is a schematic representation of the role of big data and information in medical knowledge.

Small amounts of data provide a lot of insight into the present. For example, an app for handling pain secretly collects data on the user, who is a fitness enthusiast, and delivers it to the user and his clinician [32]. Smartphones may track eating habits, fitness quotients, and anything else to provide clinicians with insight into a person's physical well-being in a variety of ways.

Smartphones' capabilities in healthcare are being recognized by technology businesses, and creative solutions are emerging [33]. Not content with that, the hidden mission is to tighten the protection as the data is analyzed and answers are revealed.

EHRs can be extended to patients by healthcare organizations that have implemented them. Hospitals and cases, on the other hand, make use of digital health technology to their full potential [33]. Table 11.1 differentiates the big data model from the small data model.

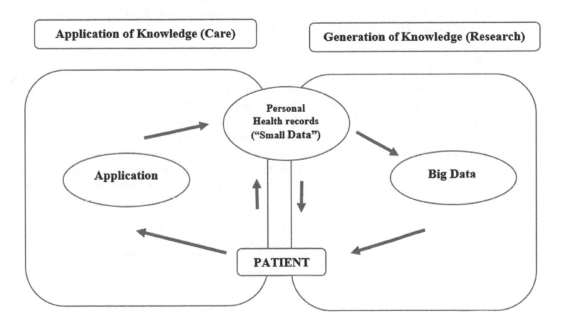

FIGURE 11.3   The circle of medical knowledge.

TABLE 11.1
Difference Between the Big Data Model and the Small Data Model

Big Data Model	Small Data Model
Where do some of the world's healthiest individuals live?	Is my diabetic treatment functioning as it should?
Are there any generic aspects that may be used to diagnose an illness?	Am I susceptible to X disease?
What impact may immunization efforts have?	Is my child's illness immunity taken care of?

11.17   INNOVATION IN MEDICAL SERVICES AND SMALL DATA

Innovative administrations see the advantages of cellphones in medical services, and creative answers are being released. The test for medical service is to subordinate small data to massive data to reveal particular medical care thataffects a large amount of collection of data.

Medical service frameworks that have controlled EHRs can transmit this to patients. Big data have vast applications in healthcare (Figure 11.4).

11.17.1   Predictions Made by Patients

For our first example of big data in healthcare, we will look at a common challenge faced by any shift executive: how many people should I have on duty at any given time? If you hire numerous people, you risk incurring excessive labor charges [47]. Very few personnel will result in poor patient examination, which could be harmful to the patients [49].

11.17.2   Electronic Health Records

Every patient has a digital record that contains information such as demographics, medical information, allergies, and laboratory test results, among other things. Proceedings are shared through protected data schemes and are accessible to both public and commercial sector providers [47]. EHRs can also send out cautions and advice when a patient needs replacement blood, investigation, or to track instructions to see if they are being followed by doctors [49].

11.17.3   Real Time

Healthcare providers educate additional cases of data analytics in healthcare to have one important feature in common: real-time alerts. Clinical decision support (CDS) software investigates health data present in hospitals, assisting doctors while they form prescriptive results [47]. Doctors prefer that patients stay away from clinics to avoid costly in-house therapies. Additionally, this data will be connected to a record on public health, permitting clinicians to associate it to data collected in a socio-economic context and regulate delivery techniques accordingly. Institutions and care supervisors will monitor this large information stream with sophisticated tools and react when the results are disturbing [46,49].

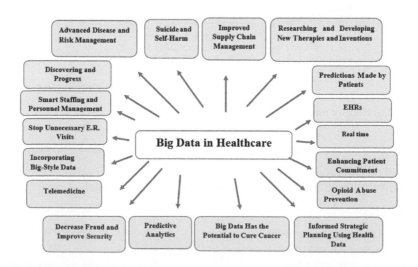

FIGURE 11.4   Application of big data in healthcare.

11.17.4 Enhancing Patient Commitment

Various parties and future patients are now interested in smart maneuvers that track each footstep, heart rate, sleeping routine, and other data indefinitely. All of this critical information is routinely combined with additional trackable information to detect hidden health hazards [47]. As an example, chronic sleeplessness with an increased pulse can specify a future possibility of heart disease. Patients are immediately involved in their own health monitoring, and insurance incentives might inspire them to live a healthy way of life (e.g., providing a rebate to persons who use smartwatches) [49]. New wearables on the market are one way to do this, as they track certain health developments and transmit them to the cloud, where clinicians can observe them. Patients with asthma or its vital signs may gain advantage from them, becoming more self-reliant and reducing unnecessary doctor visits [49].

11.17.5 Opioid Abuse Prevention

Within the USA, the fourth largest data healthcare case addresses a serious issue [49]. Here is a depressing fact: opioid overdoses have produced many more accidental deaths in the USA than traffic accidents.[47]. In a *Forbes* article, analytics guru Bernard Marr discusses the topic. Things have got so bad that Canada has confirmed opioid misuse as a "national health catastrophe"; while President Obama was in office, he set aside $1.1 billion to research remedies to the problem [49].

11.17.6 Informed Strategic Planning Using Health Data

Due to the endless ideas for incentivizing people, the practice of massive data in healthcare allows for planning [47]. Health managers can compare check-up outcomes across a wide range of demographic groups to see what variables keep patients from opting for more aggressive therapy. The University of Florida generated heat maps for a variety of conditions, including rising criminality and chronic diseases, using Google Maps and spontaneously presented public health data. Researchers then compared this information to the medical treatments available in the hottest zones. They were able to evaluate their delivery approach and add more health units to the primary problem zones as a result of this information [49].

11.17.7 Big Data Has the Potential to Cure Cancer

The Cancer Moonshot program is another excellent example of how big data may be used in healthcare [47]. Medical researchers can use a wealth of information about cancer treatment strategies and recovery amounts to identify development and management that have the maximum success rates in the world. Researchers can, for example, evaluate tumor sections in biobanks connected to patient treatment data [49].

Researchers may use this data to figure out how individual mutations and cancer proteins interact with various treatments, as well as how to recognize patterns that could lead to better patient outcomes [47]. This information can also have unintended consequences, such as discovering that the antidepressant Desipramine can help treat certain types of lung cancer. However, there are other hurdles in the way:

- Data schemes that are incompatible. Making various datasets ready to interface with one another is a marvel, therefore this is often the most essential technical obstacle.
- Concerns about patient privacy. Different rules in each state govern what information about patients can be released with or without an agreement, and each one must be directed.
- Organizations that have invested a significant amount of time and currency into establishing their cancer dataset may be hesitant to distribute it to others, even if doing so could lead to a faster therapy [49].

11.17.8 PREDICTIVE ANALYTICS

Predictive analytics has been named the most important business intelligence trend in health-care for the past two years, but its potential goes further into business and the future [47]. The objective of healthcare virtual business is to aid clinicians for data-driven conclusions and better patient care. This is especially effective in people who have a long medical past and are suffering from the variability of illnesses [49]. New AI explanations and tools could even be capable of predicting who is at risk of diabetes and, as an outcome, recommending extra screenings or weight control [49].

11.17.9 DECREASE FRAUD AND IMPROVE SECURITY

A data breach has been reported in 93 percent of healthcare businesses, according to some studies. The argument is simple: on the black market, personal information is valuable and profitable. With this in mind, many businesses are turning to analytics to mitigate security risks by recognizing changes in network traffic or additional patterns that could suggest a cyber attack [47]. Of course, big data creates safety concerns, and various people feel that using it would create businesses much more susceptible than they already are. Security advances, such as encryption technology, firewalls, and anti-virus software, have all aided in improving security. Because this answer necessitates higher security, the benefits far outweigh the risks [49].

11.17.10 TELEMEDICINE

Telemedicine has been around for more than 40 years, but it is only now, with the introduction of virtual video seminars, cellphones, and wireless devices, that it has reached full coloration. The theory refers to the use of technology to provide distant experimental facilities. More precise applications include telesurgery, in which clinicians can employ robots to perform surgery, and high-speed real-time data transfer, short of actually being present at the patient's location [47]. Clinicians use telemedicine to offer tailored management programs and prevent readmission to hospital. As previously mentioned, the use of healthcare data analytics is frequently tied to predictive analytics. This enables clinicians to anticipate acute medical occurrences and intervene before patients' circumstances deteriorate [49]. Telemedicine helps to save expenses and enhance service quality by keeping patients away from hospitals. Patients can avoid long queues, while specialists can save on time-consuming paperwork and consultations. Telemedicine also increases the accessibility of care because patients' conditions can be observed and referred to at any time [49].

11.17.11 INCORPORATING BIG-STYLE DATA

Therapeutic imaging is important, and around 600 million imaging operations are performed each year in the USA. Manually analyzing and preserving these images costs time and money because radiologists must study each image individually, although hospitals keep them for years [49].

11.17.12 HOW TO STOP UNNECESSARY EMERGENCY ROOM VISITS

BDA for healthcare is critical for saving time, money, and energy. The shortage of united medical records amongst local emergency rooms worsened the female communitt's problems, increasing the value to taxpayers and hospitals while making it more problematic for her to advocate for better care. Staff in the E.R. are familiar with items like [35,49]:

1. If the patient they're treating has had definite tests performed at additional facilities, and what the outcomes were.

2. Avoiding establishing redundant assignments if the patient is already assigned to a case manager at another facility.

3. Knowing what counsel has previously been given to the patient so that physicians can communicate with the patient in a consistent manner [49].

11.17.13 SMART STAFFING AND PERSONNEL MANAGEMENT

Patient carefulness will deteriorate, provision charges will fall, and errors will occur without constant, engaged personnel. Large data solutions in healthcare, on the other hand, can help you modernize your staff organization efforts in several important areas [47]. Time-strapped medical organizations can manage personnel while projectingdemands using the right HR analytics, resulting in better patient care. In healthcare institutions, there is far too often a lack of fluidity, with workers dispersed in the wrong places at the wrong times. This mismatch in personnel supervision could indicate that a department is either overstaffed or understaffed when it matters most, resulting in lower motivation and higher absenteeism [49].

11.17.14 DISCOVERY AND PROGRESS

The abilities, self-confidence, and skills of your team can be the transformation between life and passing away at a hospital or clinic. Doctors and surgeons are, of course, experts in their fields. Most medical institutions, on the other hand, have a diverse workforce, ranging from caretakers and organizational assistants to cardiac consultants and brain surgeons [47]. Skill or experience is almost as central as qualifications in the healthcare field. You must support continuous learning and development to maintain the institution working at its full potential. By keeping track of staff presentation across the board and documenting coaching data, you can use healthcare data analysis to determine who needs support or training and when. You will save more lives if the majority of people are prepared to change with the times—and medical data analytics can help you do just that [49].

11.17.15 ADVANCED DISEASE AND RISK MANAGEMENT

Large amounts of information are required to assess the danger of hospitalization for particular patients with persistent infections. It can also aid in the prevention of degeneration [47]. Healthcare facilities can provide effective preventative treatment and, as a result, reduce hospital admissions by delving deeper into insights such as drug kind, symptoms, and hence the frequency of medical visits. Not only will this type of risk assessment save money on in-house patient care, but it will also ensure that space and resources are available to those who need them most. This is an excellent illustration of how healthcare analytics may assist people in regaining their health and saving their lives [49].

11.17.16 SUICIDE AND SELF-HARM

Every year, almost 800,000 individuals pass away by suicide around the world. In addition, 17 percent of the world's population will self-harm at some point in their lives. These figures are concerning [47]. Even though this is a problematic subject to tackle, the use of big data in healthcare is assisting in the formation of a good shift in the field of suicide and self-harm. Healthcare institutions, as units that handle a large number of patients daily, can employ data analysis to recognize people who may be at risk of self-harm [49].

11.17.17 IMPROVED SUPPLY CHAIN MANAGEMENT

Everything else, from patient care and management to long-term savings and others, may suffer if a therapeutic organization's supply chain is compromised or detached. As a result, our broad data healthcare focuses on data analytics pfrom beginning to conclusion [47]. Analytic representation can help you make better judgments when it comes to adapting to price, decreasing supply variability, and refining the whole assembly process [49]. Medical institutions will be able to survive in the future while providing vital therapy to patients short of experiencing possibly devastating delays, problems, or blockages.

11.17.18 RESEARCHING AND DEVELOPING NEW THERAPIES AND INVENTIONS

The most recent of healthcare analytics samples focus on being utilized in the medical industry for a better, more daring future [47]. Using a combination of past, real-time, and prognostic measurements as a consistent mixture of data conception tools, healthcare specialists can discover potential assets and flaws in procedures [49].

11.18   HIGH-COST PATIENTS

One way to cut expenses is to categorize high-cost patients and managing them [31]. Cost savings have already been achieved using this strategy. However, identifying patients who are expected to be high cost has not at all times yielded the preferred results. Various Medicare demonstration programs, for example, did not reduce expenditures even though the projects were ready to categorize high-risk individuals [28]. Variability in concerns must be considered when implementing analytic tools for identifying potentially high-cost patients. Behavioral issues or socio-economic characteristics like poverty or racial marginal status may be associated with high-cost patients [29].

A third problem is putting predictions into practice by establishing which patients would benefit from intervention and which precise activities will improve their care the most [28]. To increase the probability that health care personnel will act on expectations and practically deploy the most up-to-date analytic techniques to identify potentially high-cost patients would involve making forecasts publicly available with nominal adjustments to clinical workflows [27].

Many administrations and enterprises that presently use analytic schemes have concentrated on determining the procedure that will greatly stratify the data utilizing the risk of forthcoming costs even though ignoring additional difficulties. The differences between procedures may not be considered, and an additional practical approach may be preferable to a somewhat more precise one [27].

Procedures perform best when they are drawn from and applied to parallel populations [31]. A fourth problem is figuring out how to describe in detail the many predictive model results which originate from low-risk populations. This necessitates more precise modeling, especially for population management [30]. I consider it is vital to use analytic systems to detect potentially high-cost individuals and assess their specific demands and care gaps [27].

Because an outsized number of high-risk patients for hospital admission have some form of behavioral condition, with hopelessness being chronic, it is critical to recognize and address behavioral health problems. Programs aimed at attracting high-cost patients are expensive [31].

Interventions that are typically carefully customized to a patient's unique concerns, such as transportation, medication, non-adherence, or family conflict, will be significantly more cost effective. Health-care resources are suitable progressively scarce, necessitating a larger focus on value [30]. As a result, it is critical to investigate analytic tools that can distinguish between persons who are at high risk and those who are at low risk. A quality approach could include, for example, offering all patients dismissed from hospital a follow-up appointment in a fortnight [27]. However, it would create additional sense to see the highest-risk patients within two days, whereas patients with lower risks might only need follow-up attention if desirable.

11.19   BIG DATA TRIAGE

Approximating the risk of difficulties at the time a patient initially arrives at the hospital is valuable for a variety of explanations, including bed resources and staffing management, predicting the need for a change to a more suitable unit, and shaping the total patient management approach [26].

However, calculating the score necessitates caregivers receiving training in measuring specific factors such as irritation and "color" [18].

Using recent big-data techniques that combine routinely gathered physiological parameters in newborns and many other groups allows for significantly more accurate assessments with minimum coaching and implementation [17].

It is critical to have an in-depth guideline that outlines how a triage algorithm would inform care when integrating it into the clinical workflow [26]. This method is being tested in two pilot trials at Kaiser Permanente Northern California (KPNC), a combined healthcare delivery system with powerful evidence systems. The first pilot includes the transmission of neonates for sepsis. The objective is to decrease the number of newborns who are given antibiotics that aren't necessary. Every year, hundreds of newborns are tested for early-onset sepsis.

In the initial step of the program, objective maternal data is used to allow a preliminary (before birth) risk of early-onset sepsis, which may be included in an EHR. The second phase involves combining a basic set of experimental outcomes with the estimated supported maternal data to produce a posterior replacement possibility for the risk of sepsis after birth. In the USA, combining those two measures could result in as many as 240,000 fewer neonates receiving systemic antibiotics every year.

The second KPNC experiment focuses on adult emergency department patients [26]. There are few situations when severity-of-illness scores for adult medical care patients are presented. However, the influence of the scores on triage might be minimal. This is partly because the most significant of these, the Acute Physiology and Chronic Health Evaluation (APACHE) and the Simplified Acute Physiology Score (SAPS), are based on data collected after a patient has been admitted to medical treatment.

In the second pilot, doctors working in the emergency department are given two composite scores that are standardized by various patient registers and applied to all hospitalized patients, not only those receiving medical care [18]. The primary scores reflect a patient's overall comorbidity load over the previous 12 months, while the secondary scores reflect a patient's physiological variability over the last 72 hours. Furthermore, these two scores are combined with vital signs, developments in vital signs, and additional facts, for example, the length of time a patient has been in hospital [17]. The responsible suppliers are notified if the collective knowledge suggests that a patient has an 8 percent chance of worsening within the next 12 hours. The KPNC early-onset sepsis and emergency department compound-score initiatives, in particular, are aimed at patients who are not continually watched. For the big data approaches, we have to continue to watch the patients [26]. In both cases, clinicians develop a workflow that integrates big-data components with standard components.

11.20   ADVERSE EVENTS

Another application of analytics takes place by means of anticipating which patients are at risk of various types of antagonistic outcomes. Adverse events are costly and involve significant morbidity and mortality, yet many can be avoided [50]. Adverse medication events, which are common and costly, are an area where analytics can be useful. Yet, the best efforts at anticipating which patients will experience an adversarial medication incident have been ineffective. However, by analyzing inherited and genomic data, research laboratory data, vital sign data, and other data, analytics can accurately predict which patients will experience an adversarial medication episode and discover individuals who are in the initial stages of such a situation [50].

11.21   DISEASES THAT AFFECT SEVERAL ORGAN SYSTEMS

Chronic illnesses that affect many organ systems or are systemic are among the costliest to treat. Mucosal, cutaneous (skin), renal, musculoskeletal, pulmonary, hematological, immunological, and neurological symptoms of a single disease are all possible. Scleroderma, atrophic arthritis, and systemic lupus erythematosus (L.E.) are samples of such autoimmune illnesses [51,52].

The capacity to properly forecast a patient's illness trajectory might permit a caregiver to enhance sophisticated targeting and exclusive treatments to patients who would gain advantage the most from them, decreasing the disease liability on those patients and the healthcare system. The ability of the caregiver to enhance treatment is currently restricted due to complexity stemming from clinical phenotypic variation, the range of available data, and the absence of high-precision biomarkers [53].

This section is meant for calculating algorithms that incorporate a variety of quantities collected as a measure of routine care to anticipate the evolution of a patient's illness and customize its management accordingly.

These tactics have previously proven to be successful. Multisite longitudinal registries are being established to allow for the accumulation of populaces of patients by way of a specific sickness. Experimental data networks are anticipated to take over soon the main role that archives currently play [53]. The National Patient-Centered Clinical Research Network (PCORnet), which includes numerous medical data investigation networks, is an example of such a network. As medical data networks enable EHRs to be more widely used, we can anticipate learning more about the benefits of these technologies in terms of enhancing the care of patients with such diseases.

Renal failure is unique and has a high death rate. Renal function, on the other hand, can be assessed quickly, and early alterations can appear well before significant decompensation [52]. It appears that analytics might be pooled into utilizing data on experiences with specific medications and procedures, as well as data on kidney function, vital signs, urine output, and other procedures, to categorize individuals who are at risk of decompensation.

Contamination management is frequently aided by analytics. To understand pulse variability, we have to monitor this as it can help detect severe decompensation in newborns with very low birth weights before an illness develops. Previously, simply monitoring the heart rate characteristics of neonates resulted in lower mortality and more days without use of a ventilator [53]. On the other hand, nearby space for enhancement by using progressively detailed analytics accounts for delicate signals and filters out non-essential trends, such as people who show up when you least expect it.

11.21.1 RESEARCH

In many fields, additional systematic evaluation is required in research to go from prospect to recognition. Education on tailoring explanations for high-risk patients and, as a result, the usage of numerous streams of information—specifically, with sensor technologies to predict confrontational events and therapy selection meant for patients utilizing illnesses that affect various organ systems—would be particularly beneficial. Similarly, the relevance of developing comprehensive methodologies, as well as applying and disseminating them, is still unclear. I feel there is still more work to be done in developing alternatives since payment reform will almost certainly provide considerable incentives for their adoption and diffusion.

11.21.2 DISCUSSION AND FUTURE WORK

The process of assimilating, discovering, and examining a massive quantity of complicated diverse data of varying nature—biological data, social media data, experimental data, EHR data, and social media data—is known as BDA in healthcare and medicine. BDA connects numerous domains, including medical imaging, sensor informatics, health informatics, computational biomedicine, and bioinformatics, due to the assimilation of such heterogeneous data. The significant data properties, as extra work, give a good base for developing applications that will manage big data in healthcare and medicine, utilizing encouraging software platforms [20,24].

11.22 CONCLUSION

Big data, which includes analytics, is perhaps a most important technology that will be as valuable in healthcare as it has been in other industries. The choice of the various practice cases we've explored in this chapter is frequently contested. Nonetheless, I believe that soon patientswill be among the people who provide the highest value to healthcare organizations. This broad approach to healthcare has the limitless potential of illuminating value. I believe that firms who use it across multiple domains will gain, particularly once payment reform takes effect.

REFERENCES

1. Coiera E, 2015. *Guide to Health Informatics*. Boca Raton: CRC Press.
2. European Commission. Principles of the GDPR https://ec.europa.eu/info/law/law-topic/data-protection/reform/rules-business-and-organisations/principles-gdpr_en. Accessed on 13 May 2021
3. Calvert M, Kyte D, Price G, Valderas JM, Hjollund NH, 2019. Maximising the impact of patient reported outcome assessment for patients and society. *BMJ*, Vol. 24, No. 364, k5267.
4. Food and Drug Administration. 2009. Guidance for Industry – Patient-Reported Outcome Measures: Use in Medical Product Development to Support Labeling Claims http://www.fda.gov/downloads/Drugs/GuidanceComplianceRegulatoryInformation/Guidances/UCM193282.pdf. Accessed on 14 August 2021.
5. Deshpande PR, Rajan S, Sudeepthi BL, Abdul NCP, 2011. Patient-reported outcomes: a new era in clinical research. *Perspect Clin Res.*, Vol. 2, No. 4, 137–144. doi: 10.4103/2229-3485.86879.
6. Elgendy N, Elragal A, 2014. Big data analytics: a literature review paper. *Lecture Notes in Computer Science*. Vol. 8557, 214–227. doi:10.1007/978-3-319-08976-8_16.
7. Dictionary of Quality of Life and Health Outcomes Measurement. Milwaukee: International Society of Quality of Life (ISOQOL), 2015. Accessed on 17 October 2021.
8. Data, Wikipedia, 2018. https://en.wikipedia.org/wiki/Data. Assessed on 14 October 2021.
9. Viceconti M, Hunter P, Hose R, 2015. Big data, big knowledge: big data for personalized healthcare. *IEEE J Biomed Health Inform.*, Vol. 19, 1209–1215.
10. Luo J, Wu M, Gopukumar D, Zhao Y, 2016. Big data application in biomedical research and health care: a literature review. *Biomed Inform Insights.*, Vol. 8, 1.
11. Hjollund NH et al., 2019. Health data processes: a framework for analyzing and discussing efficient use and reuse of health data with a focus on patient-reported outcome measures. *J Med Internet Res*, Vol. 21, No. 5, e12412.
12. Gour R, 2019. Best Data Architecture-The Art of Handling Big Data; The Best way to exploit Big Data. https://towardsdatascience.com/big-data-architecture-the-art-of-handling-big-data-bc565c3a7295. Accessed on 17 October 2021.
13. Andreu-Perez J, Poon CC, Merrifield RD, Wong ST, Yang GZ, 2015. Big data for health. *IEEE J Biomed Health Inform.* Vol. 19, 1193–1208.
14. Archenaa J, Anita EM, n.d. A survey of big data analytics in healthcare and government. *Procedia Comput Sci.*, Vol. 50, 408–413.
15. Borne K, 2014. Top 10 big data challenges a serious look at 10 big data v's. *Blog Post*, 11.
16. How Big Data in Health Care Influences Patient Outcomes, 2021. https://publichealth.tulane.edu/blog/big-data-in-healthcare/. Accessed on 20 October
17. Bresnick J, 2013. Data Triage is critical for effective storage strategies. https://healthitanalytics.com/news/data-triage-is-critical-for-effective-storage-strategies. Accessed on 15 September 2021.
18. Gupta V et al., 2016. Multi-Criteria Clustering for Big-Data using MR-Triage. *IRJET*, Vol. 3, No. 6, 1–6.
19. Agarwal M, Adhil M, Talukder AK, 2015. Multi-scale big data analytics for cancer genomics. *International Conference on Big Data Analytics*. Cham, Switzerland, Springer International Publishing Multi-omics 228–243.
20. He KY, Ge D, He MM, 2017. Big data analytics for genomic medicine. *Int J Mol Sci.*, Vol. 18, 412.
21. Tan SL, Gao G, Koch S, 2015. Big data and analytics in healthcare. *Methods Inf Med.*, Vol. 54, 546–547.
22. Dinov ID, Heavner B, Tang M, Glusman G, Chard K, Darcy M et al., 2016. Predictive big data analytics: a study of Parkinson's disease using large, complex, heterogeneous, incongruent, multi-source and incomplete observations. *PLoS One*, Vol. 11, e0157077.
23. Costa FF, 2014. Big data in biomedicine. *Drug Discov Today*, Vol. 19, 43340.

24. Yao Q, Tian Y, Li PF, Tian LL, Qian YM, Li JS, 2015. Design and development of a medical big data processing system based on Hadoop. *J Med Syst.*, Vol. 39, 23.

25. Kambatla K, Kollias G, Kumar V, Grama A, 2014. Trends in big data analytics. *J Parallel Distrib Comput.*, Vol. 74, 2561–2573.

26. Picon A, Chronicle SF, 2021. As animal hospitals struggle with vet shortages, pet owners worry about access to care.

27. Berkman ND, Chang E, Seibert J, Ali R, Porterfield D, Jiang L, Wines R, Rains C, Viswanathan M, 2021. Management of high-need, high-cost patients: a "Best Fit" framework synthesis. *AHRQ*, Vol. 21, No. 22, EHC028.

28. Lee NS, Whitman N, Vakharia N, Taksler GB, Rothberg MB, 2017. High-cost patients: hot-spotters don't explain the half of it. *J Gen Intern Med.*, Vol. 32, No. 1, 28–34. doi: 10.1007/s11606-016-3790-3.

29. Wammes JJG, van der Wees PJ, Tanke MAC, Westert GP, Jeurissen PPT, 2018. Systematic review of high-cost patients' characteristics and healthcare utilisation. *BMJ Open*, Vol. 8, No. 9, e023113. doi: 10.1136/bmjopen-2018-023113.

30. de Oliveira, Claire et al., 2020. High-cost patients and preventable spending: a population-based study. *JNCCN*, Vol. 18, No. 1, 23–31. doi:10.6004/jnccn.2019.7342.

31. Jacqueline LaPointe, 2017. Designing Care Models to Treat High-Need, High-Cost Patients; Researchers developed identification methods and care models that address the high-need, high-cost patient population, which represents half of healthcare spending. https://revcycleintelligence.com/news/designing-care-models-to-treat-high-need-high-cost-patients. Accessed on 24 October 2021.

32. Small Data and Big data; Deborah Eatrin, Robert V. Tishman Founder's Chair/Professor, Cornell Tech, Weill Cornell Medicine.

33. Chang A, 2021. Small Data and Big Health Benefits. https://onlinelibrary.wiley.com/doi/pdf/10.1111/jep.12350; https://research.cornell.edu/news-features/small-data-and-big-health-benefits. Accessed on 25 October 2021.

34. Pastorino R, De Vito, C, Migliara G, Glocker K, Binenbaum I, Ricciardi W, & Boccia S. 2019. Benefits and challenges of Big Data in healthcare: an overview of the European initiatives. *Europ J Pub Health*, Vol. 29, No. 3, 23–27. doi:https://doi.org/10.1093/eurpub/ckz168.

35. Norah A, Basem A, Adnan, G, 2017. Applicable light-weight cryptography to secure medical data in IoT systems. *J Res Eng Appl Sci (JREAS)*, Vol. 2, 50–58. doi:10.46565/jreas.2017.v02i02.002.

36. Krishnankutty B et al., 2012. Data management in clinical research: an overview. *Indian J Pharmacol.*, Vol. 44, No. 2, 168–172. doi:10.4103/0253-7613.93842.

37. Yang, Jin et al. 2020. Brief introduction of medical database and data mining technology in big data era. *JEBM*, Vol. 13, No. 1, 57–69. doi:10.1111/jebm.12373.

38. Yamamoto K. 1988. Design and use of medical record databases. *Medical Informatics Medecine et informatique*, Vol. 13, No. 1, 35–41. doi:10.3109/14639238809003573.

39. Gao, Y et al., 2021. Machine Learning and Blockchain Technology for Smart Healthcare and Human Health. doi:10.1155/2021/6656204.

40. Pranjal Bora, April 20, 2021; Big Data in Healthcare: All You Need to Know.

41. Shukla S, Kukade V, Sofia M, 2015. Big Data: concept, handling and challenges: an overview. *Int J Comp Appl.*, Vol. 114, 6–9. doi:10.5120/20020-1537.

42. Siddharth, 2017. Big Data in Healthcare – Challenges and Opportunities.

43. Wang J, Qiu M, Guo B, 2017. Enabling real-time information service on telehealth system over cloud-based big data platform. *J Syst Arch.*, Vol. 72, 69–79.

44. Tsuchiya S, Sakamoto Y, Tsuchimoto Y, Lee V, 2012. Big data processing in cloud environments. *FUJITSU Sci Technol J*, Vol. 48, No. 2, 159–168.

45. Agrawal D, Bernstein P, Bertino E, 2012. Challenges and opportunities with big data. A community white paper.

46. What is Big Data. IBM, New York, 2013. http://www-01.ibm.com/software/data/bigdata/

47. Mehedi Hasan, Top 20 Examples and Applications of Big Data in Healthcare.

48. Johnson BT, Reynolds HT, Mycoff JD, 2015. *Political Science Research Methods*, CQ Press.

49. Sandra Durcevic, Explore the Power & Potential of Professional Social Media Dashboards, 2020.

50. Di Giovanni R, Cochrane A, Lewis DJ, 2022. Adverse events in the digital age: finding the sharpest tool in the box. *Ther Innov Regul Sci.*, Vol. 56, No. 1, 23–37. doi:10.1007/s43441-021-00337-1.

51. Bates DW, Saria S, Ohno-Machado L, Shah A, Escobar G, 2014. Big data in health care: using analytics to identify and manage high-risk and high-cost patients. *Health Affairs (Project Hope)*, Vol. 33, No. 7, 1123–1131. doi:10.1377/hlthaff.2014.0041.
52. Six cases where big data can reduce healthcare costs, 2014.
53. Shankar RS et al., 2018. An efficient algorithm for multimodal epidemic liability prediction over big data. *Int J Pure Appl Math.*, Vol. 119, No. 18, 207–223.

Index

Note: Page numerals *italics* refer to figures and pages in **bold** refer to tables.